Richard Frederick Littledale

The Petrine Claims

A critical inquiry

Richard Frederick Littledale

The Petrine Claims
A critical inquiry

ISBN/EAN: 9783337063016

Printed in Europe, USA, Canada, Australia, Japan

Cover: Foto ©Thomas Meinert / pixelio.de

More available books at **www.hansebooks.com**

A Critical Inquiry

BY

RICHARD FREDERICK LITTLEDALE,
LL.D., D.C.L.

"Nos ergo, qui sumus vocamurque Christiani, non in Petrum credimus, sed in Quem credidit Petrus."
S. AUGUSTINUS. *De Civitate Dei*, xviii. 54.

Published under the Direction of the Tract Committee.

LONDON:
SOCIETY FOR PROMOTING CHRISTIAN KNOWLEDGE,
NORTHUMBERLAND AVENUE, CHARING CROSS, W.C.
43, QUEEN VICTORIA STREET, E.C.
BRIGHTON: 135, NORTH STREET.

NEW YORK: E. & J. B. YOUNG & Co.
1889.

TO

WILLIAM STUBBS, D.D.

LORD BISHOP OF OXFORD,

HISTORIAN OF THE ENGLISH CONSTITUTION,

THIS STUDY IN THE CONSTITUTIONAL HISTORY OF THE CHURCH

IS, WITH HIS PERMISSION,

INSCRIBED.

PREFACE.

THE scope and method of this treatise (itself a corrected reissue of a series of articles which appeared in the *Church Quarterly Review* in 1878-1884) differ from those of other works bearing on the Roman Catholic controversy, in that it does not touch the theological side of the matters in debate, save incidentally and subordinately; and is solely occupied with the legal aspect of the claim laid by the Papacy to sovereign authority over the Church Universal.

For this claim is much more than a mere speculative theory, or even than a dogmatic principle; it is a legal maxim of the widest range and the most detailed application, directly affecting every matter and every act within the spiritual domain, whether belonging to the sphere of faith or to that of discipline. The questions of the authority of Creeds and Councils, of the competence of all ecclesiastical officers, of the valid administration of Sacraments, of the legitimacy of forms of devotion, of the terms of communion requisite to Church membership, and all cognate ones, are inextricably bound up with this single proposition, which is thus of supreme legal importance.

That being so, and the "Privilege of Peter" being alleged as conveying no mere honorary Primacy, but as concentrating the whole government and jurisdiction over the Church Universal in the person of the Pope for the time being, it is removed from the sphere of dogma and from that of speculation into that of practical and legal action, and therefore must be examined and tested by legal methods, in order to ascertain its credentials.

The claim usually takes two forms: that it is based on and warranted by a Divine charter, contained in Holy Scripture; and that it has been in fact enjoyed and exercised, with the full recognition and approval of ancient Christendom, for a period so long and unbroken as to add a title by prescription to reinforce that conferred by the original charter.

The following pages are exclusively concerned with an investigation of these two theses, in their Scriptural, conciliar, and historical aspects; and the principles laid down by the Roman Canon Law have been applied throughout to guide the inquiry and determine the conclusions on purely legal grounds, as open to less dispute, and admitting of less evasion, than the theological treatment of the controversy has usually proved.

R. F. L.

CONTENTS.

CHAPTER I.

Legal Evidence of Scripture.

The Papal claims pushed to their final goal by the Vatican decrees—Roman controversy henceforward limited to a single issue—Claim that the Church of Rome is the whole Church—Language of the Vatican decrees—Three concurrent tests of divine privilege—Vatican decrees on the Papal claims—Need of conclusive evidence to prove them—Evidence as to St. Peter all contained in the New Testament—Rules of the Roman Canon Law to govern claims of privilege—The Petrine Charter in the New Testament—As expressed in Christ's words—As implied by Christ's actions—As evidenced by St. Peter's own conduct after the Ascension—As attested by St. Peter's language—St. John and St. Paul more dogmatic in teaching than St. Peter—Greater bulk and importance of the Pauline writings—Evidence of St. Paul as to the constitution of the Apostolic Church—Claims to authority made by St. Paul—Disciplinary rules laid down by him—Result of comparison between the positions of SS. Peter and Paul—Obscurity of wording in the alleged Petrine Charter—Bellarmine's argument—Its legal invalidity—The epithet "Rock" in Scripture—The rank and privileges of Jerusalem under the Mosaic dispensation—No reason for any similar privilege under the Gospel—Slight and unemphatic mention of Rome in New Testament—No direct connexion with St. Peter—Doubtfulness of identifying Babylon and Rome—No evidence for the Petrine Claims deducible from the letter of Scripture, viewed as a legal document alleged in proof .... *page* 1

CHAPTER II.

LEGAL EVIDENCE OF LITURGIES AND FATHERS.

The general belief and practice of the Christian Church may be accepted as evidence in the absence of express Scriptural statement—Evidential value of such testimony—Recapitulation of the points to be proved in order to establish the Petrine Claims—Five main sources of inquiry—What sort of evidence is inadmissible—Evidence of the Liturgies—Authority of the Fathers as witnesses—Patristic interpretations of the three great Petrine texts—Evidential value of honorific epithets of St. Peter .... *page* 60

CHAPTER III.

LEGAL EVIDENCE OF CONCILIAR DECREES.

Authority attributed to the Councils by the Church of Rome—Apostolic Canons know no rank superior to Metropolitan—Council of Nice implies limitation of Roman Patriarchate—

CONTENTS.

Council of Sardica—Its Canons, granting appellate jurisdiction to Rome, almost certainly forged in the Papal interest—Second General Council of Constantinople exclusively Eastern—Recognises no appellate jurisdiction in Rome—Concedes second place in the hierarchy to Constantinople—Council of Carthage in 418 repudiates Papal jurisdiction, rejects the alleged Sardican Canons, and prohibits appeals beyond sea—Council of Carthage in 424 renews the repudiation of Papal jurisdiction—Third General Council of Ephesus held because of the failure of the Pope to settle the Nestorian question—Takes no account of the Papal deposition of Nestorius—Enacts a Canon forbidding all bishops to extend their jurisdiction over fresh territory—Fourth General Council of Chalcedon constitutes an appellate system incompatible with the Roman claims—Enacts a canon alleging the Roman Primacy to be a merely human grant on political grounds—Maintains and reaffirms it against the protest of the Papal Legates—Conclusions which flow from this enactment—Proof of the historical truth of the Canon—Language of St. Irenæus as to the precedency of Rome—Its most probable interpretation—Roman synods in the fifth century—Trial of Pope Symmachus—Councils of Gaul and Spain in the sixth century—Unfavourable to Petrine Claims—Fifth General Council of Constantinople—Condemns Pope Vigilius—Roman Councils in sixth century—Councils of Gaul and Spain in the seventh century—Sixth General Council of Constantinople—Condemns Pope Honorius as a heretic—Roman attempts to set aside this condemnation—Disproof of such attempts—Evidence of the Council of Frankfort against the Papal claims—Synod of Rome in 963 deposes Pope John XII.—Council of Sutri in 1046 deposes three rival Popes—Council of Pisa in 1409 deposes and excommunicates two rival Popes—Council of Constance in 1415 deposes three rival Popes—Council of Basle, though not canonically recognised, of great value as historical testimony—Its anti-Papal enactments—Legal effect of the deposition and election of Popes at Pisa and Constance ... *page* 91

CHAPTER IV.

Legal Evidence of Acts, Conciliar, Papal, and Patristic.

Negative evidence legally stronger than positive evidence in questions of claim – Growth of Papal power an incidental disproof of its divine origin—Second Century : Debate between St. Polycarp and St. Anicetus—Pope Victor I. and the Asiatic Churches—Language of St. Irenæus on the question—Third Century : Evidence of Tertullian—Evidence of St. Hippolytus—Grave **charges against Popes Zephyrinus** and Callistus—**Evidence of St. Cyprian—Two distinct and** contrasted classes of statement in his writings—His actions show how they are to be harmonized—Resistance of St. Cyprian and the Church of Carthage to the Roman Church—Attitude of St. Firmilian—Further **acts** of St. Cyprian — **Interference in Spanish Church**—Errors committed by the Pope in this case—**Forgeries in the text of** St. Cyprian—Paul of Samosata—Fourth **Century** : Polity of the Christian Church in the era of Constantine the Great—Indirect disproof of Papal supremacy—Councils incompatible with a spiritual monarchy—Position accorded to the Emperor in the Church—Constantine the Great and the Donatists—Council of **Nice** convoked by the Emperor, not by the Pope—Hosius of **Cordova** its president—Proof that he was **not co-Legate of the** Pope—What the rank of the real **Legates at the Council shows—Confirmation** of the Council **by the Emperor—Validation of Councils by** dispersive acceptance of their decrees—Not restricted to the Pope—Papal confirmation insufficient alone—Council of Antioch—Canons **of Antioch** force their way to acceptance **in the teeth of Papal rejection—Fall of Pope** Liberius—**Proofs of his actual complicity in heresy—Second General Council of Constantinople —Convoked by the** Emperor—Its president a prelate excommunicated by the Pope—Confirmed by the Emperor alone—**Proof that there was no Roman** confirmation of the Council —**Language of Gregory** the Great, distinguishing between its **Canons and its** dogmatic Decrees—St. Ambrose and Maximus the Cynic—Local Council of Constantinople in 382—Rejects the interference of the Roman Church in Eastern elections to patriarchal Sees, and alleges Jerusalem to be the "Mother of all Churches"—St. Chrysostom's ecclesiastical position... *page* 125

CHAPTER V.

LACK OF PROOF FOR ST. PETER'S EPISCOPATE AT ROME.

Distinction between privilege and prescription—Evidence of Revelation essential to establish a claim of divine privilege—Silence of Scripture as to any relation of St. Peter to Rome—Conjectural solutions of the historical difficulties—Negative arguments from the **Pauline Scriptures—Ante-Nicene testimony to the presence of St. Peter at Rome—Analysis of its** elements—It affords no proof of the Roman episcopate **of St.** Peter—Nor of his devolution of any peculiar privilege to the Bishops of Rome—Evidence of Eusebius—The Chronicon of Eusebius the real basis of the Ultramontane claim—Uncertainty of its testimony—Obvious **source of the tradition as to** the foundation of the Roman Church by **St. Peter—Petrine** episcopate not distinctly asserted till post-Nicene times—Contradiction of Optatus and St. Epiphanius on the **leading details** of the story—Further contradiction **by Rufinus—Chro**nological difficulty as to **the** date of **St. Linus—St. Jerome** the first to formulate the legend **of St. Peter's** twenty-five **years'** episcopate at Rome—Internal disproofs of his account —No valid legal evidence adduced so far for St. Peter's epis**copate**—The case of the Popes still weaker—No clause in the Petrine texts other than personal, without words giving right of transmission—Such transmission expressly provided for in three leading Scriptural charters of privilege—St. **Peter thus not** empowered to transmit any peculiar grant made to him personally—Refutation of the plea that the Petrine right of transmission may have been part of the unwritten revelations of the

Great Forty Days—None of the requirements of Canon Law for validity satisfied by this theory—Twelve irreconcilable accounts in ancient writers as to the order and succession of the early Popes of Rome—Legal results of the consequent uncertainty—Legend of the nomination and **consecration of St. Linus** or St. Clement by St. Peter fatal to St. **Peter's own local** episcopate—Legal results of St. Paul's alleged survivorship of St. Peter—Probable solution of the conflicting lists of early Popes—Jewish and Christian Churches at Rome—Dual Bishopric probable—Petrine succession would end with extinction of Jewish Church of Rome—Results of the inquiry thus far .... *page* **170**

CHAPTER VI.

Dawn of the Papal Monarchy.

The fifth century a transitional period in secular and ecclesiastical politics—Causes which tended to increase Papal authority at this time—Recurrent sophism in the Ultramontane argument—Appeal of St. Chrysostom to Pope Innocent I.—Its evidential value much exaggerated—Milan and Aquileia included in the appeal—Pope Innocent's action proves his lack of supreme jurisdiction—His large claims **over** Eastern Illyricum and Gaul—His Decretal to Decentius of Gubbio attests the manu**facture of a** factitious tradition at Rome—Disproof in the **contemporary** witness of St. Jerome—Attempted encroach**ment of** Innocent upon the North **African** Churches—His **conduct** during the Pelagian controversy disproves the Papal claim to supreme teachership—Innocent I. the real founder of the Papal monarchy—His claims promptly resisted—Pope Zosimus sides with the Pelagians—Compelled to retract by St. Augustine and the **North** African Church—His failure to exercise jurisdiction **in** Gaul—Letter of the Church of Carthage to Pope Celestine I. in 424 in direct conflict with the Vatican decrees—Third General Council **of** Ephesus—

Convoked by the two Emperors—Its convocation in itself a disproof of Papal supremacy—Evidence of the growth of Papal authority since the Council of Nice—The Pope's proxy entrusted to St. Cyril of Alexandria, President of the Council —Papal condemnation of Nestorius disregarded—Decree of the Council worded by the Papal Legates—Its design nullified by other Conciliar utterances—Pope Celestine's doctrinal teaching in direct conflict with that of Clement XI.—Proof of its historical authenticity—Leo **the Great, first theologian** among the Popes—Originator of preaching in the churches of Rome—Absence **of** oral religious teaching **at Rome** till the fifth **century disproves** its title to be the teaching centre of **Christendom**—Leo's ambition for his See—His dealings with St. Hilary **of** Arles—Violates **the** canon law, and persecutes St. Hilary—Causes which made such lawlessness more feasible in the West than in **the** East—Leo applies **to** the Emperor for an edict to strengthen his hands against the Gallican Church —This edict the beginning of Papal supremacy in the West —Not applicable to Great Britain—Leo's rank as a theologian—Robber Synod of Ephesus—Indirectly advances **Papal** authority—Attempt of Leo to extend his power **over the** Eastern Churches—Letter of Theodoret in illustration of the Greek view as to the position of Rome—Fourth **General** Council of Chalcedon convoked against the express remonstrance of the Pope—He is obliged to accept it and to send legates—Gives them instructions to endeavour to depress the See of Constantinople—Early proceedings of the Council— Papal gains and losses—Attempt to get the Tome of St. Leo received without discussion, as binding in virtue of its Papal origin—Failure of the scheme—Enactment of Canon XXVIII., on the nature of the Roman Primacy, and the rank of Constantinople—Carried in opposition to the legates—Anger of Leo—His attempt to quash the Canon—Bad faith of his alleged objections to it—His acceptance of the dogmatic decrees of Chalcedon destroys his case against the Canon, viewed as involving doctrine—The Canon still valid, and virtually reaffirmed in respect of the precedency of Constantinople by the Roman Church at a later time—Pope Hilarus—His endeavours to augment Papal power in Gaul—His irregular interference in the Spanish Church—Pope Simplicius—Pope Felix III. and the Emperor Zeno—Felix attempts to exercise jurisdiction over Acacius of Constantinople—Professes to depose him from his rank—This a novel departure in Church history—Felix the author of the first great schism in the Catholic body—Gelasius I. follows in the steps of Felix III. —Exorbitant claims made by him .... *page* 203

CHAPTER VII.

Legal Breaks in the Chain of Prescription.

Transfer of the seat of the Empire to Constantinople favourable to the growth of Papal authority—The statecraft of the Empire more ancient and disciplined than that of the Church— The conditions of the struggle between Church and State reversed in the West under the barbarian kinglets—The Church aspires to supremacy in temporal affairs—Close of the fifth century—Negotiations of Pope Anastatius II. with Constantinople—Disputed election of Pope Symmachus—The dispute referred to Theodoric the Ostrogoth—Earlier precedent under Odoacer—Impeachment of Pope Symmachus—Synod of the "Incongruous Acquittal"—Ennodius of Pavia on the "hereditary innocence" of the Popes—His view accepted in an Italian Synod—Breach between Pope Symmachus and the Emperor Anastatius — Recrudescence of Eutychianism— Appeal of the Eastern Bishops to Rome—Anastatius compelled to abandon his policy—Opens communications with Pope Hormisda—The Pope endeavours to impose hard terms on the East—Accession of the Emperor Justin—He forces the Formulary of Hormisda upon the clergy of the Empire— Motive of his action—He persecutes the Arians—King Theodoric sends Pope John I. to obtain a cessation of the persecution—The Pope is thrown into prison on his return to Italy, and dies therein—Appointment of Felix IV. as Pope—Disputed election of Boniface II.—He attempts to nominate his own successor, but fails—Unsuccess of the Formulary of Hormisda in the East—Bribery in the Roman Church—Its bearing on the Petrine Claims—Pope Hormisda **commits** himself to heresy—Is compelled to retract by the concurrent action of Justinian and the chief theologians of the time—Complimentary language of Justinian while compelling the Pope to retract—Pontificate of Agapetus—Evidence afforded by his acts as to the meaning of Papal appeals to the authority of the Canons—Agapetus at Constantinople—Election of Pope Sylverius—Plot against him between Vigilius and **the** Empress Theodora'—Simoniacal **intrusion of** Vigilius into the **Papal** Chair—Murder of Pope Sylverius—The com**munion of** Vigilius renounced by several national Churches—Intrusion of Pelagius I.—His repudiation by the Western Churches—Schism of Aquileia—Failure of attempts to establish prescription for Papal authority down to the Pontificate of Gregory the Great .... *page* 260

CHAPTER VIII.

FINAL COLLAPSE OF THE PAPAL SUCCESSION.

Steady growth of Roman influence in the Western Church—The Pope must produce a *de jure* title as **well a** *de facto* one—Nullity in a Pope's title voids all **that part** of the electorate **to** the Papacy which owes its franchise **to** him—A doubtful **Pope is** no-Pope—What constitutes nullity—Citations in proof **from** Canon Law—Bull of Pope Paul IV.—The earlier cases **of** nullity **not** subversive of the whole succession—Alleged reply of **Dinoth** of Bangor-Iscoed to St. Augustine of Canterbury—Proof of the complicity of Pope Honorius in heresy—Controversy on image-worship—Condemnation of Hadrian I. and Gregory II. by a commission of Gallican Divines—Pontifica*t*e of Nicolas I.—He adopts **the False** Decretals—The

Papacy in the ninth century—Pope Formosus—His posthumous trial and condemnation—Alternate reversals and renewals of his sentence by subsequent Popes—Eleven false Popes intruded for sixty successive years in the tenth century—Total breach with the older line of succession—No Petrine line possible since that date—Second era of intrusions in the eleventh century—The electorate restricted to the Cardinals by Pope Nicolas II.—Motives for the change of franchise—Its practical result contrary to the anticipated one—Disputed elections of Innocent II. and of Alexander III.—The **Papacy** at Avignon—Probable effect of non-residence as a defect in title—The Great Schism—All the Popes elected during its continuance doubtful—Councils of Pisa and Constance—Doubtful election of Pope Martin V.—At best a wholly new departure, constituting a new Papacy with no older title—Simoniacal elections of Innocent VIII., Alexander VI., and Julius II. destroyed the electorate, as all the Cardinals who elected Leo X. derived their title from one or another of the simoniacal no-Popes—This flaw final and irremediable—No valid election since 1484—Defect not made good by the acceptance of the titular Popes by the Roman Church—Summary of the whole case against the Petrine Claims...... *page* 304

Table of Legal Flaws in the Papal Succession .... *page* 343

NOTE ON THE FALSE DECRETALS .... *page* 347

ERRATA.

Page 38, one line from bottom, *for* "*Ecclesie*" *read* "*Ecclesiâ.*"

Page 55, four lines from bottom, *for* "any" *read* "no."

Page 132, line 29, *after* "principal Church," *add* "whence priestly unity has its origin."

Page 159, line 10, *dele* "with all the more force . . . *de facto.*"

Same page, line 26, *for* "so that" *read* "nay, more."

Same page, line 29, *after* "that purpose," *insert* new matter :—

"The letter of Pope Julius, in reply to the Council of Antioch, shows at once the extent and the limitations of the Papal claims as then urged. He writes thus:

"'If, on the whole, some fault was committed by those persons, the judgment ought to have taken place in accordance with the ecclesiastical canon, and not as it did take place. Letters should have been written *to all of us,* that so a just sentence might be decreed by *all.* . . . And, especially as regards the Church of Alexandria, why was no letter written to us? Do you not know that such was the custom, that we should first be written to, and thus a just sentence might be decreed from this place?' (St. Athanasius, *Adv. Arianos,* 35)."

Page 163, line 3, *after* "Roman Breviary" *add* "(Aug 14)."

Page 181, line 21, *for* "338" *read* "339."

Page 181, line 29, *after* "Scaliger," *insert* "with whom Bishop Lightfoot substantially agrees (Smith, *Dict. Christian Biog.* II. 325, col. ii.)."

Page 182, line 16, *insert* new paragraph between (*d*) and (*e*) as under :—

(*e*) "But of the rest that accompanied Paul . . . . Linus, whom he has mentioned in his Second Epistle to Timothy as his companion at Rome, has been before shown to have been the first after Peter that obtained the episcopate at Rome (*Hist. Eccl.* iii. 4)."

Then, *for* (*e*) and (*f*) *read* (*f*) and (*g*), and *for* "These six passages" *read* "seven."

Page 192, line 21, *for* the reference in paragraph 4, "Euseb. *Hist. Eccl.* iii. 21," *read* "iii. 2, 4, 21."

Page 358, col. i., line 31, *for* "126" *read* "127."

Page 362, col. ii., line 2, *for* "227" *read* "225 n."

THE PETRINE CLAIMS.

CHAPTER I.

THE LEGAL EVIDENCE OF SCRIPTURE.

Pius IX., the Pontiff under whose auspices was completed the building of Papal autocracy in spiritual matters, planned, in part at least, by Pope Leo I. more than fourteen hundred years ago, carried on by the genius of Gregory VII., by the lofty ambition of Innocent III., by the more worldly policy of Boniface VIII., and diligently laboured at ever since the first beginning of the Counter-Reformation by the persistent toil of the Jesuit body from Bellarmine to Franzelin, bequeathed to his successor, to whom he failed to hand down the temporal crown he wore himself, a more absolute spiritual empire than he had inherited in his turn from Gregory XVI. One thing is clear, that the Papal claims can be practically advanced no further, as their logical goal has been attained, and those controversial debates which formerly ranged over almost the whole domain of theology may be henceforward concentrated on one topic alone, since whatever within the sphere of faith and morals is found existing uncensured in the Latin Obedience must be regarded as having the sanction of infallibility at its back, and as being therefore unassailable by loyal Catholics within that fold, and by all external opponents who are not prepared to join issue on the preliminary question. And, notably, the controversy between the Church of Rome and the Church of England, though it has not really changed since it originally began, has been limited, since the Vatican Council of 1870, to one definite issue, so far as Roman Catholic controversialists are concerned. That issue is the formal claim, first openly put forward by Boniface VIII. in his Bull *Unam Sanctam*, that the Roman Church is not merely "the mother and mistress of all Churches," the largest, most august, and most authoritative portion of the Christian body, occupying, so to speak, the position of the eldest son who succeeds to the titles and to the entailed estates of his father—albeit the younger have minor independent legacies bequeathed to them—but that she is the *whole* Church, the sole legitimate offspring and heir, so that wherever in the course of Holy Scripture or of the Fathers "the Church" is spoken of as clothed with any graces or privileges, the meaning is absolutely limited to the Church in communion with and under the authority of the Pope of Rome, and excludes all other Christian societies as mere sects and schisms from the unity of the One Body of Christ.[1] All other pleas which are raised by Roman controversialists against other portions of Christendom are purely incidental and subordinate, whether urged against their orthodoxy, their possession of a valid ministry, or their practical working. No unimpeachability on all these heads makes the least difference in the conduct of the Roman Church towards them. In every case her policy is the same—to enter on their domains, to deny their claims and rights, and to substitute a rival organization and worship for that which she finds established amongst them. This conduct she justifies on the alleged ground of superior right, conferred by special Divine privilege, and proved by the clear witness of revelation, as well in Holy Scripture as in the historical tradition of Christendom.

---

[1] This conflicts with the admission of Pope Innocent III. : "That is called the Church Universal which consists of all the Churches, and is named from the Greek word, Catholic. And in this sense of the word the Roman Church is not the Church Universal, but a part of the Church Universal" (Ep. ccix).

It will simplify the inquiry to set down the latest authoritative utterances on the subject of revelation, as embodied in the decrees of the Vatican Council itself :—

1. "Supernatural Revelation, according to the faith of the Universal Church, as declared by the Holy Council of Trent, is contained in written books, and in the unwritten traditions, which, having been received by the Apostles from the mouth of Christ himself, or having been, as it were, handed down from the Apostles themselves at the dictation of the Holy Spirit, have arrived even unto us."—*Conc. Trid. Sess.* iv. *Decr. de Can. Script.*)

2. "And these entire books of the Old and New Testament, with all their parts, as they are set forth in the decrees of the said Council, and as they are contained in the old Latin Vulgate edition, are to be received as holy and canonical. These the Church holds to be holy and canonical, not because, having been compiled by mere human industry, they were afterwards approved by her authority, nor merely because they contain revelation with no admixture of error, but because, having been written by the inspiration of the Holy Spirit, they have God for their author, and have been delivered as such to the Church herself. . . . That is to be held as the true sense of Holy Scripture which Holy Mother Church hath held and does hold, to whom it belongs to judge of the true sense and interpretation of Holy Scripture, *and therefore that it is permitted to no one to interpret Holy Scripture contrary to this sense*, nor, likewise, contrary to the unanimous consent of the Fathers."—(*Conc. Vatic. Sess.* iii. cap. 2.)

The last clause is somewhat obscurely worded, and it is well to cite in explanation the different wording of the third clause of the Tridentine Profession of Faith, commonly called the Creed of Pius IV., which runs thus :—

"I also admit Holy Scripture according to that sense which Holy Mother Church has held and does hold, to whom it belongs to judge of the true sense and interpretation of the Holy Scriptures ; *neither will I ever take and interpret them otherwise than according to the unanimous consent of the Fathers.*"

This creed (seriously differing from the Vatican decree in the clause above italicised) has to be formally professed by all bishops and clergy in the Roman Church, and by all lay converts who are sufficiently educated to understand it.

What we have established so far is, that any claim of

privilege, in order to be accounted Divine in the Church of Rome, and warranted by Revelation, must be based (*a*) on Holy Scripture, (*b*) on the historical tradition of the Church, (*c*) on the *unanimous* consent of the Fathers. This excludes all visions and quasi-revelations, as also expressions of ecclesiastical opinion later than the time of St. Bernard, who is accounted the last of the Fathers, and who died in 1153, as evidence of *Divine* right, which must be proved by these three concurrent testimonies.

The claims set forward in the Vatican decrees on the Constitution of the Church are as follows:—

1. "If any one shall say that blessed Peter the Apostle was not appointed by Christ the Lord the Prince of all the Apostles, and the visible Head of the whole Church Militant; or that he received a primacy of honour only, and not directly or immediately one of true and proper jurisdiction from the same our Lord Jesus Christ, let him be anathema."

2. "If any should say that it is not by the institution of Christ the Lord Himself, or by Divine right, that blessed Peter should have a perpetual line of successors in the primacy over the Church Universal, or that the Roman Pontiff is not the successor of blessed Peter in this primacy, let him be anathema."

3. "None may reopen the judgment of the Apostolic See, than whose authority there is none greater; nor can any lawfully review its judgment; therefore they err from the right course who assert that it is lawful to appeal from the judgments of the Roman Pontiffs to a General Council, as to an authority higher than that of the Roman Pontiff. If, then, any shall say that the Roman Pontiff has the office merely of inspection or direction, but not full and supreme power of jurisdiction over the Universal Church, not only in things which belong to faith and morals, but also in those which relate to the discipline and government of the Church spread throughout the world; or assert that he possesses only the chief part, and not the entire fulness of the supreme power; or that this power which he enjoys is not ordinary and immediate, both over each and all the Churches, and over each and all the pastors and faithful, let him be anathema."

4. "The Sacred Council approving, we teach and define that it is a dogma divinely revealed, that the Roman Pontiff, when he speaks *ex cathedrâ*, that is, when discharging the office of Pastor and Doctor of all Christians, by virtue of his supreme Apostolic authority, he defines a doctrine regarding faith or morals to be held by the Church Universal, by the Divine assistance promised to him in blessed Peter, is possessed of that infallibility with which the Divine Redeemer willed that His Church should be endowed for defining doctrine

concerning faith or morals; and that, therefore, such definitions of the Roman Pontiff are irreformable of themselves, and not from the consent of the Church. But if any one—which God avert—presume to contradict this our definition, let him be anathema."

In proportion as these claims are vast and startling, the proofs alleged need to be abundant, clear, and conclusive, and every step in the process must be rigorously established by convincing evidence of its Divine origin and institution, as distinguished from mere ecclesiastical powers of human origin, arrangement, and concession. For the claim is that it is nothing less than divinely revealed, and that not by any such visions and miracles as are alleged on behalf of particular devotional practices in modern times, but by the threefold testimony of Scripture, Church history, and the writings of the Fathers.

Further, as the entire claim of Papal Infallibility rests avowedly on asserted heirship to St. Peter, and right of succession to all his privileges, while no allegation is made that those privileges have been specifically re-granted to any Pope since his time, much less increased, developed, and amplified in any manner, it follows that the Pope can claim no more than is plainly discoverable as conferred upon and exercised by St. Peter himself. But the whole of the evidence now extant upon this head is confined to the books of the New Testament. The few meagre and uncertain notices of St. Peter's life which have come to us from uninspired writers do not touch this question of his primacy, jurisdiction, and transmission of his powers at all. Consequently, the Gospels, Acts, and Epistles contain not only his whole charter of privilege, but our whole means of ascertaining what he actually enjoyed and exercised in virtue of that charter.

For the Roman claims, then, to have any firm basis, this evidence must establish clearly and expressly, and not by mere possible implication or inference, the following points:—

1. That St. Peter was given by Christ a primacy, not of honour and rank alone, but of direct and sovereign jurisdiction over all the other Apostles.

2. That this primacy was not limited to St. Peter's person only for his lifetime, but was conferred on him with power to bequeath it to his successors.

The subsequent question, as to whether he did actually so bequeath it to the Bishops of Rome, belongs to a later date in Church history than that comprised in the New Testament period, and must be deferred for the present. It is our business now to examine the charter, conveyance, and exercise of that which in the language of modern Roman theologians is called the "Privilege of Peter." The reason why the proof of it needs to be express and clear, is because *privilege*, being a private exception to the usual public course of law, either in the form of exemption from some burden generally imposed, or of enjoyment of some benefit generally withheld, is essentially an invidious thing, and requires fuller proof than any other right before it can be allowed as valid. Consequently, the Roman Canon Law (by which an exclusively Roman claim cannot reasonably or even plausibly refuse to be tested[1]) has laid down the following broad rules (amongst others) to govern all cases of the sort:—

1. The authoritative document containing the privilege must be produced.—(*Decret. Greg. IX.;* lib. v. tit. xxxiii.)

2. Its wording must be certain and manifest, not obscure or doubtful.—(*Decret. Greg. IX.;* lib. v. tit. xl. 25.)

3. It must be construed in the most strict and literal sense.—(*Reg. Juris.;* vi. and xxviii.; *Fagnan. de Past. et Prælat.* 7; *Zypæus de Privil. Consult.* 1.)

4. If personal, it follows the person [not the office]; and it dies with the person named in it.—(*Boniface VIII. De Regulis Juris.;* reg. vii.)

5. It may not be extended to any other person, because of identity or similarity of reason, unless such extension be

---

[1] As by pleading that the Petrine privilege, being older than the Canon Law, cannot be subject to its rules. For the question is as to the devolution of this privilege to the reigning Pope, whose claim to it must be subject to the tests of contemporary Canon Law. And the claim itself was not formulated definitely till the fifth century.

expressly named in it.—(*Decret. Greg. IX.;* lib. v. tit. xxxiii. 9.)

6.—It may not be so interpreted as to deny, interfere with, or encroach upon the rights and privileges of another. —(*Decret. Greg. IX.;* lib. v. tit. xxxiii. 4.)

7. It is forfeited by any excess or abuse in its exercise.— (*Decret.* ii. xi. 3, lx.)

Let us now examine the evidence of Holy Scripture, not mainly from a theological point of view, but rather from a legal one, as the principal document tendered in proof of claim. Our Lord's charter to St. Peter is held to be contained in three clauses of the Gospels:—

1. "And Jesus answered and said unto him, Blessed art thou, Simon Bar-jona: for flesh and blood hath not revealed it unto thee, but My Father which is in heaven. And I say also unto thee, That thou art Peter, and upon this rock I will build My church; and the gates of hell shall not prevail against it. And I will give unto thee the keys of the kingdom of heaven: and whatsoever thou shalt bind on earth shall be bound in heaven: and whatsoever thou shalt loose on earth shall be loosed in heaven."—St. Matthew xvi. 17-19.

2. "And the Lord said, Simon, Simon, behold, Satan hath desired to have you, that he may sift you as wheat: But I have prayed for thee, that thy faith fail not: and when thou art converted, strengthen thy brethren."—St. Luke xxii. 31, 32.

3. "So when they had dined, Jesus said to Simon Peter, Simon, son of Jonas, lovest thou me more than these? He saith unto Him, Yea, Lord; Thou knowest that I love Thee. He saith unto him, Feed My lambs. He saith to him again the second time, Simon, son of Jonas, lovest thou Me? He saith to Him, Yea, Lord; Thou knowest that I love Thee. He saith unto him, Feed My sheep. He saith unto him the third time, Simon, son of Jonas, lovest thou Me? Peter was grieved, because He said unto him the third time, Lovest thou Me? And he said unto Him, Lord, Thou knowest all things; Thou knowest that I love Thee. Jesus saith unto him, Feed My sheep."—St. John xxi. 15-17.

This is the sum of the charter. If we look somewhat more minutely into it, we shall find that certain portions of it are not peculiar to St. Peter, but are common to others. First we are told that in what appears to be the interval between St. Peter's going away to pay the tribute money for Christ and himself (St. Matthew xvii. 27) and his return to the other Apostles, when he put his question to Christ on the forgiveness of injuries, our Lord conferred the same power of binding and loosing on the remaining Apostles, apart from St. Peter, saying :—

> "Verily, I say unto you, Whatsoever ye shall bind on earth shall be bound in heaven: and whatsoever ye shall loose on earth shall be loosed in heaven."—St. Matthew xviii. 18;

and again bestowed it on all the Apostles, collectively, after His Resurrection—

> "Then said Jesus to them again, Peace be unto you: as My Father hath sent Me, even so send I you. And when He had said this, He breathed on them, and saith unto them, Receive ye the Holy Ghost: Whosesoever sins ye remit, they are remitted unto them; and whosesoever sins ye retain, they are retained."—St. John xx. 21-23.

Accordingly, the clause as to binding and loosing in St. Matthew xvi. 19 is no part of the especial *privilege* of Peter, and constitutes no difference between him and the remaining Apostles.

The second passage, that from St. Luke, so far from exalting St. Peter, actually puts him below the level of his colleagues, as the context shows. All of them are to be tried and sifted by Satan like wheat. Peter is the only one whose actual fall and denial of his Lord is foretold—cowardly flight being the worst fault of the other Apostles—and thus he is the only one who stands in need of "conversion." And he is bidden, when this necessary repentance and change have taken place in himself, to support, by his newly-revived zeal, his yet unfallen brethren, lest they should sin as he had just done. To fortify them by confession of his own weakness is in no respect akin to exercising authority over them.

The third passage (apart from the difficulty that in the only one place of Holy Writ where the Apostles are spoken of as "sheep," St. Peter is included amongst them, and not separately named as their shepherd:—"Behold I send you forth as sheep in the midst of wolves," St. Matthew x. 16) in like manner confers no exceptional privilege, because we have it twice attributed to the ordinary ministers of the Church—the Elders, far below the Apostles in power and dignity, while one of these two attributions is made by St. Peter himself. The clauses are, first, St. Paul's address to the Elders of the Church at Miletus:—

"Take heed therefore unto yourselves, and to all the flock, over the which the Holy Ghost hath made you overseers, to feed the church of God, which He hath purchased with His own blood."—Acts xx. 28;

and next, St. Peter's similar exhortation :—

"The elders which are among you I exhort, who am also an elder, and a witness of the sufferings of Christ, and also a partaker of the glory that shall be revealed: Feed the flock of God which is among you, taking the oversight thereof, not by constraint, but willingly; not for filthy lucre, but of a ready mind; neither as being lords over God's heritage, but being ensamples to the flock."—1 St. Peter v. 1-3.

And, in truth, part of the immediate context of St. John xxi. 17, which has been generally overlooked in this connexion, furnishes incidental but adequate disproof of the Ultramontane gloss :—

"Then Peter, turning about, seeth the disciple whom Jesus loved following; which also leaned on His breast at supper, and said, Lord, which is he that betrayeth Thee? Peter seeing him, saith to Jesus, Lord, and what shall this man do? Jesus saith unto him, If I will that he tarry till I come, what is that to thee? follow thou Me."—St. John xxi. 20-22.

It is obvious that if St. Peter had received jurisdiction over St. John only a few minutes before, his question was perfectly legitimate and reasonable, and merited a reply, as being his concern, because affecting one for whom he had been just made responsible. But the answer he actually receives can denote nothing short of St. John's entire independence, and the restriction of St. Peter's own commission to attending to his own specific and limited share of Apostolic work, with no right of control over St. John.

There remains, therefore, so far, as the whole charter of special Petrine privilege, only the one passage :—

"And I say also unto thee, That thou art Peter, and upon this rock I will build My Church; and the gates of hell shall not prevail against it. And I will give unto thee the keys of the kingdom of heaven."—St. Matthew xvi. 18.

But before we enter on the question of its interpretation, to be considered later, even if we take St. Peter to be the rock, it appears that even this title does not stand alone in such sort as to constitute a gift of sovereign authority. For this same attribute of being foundations of the Church is in two other places ascribed to the Apostles generally, once by St. Paul:—

"Now therefore ye are no more strangers and foreigners, but fellow-citizens with the saints, and of the household of God; and are built upon the foundation of the Apostles and Prophets, Jesus Christ Himself being the chief corner stone; in Whom all the building fitly framed together groweth unto an holy temple in the Lord."—Eph. i. 19-21;

and again by St. John:—

"And the wall of the city had twelve foundations, and in them the names of the twelve Apostles of the Lamb."—Rev. xxi. 14;

where, moreover, it is not unworthy of notice, that the *first* stone, a jasper, is much inferior in beauty and value to some of the remainder, as the sapphire, emerald, and chrysolite, which severally form the second, fourth, and seventh foundations.—Rev. xxi. 19, 20. As to the clause about the power of the Keys, see later, Chap. II.

Nevertheless, as the whole New Testament ought, for the purposes of this inquiry, be construed as a single document, there may be other expressions and indications in it from which the extent of the Petrine charter may be reasonably inferred, and if a collation of them give any more specific authority to St. Peter than is visible thus far, it must be read into and incorporated with that charter. Conversely, if the additional evidence point to a strict and narrow construction, or even to further limitation, of it, that too must needs be taken as conditioning its terms.

The first piece of evidence, then, is that *immediately after* the bestowal by Christ of whatever gift or privilege is conferred by St. Matthew xvi. 18, 19, and most probably in the course of the very same conversation, as appears from a comparison of St. Mark viii. 27-34, by far the sternest rebuke ever uttered to an Apostle by Christ falls on St. Peter:—

"From that time forth began Jesus to shew unto His disciples how that he must go unto Jerusalem, and suffer many things of the elders and chief priests and scribes, and be killed, and be raised again the third day. Then Peter took Him, and began to rebuke Him, saying, Be it far from Thee, Lord: this shall not be unto Thee. But He turned, and said unto Peter, Get thee behind Me, Satan: thou art an offence unto Me: for thou savourest not the things that be of God, but those that be of men."—St. Matthew xvi. 21-23.

This proves at the least that St. Peter did not acquire in virtue of that previous charter the gift of infallibility, nor even that of not directly contravening the will of God. And so evident is this deduction, that a modern infallibilist has endeavoured to escape from it by alleging that the Peter of the second clause was a different person from the Simon Bar-jona or Peter of the first one.

Next, if the passage St. Matthew xvi. 17-20, be, as it is from a Roman Catholic point of view, one of the most significant and important items of Divine revelation, we are entitled to expect to find it emphasized by the other Evangelists.

If it lay outside their plan, and they made no reference whatever to this conversation at Cæsarea Philippi, no conclusion either way could be drawn from their silence, any more than from St. John's omission of the Last Supper or the Ascension.

But St. Mark and St. Luke both do embody St. Peter's confession of Christ in their narratives, yet leave out entirely all reference to the words "Thou art Peter," &c.,—St. Mark viii. 27-34, St. Luke ix. 18-23. Hence it is clear that in their minds the important part of the conversation was the declaration of our Lord's person and office, not the definition and scope of St. Peter's privilege. Nor is this all. The received tradition of the Roman Church is that St. Mark was the disciple of St. Peter, and wrote his Gospel by St. Peter's directions and under his supervision.

But St. Mark, while *omitting* the words "Thou art Peter," &c., *inserts* the words "Get thee behind me, Satan; for thou savourest not of the things that be of God, but the things that be of men."—St. Mark viii. 33.

The inevitable inference from this most weighty fact is that St. Peter himself did not consider the words of Christ in St. Matthew xvi. 17-20 necessary to be communicated by St. Mark to those for whom his Gospel was written, and therefore it is clear that he did not attach the meaning to them which Roman controversialists now allege as the true one; since, had he done so, he was bound for the highest reasons to make his peculiar commission known, precisely as an ambassador is required to produce his credentials, and the governor of a colony to exhibit his patent from the Crown, at his entry upon his office. Nor can such a breach of duty as silence under such circumstances be excused by attributing it to St. Peter's humility, because the truest humility is implicit obedience to God's commands, whether tending to exalt or abase him to whom the command is given.

Further, St. Peter uses language in his own Epistles which implies, if not ignorance on his part as to any special privilege attaching to his own person, at any rate abstinence from pressing it, and that to the extent of employing phrases which seem to exclude it, so far as it is held to be based either on St. Matthew xvi. 18, or on St. John xxi. 15-17. For in the first place, he seems to recognise no foundation of the Church save Christ himself:—

"If so be ye have tasted that the Lord is gracious. To Whom coming, as unto a living stone, disallowed indeed of men, but chosen of God, and precious, ye also, as lively stones, are built up a spiritual house, an holy priesthood, to offer up spiritual sacrifices, acceptable to God by Jesus Christ. Wherefore also it is contained in the scripture, Behold I lay in Sion a chief corner stone, elect, precious: and he that believeth on Him shall not be confounded."—1 St. Peter i. 3-6.

And in the next place he names only one Chief Shepherd and Bishop—

"Who His own self bare our sins in His own body on the tree, that we, being dead to sins, should live unto righteousness: by Whose stripes ye were healed. For ye were as sheep going astray; but are now returned unto the Shepherd and Bishop of your souls."—1 Peter ii. 24, 25.

With this may be contrasted the language of Pius IX., who, in a public address, applied to himself the text St. John xiv. 6,—"I am the Way, the Truth, and the Life,"[1] words which cannot by any accommodation be applied save to Him Who spoke them, as two of them denote incommunicable attributes; whereas St. Peter might have found justification for claiming the titles of "Foundation of the Church" and "Chief Shepherd," as his own, had he thought they belonged to him.

The next question to consider is, what additional light the language of our Lord in the Gospels sheds on the extent and nature of the privilege of Peter. First, then, soon after the utterance in St. Matthew xvi. 18, and just before the bestowal of the power of binding and loosing on all the Apostles in St. Peter's absence, the question of precedence in Christ's kingdom is raised, and is answered by our Lord in terms inconsistent with the opinion that the disciples understood Him to have already settled that point, or that He had in fact done so, whether they understood Him or not:—

"At the same time came the disciples unto Jesus, saying, Who is the greatest in the kingdom of heaven? And Jesus called a little child unto Him, and set him in the midst of them, and said, Verily I say unto you, Except ye be converted, and become as little children, ye shall not enter into the kingdom of heaven. Whosoever therefore shall humble himself as this little child, the same is greatest in the kingdom of heaven."—St. Matt. xviii. 1-4.

A little later Christ puts all the Apostles on the same level:—

"Then answered Peter and said unto Him, Behold, we have forsaken all, and followed Thee; what shall we have therefore? And Jesus said unto them, Verily I say unto you, That ye which have followed Me, in the regeneration when the Son of man shall sit in the

---

[1] Reported in the *Observateur Catholique* of April 1, 1866, page 357; textually cited by Quirinus, Letter XXIII. (p. 285 of English version).

throne of His glory, ye also shall sit upon twelve thrones, judging the twelve tribes of Israel."—St. Matt. xix. **27**, 28.

This text has a further bearing on the question, as establishing that Christ's grants are conditional and forfeitable, not indefeasible, since one of the twelve to whom these words were spoken was Judas Iscariot.

Thirdly, comes the application of the mother of SS. James and John on behalf of her children:—

"Then came to Him the mother of Zebedee's children with her sons, worshipping Him, and desiring a certain thing of Him. And He said unto her, What wilt thou? She saith unto Him, Grant that these my two sons may sit, the one on Thy right hand, and the other on the left, in Thy kingdom. But Jesus answered and said, Ye know not what ye ask. Are ye able to drink of the cup that I shall drink of, and to be baptized with the baptism that I am baptized with? They say unto him, We are able. And He saith unto them, Ye shall drink indeed of My cup, and be baptized with the baptism that I am baptized with: but to sit on My right hand, and on My left, is not Mine to give, but it shall be given to them for whom it is prepared of My Father. And when the ten heard it, they were moved with indignation against the two brethren. But Jesus called them unto Him, and said, Ye know that the princes of the Gentiles exercise dominion over them, and they that are great exercise authority upon them. But it shall not be so among you: but whosoever will be great among you, let him be your minister; and whosoever will be chief among you, let him be your servant; even as the Son of man came not to be ministered unto, but to minister, and to give His life a ransom for many."—St. Matt. xx. 20-28.

Here it is to be noticed that the request of Salome was not for a mere honorary distinction, but for substantial office and authority, since in Eastern kingdoms, even to this day, the two principal ministers of State ranking next in authority to the monarch are styled "Vizir of the right hand" and "Vizir of the left hand." Obviously, Christ's answer, on the Roman hypothesis, must have been that He had already given away the right-hand post to St. Peter, and did not intend to create a left-hand one. What He does say is to declare explicitly that no one of them should exercise authority over the others, consequently that He had *not* given St. Peter any jurisdiction over the Apostolic college.

Nevertheless, so persistent amongst the Twelve was the

carnal way of viewing Christ's kingdom as modelled on the pattern of earthly monarchies, that this very same question crops up again at the Last Supper—a time when a peculiar solemnity and sacredness attaches to every word of Christ, and when, if ever, we might expect Him to nominate the chief who should rule His Church after His departure. What we do find, however, is a precise reiteration of His former explanation, a renewal of His former promise of equal dignity:—

"And there was also a strife among them, which of them should be accounted the greatest. And He said unto them, The Kings of the Gentiles exercise lordship over them; and they that exercise authority upon them are called benefactors. But ye shall not be so: but he that is greatest among you, let him be as the younger; and he that is chief, as he that doth serve. For whether is greater, he that sitteth at meat, or he that serveth? is not he that sitteth at meat? but I am among you as he that serveth. Ye are they which have continued with Me in My temptations. And I appoint unto you a kingdom, as My Father hath appointed unto Me; that ye may eat and drink at My table in My kingdom, and sit on thrones judging the twelve tribes of Israel."—St. Luke xxii. 24-30.

After supper, He says, still marking their perfect equality "I am the vine, ye are the branches."—St. John xv. 5.

The last utterance of Christ which directly bears upon the question of privilege is the final commission to the Apostles before the Ascension:—

"Then the eleven disciples went away into Galilee, into a mountain where Jesus had appointed them. And when they saw Him, they worshipped Him; but some doubted. And Jesus came and spake unto them, saying, All power is given unto Me in heaven and in earth. Go ye therefore, and teach all nations, baptizing them in the name of the Father, and of the Son, and of the Holy Ghost: teaching them to observe all things whatsoever I have commanded you: and, lo, I am with you alway, even unto the end of the world. Amen." St. Matt. xxviii. 16-20.

Here, as before, no distinction is made between them, and no hint is given that they should look to St. Peter as their chief.

There is, however, yet another important saying of our Lord's which touches the subject from another side, and not less significantly.

It is to be remembered, that as the Gospel is the harmonious development and spiritual fulfilment of the typical Mosaic Law, we are entitled to look for some parallel in the Gospel for every salient type or incident under the Law, with, however, this weighty and invariable difference, that the antitype is never *identical* with the type, but belongs to a less carnal and more spiritual order, so that there is never an exact reproduction of the earlier ordinance; as the Holy Eucharist, when compared with the animal sacrifices, exemplifies, and still more the substitution of Christ for the Levitical High Priests (Heb. vi. 20; vii. 15–28; viii. 1–6). Now the two greatest Old Testament types of Christ are Moses, as lawgiver and prophet, and David, as king and prophet. Each of these takes measures to appoint his successor before his own death, and to secure his acceptance by the nation. The delegation by Moses to Joshua is recorded in Numbers xxvii. 15-23, and in Deut. xxxi. 23; the action of David is recorded in 1 Kings i. 32–35; and in each case the action is most formal and explicit.

Now these two examples have three points in common: (*a*) they take place just before the deaths of the chief actors; (*b*) they are express and unambiguous in their designation of the successor's name; (*c*) they are attended by public ceremonial solemnities. And we are justified, by the analogy of faith, in looking for some cognate action on Christ's part, only this analogy would be violated, not observed, by a precise agreement in the human element of the proceeding.

Accordingly, we do find it, and exactly in the higher plane to be expected. On the night before His death, Christ formally designates His Vicar on earth, and that in the most precise and definite terms, to the necessary exclusion of any other :—

"And I will pray the Father, and He shall give you another Comforter, that He may abide with you for ever; even the Spirit of truth; whom the world cannot receive, because it seeth Him not, neither knoweth Him: but ye know Him; for He dwelleth with you, and shall be in you. . . . . But the Comforter, which is the Holy

Ghost, Whom the Father will **send in my** name, He shall teach you all things, and bring all things to your remembrance, whatsoever I have said unto you. . . . . But when the Comforter is come, Whom I will send unto you from the Father, even the Spirit of truth, which proceedeth from the Father, He shall testify of Me. . . . . Nevertheless I tell **you** the truth; It **is** expedient **for you that I go away**: for if I go not away, the Comforter will not come unto you; **but if I depart, I** will send Him unto you. . . . . Howbeit when He, the Spirit of truth, **is** come, He will guide you into all truth: for He shall not speak of Himself; but whatsoever **He** shall hear, that shall He speak: and He will show you things **to** come. He shall glorify Me: for He shall receive of Mine, and shall show it unto you. All things that the Father hath **are** Mine: therefore said I, that He shall take of Mine, and show it **unto you.**"—St. **John** xiv. 16, 17, 26; **xv.** 26; xvi. 7, 13, 14, **15.**

The formal installation of this **Vicar of Christ is** also recorded:—

"And when the day of Pentecost was fully come, they were all with one accord in one place. And suddenly there came **a sound** from heaven as of a rushing mighty wind, and it filled all the **house** where they were sitting. And there appeared **unto** them **cloven** tongues like as of fire, and it sat upon each of them. **And** they **were** all filled with the Holy Ghost, and began to **speak with other** tongues, as the Spirit gave them utterance."—Acts ii. **1-4.**

The parallel thus holds good in all the three particulars common to the appointments of Joshua and Solomon, besides fulfilling **the** further condition essential to its Gospel character, of belonging to a higher **order of things, inasmuch** as a Divine Being—not a mere **man, however commissioned**—is sent to occupy the **place of the departed** Lawgiver and King. The nomination **of any Apostle** would **have** left the act of Christ on **exactly the same** level as those of Moses and David,—or **rather, on** a much lower one, since **the** interval between **Him** and **St.** Peter is much vaster than that between Moses **and** Joshua, or David and Solomon—and thus it would have provided no real antitype for **the** type and shadow under the old Covenant.

This being so, to demand, much more to constitute, what the Vatican Council styles a "Visible Head of the Church Militant" is, in effect, to refuse the Head so nominated and appointed by Christ, and to commit the sin of the Jews when they twice rejected the Lord because of His invisibility, desiring some object of worship and some leader more cognisable by the senses, saying first to Aaron :—

"Up, make us gods, which shall go before us; for as for this Moses, the man that brought us up out of the land of Egypt, we wot not what is become of him."—Exodus xxxii. 1 ;

and later, demanding a king, in order to be like the nations round them, as recorded in 1 Sam. viii. 4-7.

This closes the evidence derivable from *words* of our Lord in the Gospels as to any peculiar charter of privilege bestowed on St. Peter. But *acts*, in such a matter, would be equally valid as testimony, and must also be taken into account. Our next step, therefore, is to ascertain what direct personal distinctions are, by the immediate *action* of Christ Himself, conferred on St. Peter, and recorded in the Gospels. They are as follows :—

1. St. Peter's name stands *first* in the three lists of the Apostles given in the synoptic Gospels, St. Matthew x. 2 ; St. Mark iii. 16 ; St. Luke vi. 15. This, coupled with the fact that the name of Judas Iscariot stands *last* in these same three lists, points to a priority of some kind, albeit not defined clearly.

2. He is chosen as a companion and witness to Christ on three important occasions, from which the general body of the Apostles was excluded—(*a*) the Transfiguration—St. Matt. xvii. 1 ; St. Mark ix. 2 ; St. Luke ix. 28 ; (*b*) the raising of Jairus's daughter—St. Mark v. 37 ; St. Luke viii. 51 ; (*c*) the Agony in the Garden—St. Matt. xxvi. 37 ; St. Mark xiv. 33.

3. He is directed to pay the tribute-money for Christ and himself, and is thus specially coupled with our Lord— St. Matt. xvii. 27.

4. He is sent to prepare the upper chamber for the Passover—St. Luke xxii. 8. These are all the instances discoverable.

(i.) As to the first of these distinctions, St. Peter's priority in the lists of Apostles, where we might naturally look in his stead either for the name of St. Andrew, as the first called of the Twelve, and himself the first to call another to Christ (St. John i. 40, 41), or else of St. John, because of his special prerogative as "the disciple whom Jesus loved" (St. John xiii. 23; xix. 26; xx. 2; xxi. 7, 20), undoubtedly denotes some precedence, and were any jurisdiction over the other Apostles attributed to St. Peter elsewhere, it would serve as collateral evidence in proof of his claim. But the entire silence of the Gospels on this head forbids us to read any such clause into the statement, and shows that, instead of the order of names in the lists serving as a key to interpret the remainder of the notices concerning St. Peter in the Gospels, it must itself be interpreted by them, if the extent of St. Peter's privilege be inferred from the information they supply. In the analogy of any cognate lists, so far as Holy Scripture is concerned—such as those in Genesis, Numbers, and Chronicles — only genealogical order of seniority is denoted, and no difference of authority over the deacons appears in the case of St. Stephen (Acts vi. 5), nor over the Seven Churches in that of the Angel of the Church of Ephesus (Rev. i. 2; ii. 1); while in lists belonging to civil life, say, for example, such as the roll of English dukes, the order denotes merely social precedence, not inequality of rank and honour, far less official superiority, and the subordination of all the lower names on the roll to the authority of that which stands first. There are, moreover, two items of evidence discoverable in the lists of the Apostles, which materially weaken the argument drawn from the order of the names. They are that, unquestionably, St. James and St. John occupy a more prominent place in the Gospels than any other Apostle except St. Peter himself, and seemingly enjoy some degree of priority. But in two out of the three lists (St. Matt. x. 2, and St. Luke vi. 14), St. Andrew is placed next after St. Peter, and described as his brother, while in St. Mark's Gospel alone (chap. iii. 16, 17) is the actual order of rank observed, and the qualifying description of St.

Andrew omitted—another incidental proof of St. Peter's care not to magnify his office. In like manner, St. Matthew, out of humility, places his own name after that of St. Thomas (St. Matt. x. 3), albeit he is put before St. Thomas in the lists of St. Mark (iii. 18) and St. Luke (v. 15). Consequently, these variations of the order forbid us to assume that any strict gradation of rank is implied, since otherwise the Evangelists would not have ventured to deviate from the series of the original appointment.

(ii.) As regards the three occasions on which St. Peter is specially chosen to accompany Christ, St. James and St. John share the distinction with him.

(iii.) The tribute-money seems to couple him more individually with Christ; but an inquiry into the circumstances of the case deprives it of all importance for the matter at issue. For the event happened at Capernaum (St. Matt. xvii. 24), and a comparison of St. Mark i. 21, 29, shows that St. Peter's house was in that town: "And they went into Capernaum; and straightway on the Sabbath day he entered into the synagogue, and taught. . . . And forthwith, when they were come out of the synagogue, they entered into the house of Simon and Andrew." The tax-collectors at Capernaum, going from house to house to demand the temple-tribute, come to St. Peter's dwelling in its turn, and call on him, in his character of householder, to answer for his guest as well as for himself, in order that if he were a loyal Jew, and consequently morally liable to the tribute, it might be levied on Him also; and knowing that Christ was then abiding in the house, they ask Peter, "Doth not your Master pay tribute?"—(St. Matt. xvii. 24). Accordingly, Christ accepts the position, and in his capacity as St. Peter's guest, enables him to acquit himself of his twofold responsibility in respect of the tax. Yet the relation is one which does not arise out of His spontaneous action for the purpose of honouring St. Peter, but from the accidental coincidence in time, so to speak, of the application to St. Peter for payment and our Lord's visit to his house. And, further, both Christ and St. Peter were, in this instance, alike subordinated to the Jewish law, which naturally treated them as on exactly the same footing below itself, and recognised no distinction of liability between them; so that no inference whatever can be drawn from the narrative as to their relation to each other under the Gospel, and it remains that the sole reason for the commemoration of the event is to record the miracle of the fish.

(iv.) Finally, St. John is coupled with St. Peter in the errand to prepare the Passover, so that here, too, no special privilege is discernible.

This concludes the evidence obtainable from the four Gospels, and it is manifest so far that no jurisdiction over the Church was clearly bestowed on or unquestionably exercised by St. Peter. And yet the analogy of the Old Testament justifies us in looking for the exact reverse of both these propositions, if the hypothesis of the special charter be sound. For in the Old Testament there are no fewer than three Divine and exceptional charters of privilege bestowed, in all of which the terms of gift are precise and unambiguous, and in all of which, moreover, the right of transmission of the privilege by inheritance is expressly provided for and assured. These are (*a*) the covenant with Abraham and his seed, Gen. xii. 1-3, renewed in Gen. xvii. 6-8, and xxii. 16-18, confirmed to Isaac, Gen. xxvi. 3, 4, 5, and to Jacob, Gen. xxviii. 13, and xxxv. 11, 12; (*b*) the grant of the priesthood to Aaron and his descendants, Exod. xxviii. 1, confirmed by miracle, Numb. xvi. 31-40, xvii. 5, 8, and amplified in detail, Numb. xviii. 1-8; (*c*) the grant of the kingdom of Israel to David and his posterity, 1 Sam. vii. 1-16, renewed to Solomon, 1 Kings, ix. 2, 6. It is contrary to the analogy of faith that the Law should be clear, definite, and literal in a certain respect, and that the Gospel, in a perfectly cognate and similar one, should be obscure, indeterminate, and typical, veiling the grant itself in mystical and enigmatic phrases, and passing over in entire silence the question of transmission. And, regarded from a legal point of view (which the plea of a Divine right conveyed by a formal grant makes necessary to the Ultramontane argument), there is no conclusion possible from this marked departure from these three leading precedents, or, so to speak, exemplifications of form, save that no similar powers were bestowed, or intended to be bestowed, and conveyed by the grant to St. Peter, seeing that the grantor in all four cases is the same Divine Person, so that we have a right to look for identical action and similar wording.

But it may not unreasonably be argued in reply, that as it is St. Peter's peculiar office and dignity to be the Vicar of Christ, we cannot fairly expect to find him discharging that function while Christ is Himself present with His Church on earth, just as we do not look for moonlight when the sun is shining in its strength, albeit at night the moon far excels the stars singly or collectively. It is after the constitution of the Church on the Day of Pentecost, and thenceforward, that we must look for proofs of St. Peter's authority. And it is perfectly true that he does at once assume a prominence in the narrative of the Acts of the Apostles, much exceeding anything recorded in the Gospels. The instances are as follows:—

1. He proposes, between the Ascension and Pentecost, the filling up of the vacancy left by Judas Iscariot in the College of Apostles.—Acts i. 15, 21, 22.

2. He preaches the first missionary sermon to the Jews on the Day of Pentecost.—Acts ii. 14, 38.

3. He works the first miracle of the Church, on the lame man at the Temple Gate—(Acts iii. 6), and two others of the very few recorded in the Acts (ix. 32-42).

4. He preaches the second missionary sermon to the Jews.—Acts iii. 12.

5. He is spokesman for himself and St. John before the Sanhedrin.—Acts iv. 8.

6. He passes judgment on Ananias and Sapphira.—Acts v. 3-11.

7. He is a second time spokesman for the Apostles before the Sanhedrin.—Acts v. 29.

8. He preaches the first missionary sermon to the Gen-

tiles, and causes his converts from amongst them to be baptized.—Acts x. 34, 48.

9. He argues in the Council of Jerusalem for the relaxation of the ceremonial law in the case of Gentile Christians. —Acts xv. 7.

10. St. Paul, at the outset of his regular ministry, after his three years' sojourn in Arabia, goes up to Jerusalem to consult St. Peter.—Gal. i. 18.

Most of these acts are evidence of important and prominent station, and (2) and (8) of a distinction in honour greater in some respects than was accorded to any other Apostle. But not one of these acts singly, nor all of them collectively, can furnish a tittle of proof in favour of a primacy of jurisdiction. And it will be shown later that even the two acts which do confer peculiar lustre on St. Peter's name, are interpreted by ancient Christian writers in a sense adverse to the claim of supremacy.—See Chap. II.

(i.) The narrative of the election of St. Matthias, so far from helping to establish any claim to sovereign authority on St. Peter's behalf, furnishes one weighty item of evidence against it. Nothing is clearer than that if he had succeeded in any special sense to Christ's authority over the Church, as His Vicar, and if, in consequence, the Apostolic College bore any such relation to him, as, for instance, the College of Cardinals does to the Pope—and the Ultramontane theory requires no less—St. Peter would have filled up the vacant place of Judas on his own authority, as the Pope deals with a vacant Cardinal's hat, or as Solomon, when clothed with David's twofold office of king and prophet, dealt with the high-priesthood, when he put Zadok the priest into the room of Abiathar (1 Kings ii. 26, 27, 35). But nothing of the sort meets us. St. Peter's share in the transaction is strictly confined to suggesting the necessity of designating a successor. The whole College unites in nominating two candidates, and the actual election is decided in quite another way than by the voice of its president, so that there is no likeness even to the mode commonly observed in episcopal elections now a-days by the

Roman Catholic Church in countries where it is disconnected from the State, namely, that the electors to a vacant see submit three names to the Pope, who may select one, or, at his pleasure, set them all aside, and appoint some fourth person, whom none of the electors had chosen, as was exemplified by the appointment of Dr. Manning to the titular see of Westminster in 1865, to the prejudice not merely of the freedom of election, but of the vested rights of Archbishop Errington as coadjutor of Cardinal Wiseman *cum jure successionis*. The narrative in the Acts runs thus:—

"Wherefore of these men which have companied with us all the time that the Lord Jesus went in and out among us, beginning from the baptism of John, unto that same day that He was taken up from us, must one be ordained to be a witness with us of His resurrection. And they appointed two, Joseph called Barsabas, who was surnamed Justus, and Matthias. And they prayed, and said, Thou, Lord, Which knowest the hearts of all men, shew whether of these two Thou hast chosen, that he may take part of this ministry and apostleship, from which Judas by transgression fell, that he might go to his own place. And they gave forth their lots; and the lot fell upon Matthias; and he was numbered with the eleven apostles."—Acts i. 21-26.

(ii.) Preaching a sermon to convert outsiders to the Church is in no respect akin to exercising jurisdiction over those within the Church.

(iii.) Nor is a miracle of healing, also performed on one outside the Church, an act of internal jurisdiction.

(iv.) This case is identical with ii.

(v.) A plea in self-defence before an alien and external tribunal is not an act of internal jurisdiction.

(vi.) The sentence on Ananias and Sapphira is unquestionably an example of coercive jurisdiction for the punishment, by Divine authority, of offences against religion. But (*a*) it is an extraordinary and miraculous judgment in a wholly exceptional case, not an act of habitual and general jurisdiction; (*b*) it is inflicted not on an Apostle, nor on any office-bearer in the Church, but on two lay persons belonging to the particular local congregation over which St. Peter was then presiding, so that it affords no clue to the extent of his authority over other Apostles, or even over lay folk void of offence; (*c*) the authority exercised is in any case not visibly different in kind or degree from that of St. Paul, when he smote Elymas the sorcerer with blindness (Acts xiii. 6–12), or when he delivered Hymenæus and Alexander unto Satan, **that** they might learn not to blaspheme (1 Tim. i. 20); while it **is** actually less than that which St. **Paul** exercised in the case of the incestuous Corinthian, because on that occasion the Apostle acted as a judge of appeal, not of first instance, and decided the case from a distance, and not on the spot.—1 **Cor. v. 3.**

(vii.) **Is** identical **with v.**

(viii.) Is identical **with** ii., **with, however, a** noteworthy hint of St. Peter's responsibility to the Apostolic College: "**Can any man** forbid water," &c. (Acts. x. 47), words **which** imply that had no miracle attested his action, it might be disallowed at Jerusalem, in despite of his Apostolic office.

(ix.) This establishes no more than St. **Peter's right to a** voice in the assembly. He does not open the debate, for he does not begin to speak till "after there had been much disputing" (Acts xv. 7), nor—what is more significant—does he close it, as will be shown presently.

(x.) St. Paul's consultation of St. Peter merely helps to establish what is not disputed, the prominence and weight which St. Peter's position gave him in the Church, that is to say, his primacy of honour. Whether it implied any obligation on St. Paul's part to be bound **by** St. Peter's decision, will be **seen presently** from an examination of another statement **made** by **St. Paul in the very** same Epistle, nay, in the **very** same part of its argument.

So far, then, the case of Ananias and Sapphira is the only example of anything resembling the exercise of actual jurisdiction and authority by St. Peter, and, as has been pointed out, **it is a** purely local instance, proving no more than the right **of a** pastor to rebuke and excommunicate one of his own immediate and local flock; **a** very slender result of the Petrine charter of privilege, if **it** be what is alleged.

On the other hand, **there are** three proofs in the Acts

that establish more than mere failure of evidence as to St. Peter's exercise of supreme jurisdiction, because they show that it was not his to exercise at all. First stands the narrative of the mission to Samaria :—

"Now when the apostles which were at Jerusalem heard that Samaria had received the word of God, they sent unto them Peter and John : who, when they were come down, prayed for them, that they might receive the Holy Ghost : (for as yet He was fallen upon none of them : only they were baptized in the name of the Lord Jesus). Then laid they their hands on them, and they received the Holy Ghost."—Acts viii. 14-17.

It is a maxim admitting of no exception in human affairs that the sender is greater than the sent, and therefore the Apostolic Church at Jerusalem was in its totality greater than St. Peter, whatever his rank in relation to its separate members may have been. It would be simply impossible to produce a parallel from the modern Roman Church in which such a phrase as "The College of Cardinals at Rome, having heard that a dispute as to liturgical questions had arisen at Lyons, sent the Pope and Cardinal Tale to settle it," would be so much as conceivable.

Secondly, when St. Peter had baptized Cornelius and some other Gentiles, the remaining Apostles and brethren, instead of submissively accepting his decision, called him to account for the innovation ; and he, in turn, instead of simply citing his privilege and bidding them obey, admitted his responsibility to them, by defending himself at length, recounting the circumstances of his vision :—

"And the apostles and brethren that were in Judæa heard that the Gentiles had also received the word of God. And when Peter was come up to Jerusalem, they that were of the circumcision contended with him, saying, Thou wentest in to men uncircumcised, and didst eat with them. But Peter rehearsed the matter from the beginning, and expounded it by order unto them," &c.—Acts xi. 1-5.[1]

The third item of disproof is even weightier. It is that

---

[1] Gerson cites this passage as proving St. Peter's accountability to the Church, and the compulsion he was under of giving satisfactory reasons for his action : "Ut scilicet paratus esset coram totâ rationem reddere. . . . alioquin non sibi credidisset ecclesia."—*De Auferibilitate Papæ ab Ecclesia.* Consid. 12.

the presidency and deciding voice in the Council of Jerusalem belong to St. James, and not to St. Peter, who is no more than an influential debater, on a level with St. Paul and St. Barnabas. St. James terminates the discussion with an authoritative ruling, Acts xv. 19, "Wherefore my sentence is," or as it would be more tersely and literally rendered, "Wherefore I *decide*" (Gr. ἐγὼ κρίνω; Vulg. *ego judico*), whereas the words he uses of St. Peter's argument are merely "Simeon hath declared," &c., where the exact rendering is no more than "stated" or "related" (Gr. ἐξηγήσατο; Vulg. *narravit*). And the decree of the Council is strictly corporate in its terms, implying absolute equality in the authority of its framers:—

"Then pleased it the apostles and elders, with the whole church . . . . The apostles and elders and brethren send greeting . . . . It seemed good unto us, being assembled with one accord, to send . . . . For it seemed good to the Holy Ghost, and to us . . . . Fare ye well."—Acts xv. 22.

It will not avail here to argue that the presidency was conceded to St. James out of courtesy to his local rights as Bishop of the diocese of Jerusalem, even though his superior was present, much as in Church Congresses the diocesan is chairman, no matter what prelates of higher rank may attend; simply because this was not in any sense a local assembly for diocesan purposes, nor a merely consultative gathering, not intended to come to any decision, but a Council met to consider a question of first-rate importance to Christianity, and to formulate a binding decree respecting it for the whole Catholic Church of the time; while St. Peter's presence and active share in the proceedings excludes any rebutting plea based on his relation to the Council; nor is any hint discoverable that St. James did but give voice to St. Peter's decision. This piece of evidence becomes all the more weighty, if we follow the received and highly probable tradition of the ancient Church, that St. James was not one of the original Twelve Apostles, but the "Lord's brother."—Gal. i. 19.

The next step in the inquiry is to ascertain what claims St. Peter himself, by his acts or writings, makes to supreme personal authority, as ruler or teacher of the Church, as it is certain that he could not justifiably conceal nor even minimise a Divine charter of the sort, forming an integral part of the constitution of Christ's Kingdom. Any acts or words of the kind would serve as an inspired comment on the terms of his commission, and should rightly be read into it as its measure and explanation.

These are exactly three passages of Holy Scripture which are relevant to this part of the discussion. They are these:—

1. "And as Peter was coming in, Cornelius met him, and fell down at his feet, and worshipped him. But Peter took him up, saying, Stand up; I myself also am a man."—Acts x. 25, 26.

2. "The elders which are among you I exhort, who am also an elder, and a witness of the sufferings of Christ, and also a partaker of the glory that shall be revealed."—1 St. Peter v. 1.

3. "Wherefore I will not be negligent to put you always in remembrance of these things, though ye know them, and be established in the present truth. Yea, I think it meet, as long as I am in this tabernacle, to stir you up by putting you in remembrance; knowing that shortly I must put off this my tabernacle, even as our Lord Jesus Christ hath showed me. Moreover, I will endeavour that ye may be able after my decease to have these things always in remembrance."—2 St. Peter i. 12-15.

It is to be observed that the phrase "who am also an elder," in the second of these citations, is simpler and humbler in the original and in the Vulgate, which have severally συμπρεσβύτερος and *consenior* = "a fellow-elder"; so that here St. Peter does not press even his apostleship.

Obviously, these three citations, so far from strengthening the case for the supremacy, rather weaken it. To say the least, nothing can be extracted from them which denotes consciousness on St. Peter's part of his especial and singular privilege, while the language of the third quotation is that of a man who is seizing a final opportunity of warning his flock personally for the last time, in hopes that his latest words may have permanent influence; not that of a dying monarch and lawgiver, who had provided for all contingencies to the latest hour of time, by bequeathing infallible judgment and absolute power to a line of successors, heirs to his transmissible and inalienable privilege.

Moreover, if, as we are further assured, the plenitude of teaching as well as of ruling is vested in St. Peter and his successors, we are entitled to look for evidence of this fact also in Holy Scripture. St. Peter's own writings will in that case be our chief storehouse of doctrinal and disciplinary instruction; or else the authority of St. Peter will be found specifically given to the other Scriptural documents as their warrant. Here, again, if no writings of St. Peter had come down to us, we might perhaps assume that St. Mark's Gospel (itself the briefest and, in some sense, least important of the four) embodied for us the whole of Petrine teaching, but the existence of the two Epistles of St. Peter bars that plea. What do these Epistles yield us on examination?

They prove to be exclusively moral and hortatory, except in three passages, which only are, so to speak, classical texts supplying information on doctrinal matters not elsewhere set down in equivalent terms. They are these:—

1. "For Christ also hath once suffered for sins, the just for the unjust, that He might bring us to God, being put to death in the flesh, but **quickened** by the Spirit. By which also He went and preached **unto** the spirits in prison; which sometime were disobedient, when once the long-suffering of God waited in the days of Noah, while the ark was a-preparing; wherein few, that is, eight souls, were saved by water. The **like** figure whereunto, **even** baptism, doth also **now** save us (not the putting away of the filth of the flesh, **but the** answer of a good conscience toward God), by the resurrection of Jesus Christ: Who is gone into heaven, and is **on the** right hand of God, angels and authorities and powers being **made** subject **unto** Him."—1 St. Peter iii. 18–22.

2. "For this cause was the Gospel preached **also** to them that are dead, that they might be judged according **to men** in the flesh, but live according **to** God in the spirit."—1 St. Peter iv. 6.

3. "**And** account that the long-suffering of our Lord is salvation; **even as** our beloved brother Paul also according to the wisdom given unto him hath written unto you; as also in all his epistles, speaking in them of these things; **in** which are some things hard to be understood, which they that are unlearned and unstable wrest, as they do also the other scriptures, unto their own destruction."—2 St. Peter iii. **15, 16.**

And there is a fourth passage, noticeable as the only one worded in an authoritative fashion, but remarkable for its collective and, as it were, impersonal wording "us the apostles," contrasted with the first person singular of St. Paul and St. John :—

"This second epistle, beloved, I now write unto you; in both which I stir up your pure minds by way of remembrance: that ye may be mindful of the words which were spoken before by the holy prophets, and of the commandment of us the apostles of the Lord and Saviour."—2 St. Peter iii. 1. 2.

This, then, is the sum of the direct instruction in matter of doctrine, as distinguished from devotional and moral exhortation, peculiar to these Epistles, which St. Peter has given to the Church—two sentences giving some information as to the souls of those who died before the coming of Christ, one declaration of the nature and effect of Baptism, and one warning against misinterpreting St. Paul's writings. There is no disciplinary instruction whatever. On the other hand, if we turn to the Epistles of St. James and St. John, even without taking account of the latter Apostle's Gospel and Apocalypse, we shall find a larger element of both discipline and doctrine than in St. Peter's writings. Thus, for example, in the second chapter of St. James's Epistle, a rule is laid down about the equality of rich and poor in Christian assemblies :—

"My brethren, have not the faith of our Lord Jesus Christ, the Lord of glory, with respect of persons. For if there come unto your assembly a man with a gold ring, in goodly apparel, and there come in also a poor man in vile raiment: and ye have respect to him that weareth the gay clothing, and say unto him, Sit thou here in a good place; and say to the poor, Stand thou there, or sit here under my footstool: are ye not then partial in yourselves, and are become judges of evil thoughts?"—St. James ii. 1 4,

In another place a rule is laid down about the anointing the sick and the duty of confession :—

"Is any among you afflicted? let him pray. Is any merry? let him sing psalms. Is any sick among you? let him call for the elders of the church; and let them pray over him, anointing him with oil in the name of the Lord: and the prayer of faith shall save the sick, and the Lord shall raise him up; and if he have committed sins, they shall be forgiven him. Confess your faults one to another, and pray one for another, that ye may be healed. The effectual fervent prayer of a righteous man availeth much."—St. James v. 13-16.

And, perhaps more significantly than these passages, the error of those who perverted St. Paul's teaching is combated directly, and not by way of broad general statement, whereby we learn that their error was Antinomianism, and it is not too much to **say** that, as an element of Christian teaching, St. James's doctrine of **the necessity of works** as a proof and fruit of faith, laid down **in Chapter ii. 14-26**, in correction of **the** misuse which had been **made** in the Early Church, as it has been in modern times also, of St. Paul's language in the Epistles to the Romans and Galatians, is of incomparably greater practical importance, and has occupied a much larger space **in** Catholic theology, than **the** above-cited words of St. Peter.

So, too, if we examine the Epistles of St. John, we shall find more explicit dogmatic teaching and clearer references to ecclesiastical discipline than in St. Peter's writings. There is, chiefly in the First Epistle, the doctrine of the Incarnation and of the Homoousion clearly laid down (1 St. John i. 1, 2; ii. 22, 23; iv. 3, 15; v. 6, 10, 12); while in the Second and Third we have these intimations of discipline :—

" Whosoever transgresseth, and abideth not in **the** doctrine of Christ, hath not God. He that abideth in **the doctrine of** Christ, he hath both the Father and the Son. **If** there **come** any unto you, and bring not this doctrine, receive him **not into your** house, neither bid him God speed: for he that biddeth **him God** speed is partaker of his evil deeds."—2 St. John, 9-11;

and

" I wrote unto **the** church: but Diotrephes, who loveth to have the pre-eminence among them, receiveth us not. Wherefore, if I come, I will remember his deeds which he doeth, prating against us with malicious words; **and** not content therewith, neither doth he himself receive the brethren, and forbiddeth them that would, and casteth them out of the church."—3 St. John, 9, **10**.

That is to say, in effect, if the two Epistles of St. Peter had been lost, as the Epistle to the Church of Laodicea has been lost (Coloss. iv. 16), albeit much food for devout meditation would be gone, no practical difference in the sum and colour of Christian teaching would be discernible, except as to the one speculation concerning the spirits of the pre-Christian patriarchs—a conclusion wholly inconsistent with the position of Universal Teacher claimed for St. Peter by Roman controversialists, and yet indisputable as matter of fact. For Christianity, as we know it, is Pauline and Johannine all but exclusively, and if there be a Petrine element, it is so obscure as to be matter of conjecture, not of knowledge.[1]

There remains still a great mass of yet uncited Scripture testimony, which is perhaps weighter than all that has thus far been adduced, namely, that which consists of the life and writings of St. Paul.

That superior prominence in the narrative of the Apostolic Church, already named as evident of St. Peter from the moment of the Ascension, is not prolonged throughout. His leadership and chief share in guiding the fortunes and in moulding the shape of the infant community, end, so far as Scripture records for us, with his admission of the Gentiles into Church fellowship. From the time of St. Paul's return to Jerusalem, after the three years of retirement in Arabia, which followed his conversion (Gal. i. 17), he completely overshadows St. Peter in the narrative of the Acts of the Apostles, to such an extent, indeed, that no

---

[1] Indeed, if to be found now at all, it is in the literature of the Syrian Churches, influenced by the once famous schools of Edessa and Nisibis, whose Petrine tone is probable evidence that the "Babylon" of St. Peter's First Epistle is the ancient city of Mesopotamia, in their neighbourhood, and not Rome; in which case the one possible link of *Scriptural* evidence to connect him with that See fails. And whether or not, as these Syrian Churches severed themselves from Catholic unity in hostility to the Councils of Ephesus and Chalcedon, and have remained separated ever since, they are proof that adherence to Petrine teaching does not necessarily connote orthodoxy or Catholicity in all respects.

mention whatever of the elder Apostle occurs after the account of his deliverance from prison (Acts xii. 3-17), except his speech at the Council of Jerusalem in Acts xv. 7-11, already referred to; whereas the whole latter portion of the Acts, including Chapters xiii.-xxviii., with the exception of part of Chapter xv., is entirely devoted to recording the actions and missionary travels of St. Paul—an amount of direct biographical record not paralleled by any human lives in Holy Writ save those of Moses and David. And if it be urged that this circumstance is due to the "accident," so to speak, of St. Luke, the compiler of the Acts, having been the chosen companion of St. Paul (Coloss. iv. 14; 2 Tim. iv. 11), the reply is obvious, that St. Peter, too, had an Evangelist in his train, "Marcus, my son" (St. Peter v. 13), so that they were on an equal footing in that respect; and, had the events of St. Peter's life been as important for us to know as those of St. Paul, it would doubtless have pleased the Holy Ghost to have inspired St. Mark to write them for our edification. Yet, on the Ultramontane hypothesis, every act and word of St. Peter must needs be of vital interest, and especially everything which took the shape of a dogmatic instruction or a disciplinary regulation, as moulding the Church for all time.

The second fact which meets us under this head is the great bulk of St. Paul's writings, here again only paralleled by Moses, even if we exclude the Epistle to the Hebrews as not St. Paul's, albeit Pauline in its doctrine. Apart from the Pentateuch, Isaiah, with its 66 chapters of 1,302 verses, is the largest product of a single author in the Old Testament; for the Psalter, with its 150 Psalms of 2,500 verses, is the work of several hands besides that of David; while St. Paul's Epistles occupy 87 chapters, with 2,023 verses, and if the Hebrews be added in, 100 chapters, with 2,325 verses, as compared with the eight chapters of 166 verses in St. Peter's two Epistles. Further, St. Luke's, or the Pauline, Gospel, exceeds St. Mark's, or the Petrine, in the ratio of 24 chapters, with 1,151 verses, to 16 chapters, with 678 verses; and there are the 28 chapters of 1,007 verses in the Acts, also Pauline in source, to be added in besides, making a grand total of 152 chapters, with 4,483 verses, as against 24 chapters, with 844 verses.

In the third place, not only are the directly Pauline writings fourteen times in excess of the Petrine in mere bulk, but they are of enormously greater literary and theological importance, being not merely replete with doctrinal statements and disciplinary enactments, such as are noticeably absent from St. Peter's Epistles, but having in truth been incomparably the most powerful factor in moulding the life and tenets of the Christian Church, which has drawn, for example, by far the greater part of its teaching on grace, election, and free-will, on the moral and dogmatic results of Christ's Resurrection, on the nature of Baptism, on the unity of the Church, on the operations of the Holy Spirit, on the place of tradition as an element of doctrine, on the relation of the Law to the Gospel, and also on the fundamental principles of ecclesiastical discipline, from the Epistles of St. Paul, for his Pastoral Epistles are our chief repertory of knowledge as to the rules of Church government which prevailed in the earliest times. So thoroughly did the Fathers realise this pre-eminence of St. Paul as the Teacher of the Church, that wherever we find "the Apostle" referred to by them, with no specification of person, they always mean St. Paul. So Eusebius, *Hist. Eccl.*, vi. 36; so Theodoret, *Hæret. Fab.*, ii. 7; so St. Augustine, *Cont. Epist. Pelag.*, saying, "So, when 'Apostle' is said, if it be not expressed what Apostle, none is understood save Paul;" so St. Chrysostom, *Hom.* iv. *in Act. Apost.*, observing, "When you say *Apostle*, at once all think of him [Paul], just as when you say *Baptist* they think of John." And this custom prevails in the Oriental Churches to the present day, where "the Apostle" means the Book of St. Paul's Epistles. Similarly, St. Luke's Gospel is far more important than St. Mark's, which, save for a few passages, might be described as a short recension of St. Matthew, and could, so to speak, be more easily dispensed with than any of the others.

It is difficult, if not impossible, to reconcile this broad fact with the position now claimed for the Popes as chief teachers of the Church in virtue of their heirship to St. Peter, for it is simply indisputable that St. Peter either did not fill this office at all in the primitive Church, or that by divine intervention he was set aside in it, and the records of his occupancy destroyed, leaving the apparent dignity, as well as the actual influence, in the hands of St. Paul, so far, at any rate, as the Biblical notices guide us; thus carrying out under the New Testament that rule of the first being last and the elder serving the younger, laid down by Christ, and evidenced in the Old Testament in the cases of Cain and Seth, Ishmael and Isaac, Esau and Jacob, Reuben and Joseph or Judah, Aaron and Moses, Eliab and David, Adonijah and Solomon.

It has been alleged, indeed (by Cardinal Manning, in a sermon preached on July 3, 1887), that whatever share the other Apostles had in authority over the Church was "always in union with, and in dependence upon, Peter, who was their head." But this assertion (which first appears in the writings of Pope Leo I., *Serm.* iv. 2; *Epp.* x. 1) is not merely without sustaining evidence in all cases, but is directly refuted by the explicit language of St. Paul, who declares that he received his Apostleship and his doctrine directly from Christ Himself, as will be cited presently, when we examine St. Paul's evidence touching his own powers (*n* and *o*).

Such is the general result of this remarkable contrast in the parts severally played by the two Apostles in the New Testament, but there is in addition some important evidence obtainable from St. Paul's writings; first, as to the true measure and limits of St. Peter's official authority; and secondly, as regards the extent of St. Paul's own powers.

The first class of these testimonies is comprised in the following paragraphs :—

i. "Now I beseech you, brethren, by the name of our Lord Jesus Christ, that ye all speak the same thing, and that there be no divisions among you: but that ye be perfectly joined together in the same mind and in the same judgment. For it hath been declared unto me of you, my brethren, by them which are of the house of Chloe, that there are contentions among you. Now this I say, that every one of you saith, I am of Paul; and I of Apollos; and I of Cephas; and I of Christ. Is Christ divided? was Paul crucified for you? or were ye baptized in the name of Paul?"—1 Cor. i. 10-13.

ii. "Therefore let no man glory in men. For all things are yours; whether Paul, or Apollos, or Cephas, or the world, or life, or death, or things present, or things to come; all are yours; and ye are Christ's; and Christ is God's."—1 Cor. iii. 21-23.

iii. "When they saw that the gospel of the uncircumcision was committed unto me, as the gospel of the circumcision was unto Peter; (for He that wrought effectually in Peter to the apostleship of the circumcision, the same was mighty in me toward the Gentiles:) and when James, Cephas, and John, who seemed to be pillars, perceived the grace that was given unto me, they gave to me and Barnabas the right hands of fellowship; that we should go unto the heathen, and they unto the circumcision. Only they would that we should remember the poor; the same which I also was forward to do. But when Peter was come to Antioch, I withstood him to the face, because he was to be blamed. For before that certain came from James, he did eat with the Gentiles: but when they were come, he withdrew and separated himself, fearing them which were of the circumcision. And the other Jews dissembled likewise with him; insomuch that Barnabas also was carried away with their dissimulation. But when I saw that they walked not uprightly according to the truth of the gospel, I said unto Peter before them all, If thou, being a Jew, livest after the manner of Gentiles, and not as do the Jews, why compellest thou the Gentiles to live as do the Jews?"—Gal. ii. 7-14.

iv. "And God hath set some in the church, first apostles, secondarily prophets, thirdly teachers, after that miracles, then gifts of healings, helps, governments, diversities of tongues."—1 Cor. xii. 28.

v. "And He gave some, apostles; and some, prophets; and some, evangelists; and some, pastors and teachers; for the perfecting of the saints, for the work of the ministry, for the edifying of the body of Christ."—Eph. iv. 11, 12.

From these five passages we collect the subjoined facts, as divinely revealed.

a. It was a mark of schism to adhere specifically to St. Peter, so as to form a separate school or party in the Church; instead of this very choice being treated, as it is by Ultramontanes now, **as** the one peculiar **note and test** of Catholic fellowship and of covenant with God.

b. The Christian body is not St. Peter's domain, but he himself, contrariwise, as part of that **body, belongs to the** whole, and is included in its possessions, **as it in turn is** included in Christ's.

c. Instead of the Church Universal being, **so to speak,** St. Peter's diocese, he was divinely restricted **to the Circumcision, that is to say, the** Church of Jewish converts, **and had** no jurisdiction whatever over the Gentiles, and, consequently, **as** no subsequent enlargement of this restriction **is recorded either by Scripture or by** other sources **of revelation, he could not transmit to any of** his successors a wider authority than that here named as his limit. The restriction is nowhere explained to us, and looks **at** first sight somewhat inconsistent with St. Peter's priority in making Gentile converts; but it is probably analogous to the subdivision of a too extensive diocese in our own day, whereby the **original** bishop gradually **finds one** district after another **withdrawn** from his jurisdiction, not **in the** least by way of slight or penalty, but as a matter of necessity. Whatever be the cause, nevertheless such withdrawal deprives him of episcopal rights over the severed districts, unless saved to him in the capacity of Metropolitan by express provision; nor can he transmit his original rights over the whole unbroken diocese to his successors. There are three modern and familiar instances, Australia, Cape Town, and Rupertsland, **in the** history of the Anglican Church in the colonies. **The inference, so** far, is that St. Peter had no Gentile **jurisdiction to** transmit, for the **separate "** Church of **the Circumcision "** did not merge in the general Christian **body till the reign of** Hadrian, fifty **years** after St. **Peter's death.**

d. The order **of** the three Apostolic names, "James, Cephas, John," **cited** by St. Paul, seems to imply either equality of rank amongst them, or else that St. James, as head of the principal Church of the Circumcision **at Jerusalem, was** now in some sense St. Peter's ecclesiastical superior. And his view is supported **by** the words cited above (iv.), which tell us (Gal. ii. 12) that St. Peter's line of policy at Antioch was through fear of St. James's legates, a fear not easily explicable on any ground save that of some accountability on his part to them. There is one further item of evidence, too slight for independent importance, but cumulative, which makes in the same direction, namely, that when St. Peter was released from prison he directed the people at St. Mark's house to "Go, shew these things unto James and to the brethren" (Acts xii.)—words which may imply that he was in some way bound to report himself to what, in modern language, would be called the Bishop and Chapter of the see.

e. Next, there is at once the full disproof of St. Peter's infallibility and of his supremacy. He decides wrongly on an important question of faith and morals—for even if we accept the view of St. Jerome and others, that the debate was pre-arranged between St. Paul and himself, he was assigned the worse cause—as is established by the Church having ever since taken St. Paul's view of the situation, and he is withstood face to face, not submitted to, by the younger Apostle, who, had he been in the wrong, would have had his rebellion—for it would have been no less— as clearly censured in Holy Writ as St. Peter's denial of Christ, to warn all others by so terrible a fall, instead of standing as it does now, by the will of the Holy Ghost, as a proof of St. Paul's zeal and loyalty for the truth of the Gospel, and a ground of justifiable satisfaction to himself.[1]

f. Lastly, the sketch which St. Paul gives of the divinely-ordered constitution of the Church becomes more than merely defective if there were any office and authority higher than that of an Apostle instituted by Christ, and forming the immediate link of connexion—the neck, so to speak—between the Head and the Body.

It is clear, then, that in his capacity of Doctor of the

---

[1] Gerson says that there was a direct appeal on St. Paul's part against St. Peter to the Church, and that if St. Peter had persisted he would have been liable to condemnation by the Church. "Unde et si Petrus desistere noluisset, fuisset ab Ecclesie condemnandus."—*An liceat in Causis Fidei a Papâ appellare?*

Gentiles, and chief theologian of the primitive Christian Church, St. Paul, who expressly states himself to "have kept back nothing that was profitable," and to "have not shunned to declare the whole counsel of God" **(Acts xx. 20, 27)**, not merely avoids any allusion in his copious writings to the "privilege of Peter," but uses language so manifestly inconsistent therewith as to necessarily mislead all in that day to whom those writings might come, supposing that privilege to be a matter of Divine truth; while the silence of St. James also, as indeed **of all the other** New Testament writers, **may be** taken **as proof that** this was not **one of St.** Paul's misconstrued **teachings which** had been **perverted,** and needing correction **at some** other hand, but **the** received doctrine of Apostolic days.

There is besides this direct Pauline gloss on the alleged privilege of Peter, an indirect one, even fuller in its statements, and scarcely less convincing in its form. **It is** quite possible to argue that we have no right to draw conclusions from St. Peter's marked reticence as to his own supremacy, because **we are** not in **a** position **to** judge what kind of acts and **language** he would have used to enforce it, and we are not justified in treating our mere guess-work **as to** what would or would not have been fit and proper for **him** to say and do, as if it were a solid piece of evidence. **In** truth, this mode of reasoning (technically called the *à priori* argument) is itself the mainstay of every Roman controversialist who pleads **the** *practical necessity* of **a** visible and infallible Head of the Church, **as a** proof that such a **head** does really exist, **so** that the objection is not valid from that quarter; but **it** may be allowed to pass, since it can readily be dispensed with, inasmuch as St. Paul supplies us with all the illustration required.

The peculiar **and** altogether exceptional mode of St. Paul's appointment to the Apostolic office, and the leading part he took against the Judaizing school in the infant Church, caused his rank to be frequently called in question, and his authority disputed. Hence, he was obliged to magnify his office, and to insist on his **powers** and privileges, and that frequently; **albeit** there could **be no** such imperative obligation for him to do so, as for St. Peter to do the like, if it were true, as we are now told, that the whole relation of every human soul to the Father and Christ depends on, and is inextricably bound up with, its relation to the See of Peter. The rejection of St. Paul might be and in fact was, perfectly consistent with acceptance of Christianity and with membership of the Church, for it did not involve the extrusion of the Judaizers who refused to acknowledge him, but the rejection of St. Peter, on the Ultramontane theory, would have been apostasy from the Faith itself. St. Peter would, therefore, have been bound, if not on his own behalf, yet on that of his successors, to allege his peculiar charter as plainly as St. Paul does his Apostolic character.

Let us now collect and examine the most salient instances of this vindication of his rights by St. Paul:—

a. "Paul, a servant of Jesus Christ, called to be an apostle, separated unto the gospel of God (which he had promised afore by his prophets in the holy scriptures), concerning his Son Jesus Christ our Lord, which was made of the seed of David according to the flesh; and declared to be the Son of God with power, according to the spirit of holiness, by the resurrection from the dead: by Whom we have received grace and apostleship, for obedience to the faith among all nations, for His name: among whom are ye also the called of Jesus Christ: to all that be in Rome, beloved of God, called to be saints: Grace to you and peace from God our Father, and the Lord Jesus Christ."—Rom. i. 1-7.

b. "For I speak to you Gentiles, inasmuch as I am the apostle of the Gentiles, I magnify mine office."—Rom. xi. 13.

c. "Nevertheless, brethren, I have written the more boldly unto you in some sort, as putting you in mind, because of the grace that is given to me of God, that I should be the minister of Jesus Christ to the Gentiles, ministering the gospel of God, that the offering up of the Gentiles might be acceptable, being sanctified by the Holy Ghost. I have therefore whereof I may glory through Jesus Christ in those things which pertain to God. For I will not dare to speak of any of those things which Christ hath not wrought by me, to make the Gentiles obedient, by word and deed, through mighty signs and wonders, by the power of the Spirit of God; so that from Jerusalem, and round about unto Illyricum, I have fully preached the gospel of Christ. Yea, so have I strived to preach the gospel, not where Christ was named, lest I should build upon another man's foundation."—Rom. xv. 15-20.

CHAP. I.] LEGAL EVIDENCE OF SCRIPTURE.   41

d. "I write not these things to shame you, but as my beloved sons I warn you. For though ye have ten thousand instructors in Christ, yet have ye not many fathers: for in Christ Jesus I have begotten you through the gospel. Wherefore I beseech you, be ye followers of me. For this cause have I sent unto you Timotheus, who is **my beloved son**, and faithful in the Lord, who shall bring you into **remembrance of my ways** which be in Christ, as I teach everywhere in every church. Now some are puffed up, as though I would not come **to** you. But I will come to you shortly, if the Lord will, and will know, not the speech of them which are puffed up, but the power. For the kingdom of God is not in word, but in power. What will ye? shall I come unto **you** with a rod, or in love, and **in the** spirit of meekness?"
—1 Cor. iv. **14-21**.

e. "For **I** verily, **as** absent **in** body, but present in **spirit**, have judged already, as though **I** were present, concerning **him** that hath so done this deed. In the **name** of our Lord **Jesus** Christ, when ye **are** gathered together, and my spirit, with the power of our Lord Jesus Christ, to deliver such an one unto Satan for the destruction of the flesh, that the spirit may be saved in the day of the Lord Jesus."
—1 Cor. v. 3·5.

f. "But as God hath **distributed to every man, as the Lord hath** called every one, so let him walk. **And** so **ordain I** in all [the] **churches.** (Gr. καὶ οὕτως ἐν ταῖς ἐκκλησίαις πάσαις διατάσσομαι: Vulg. *et sicut in omnibus ecclesiis doceo*)."—**1** Cor. vii. 17.

g. "Be ye followers of me, even as I also am of Christ. **Now I** praise you, brethren, that ye remember me in all things, and keep the ordinances, as I delivered them to you."—1 Cor. xi. 1, 2.

h. "Now concerning the collection for the saints, as I have given **order** to the churches of Galatia, even so do ye. Upon the first day **of the** week let every one **of** you lay by him in store, as God hath prospered him, that there be no gatherings when I come. And when I come, whomsoever ye shall approve by your letters, **them** will I send to bring your liberality unto Jerusalem. **And if** it **be meet** that I go also, they shall go with me."—1 Cor. **xvi. 1-4**.

i. "For to this end also did I write, **that I** might know the proof of you, whether ye be obedient **in all** things. To whom ye forgive anything, I forgive also: for if I forgave anything, **to** whom I forgave it, for your sakes forgave I it in the person of Christ."—2 Cor. ii. 9, 10.

j. "For I suppose I was not a whit behind the very chiefest apostles."—2 Cor. xi. 5.

k. "Beside those things **that are** without, **that which cometh upon** me daily, the care of all the churches." (Gr. ἡ μέριμνα πασῶν **τῶν** ἐκκλησιῶν: Vulg. *solicitudo omnium ecclesiarum*.)—2 Cor. xi. 28.

l. "I am become a fool in glorying: ye have compelled me: for I ought to have been commended of you: for in nothing am I behind the very chiefest apostles, though I be nothing. Truly the signs of **an** apostle **were** wrought **among you in** all **patience**, in signs, and wonders, and mighty deeds. For what is it wherein ye were inferior to other churches, except it be that I myself was not burdensome to you? forgive me this wrong."—2 Cor. xii. 11-13.

m. "This is the third time I am coming to you. In the mouth of two or three witnesses shall every word be established. I told you before, and foretell you, as if I were present, the second time; and being absent now I write to them which heretofore have sinned, and to all other, that, if I come again, I will not spare: since ye seek a proof of Christ speaking in me, which to you-ward is not weak, but is mighty in you..... Therefore I write these things being absent, lest being present I should use sharpness, according to the power which the Lord hath given me to edification, and not to destruction."—2 Cor. xiii. 1-3, 10.

n. "Paul, an apostle, (not of men, neither by man, but by Jesus Christ, and God the Father, who raised him from the dead)."—Gal. i. 1.

o. "But I certify you, brethren, that the gospel which was preached of me is not after man. For I neither received it of man, neither was I taught it, but by the revelation of Jesus Christ."—Gal. ii. 11, 12.

p. "Those things, which ye have both learned, and received, and heard, and seen in me, do: and the God of peace shall be with you."—Philipp. iv. 9.

q. "Now we command you, brethren, in the name of our Lord Jesus Christ, that ye withdraw yourselves from every brother that walketh disorderly, and not after the tradition which he received of us..... And if any man obey not our word by this epistle, note that man, and have no company with him, that he may be ashamed."—2 Thess. iii. 6, 14.

r. "Thou, therefore, my son, be strong in the grace that is in Christ Jesus. And the things that thou hast heard of me among many witnesses, the same commit thou to faithful men, who shall be able to teach others also."—2 Tim. ii. 1, 2.

s. "For this cause left I thee in Crete, that thou shouldest set in order the things that are wanting, and ordain elders in every city, as I had appointed thee."—Tit. i. 5.

Besides all these statements of St. Paul's apostolic authority, we find disciplinary enactments, which need not be cited in detail, laid down by him on the following points:—

1. Observance of Jewish distinctions of food and of days, Rom. xiv. 1-6, 21; Coloss. ii. 16.
2. Lawsuits between Christians, 1 Cor. vi. 1-4.
3. Marriage-tie between Christians and heathens, 1 Cor. vii. 12-17.

4. Lawfulness of using pagan sacrifices as food, 1 Cor. viii.; x. 27-28.

5. Head-dress of men and women at public prayer, 1 Cor. **xi. 4-16**.

6. Preparation for Communion, 1 Cor. xi. 28.

7. Vernacular language in public worship, 1 Cor. **xiv.** 15-19.

8. Order in public worship, 1 Cor. xiv. 27-33, 40.

9. Women forbidden to preach, 1 Cor. xiv. 34, 35.

10. Weekly offertory, 1 Cor. **xvi. 2**.

11. Intercessory prayer, 1 **Tim. ii. 1, 2**.

12. **Dress** and conduct **of women,** 1 **Tim. ii.** 9-15.

13. Qualifications **of** bishops **and deacons,** 1 Tim. iii. 1-13; Tit. i. 7-9.

14. Qualification of Church widows, 1 Tim. v. 9-13.

15. Excommunication of **heretics** after two admonitions, Tit. iii. 10.

These disciplinary **rulings need not be further considered,** but **it is important to** cite them as showing what **kind of** matters we might **fairly** expect to have found in St. Peter's Epistles had he been **supreme ruler as well** as chief **teacher** in the Church of Apostolic times. Yet **it** is desirable **to** emphasize certain results of the fuller citations just given, excluding such of those texts as we may fairly hold to denote no more than the degree of rank and power common to the Apostolic body, albeit even these are not paralleled by anything in St. Peter's Epistles.

a. St. Paul alleges himself **to be "not a** whit [*al.* in nothing] behind the very chiefest Apostles," making no exception in favour of St. Peter or **St. James.** See *ante* (*j*).

b. He **states** that his **Apostolate and** his teaching are both directly from Christ **Himself,** and not mediately (like St. Matthias's) through other Apostles, thus showing that he was entirely independent of St. Peter (*n* and *o*).

c. He claims the whole field of the "Church of the Uncircumcision" **as his** own, to the direct and specified *exclusion* of St. Peter, alleging himself further to be "*the,*" not *an,* "Apostle of the Gentiles" (*b* and *c*).

d. In virtue of this claim, he demands the obedience of the *Roman Church*, giving no hint throughout the Epistle to it of any superior, previous, or co-existing claim on St. Peter's part (*c*).

e. He tells the Church of Corinth that the only particular in which it was inferior to any other Church was that he did not permit it to defray his expenses. He gives no hint that Antioch or Rome, as St. Peter's see, had any priority or authority over Corinth (*l*).

f. He declares that the "care of *all* the Churches" is his daily task (*k*).

g. He ordains rules to be observed "in *all* the Churches" (*f*).

h. He sends his legates with plenary powers to act for him, alleges his commission to them as their full warrant, and, unlike St. Peter (2 Pet. i. 13–15), provides at least one personal successor to himself, to transmit his teaching authoritatively (*r* and *s*).

i. He directs the excommunication of all persons who refuse to accept his injunctions as being in effect those of Christ Himself (*q*).

Now, if it were St. Paul who is alleged to have been the infallible and sovereign head of the Church Militant on earth, it would be extremely easy to support such an allegation by the cited passages, all of which are at least consistent with such a theory, and some of which even seem to force it on our attention. Nevertheless, no such allegation has ever been made on St. Paul's behalf.[1] We can guess what use would have been made of it on St. Peter's behalf, had such evidence been producible from the Petrine Epistles.

Further, not only are we justified in saying that the claim made for St. Peter absolutely requires the production of some at least equivalent, if not yet more cogent, Scriptural testimony, confessedly non-existent, but that the Pauline assertions, *a, b, c, d, e, f,* and *g,* are wholly inconsistent with

[1] See, however, a statement by St. Peter Damiani in Chapter v. p. 184.

and destructive of the alleged "Privilege of Peter," as stated by the modern Church of Rome, unless some overwhelmingly rebutting evidence, unequivocally bearing the stamp of Divine revelation, can be adduced in its favour from some other quarter than Holy Scripture—a question to be considered later.

The charter of Privilege, so far, is shown to be restricted to the words in St. Matt. xvi. 18, "Thou art Peter, and upon this rock I will build My Church." This sentence obviously does not satisfy the second condition—that of clearness—laid down by the Canonists, as necessary to fulfil the legal requirements of a claim of privilege, because there is confessedly an ambiguity in its wording, which is not certain, manifest, and unmistakable in meaning.

The ambiguity consists in a play upon words, so to speak, visible in the Greek text, which runs thus: Σὺ εἶ Πέτρος, καὶ ἐπὶ ταύτῃ τῇ πέτρᾳ οἰκοδομήσω μου τὴν ἐκκλησίαν: a peculiarity reproduced by the Vulgate, which translates thus: *Tu es Petrus, et super hanc petram ædificabo ecclesiam meam.*

With this compare the partially parallel passage in St. John i. 42, "And when Jesus beheld him, He said, Thou art Simon the son of Jona: thou shalt be called Cephas, which is by interpretation, A stone." Here the Greek runs: Σὺ κληθήσῃ Κηφᾶς, ὃ ἑρμηνεύεται Πέτρος; and the Vulgate: *Tu vocaberis Cephas; quod interpretatur Petrus.*

Obviously, to warrant the stress laid by Roman theologians on this obscure saying of our Lord's, the *same* word ought to be used in both clauses of the sentence, and it should run in the Greek: Σὺ εἶ Πέτρος, καὶ ἐπὶ τούτῳ τῷ πέτρῳ, κ.τ.λ., or else Σὺ εἶ πέτρα in the first clause; and in the Vulgate: *Tu es Petrus, et super hunc Petrum, &c.,* or else we ought to have *Tu es Petra* in the earlier member. As the clauses actually stand, there is contrast as well as likeness implied, and the *stone*, although akin to the *rock*, is something different and apart from it, less in dimensions, stability, and importance, for though πέτρος is used with extreme rarity in Attic Greek to signify a rock, it is never so found in the LXX. or the New Testament.

An ingenious reply was devised by Cardinal Bellarmine to this objection, which has been frequently reproduced since his time. It is that our Lord, speaking in Syriac or Aramaic, actually did use the same word in both clauses, saying, "Thou art *Cepha*, and upon this *Cepha* I will build My Church." The answer to this is fivefold. (1) It is matter of reasonable conjecture and high probability only, not of absolute certainty, that our Lord did use, or must have used, the same word, and indeed that He spoke in Syriac or Aramaic at all, and not in Greek. (2) In any case, if His original words are *not* those of the Greek St. Matthew, they are for ever lost to us, and since the very first and fundamental rule of Canon law as to any privilege is that the document containing it must be produced, this plea is barred. (3) For us, St. Matthew's Greek is the original text, and not a mere translation, so that even *if* we were sure of the unproved assertion made by Bellarmine, we should yet be compelled to accept St. Matthew's variation of the two words, as divinely inspired for the express purpose of marking a difference which the Syriac failed to accentuate or suggest. (4) In any case, no Roman Catholic is at liberty to raise the plea at all, because he is certainly bound by the decrees of Trent, and perhaps by those of the Vatican, to accept the "old Latin Vulgate edition as holy and canonical" (*Conc. Vatic. Constit. de Fide*, cap. ii.), and inasmuch as this version marks the antithesis between *Petrus* and *petram*, Roman Catholics are barred from asserting their identity. (5) Lastly, as regards those not so restricted, and who are at liberty to look at the question as a purely textual and grammatical one, the reply is direct and conclusive, that both the Hebrew *Cepha* (כֵּיפָא) and the Peshîttâ Syriac *Kîphâ* (ܟܐܦܐ), when they mean rock or stone, are of the feminine gender, which Cephas, or Peter, as a masculine noun denoting a man's name, certainly is not, either in Syriac or Greek; and in the ancient Syriac version of this very passage, St. Matt. xvi. 18 (doubtless the most trustworthy gloss obtainable), the feminine pronoun is found united with the second *Cepha* thus, ܟܐܦܐ ܗܕܐ (*hádhe* Kiphâ = *hanc* petram), not ܗܢܐ (*hana* = *hunc Petrum*), which Bellarmine's argument would require.[1]

If the question be now regarded from another Biblical standpoint, the result is not more favourable to the Ultramontane claim. The theological principle known as the analogy **of** faith, already referred to, demands that the **Gospel** shall always be **at** the **very** least on **an** equality **with** the Law, **and that,** wherever possible, it shall **move** in **a** higher plane, **but** that it shall never descend under any circumstances whatever to **a** lower level, far less substitute a type for **a** reality, a shadow for **a** substance.

Now, wherever in the Old Testament the word *rock* is spiritually used to denote either the basis and strength of the Hebrew Church, or the refuge and confidence **of a** single believer, it invariably means none save Almighty God Himself, **in** which sense it occurs no fewer than thirty-five times.

Here **are a few** select examples:—

1. "He is the rock, His work is perfect: for all His ways are judgment: a God **of** truth and without iniquity, just and right is He."—Deut. xxii. 4.

2. "Of the Rock that begat thee thou **art** unmindful, and hast forgotten God that formed thee."—Deut. xxxii. 18.

---

[1] This Peshittâ version (which in this place agrees precisely with the Curetonian Gospels), assuming that Christ spoke Syro-Aramaic, is probably the nearest reproduction extant of His exact words, and is at any rate good authority for the interpretation of St. Matt. xvi. 18, in the second century. And it is very noteworthy that in two other extremely old Syriac versions, the Palestinian Lectionary, published by Count Miniscalchi Erizzo from a Vatican MS., and the "Philoxenian" version by Thomas of Heraclea (A.D. 533), the Greek word *Petros* occurs in the first clause in Syriac letters; while the native word *Kîphâ* is in the second clause of the Palestinian version, and its synonym *shu'â* in the second clause of the Philoxenian, thus studiously avoiding even the chance of identifying the Rock with Peter.

3. "There is none holy as the Lord: for there is none beside Thee: neither is there any rock like our God."—1 Sam. ii. 2.

4. "The Lord is my rock, and my fortress, and my deliverer; the God of my rock. For who is God, save the Lord? and who is a rock, save our God?"—2 Sam. xxii. 2, 3, 32.

5. "The God of Israel said, the Rock of Israel spake to me, He that ruleth over men must be just, ruling in the fear of God."—2 Sam. xxiii. 3.

6. "Truly my soul waiteth upon God: from Him cometh my salvation. He only is my rock and my salvation; He is my defence; I shall not be greatly moved."—Psalm lxii. 1, 2.

7. "Trust ye in the Lord for ever, for in the Lord Jehovah is the Rock of ages."—Isa. xxvi. 4 (marg.).

8. "Is there a God beside Me? yea, no Rock, I know not any.'—Isa. xliv. 8 (marg.).

The remaining examples are Deut. xxxii. 15, 30, 31; 2 Sam. xxii. 47; Psalm xviii. 2, 31, 46; xix. 14 (marg.); xvii. 5; xxviii. 1; xxxi. 2, 3; xlii. 9; lxi. 2; lxii. 2, 7; lxxi. 3 (marg.); lxxiii. 26 (marg.); lxxviii. 35; lxxxix. 26; xcii. 15; xciv. 22 (marg.); xcv. 1; Isa. viii. 14; xxx. 29 (marg.); li. 1; Hab. i. 12 (marg.).

Even if this remarkable identity of spiritual application were not preserved, we have three authoritative glosses in the New Testament itself—one by our Lord, given with slight verbal differences by St. Matthew vii. 24, 25, and St. Luke vi. 47, 48:—

"Therefore whosoever heareth these sayings of Mine, and doeth them, I will liken him unto a wise man, which built his house upon a rock; and the rain descended, and the floods came, and the winds blew, and beat upon that house; and it fell not: for it was founded upon a rock."

"Whosoever cometh to Me, and heareth My sayings, and doeth them, I will show you to whom he is like: He is like a man which built an house, and digged deep, and laid the foundation on a rock: and when the flood arose, the stream beat vehemently upon that house, and could not shake it: for it was founded upon a rock."

St. Paul supplies the others, 1 Cor. x. 4, and 1 Cor. iii. 2:—

"They drank of that spiritual Rock that followed them: and that Rock was Christ."

"For other foundation can no man lay than that is laid, which is Jesus Christ."

If it had so happened that these New Testament illustrations of the meaning of St. Matthew xvi. 18 were absent, and that in their stead others were found which seemed to warrant, or even to enforce, the Ultramontane interpretation, then in that case there would be here the only exception, and that a wholly unaccountable one, to the rule which insists that the Gospel plane must be higher than the Mosaic, wherever a higher plane is conceivable and possible. For extol as we may the privilege of Peter, clothe him with one semi-divine attribute after another, magnify as we choose his share in the establishment of Christianity, and his authority over the Apostolic Church; nevertheless, the interval between him and God cannot be appreciably abridged, the finite cannot be stretched so as even to suggest the infinite. And if the Infinite and Almighty was the Rock of Israel, while Peter is the rock of Christendom, then the Gospel has sunk unspeakably and immeasurably below the Law. Even in human affairs, every one acknowledges the wide difference—perfectly measurable though it be—there is between the personal visit of a king, coming in a recognised and public fashion to his subjects, and that of a mere viceroy, though loaded with titles, decorated with orders, and clothed with plenipotentiary powers; and no one could be persuaded that equal favour had been shown to two cities, one of which had welcomed the sovereign as a personal guest, while the other had perforce to put up with his deputy. So ends our inquiry into that part of the evidence for the personal privilege of Peter which is professedly based on Holy Scripture, regarded in the light of a purely legal document of absolutely indefeasible authority, and as the main evidence adduced in support of the claim. It is obvious that unless some corroborative testimony of equally high and indisputable character can be discovered, the case is not made out, and does not even satisfy several of the tests of validity exacted by the Roman Canon Law itself in all claims of privilege.

The next branch of the inquiry is to ascertain whether Scripture yields any more satisfactory proof of divinely granted primacy and supremacy on behalf of the **See, as distinguished from the Pope, of Rome.** This done, the Scriptural argument will be closed, and it will then remain **to inquire** finally whether the other **evidence producible,** apart from **Scripture,** is of **such a kind as to create a** reasonable **presumption in favour of the Divine,** or at least Apostolical, **character of Papal supremacy, analogous to that which exists for infant baptism, for the tenet of Eucharistic** sacrifice, or for Sunday observance.

We **will** therefore first discuss that part of the **Papal claims** (also adduced as resting on express Divine revelation) which alleges the indefeasible primacy of the city and **see of** Rome, asserted to **be** so indissolubly bound up with **the Petrine** privilege that even **to suggest that** the Chief **Patriarch of** the Christian Church **might have** his see transferred to some other city, say **Jerusalem, in time to** come, is to incur the Vatican anathemas.[1] **If this be so, we** shall certainly find **clear** analogical preparation **for it in the** Old Testament, and **evident** development **of the idea in the New.**

At first, **then, there** appears no centre of worship whatever. The altar depends **for** its locality on the **casual halt** of the nomad **Patriarchs (Gen. xii. 7;** xiii. 18; xxi. 33); and the **earliest intimation of** a more settled shrine is found in Jacob's vow at Bethel (Gen. xxviii. 16–22). During **the Exodus** the Tabernacle was the travelling "field-chapel" of the Israelite host (Numb. ii. **17; x. 17, 21).** But in the **book** of Deuteronomy repeatedly occurs a declaration that a national centre of worship would be **set up in Canaan,** where alone the rites of sacrifice could be lawfully and acceptably performed. One citation will suffice:—

> "But **when ye** go over Jordan, and dwell in the land which the Lord **your God** giveth **you to** inherit, and when He giveth you rest from **all your** enemies **round about,** so that ye dwell in safety; then **there shall be** a place which **the Lord your** God shall choose to cause His **Name to** dwell there; **thither shall ye** bring all that I command

---

[1] Conc. Vatican, Canon II. de Ecclesiâ.

you ; your burnt offerings, and your sacrifices, your tithes, and the heave offering of your hand, and all your choice vows which ye vow unto the Lord."—Deut. xii. 10, 11.

For a considerable time, however, this central shrine was not absolutely fixed and permanent. Shiloh, its first seat (Josh. xviii. 1), remained such from the time of Joshua till the Philistine capture of the Ark (1 Sam. iv. 4, 11), which was restored to Kirjath-Jearim (1 Sam. vii. 1, 2), whence, after **a long interval,** David translated it to Jerusalem (2 Sam. **vi. 2,** 12), its **final seat.** With the building **of** Solomon's temple begins **the great** series of Divine promises of permanence for **this** great national shrine, conditioned from the very first, however, by possibilities of forfeiture (1 Kings ix. 1–9). To this sacred place the strict theory of the Law, albeit necessarily relaxed by dispensations, enjoined every adult male of the Hebrew nation to make pilgrimages thrice every year :—

"Three times in a year shall all thy males appear before the **Lord** thy God in the place which He shall choose ; in the **feast of unleavened** bread, and in the feast of weeks, and in the feast of tabernacles : **and** they shall not appear before the Lord empty."—Deut. xvi. 16.

And as a practical **fact,** even when the nation, in the postexilic period, had long ceased to be included within the borders of Palestine, one visit, at least, in a lifetime was as much the **desire of** every devout Jew as **the** pilgrimage to Mecca is **of** the fervent Moslem in our own day.

What is especially noticeable about the series of prophecies concerning Jerusalem, both before **and after** its overthrow by the Chaldeans, is that its restoration to more than **its** former glory is always foretold in explicit terms. And **after** deducting all the passages of this kind, which may fairly be explained in the literal sense by the rebuilding under Ezra and Nehemiah, or in the spiritual order by the manifestation of Christ at Jerusalem, and the origin of the Gospel thence as its local source, such as

"And it shall come to pass in the last days, that the mountain **of** the Lord's house shall be established in the top of the mountains, and shall be exalted above the hills; and all nations shall flow unto it. And many people shall go and say, Come ye, and let us go up to the mountain of the Lord, to the house of the God of Jacob; and He will teach us of His ways, and we will walk in His paths: for out of Zion shall go forth the law, and the word of the Lord from Jerusalem."—Is. ii. 2, 3,

there remains a residuum not capable of being so treated, in which indefeasible supremacy **appears to** be promised. Here are a few examples:—

"**Look** upon Zion, **the** city of our solemnities: thine eyes shall **see** Jerusalem a quiet habitation, a tabernacle that shall not be taken **down**; not one of the stakes thereof shall ever be removed, neither **shall** any of **the** cords thereof be broken."—Is. xxxiii. **20.**

"And the sons of strangers shall build thy walls, **and** their kings **shall** minister unto thee; for in My **wrath** I smote thee, but in My favour have I had mercy on thee. Therefore thy gates shall be open continually; **they** shall **not** be shut day nor night; that men may bring unto thee the forces of the Gentiles, and that their kings may be brought. For the nation and kingdom that will not serve thee shall perish; yea, those nations shall be utterly wasted. The glory of Lebanon shall come unto thee, the fir tree, the pine tree, and the box together, to beautify the place of My sanctuary; and I will make **the** place of My feet glorious. The sons also of them that afflicted thee shall come bending unto thee; and all they that despised thee shall bow themselves down at the soles **of** thy feet; and they shall call thee, The city of the Lord, The Zion **of** the Holy One of Israel. Whereas thou hast been forsaken and hated, so that no man went through thee, I will make thee **an** eternal excellency, a joy of **many** generations."—Is. lx. 10-15.

"And I will make her that halted a remnant, and her that was cast far off a strong nation: and the Lord shall reign over them in mount Zion from henceforth, even for ever. And thou, O tower of the flock, the stronghold of the daughter of Zion, **unto thee** shall it **come, even the** first dominion; the kingdom **shall come to** the **daughter** of Jerusalem."—Micah iv. 7, 8.

"**And** it shall come to pass, that every **one that** is left of all the **nations** which came against Jerusalem shall **even** go up from year to year **to** worship the King, the Lord of hosts, **and** to keep the feast of tabernacles. And it shall be, **that** whoso will not come up of all **the** families of the earth unto Jerusalem to worship the King, the Lord **of** hosts, even **upon** them shall be no **rain.**"—Zech. xiv. 16, 17.

There are only four possible ways of explaining these statements:—(a) They are not inspired prophecies at all, but the mere fervent wishes and guesses of Hebrew enthusiasts; (b) their fulfilment is yet future, and points to the restoration of Jerusalem as the central shrine of the world; (c) they are conditional, albeit the condition is not verbally expressed, and their promises have been forfeited by Jewish unbelief; (d) they are typical of another and holier Jerusalem. The Roman controversalist is estopped from accepting either (a) or (b). If he accept (c), he destroys the argument for the indefeasibility of the similar position claimed for Rome, and he is thus practically limited to (d), and is bound to show that Rome, by reasonable implication, if not by necessary consequence, fulfils the needful conditions as the antitype of this Old Testament type.

What evidence does the New Testament yield on this head?

(a) There is absolutely but one passage in the Gospels which can be said to bear on the inquiry, since our Lord's mention of Jerusalem as "the city of the Great King" (St. Matt. v. 35) does not decide it. That passage is the speech of Christ to the Samaritan woman at the well of Sychar:—

"The woman saith unto Him, Sir, I perceive that Thou art a prophet. Our fathers worshipped in this mountain; and ye say, that in Jerusalem is the place where men ought to worship. Jesus saith unto her, Woman, believe me, the hour cometh, when ye shall neither in this mountain, nor yet at Jerusalem, worship the Father. Ye worship ye know not what: we know what we worship: for salvation is of the Jews. But the hour cometh, and now is, when the true worshippers shall worship the Father in spirit and in truth: for the Father seeketh such to worship Him. God is a Spirit: and they that worship Him must worship Him in spirit and in truth."—St. John iv. 19-24.

The only interpretation of this passage which will fairly stand is that it points to the decentralisation and delocalisation of worship under the Gospel, in direct contrast to the usage under the Law. And, as a fact, such decentralisation has actually taken place. It is one of the chief boasts of the Roman Church that no minute of any day from year to year passes during which the highest rite of Christian worship is not being actually celebrated, in one part or other of the world, by her priests; and a popular lithographic print, to be procured in Parisian shops for *objets de religion*, is the "Dial of the Eucharist," showing at what place Mass is being said as each hour comes round at the meridian of Paris, whether it be Edinburgh, Vienna, Moscow, Damascus, Calcutta, Pekin, Melbourne, San Francisco, Buenos Ayres, or Capetown.

Hence, the chief motive for the peculiar regard paid to Jerusalem no longer exists, for the political accident of its being the capital of the Davidic line of kings had nothing to do with its religious sacredness as the one place of lawful sacrifice. To retain another city in a similar position, when all monopoly of this peculiar kind has been abolished for nearly two thousand years, would have no adequate motive whatever.

(*b*) Next, what does the letter of the New Testament tell us about Rome? Is there anything which foretells its coming dignity, or its relation to St. Peter? No syllable in the Old Testament supplies so much as a hint on the subject. While there are many prophecies implying that a Gentile *nation* will succeed to, or partake the privileges of, *Israel*, there is none to suggest that any Gentile *city* should ever supplant *Jerusalem*. Rome is named exactly nine times in the New Testament, as under:—

1. "Strangers of Rome, Jews and proselytes" (included amongst the concourse at St. Peter's sermon on the day of Pentecost).—Acts ii. 10.
2. "Claudius had commanded all Jews to depart from Rome."—Acts xviii. 2, 3.
3. "After these things were ended, Paul purposed in the spirit, when he had passed through Macedonia and Achaia, to go to Jerusalem, saying, After I have been there, I must also see Rome."—Acts xix. 21.
4. "And the night following the Lord stood by him, and said, Be of good cheer, Paul: for as thou hast testified of Me in Jerusalem, so must thou bear witness also at Rome."—Acts xxiii. 11.
5. "We came the next day to Puteoli: where we found brethren, and were desired to tarry with them seven days: and so we went towards Rome."—Acts xxviii. 13, 14.

6. "And when we came to Rome, the centurion delivered the prisoners to the captain of the guard: but Paul was suffered to dwell by himself with a soldier that kept him."—Acts xxviii. 16.

7. "To all that be in Rome, beloved of God, called to be saints: Grace to you and peace from God our Father, and the Lord Jesus Christ."—Rom. i. 7.

8. "I am debtor both to the Greeks and to the Barbarians; both to the wise and to the unwise. So, as much as in me is, I am ready to preach the gospel to you that are at Rome also."—Rom. i. 14, 15.

9. "The Lord give mercy unto the house of Onesiphorus; for he oft refreshed me, and was not ashamed of my chain: but, when he was in Rome, he sought me out very diligently, and found me."—2 Tim. i. 16, 17.

Now seven of these nine passages are exclusively concerned with some relation of St. Paul, not St. Peter, to Rome; and next, of the other two, one is merely intended to explain the presence of Aquila and Priscilla in Corinth, instead of their being at home in Italy; while the remaining one alone, itself the first cited, has any connexion, even indirectly, with St. Peter, and then no more than is equally shared by Cappadocia, Pontus, Egypt, Libya, and the rest of the catalogue in Acts ii. 9-11. Not one of them so much as hints at any spiritual pre-eminence, actual or future, attaching to Rome.

And it would be difficult to find a more remarkable contrast than this brief, meagre, cold, and matter-of-fact way in which the imperial mistress of the world is thus casually referred to in Scripture presents, when compared with the lavish terms of admiration, love, and reverence with which the Prophets greet Jerusalem, nay, even with their recognition of the material splendour and might of Nineveh and Babylon. Not only do the Apostles pass its secular marvels over in utter silence, but no hint of its future spiritual glories escapes from them.

Is there, then, anything lacking? Does Jerusalem alone of the great Old Testament types find any antitype under the Gospel? Certainly she does find one, only, as before, the analogy of faith holds good, and the type is eclipsed utterly by the antitype, belonging, as it does, to the higher spiritual order. Rome, the centre and strength of the carnal world-power, the last stronghold of classical heathenism, when even in the days of St. Leo the Great, in the very middle of the fifth century, professed Christians (the great Pope tells us in his seventh Christmas Sermon), when actually climbing the ascent up to the high altar of St. Peter's own Basilica, used to turn round on the steps and solemnly bow down in worship to the Sun-God; Rome, the last powerful enemy of the Cross, would, if put in the stead of Jerusalem, have been in one sense a greater declension than Peter put as the Rock instead of God; for Peter was, at any rate, a glorious saint, but all Rome's spiritual memories were of idolatry, cruelty, and lust, contrasting with the glory of Jerusalem not merely in the far distant past, but as the City in which the Great King manifested his countenance, fulfilled his work, and endowed His Church with the gifts of the Holy Spirit.

No such degradation from the loftier ideal is to be found. "Here," says the Apostle, "we have no continuing city, but we seek one to come."—Heb. xiii. 14. And what that is, let him tell us more at length:—

"But ye are come unto Mount Sion, and unto the city of the living God, the heavenly Jerusalem, and to an innumerable company of angels, to the general assembly and church of the firstborn, which are written in heaven, and to God the Judge of all, and to the spirits of just men made perfect, and to Jesus the mediator of the new covenant, and to the blood of sprinkling, that speaketh better things than that of Abel."—Heb. xii. 22.

It is this "Jerusalem above [which] is free," according to St. Paul, "which is the mother of us all," Gal. iv. 26: the only "mother and mistress of all Churches" known to him. And only to this city are men under the Gospel to go on pilgrimage, because—

"Now they desire a better country, that is, an heavenly: wherefore God is not ashamed to be called their God: for He hath prepared for them a city."—Heb. xi. 16.

What it is like St. John tells us in the glowing language at the close of the Apocalypse, wherein the jasper walls, jewelled foundations, gates of pearl, and golden streets of the Heavenly City are depicted.

Such is all that is directly obtainable from the clear letter of Scripture.

There is one isolated fragment of testimony adducible, and adduced, on the Ultramontane side, namely, this verse of the first Epistle of St. Peter:—

"The church that is at Babylon, elected together with you, saluteth you; and so doth Marcus my son."—1 St. Peter v. 13.

The received opinion in the Roman Church, based on very early tradition (beginning with Eusebius, and from an erroneous interpretation of his statement, supposed to be ascribed by him to St. Papias and St. Clement of Alexandria, whom he, in fact, cites only as attesting the Petrine origin of St. Mark's Gospel, as Valesius has pointed out in his note upon the passage), and also on arguments which have some weight and cogency, is that Babylon here stands for Rome. On the whole, there is something to be said for this view, and against the alternatives of the Mesopotamian Babylon and of Cairo, which have been suggested (and, in the former instance, supported by very cogent arguments) by eminent scholars, such as Archbishop de Marca and Bishop Pearson,[1] though at best there is only conjecture, not proof, while the Sinaitic MS. supplies the word "church," formerly supposed to be missing in the Greek, and thus refutes the theory of Calvin that St. Peter is speaking in this verse, not of the Church, but of his wife, as "*she* who is elect at Babylon." But the passage, nevertheless, cannot be pleaded in evidence of privilege, because (1) it is unquestionably obscure and ambiguous, not clear and manifest; because (2) it does not specify any *official*

---

[1] These are (1) the absence of symbolical language elsewhere in this Epistle; (2) the large Jewish population then at Babylon (Joseph. "Antiq.," xv. 3; xvii. 2; xviii. 1), while the Jews had been driven out of Rome by Claudius, so (3) that St. Peter, as Apostle of the Circumcision, would more naturally go elsewhither.

connexion between St. Peter and the Church at Babylon, wherever that may have been; and because (3) even if these two facts were otherwise, the adjective "elect together," συνεκλεκτή, Vulg. *coëlecta*, denotes absolute equality of spiritual condition with those other Churches of "Pontus, Galatia, Cappadocia, Asia, and Bithynia," enumerated in the opening words of this Epistle as those to which it is addressed. And lastly (4), it is the evil case of Babylon that, whether in the Old Testament or the New, there is not one word ever spoken in its favour. Egypt and Assyria, often condemned, have, at any rate, some sets-off to show, as Isaiah xix. 18–24; Ps. lxviii. 31; Micah vii. 12; but for Babylon, from Isaiah to Revelation, there is nothing but denunciations of judgment, destruction, and woe: no hint of so much as a remnant to be delivered out of it, save of such as, being mere exiles and captives there, are not of its citizens (Rev. xviii. 4; *cf.* Ps. lxxxvii. 4; Isa. xlviii. 20; Jer. li. 6, 45); no promise of a spiritual growth to spring up when the earthly one is cut down. And therefore, if the types of the Old and New Testament are to count for anything in the evidence, this identification of Babylon and Rome is fatal to any claim of privilege urged on behalf of the latter on the ground of Divine favour and revelation.

The last item of the evidence is that, in the closing book of the Sacred Canon, there is total silence as to any central court of appeal for the Seven Churches, any supreme visible authority to which each Angel is subject. The visitation, so to speak, of each Church is made directly by Christ Himself, and not by any Vicar of His upon earth; and even the Apostle St. John acts as merely communicating a message, not as personally enforcing it.

No case, therefore, can be established from the Holy Scriptures, regarded in the legal point of view as a single document proffered in evidence of the Petrine privilege, and as the chief item of that evidence, since being the most authoritative and indisputable form of Divine revelation; and therefore unless it can be conclusively shown that this *primâ facie* failure to prove the claim thereby is fully repaired by evidence of equivalent weight, as marked in its broader outlines, and as cumulative in its minor indications, as that which has been marshalled above, it remains that Christ as the Rock, and the Heavenly Jerusalem as the Mother of all the Churches, are alone set forth and recognised in these capacities by the inspired writers of the New Testament. And that because the one possible plea in bar of judgment which might be adduced under other circumstances, that of Development, is inapplicable here, first, because a "charter of privilege" cannot be developed at all, but must have been clearly granted from the first in explicit terms, unlike a mere right of prescription, which may grow through user in course of time; and next, because in this particular instance the comparison of the evidence shows that there is nothing to develope.

So far, then, as the Papal claim is alleged to be of Divine privilege, given by revelation, the Scriptures, treated as the chief document in evidence of claim, fail to satisfy the requirements of Roman Canon Law; for (1) they afford no testimony whatever as to the annexation of privilege to the Roman See, or its transmission from St. Peter to any of his successors; (2) the evidence as to his own primacy is obscurely and enigmatically worded; (3) so far as its wording does go, it is a personal, not an official grant, and thus dies with the original grantee; (4) if continued in the Ultramontane sense, it encroaches on St. Paul's privileges, which are more clearly worded.

Wherever the proof may be found, therefore, it is certainly not in the Scriptures.

CHAPTER II.

LEGAL EVIDENCE OF LITURGIES AND FATHERS.

ALTHOUGH the investigation of the letter of Scripture yields such extremely slender results in favour of the privilege of St. Peter, yet it may be, and in fact is, argued that there is such a body of other incontestable evidence on its behalf in existence, proving its recognition and acceptance from the very first, as to amount to proof of Divine revelation; on the principle that the universal prevalence of a certain interpretation of Scripture at the hands of the body which is the custodian and witness of Scripture, and of an unbroken practice based on that interpretation, is as truly proof of its being a revealed part of the Gospel of Christ as any statement found in the express words of Scripture itself. Exactly so, there are certain statutes in the English law whose wording is far from being clear to the lay mind, and whose clauses seem to go but a very small way towards covering the whole subject-matter concerned, but where a perfectly consistent series of decisions in the law-courts, dating from the original enactment, and an unbroken usage in entire harmony therewith, serve as proof to every one that these Acts have in fact one unquestioned meaning, itself as much part of the law of the land as if verbally embodied in their wording.

Examples of the kind referred to may be found in ecclesiastical matters also. The observance of Sunday, the baptism of infants, the institution of episcopacy, do not rest on clear and express warrant of the letter of Scripture. They are instances of an universal identity of interpretation of that letter, resulting in an universal identity of practice all over the Christian world from its earliest times.

And to all who accept the Church as being a divinely

established and guided body, such evidence is sufficient; while even those who regard it merely as a human organization, are constrained to admit that whatever exhibits such complete unison and such an unbroken prescription, must fairly represent the mind of the first Christian teachers, and be clothed with whatever authority they possessed.

If, then, any such harmonious testimony to the Privilege of Peter be producible as that which can be found for Sunday observance, for infant baptism, and for episcopacy, with a like absence of rebutting evidence, it will, to say the least, very nearly counterbalance the adverse construction which a comparative survey of the bare letter of Scripture forces on the theologian's attention.

"Very nearly," but not quite. And only "very nearly," for these reasons: (1.) The claim in this individual instance is a special *privilege* by a deed, so to say, of particular grant or donation, to which impugners are referred as the paramount evidence and authority. The claim on behalf of Sunday observance, or of infant baptism, does not rest on any such definite warrant at all, but on unbroken *prescription* (that is, long use and custom). Now, it is a maxim of Canon Law that *privilege* and *prescription* cannot be simultaneously pleaded on behalf of the same claim; for the man who bases his demand on a deed of privilege is held to renounce his right of prescription—(*Decret. Greg. IX.*, lib. ii. titt. xxvi. and xxvii. 19). (2.) That which expresses the mind of the Church only, and is not directly matter of Divine revelation, may be conceivably altered by the consent of the whole body, as if, suppose, the distinction between Metropolitans and Bishops were abolished. But it is not competent for even the whole body to alter, either by enlargement or diminution, whatever it acknowledges to be divinely revealed, as is the case with the books of the Old and New Testament.

The most, therefore, which could be derived from such a consensus of authorities, each indefinitely inferior in weight to any New Testament writer, and all collectively not nearly equalling the aggregate witness of the New

Testament, would be a very strong presumption, **but still far short** of Divine certainty, in favour of a particular opinion or usage; **unless** this consensus went the whole length of asserting that the **matter** alleged is a divinely revealed dogma **of** Christianity. And this is the least which would **make amends for the indirectness and obscurity**, to say no more, of the evidence for the Privilege of Peter as found in the Scriptures.

Before beginning the investigation of such evidence **as is** tendered or producible, it is expedient to set down **once more the** links which must be, one and all of them, conclusively established before the claim will bear the weight of **Papal supremacy or** infallibility, and also to state the sources **of** inquiry, and the classification of testimony.

First, then, it must be shown that **there** is full agreement amongst the Fathers, **that St. Peter was the** Rock of the Church, was **infallible, and was** invested with direct jurisdiction over all **the other Apostles, and not** with a **mere** primacy of **honour.**

Next, that this supreme jurisdiction and infallible character were **not personal only, but capable of being devolved and transmitted to his successors.**

Thirdly, **that St. Peter was local** and diocesan Bishop of Rome.

Fourthly, that as a matter of fact he did professedly and expressly transmit his privilege to the Bishops **of Rome,** constituting them his **heirs** and successors.

Fifthly, that the Christian Church did, in fact, from the earliest times, recognise and submit to this infallible supremacy as of Divine institution.

There are several collateral issues, **scarcely** less important, **but it** will suffice to examine these **five links, the** failure of any **one of which is** fatal to the whole claim.

As to the sources of inquiry, they are: (1.) The ancient Liturgies. (2.) **The** writings of the Fathers from St. Ignatius **and other sub-**Apostolic authors down to Venerable Bede, A.D. 735. (3.) The canons, decrees, and acts **of** Councils, **and,** mainly, the six undisputed General Councils.

(4.) The admissions and acts of Popes and others. (5.) All such events in Church history as illustrate the meaning of phrases used by the Fathers.

As to the classification of testimony, nothing that does not help to prove some one of the five links just named is relevant. For example, no quotations which are simply laudatory of St. Peter, but which go no further than ranking him foremost of the Apostles, and none which speak of the Roman Church as an Apostolic See, but do not attribute to it a preponderating authority in Christendom, are to the point. They may be, and constantly are, adduced as though they helped to prove the privilege of Peter; but in fact they do nothing of the sort. Foremost amongst such irrelevant citations are those which speak of St. Peter as " Prince of the Apostles." The modern use of the word " Prince," to denote superior and even sovereign rank, naturally misleads those who do not know that the Latin *princeps*, from which it is derived, has no such necessary meaning, but originally denoted no more than " first in time or order." And in this sense, just as St. Peter is called " Prince of the Apostles," as indeed St. Andrew is also by St. Jerome on Psalm lxviii., so is St. Stephen called " Prince of the Martyrs," without any superior authority being thereby attributed to him over them. The mistake generated in this way may be compared to that which would be caused if some person, noticing in a Peerage that the Duke of Norfolk is " Premier " Duke and Earl of England, were not merely to suppose that he is the holder of the first Dukedom and Earldom ever created in England, but that he and the Dukes his predecessors have always been the heads of the Executive, as Prime Ministers of the Crown, because such is a modern use of the word " Premier."

Once more.—It must be steadily borne in mind that no quotation which merely goes to show that St. Peter stands forth conspicuously as the representative of the unity and authority of the Church, and as for a time its most prominent member, is of the least value either in behalf of the alleged privilege. What is needed is proof that St. Peter represents, not the Church, but Christ ; that he is, in short, in his double relation to the Head and to the Body, not what (to borrow a parallel from civil society) the President of a Legislative Chamber is, but what a Regent under an absolute monarchy is, in the absence of the King.

Again, no testimony of a writer who uses inconsistent and incompatible language on the points in debate can be received in favour of the claim, unless his affirmative words be later than, and in formal retractation of, his negative ones.

Fourthly, no Pope can be accepted as evidence in his own favour, because of the universal maxim of law, "No man may be judge in his own cause." But admissions made by Popes adverse to their own alleged privilege are good proof against it ; just as, in a common question of ownership, say of a purse picked up in the street, a disclaimer of right in it carries conviction of the speaker's truth much more perfectly than an assertion of ownership would do, because, in the former case, the statement is against the interest of the person who makes it.

Fifthly, words must be invariably brought to the test of deeds. It is a common device of Protestant controversialists, for example, to dilute and minimise the strong language of certain Fathers on the Holy Eucharist by describing it as merely rhetorical metaphor, not to be literally construed. But when this language is brought to the test of the ancient Liturgies, which, both in their words and acts, denote the practical belief of the Churches which used them, it is at once found that the Fathers are actually less fervid and, so to say, "extreme," than the Liturgies in their diction. It will be shown later what light the acts of Tertullian, of St. Cyprian, of St. Augustine, and other eminent Christian writers, shed on their language with regard to the Petrine claims.

The importance of the Liturgies as sources of evidence is due not only to their great antiquity, but still more to the fact that they testify to a great deal more than any patristic citations can do, for what whole Churches and nations said officially and authoritatively every day for several centuries together **is** much weightier than what a single ecclesiastical writer said but once, and that **perhaps** informally, **and** almost certainly in his private capacity, pledging **no one** but himself. The nearly universal custom in these Liturgies of commemorating the most **eminent** Saints by name in the oblation is important to **bear in** mind, as it must certainly have led to the specific **mention** of St. Peter in most, if not all of them, if his **rank be as** alleged by Ultramontanes.

It will **not** be necessary to cite **all the extant** Liturgies, **for a** comparatively small number of extracts will display **the** whole evidence :—

a. Liturgy of St. James, or norm of Palestine.—In the course of the Prayer of Invocation **of** the Holy Ghost on the oblations occur these two highly significant passages :— (1.) "For the stablishing of thy Holy Catholic Church, which *Thou hast founded on the rock of the faith*, that the gates of hell may not prevail against it." (2.) "Especially for the glorious Zion, the *Mother of all the Churches*."

b. **Liturgy** of St. Mark, or norm of Egypt.—There are three items of evidence in **this** document :—(1.) The first place in the commemoration of ecclesiastical persons **is** assigned to the **Pope or** Patriarch of Alexandria, who is described in **one** passage as "pre-ordained to rule over Thy Holy Catholic and Apostolic Church." (2.) The only Saints commemorated by name are the Blessed Virgin and St. Mark, as founder of the See **of** Alexandria. **(3.)** The order of commemoration **of places** gives the first rank to Jerusalem, the second, perhaps **to** Rome, but as probably to Constantinople at a later time, **and** the third to Alexandria, thus :—"Remember, O Lord, the Holy city of our God, Jesus Christ, *and the imperial city*, and this city of ours."

c. Liturgy **of** the **Holy** Apostles, or Nestorian norm of Persia.—No evidence.

d. Liturgy of St. Clement.—One clause alone in this ancient document—and that most probably an interpolation by the anonymous compiler of the Apostolical Constitutions some time in the fourth century—is relevant, and it puts the Bishop of Jerusalem first, of Rome second, and either of Antioch or Alexandria third, thus:—"For every episcopate under heaven of those who rightly divide the word of Thy truth, let us make our supplication; and for our Bishop James and his parishes, let us make our supplication; for our Bishop Clement and his parishes let us make our supplication; for our Bishop Evodius [*al.* Anianus] and his parishes, let us make our supplication."

e. Liturgy of St. Basil the Great, or norm of Syro-Greek Church.—No evidence, save that the Blessed Virgin and St. John Baptist are the only saints commemorated by name, and that the local prelate is the first named in the Great Intercession.

f. Liturgy of St. Chrysostom, or norm of Constantinople.—As St. Basil.

g. Coptic St. Basil, or norm of the Coptic Church.—(1.) In the Prayer of Absolution the Twelve Apostles are mentioned collectively, and next St. Mark is named specifically, followed by some other names. (2.) The Pope of Alexandria occupies the first place in the Intercession. (3.) There is a prayer in honour of St. Paul after the Epistle, as being the chief preacher of the Gospel. (4.) In a copious commemoration of Saints, the only New Testament names are St. Mary, St. John Baptist, St. Stephen, and St. Mark. (5.) In the Prayer of Absolution to the Father, the text St. Matt. xvi. 18, 19, is embodied thus:—". . . . Thou art He Who sayest to Peter our father, by the mouth of Thine only begotten Son our Lord Jesus Christ, 'Thou art Peter . . . . loosed in heaven'; so then, O Lord, let my father and brethren be absolved out of my mouth, by Thy Holy Spirit, O merciful lover of men."

The ground of the citation here, therefore, is not to allege any special privilege of Peter, but to base on the grant of the power of binding and loosing to the whole Church in his person the right of the individual celebrant o pronounce absolution.

h. Ordo Communis, or norm of Syro-Jacobites.—(1.) There is an exclamation after the Epistle, "Glory to the Lord of Paul, of the Prophets, and of the Apostles." (2.) The Four Evangelists are commemorated by name after the Gospel has been read. No mention of St. Peter occurs. A variant of this rite has a Canticle in which are the words: "Blessed be Christ, who built His Church upon Simon," but this seems to be a Maronite copy, altered under Latin influence.

i. Syriac St. James.—"Remember, O Lord, the holy Bishops . . . . who from James, *first of Bishops*, Apostle and Martyr, unto this day have preached the word," &c.

j. Syriac St. Peter the Apostle. I. and II.—The former of these commemorates only St. Mary, St. John Baptist, and St. Stephen by name; the latter St. Mary alone. They contain no other evidence.

k. Armenian Liturgy.—St. Mary, St. John Baptist, St. Stephen, and the Apostles Thaddeus and Bartholomew, are the only New Testament Saints enumerated.

l. Liturgy of Malabar, or norm of Christians of St. Thomas.—The only Apostle commemorated by name is St. Thomas.

m. Liturgy of Nestorius.—No evidence.

n. Ambrosian Missal.—No relevant evidence, even in the office of SS. Peter and Paul, but there is one phrase in the *Oratio super sindonem* for St. Peter's Chair at Rome, worded thus:—"O God, Who didst this day hallow the Pontificate of Thy blessed Apostle Peter, grant that Thy Church, spread throughout the world, may be always ruled by his governance [*ejus magisterio gubernari*], from whom it derived the beginning of religion." But this is an interpolation in the sixteenth century, being absent from the Ambrosian Missal in 1475, though it is found in one of 1522. It is thus far too late to have any evidential value.

o. Mozarabic Missal, or norm of Spanish Church (tampered with by Cardinal Ximenes in 1500).—(1.) St. Peter, "Prince of the Apostles," is specially named, along with St. Mary, in a prayer for absolution at the beginning of the office. (2.) The Pope of Rome is alone specified by name as joining in the act of oblation which all the clergy are said to offer. (3.) St. Peter is named in the commemoration of Saints at the head of the Apostles and Evangelists, but after St. Mary, St. Zacharias, St. John [Baptist], and Holy Innocents. (4.) The Collect for St. Peter's Chair begins :—"O God, Son of God, Who didst exalt Peter upon Thyself, the most solid Rock, and upon Peter the Church," &c.

p. Gallican Missal.—This office does, indeed, in a collect speak of St. Peter as "fundator Ecclesiæ" ("founder of the Church"), and in the Collect for St. Peter's Chair as "caput ecclesiæ" ("head of the Church"); but in the *Contestatio* of that day are the crucial words :—" In cujus confessione est fundamentum ecclesiæ ; nec adversus hanc petram portæ inferi prævalent" (" In whose confession is the Church's foundation, nor shall the gates of hell prevail against this rock"). Mabillon cannot decide whether the feast is that of St. Peter's Chair at Rome or at Antioch (*De Liturg. Gallic.*). If the latter, it does not help the Roman claim. The point is really settled by the fact that Durandus knows of the Chair at Antioch only.—*Rat. Div. Off.* vii. 8.

q. The Old German Missal, which, however, cannot be older than the middle of the eighth century, and probably bears the marks of the strong Roman zeal of St. Boniface, is the only one which contains testimony directly favourable to the Petrine claims. In the Preface for St. Peter's Chair (itself probably a later interpolation) we read :— " From amongst which [Saints] Thou didst make ruler and keeper [*præsulem et custodem*] of Thy heavenly enclosures Blessed Peter, called to the Apostolate by the mouth of our Lord and God, Thy Word Himself, and appointed Prince of the Apostles because of his confession of Christ, Thine only begotten Son, and placed, with a change of name, in the foundation of Thine house, the right being divinely conferred on him that what he decreed on earth shall be made good in heaven." This case is specially useful as serving to show what kind of evidence we are entitled to require from the ancient Liturgies, but do not find there.

r. Roman Missal.—The evidence of this document, which is very important against the privilege, will be set down a little later under another heading, for a reason there assigned.[1]

The liturgical evidence is thus shown to be either positively against the Petrine claims, or negatively incapable of being cited in their favour, although it is quite certain that, if any such view of St. Peter's peculiar rank as Head of the Church and Vicar of Christ had prevailed as unquestionably did prevail touching St. John Baptist's exceptional position as herald and forerunner of Christ, we should find abundant and conclusive proof of it in the Liturgies.

Before entering on the second stage of inquiry—that which is concerned with the writings of the Fathers—it is expedient to say a few words about the authority they individually possess. No person can be formally enrolled amongst the Saints by canonization, unless after the strictest inquiry it be established that nothing which he wrote, even if unpublished, contained any doctrinal error whatever; or else, supposing him to have written aught which contradicted the known teaching of the Church in his day, evidence of retractation must be adduced—(*Decret. Urbani VIII.; Bened. XIV. De Serv. Dei Beatificat.* ii. 26, 2). Nevertheless, this does not make the teaching of any Saint unimpeachable, if valid grounds of objection can be stated

---

[1] But it may be said here that the festival of St. Peter's Chair at Rome does not occur in the Roman Missal and Breviary till inserted in virtue of a Bull of Paul IV. in 1538, wherein the Pope states that it had become entirely obsolete everywhere except in Gaul and Spain. The feast of St. Peter's Chair is mentioned in Canon xxii. of the Second Council of Tours in 567, but without any specified locality, and all the earlier mentions of place have Antioch, not Rome. The latter has been substituted for the former in the Gregorian Sacramentary, where the Codex Rutoldi has *Antiochia*.

against it, but only makes its tenability probable—(*Bened. XIV. De Serv. Dei Beatificatione*, ii. 32, 12). But if the Saint be also a Doctor of the Church, then his doctrine may not be impugned at all, because he has not merely taught *in* the Church, but has taught the Church itself— (*Bened. XIV. De Canonizatione*, iv. 2; xi. 11). And, accordingly, the great majority of the subjoined citations are taken from Doctors of the Church, whose authority is not open to criticism from Roman Catholics. Authors who are not counted amongst the Saints, and especially such as are charged with heresy, may be quoted to prove an historical fact, but not to establish doctrine. And nothing short of the *unanimous consent* of the Fathers may lawfully be followed by any Roman Catholic in the interpretation of Scripture—(*Creed of Pius IV.*, par. 3).

This does not mean, obviously, that the silence of even a considerable number of Fathers on any point is conclusive against it, but only that all such as do treat of it must be substantially agreed in their view, and neither contradict one another nor oppose the opinion sought to be maintained by their testimony. Of course, silence is sometimes very weighty adverse evidence, when the scope and circumstances of any patristic or conciliar document seem to call for express mention of the point in discussion, and yet no such mention is found. But it is the peculiarity of the Petrine privilege that its importance as a central dogma of Christianity (which it must be, if the relation of every human soul to God depend on its relation to the Roman See) is so great, that it could no more be left out of sight by any appreciable number of Christian writers than the Incarnation or the Atonement; and, consequently, silence is in this case a very serious contradiction.

It will be convenient, as matter of arrangement, to restrict the inquiry at first to the opinions expressed by the Fathers upon the three capital texts of Scripture which are used as the basis of the Petrine privilege; namely, St. Matt. xvi. 18; St. Luke xxii. 32; and St. John xxi. 15–17.

What, then, do the Fathers say as to the Rock of the

Church, the prayer for Peter's steadfastness, and the commission to feed the sheep?

There is a scantiness of reference to these topics in the whole ante-Nicene period which is simply unaccountable on any hypothesis of their vital or central importance. Out of the following authors and books—Ignatius, Clement, Polycarp, Hermas, Papias, Justin Martyr, Athenagoras, Tatian, Theophilus, Clementine Recognitions and Homilies, **Apostolical Constitutions**, **Irenæus, Hippolytus, Caius, Asterius,** Alexander of Jerusalem, Clement of Alexandria, Origen, Tertullian, Methodius, Lactantius, **Peter of** Alexandria, Alexander of Alexandria, **Cyprian,** Firmilian, Gregory Thaumaturgus, Dionysius of **Alexandria, and** Archelaus— only six make any reference at all to St. Matthew xvi. 18. One of these, St. Hippolytus, in his *Discourse on the Holy Theophany*, is speaking of the work of the Holy Spirit, and says, " By this Spirit Peter spake that blessed word, **'Thou art the Christ, the Son of the living God.'** By this Spirit the Rock of the Church is established." No conclusion can be drawn either way from this citation.

St. Cyprian, Doctor of the Church, in the first place where he quotes the text, Ep. xxvii., begins by saying that it serves to explain "the honour of a Bishop and the Order of the Church, ... so that the Church is founded on the Bishops." In the second citation of it, in his treatise on the Unity of the Church, he glosses it (and St. John xxi. 15, cited in the same sentence) by saying: "The Lord . . . . that He might set forth unity, He arranged by His authority the origin of that unity, as beginning from one. *Assuredly the rest of the Apostles were also the same as was Peter*, endowed with a like partnership *both of honour and power*; but the beginning proceeds from unity."

St. Firmilian actually quotes the text to prove that Pope St. Stephen was in error, folly, and blindness by permitting heretical baptisms to be counted valid, and was thereby introducing many other rocks and Churches instead of one only, at the very time that he was boasting of his succession from Peter, on whom the foundations of the Church were laid.—*Ep.* lxxv. in *Opp. St. Cypriani.*

The three remaining witnesses are the Clementine Homilies, Origen, and Tertullian. But the first of these is rejected by the Roman Church, ever since the Synod under Pope Gelasius in 494, as spurious and heretical, and therefore its testimony (chap. xix.) that St. Peter describes himself as "a firm rock, the foundation of the Church," cannot be adduced.

Nor is anything lost to the Ultramontane cause by refusing to admit this apocryphal testimony, since, even though St. Peter is the hero of its romantic narrative, St. James is described throughout as the chief bishop and arbiter of Christian doctrine, exercising authority over St. Peter himself,—a fact in itself inconsistent with the universal prevalence of the opposite view at the date of the book.

Origen says that "the Rock is every disciple of Christ, from whom they drank who drank of the spiritual rock which followed them, and on every such rock every ecclesiastical word is builded, and the plan of life according to His pattern . . . . But if thou thinkest that the whole Church is built by God on St. Peter alone, what dost thou say of John, the son of thunder, and every one of the Apostles? Or shall we dare to say that the gates of hell were not to prevail against Peter in particular, but that they were to prevail against the other Apostles and perfect ones? Is it not true for each and all, what was said before, that 'the gates of hell shall not prevail against it,' and also that other saying, 'Upon this rock I will build my Church?'" And he goes on to say that all who make St. Peter's confession of Christ their Rock, become the same as Peter.— *Comm. in St. Matt.* xvi. 18.

Tertullian alone remains, and his two citations of St. Matt. xvi. 18 are in treatises written after he fell, as is alleged, into Montanist heresy. In the former of these, *De Præscript. Hæret.* xxii., he confines himself to saying, "Peter, who is called the Rock on which the Church should be built"; but in the latter, *De Pudicitia*, xxi., he insists strongly, and at length, that the privilege of Peter died with him, and was incapable of transmission, so that he was the Rock only in the sense of founding the Church by being its first preacher, and that the power of binding and loosing, conferred on Peter alone *personally*, could not be derived to, nor exercised by, any Church claiming to be akin to Peter; while that even as regards Peter himself, his power of binding and loosing referred merely to his action in first unlocking the doors of the kingdom of heaven by administering baptism to the new converts, in abolishing part and retaining part of the Mosaic Law, and in his miracles upon the lame man and upon Ananias. And in two other places, *Adv. Jud.* ix. and *Adv. Marcion.* iv. 13, Tertullian restricts the title of Rock to Christ.

That is the whole which the ante-Nicene Church has to tell us on St. Matt. xvi. 18.

As to St. Luke xxii. 31, only four ante-Nicene writers cite it. Of these, two, St. Ignatius, in the *Epistle to the Smyrnæans*, and the Apostolical Constitutions, vi. 5. iv., actually refer to it as if worded in the plural throughout and referring to *all* the Apostles, and not to St. Peter singly, albeit the original text is in the singular. Tertullian (*De Fuga*) uses the text merely to show that the Devil's power is limited, so that he cannot tempt Christians further than he is expressly permitted. St. Cyprian quotes it twice (*Epist.* vii. 5, and *De Orat. Domini* 30), in each case employing it in proof of Christ's intercessory office for all sinners, and making no special application of it to St. Peter.

St. John xxi. 15 is but twice cited, once by St. Cyprian in the passage of the treatise on Unity already quoted above, where he alleges the commission of feeding the sheep to extend to every Apostle alike; and it occurs again in a very obscurely-worded sentence in a letter from the clergy of Rome to those of Carthage, on St. Cyprian's withdrawal during a persecution. After quoting our Lord's words about himself as the Good Shepherd, in contrast to the hireling that leaveth the sheep to the wolf and fleeth, they go on: "To Simon, too, He speaks thus: 'Lovest thou me? He answered, I do love Thee. He saith to him. Feed My sheep.' We know that these words came to pass by reason of the very act whereby he [Peter] withdrew, and the other disciples did the like."—*Ep.* ii. in *Opp. St. Cypr.* The simplest interpretation of this difficult passage is that the Roman clergy read the text in the light of a rebuke to St. Peter for fleeing and denying his Master, and as a warning not to neglect his pastoral duties another time.

This is absolutely the whole which the Fathers of the three first centuries have to tell us as to the three clauses of the Petrine grant of privilege, and apart from the ominous silence of the great majority, the words of those who do speak are of curiously little help to the claim. There is, of course, a good deal of other evidence in the writers of this early period yet to be considered, but as interpreters of the letter of Scripture, they have no more to give us on this special topic.

If the inquiry be carried down somewhat lower, still confining it strictly to the interpretation of these three texts, the case for the claim of privilege will not be strengthened:—

St. Matt. xvi. 18.

St. Hilary of Poitiers, Doctor of the Church.—"Upon this rock of the confession is the building up of the Church .... This faith is the foundation of the Church. Through this faith the gates of hell are powerless against it. This faith hath the keys of the heavenly kingdom."—*De Trinit.* vi. 36, 37.

St. Epiphanius, Doctor of the Church.—"Peter, the foremost of the Apostles, who became to us a truly solid rock, laying the foundation of the faith of the Lord, on which [faith] the Church is in all respects built. And that first because he confessed Christ, the Son of the living God, and heard that 'Upon this rock of unshaken faith I will build My Church.'"—*Adv. Hær.* lib. ii. tom. i. 8.

"He also reveals the Holy Spirit (Acts v. 3), for this befitted the first of the Apostles, the strong rock on which the Church of God is built, and the gates of hell shall not prevail against it."—*Ancor.* ix.

St. Basil, Doctor of the Church.—"The Church of God, whose foundations are upon the holy hills; for it is built upon the foundation of the Apostles and Prophets. One of these mountains was Peter, on which rock the Lord promised that He would build His Church. For sublime and lofty minds, lifted high above earthly things, are fitly styled mountains. But the lofty mind of blessed Peter is named a lofty rock, because it was deeply rooted in the faith and abode firmly and unshrinkingly the blows inflicted by temptation. All those who acquire knowledge of the Godhead, through greatness of mind, and of actions proceeding from mind, perfected in sound life, they are the tops of the mountains upon which the house of God is built. . . . . It may be that he is speaking **of** an escape from the evils he specified above; to wit, entering into the hole of the rock (Isa. ii. 19)**, that** is, the steadfastness of faith in Christ. That **is** where Moses was placed when about to see God. . . . . But **collate** whatever is said in Scripture concerning the Rock, **that** the **passage may** be cleared up for thee."—*Comm. in Esaiam*, ii. 66, 85.

ST. GREGORY NAZIANZEN, Doctor **of** the Church.—"Do you notice how, when all Christ's disciples **were** lofty and worthy of election, one is called a Rock, and is intrusted with the foundations of the Church (καὶ τοῖς θεμελίοις τῆς ἐκκλησίας πιστεύεται), while another is better loved, and rests on the bosom of Jesus, and the remaining disciples admit their superior honour?"—*Orat.* xxvi.

ST. AMBROSE, Doctor of the Church :—

"Præco diei jam sonat—
Noctis profundæ pervigil,
 . . . .
Hoc ipsa Petra ecclesiæ
Canente culpam diluit."
      Hymn, *Æterne Rerum* **Conditor.**

("Lo, even the very Church's Rock
Melts at the crowing of the cock.")

"This is that Peter to whom Christ said, '**Thou** art Peter, and upon this rock I will build my Church.' Therefore where Peter is, there is the Church; where the Church **is,** there **is no** death, but life eternal. And therefore He adds : 'The gates **of hell** shall not prevail against it ; and I will give unto **thee** the keys **of the** kingdom of heaven.' That blessed Peter, **against whom** the gates of hell prevailed not, did not close the gates **of** heaven against himself; but, on **the** contrary, destroyed the entrances of hell, and made manifest the entrances of heaven. **Being,** therefore, placed on earth, he **opened** heaven and closed hell."—*In Psalm* xl. *Enarr.* 30.

"This, then, **is** P**eter, who** answered for the other Apostles, yea, before the others, **and** therefore is called the foundation, **because he** not only knew how **to** preserve that which belonged to himself, **but** that which was common to others. Christ expressed his assent **to** him, the Father made revelation to him. For whoso speaketh truly of generation from the Father got it from the Father, and not from the flesh. Faith is therefore the foundation of the Church; for it was not said of Peter's person [*lit.* flesh], but of his faith, that the gates of hell should not prevail against it, but his confession conquered hell."—*De Incarn. Dom.* 33, 34.

"The rock is Christ. 'For they drank of that spiritual rock which followed them, and that rock was Christ.' However, He did not deny the favour of this epithet to His disciple, that he should be Peter, because he had steadfastness of constancy, firmness of faith, from the rock. Strive, therefore, that thou, too, mayest be a rock. Look, therefore, for the rock not outside thyself, but within thee. Thine act is a rock, thy thought is a rock. Thine house is built on this rock that it may not be shaken by any storms of spiritual wickedness. Thy faith is a rock: faith is the foundation of the Church. If thou be a rock, thou shalt be in the Church, because the Church is on the rock. If thou be in the Church, the gates of hell shall not prevail against thee."—*Expos. in Lucam*, vi. 97, 98.

"That starry sky . . . . is the high firmament of heaven, nor is this other firmament unlike it, of which it is said, 'Upon this rock will I build my Church.' . . . . They sucked oil out of the firm rock, for the rock was the flesh of Christ, which redeemed heaven and the whole world."—*Ep.* xliii. 9.

ST. JEROME, Doctor of the Church.—"I speak with the successor of the Fisherman and a disciple of the Cross. I, following no chief save Christ, am counted in communion with your Blessedness, that is, with the Chair of Peter. On that rock I know the Church is built. Whoso eats the lamb outside this house is profane."—*Epist. ad Damasum Papam*, A.D. 376.

"Christ is the rock, Who granted to His Apostles that they should be called rocks: 'Thou art Peter, and upon this rock I will build my Church.'"—*Comm. in Amos*, vi. 12, A.D. 392.

"But thou sayest the Church is founded on Peter, albeit the very same thing is also done upon all the Apostles, and they all receive the keys of the kingdom of heaven, and the strength of the Church is stablished on them all equally; nevertheless, one out of the twelve is chosen, that by the appointment of a head, the chance of division might be averted. . . . ."—*Adv. Jovin.* ii. A.D. 393.

"Was there any other province in the whole world which admitted the preaching of pleasure, into which the wily serpent crept, save that which the teaching of Peter had founded on Christ the Rock?"—*Adv. Jovin.* ii. circa finem, A.D. 393.

"Upon this rock the Lord founded His Church; from this rock the Apostle Peter derived his name. . . . . The foundation which the Apostle, as architect, laid is our Lord Jesus Christ alone. On this foundation the Church of Christ is built."—*Comm. in Matt.* vii. 24, 25, A.D. 398.

"As He gave light to the Apostles, that they might be called the light of the world, and they obtained other titles from the Lord, so also to Simon, who believed in Christ the Rock, He gave the name of Peter, and according to the metaphor of a rock, it is rightly said, 'I will build my Church on thee.'"—*Comm. in Matt.* xvi. 18, A.D. 398.

ST. JOHN CHRYSOSTOM, Doctor of the Church.—"'And I say unto thee, that thou art Peter, and upon this rock will I build My Church,' that is, upon the faith of his confession (τῇ πίστει τῆς ὁμολογίας.")—*Hom.* 54 *in Matt.* xxvi. sect. 2.

ST. ISIDORE OF PELUSIUM.—"Christ, Who searcheth the hearts, did not ask His disciples, 'Whom do men say that I, the Son of Man, am?' because He did not know the varying opinion of men concerning Himself, but was desirous of teaching all that same confession which Peter, inspired by Him, laid as the basis and foundation on which the Lord built His Church."—*Epist.* 235.

"Christ is the Rock, abiding unshaken, when He was Incarnate." —*Ep.* 416.

ST. AUGUSTINE, Doctor of the Church.—"At the same time while I was a priest (A.D. 392–395), I wrote a book against the Letter of Donatus . . . in which book I said in a certain place of the Apostle Peter that the Church was founded on him as on a rock, an interpretation which is also sung by the lips of many in the verses of blessed Ambrose, where he speaks of the cock, 'Lo, even the very Church's Rock melts at the crowing of the cock.' But I know that afterwards I most frequently (*sæpissime*) have thus explained what the Lord said, 'Thou art Peter, and upon this rock I will build My Church,' that it should be understood as upon Him Whom Peter confessed, saying, 'Thou art the Christ, the Son of the living God,' and that Peter, named from this Rock, represented the person of the Church, which is built on the Rock, and received the keys of the kingdom of heaven. For it was not said to him, Thou art the rock (*petra*), but thou art Peter. For Christ was the Rock, Whom Simon confessing, as the whole Church confesses Him, was called Peter."—*Retract.* i. xxi. A.D. 428.

"The first of the Apostles . . . . signified the Church universal . . . . because it is founded upon the rock, whence Peter received his name. For the rock is not from Peter, but Peter from the rock, just as Christ is not called from Christian, but Christian from Christ. Therefore it is that the Lord saith, 'Upon this rock will I build My Church,' because Peter had said, 'Thou art the Christ, the Son of the living God.' Upon this rock, this rock which thou hast confessed, I will build My Church. For Christ was the rock, on which foundation Peter himself was built. For other foundation can no man lay than that is laid, which is Christ Jesus. Therefore the Church, which is founded on Christ, received from Him the keys of the kingdom of heaven in Peter, that is, the power of binding and loosing sins."—*Tract. in Evang. Joann.* cxxiv. 5.

St. Cyril of Alexandria, Doctor of the Church.—"That which He named a rock, referring to his name, was nought else, I think, than the unshaken and most firm faith of the disciple, on which also the Church of Christ was founded and established."—*Dialog. de Trinitate*, iv.

Theodoret.—"For this reason Christ our Master suffered the first of the Apostles, whose confession he laid as the kind of basis or foundation of the Church, to be shaken and to err, and to raise him up again, teaching two things by the one act, not to trust themselves and to stablish the wavering."—*Epist.* lxxvii.

St. Leo the Great, Pope and Doctor.—"The solidity of the foundation on which the lofty building of the whole Church is erected, fails not by reason of the mass of the temple which rests upon it. For the solidity of that faith which was praised in the Prince of the Apostles is perpetual. And so, as that abides, which Peter believed in Christ, so that too abides which Christ instituted in Peter. . . . . Therefore the appointment of the Truth abides, and blessed Peter persevering in that strength of the rock which he received, hath never quitted the governance of the Church which he received. For so he was ordained before the others, that whilst he is called the Rock, whilst he is declared the foundation, whilst he is constituted doorkeeper of the kingdom of heaven, and arbiter of things to be bound and loosed . . . . we should know by the mystery of these titles what is his fellowship with Christ . . . . That confession which, inspired by God the Father in the Apostle's heart, rises above all the uncertainties of human opinions, received the firmness of the rock, which cannot be shaken by any impacts. For, throughout the Church Universal Peter daily saith, 'Thou art the Christ, the Son of the living God,' and every tongue which confesses the Lord is imbued with the authority of this voice. This faith conquers the Devil, and looses the bonds of his captives. This delivers men from the world and places them in heaven, and the gates of hell cannot prevail against it. For it has been divinely established with such firmness that neither heretical pravity was ever able to corrupt it, nor pagan unbelief to overcome it."—*Serm.* ii. on Anniversary of his Consecration.

St. Gregory the Great, Pope and Doctor.—"The Son of God is the Beginning. In this beginning the earth was founded, because the Church is founded on Him. Hence the Apostle saith, 'Other foundation can no man lay than that is laid, Jesus Christ.' Hence He Himself, the mediator of God and man, saith to the Prince of the Apostles. 'Thou art Peter, upon this Rock I will build My Church.' For He is the Rock from which Peter derived his name, and on which He said that He would build the Church.'—*Comm. in Ps.* ci. 27.

Venerable Bede.—"He received the name of Peter from the Lord, because he chose faith from a steadfast mind to Him of Whom it is written, 'And that Rock was Christ,' and ' Upon the Rock,' that is, upon the Lord the Saviour, who gave to Him, knowing, loving, and confessing Him faithfully, a share in his own Name, so that he should be called Peter, from the Rock on which the Church is built." *Hom. in Matt.* xvi. 18.

St. Gregory VII., Pope, sending a crown to Rudolf of Rheinfelden, to stir him up against the Emperor Henry IV., added the following line :—

"Petra dedit Petro, Petrus diadema Rodolpho,"
(" The Rock gave the diadem to Peter, Peter to Rodolf").
Baronius, *Ann.*

It is unnecessary to carry this chain of evidence down further, though it could be largely amplified from early and later writers.[1] It is sufficient to say that only two of the passages just cited are even patient of the Ultramontane interpretation, namely, the first citation from St. Jerome, and the fuller context of the citation from St. Leo the Great, which makes very lofty claims indeed for the Papacy. As regards St. Jerome, apart from a very old debate as to what he meant (seeing that the whole scope of the letter is an appeal to the Trinitarian teaching at Rome against the prevalent Arianism of the East, and may, therefore, be very reasonably interpreted of communion in faith with the orthodox Pope Damasus), and that the great Erasmus glosses the passage thus :—

" Not on Rome [was the Church built], as I think, for it might happen that Rome also should become degenerate, but upon that faith which Peter professed, which hitherto the Roman Church has preserved ; "

there is the weighty fact that, even if we interpret the *Epistle to Damasus* in the most hyper-Papal sense, it is

---

[1] *E.g.*—St. Gregory Nyssen, St. John Damascene, St. Isidore of Seville, Popes Hadrian I., Nicolas I., John VIII., Stephen V., Innocent II., Hadrian IV., Urban III., &c. See citations in Friedrich, *Documenta ad Illustrandum Concilium Vaticanum.* And for other mediæval and later authors of note, such as Albertus Magnus, Cardinal Hugo, &c., who do not identify St. Peter with the Rock, see Denton, *Commentary on the Gospels,* St. Peter's Day.

sixteen years earlier than the oldest of the five other contradictory passages cited from St. Jerome, whose maturer and final opinion must be judged by them, just as St. Augustine's retractation of his first view about St. Peter being the Rock, settles his judgment on that point. And it is another weighty **fact** that St. Leo, when making very large claims indeed **for** the " privilege of Peter," and for himself as Peter's heir, is obliged to contradict himself by admitting that the Catholic faith is the Church's foundation.

There is, then, not merely no " unanimous consent " of the Fathers in favour of Peter being the Rock, but there is a powerful preponderance of adverse testimony. However, though some, although but few (17 **as** against 44, and 8 more who take all the Apostles to be the Rock)[1] of the Fathers do call Peter the Rock of the Church[2]; nevertheless, *this view is not open, even as a mere pious opinion*, to any Roman Catholic. Two clauses of the Creed of Pius IV. bar it effectually—namely, the second, which binds to acceptance of " apostolic and ecclesiastical traditions, and all other observances and constitutions of the same (holy Roman) Church," and the eleventh, already cited, obliging to the definitions of the Councils, and chiefly that of Trent.

Now the Roman Missal **is a** formulary of the highest authority in the Latin Church, and not only includes many "apostolic and ecclesiastical traditions," but is the chief storehouse of " observances " in worship.

But the Collect for the Vigil of SS. Peter and Paul runs thus :—

"Grant, we beseech Thee, Almighty God, that **Thou** wouldst not suffer us, whom Thou hast established *upon the* **rock of** *the Apostolic confession*, to be shaken by any disturbances ; "

---

[1] Speech of Archbishop Kenrick **of** St. Louis at the Vatican Council. Friedrich, *Documenta*. Vol. i. p. **195.**

[2] None of those who do so, however, add anything to connect the text with the Bishop of Rome as successor or heir of St. Peter.

while the only evidence it contains capable of being cited on the other side is that SS. Peter and Paul are named together in the Confession, but after St. John Baptist; and again together in the Canon, *infra actionem*, at the head of the list of Apostles and Martyrs there commemorated.

And the Council of Trent, in its solemn decree upon the Symbol of the Faith, speaks thus, after a long preamble:

"Wherefore it [the Council] judged that the symbol of the Faith, which the Holy Roman Church uses, should be set forth in the full wording whereby it is read in all Churches, as that principle in which all who confess the faith of Christ must needs agree, and *as the firm and only foundation, against which the gates of hell shall not prevail,* which is of this sort : ' I believe in one God,' &c."

Consequently, any Roman Catholic who alleges that St. Matt. xvi. 18 refers to St. Peter's person, subjects himself to anathema, inasmuch as the Missal and the Council of Trent declare that the Rock is the faith contained in the Nicene Creed. No doubt there is a rival anathema in the Vatican decrees, awaiting those who hold the Tridentine view, but the decisions of Trent are much more certainly valid and binding in the Church of Rome than those of the Vatican, whose canonical legality is open to the most serious question, and which merely serve, by this contradiction, as a useful touchstone for Infallibility.

St. Luke xxii. 31, 32.

The next part of the inquiry is the interpretation put by the Fathers on Christ's address to St. Peter at the Last Supper, and whether they take it as a grant of infallibility and jurisdiction. There is much less evidence of any kind producible as to this text than for the preceding one, from the curious fact, familiar to all Biblical students, of the comparative paucity of comments on St. Luke's Gospel. However, there is quite enough to settle the question :

St. Hilary of Poitiers, Doctor.—"As for what he said, 'If it be possible,' &c. (St. Matt. xxvi. 39), He taught its meaning plainly in what he says to Peter : ' Behold, Satan hath desired to have you, that he may sift you as wheat, but I have prayed for thee, that thy faith fail not.' For they all had to be tried by this cup of the Lord's Passion. And the Father is besought for Peter, lest his faith should fail, that at all events the grief of repentance might not be wanting to the weakness of the sinner, for in case he did repent, then this faith would not fail in him."—*De Trin.* x. 38.

ST. BASIL THE GREAT, Doctor.—"Thou art not more honourable than blessed Peter the Apostle. For thou canst not excel in love one who loved so vehemently as to be willing to die for him. But because he spoke too confidently, when he said, 'Though all should be offended in Thee, yet will I never be offended,' he was given up to human cowardice, and fell into denial, instructed in caution by his fall, and taught to spare the weak by learning his own weakness; and to know clearly that just as when he was drowning in the sea, he was rescued by Christ's right hand, so when in danger of perishing in the stormy sea of offence through lack of faith, he was preserved by Christ's power, Who had moreover foretold him what would happen, saying, 'Simon, Simon,' &c. And Peter, thus rebuked, was fitly aided and taught to lay aside his vanity, and to spare the weak."—*Hom. de Humilitate.*

ST. AMBROSE, Doctor.—The first thing to be remarked is that St. Ambrose passes over St. Luke xxii. 31, 32 altogether in his commentary on that Gospel—a fact inconsistent with his having attached the importance or the meaning to it which it assumes when adduced as one clause of the Petrine grant of privilege. He does explain it, however, in another part of his writings:—

"Peter is winnowed, that he may be forced to deny Christ. He falls into temptation, he speaks some things full, as it were, of chaff; but he spake in word that he might be better stablished in affection. At last he wept, and washed away his chaff, and by these temptations he obtained Christ's intercession for him. . . . At length Peter is set over the Church after being tempted by the Devil. And so the Lord signifies beforehand that which came to pass afterwards, in that He chose Him to be shepherd of the Lord's flock. For he said to him: 'When thou art converted, strengthen thy brethren.' Therefore the holy Apostle Peter was converted into good corn, and was winnowed as wheat, that he might be one bread unto the family of God for our food."—*Comm. in Ps.* xliii. 41.

ST. JOHN CHRYSOSTOM, Doctor.—"Hear what He saith, 'I have prayed for thee, that thy faith fail not.' For this He said sharply reproving him, and showing that his fall was more grievous than that of the rest, and needed more help. . . . And why, if Satan desired all, did He not say concerning all, 'I have prayed for *you*?' Is it not quite plain that it is this, which I have mentioned before, that it is as reproving him, and showing that his fall was more grievous than that of the rest, that He directs His words to him?"—*Hom.* 82 *in Matt.* xxvi.

ST. AUGUSTINE, Doctor.—"'And take not the word of **truth** utterly out of my mouth' (Ps. cxix. 43). The word of truth was not utterly taken out of Peter's mouth, in whom was a type of the Church, for though he denied for a time when troubled with fear, yet he was amended by weeping, and afterwards crowned by confessing. But when he says, 'Take not,' it is to be understood, 'Suffer not to be taken;' therefore we say in praying, '**Lead us not into** temptation.' And the Lord Himself to Peter, 'I have **prayed for thee** that thy faith fail not'; that is, lest the word **of** truth be taken **out** of thy mouth *utterly*."—*Hom.* xiii. *in Ps.* cxviii.

The text is also cited several times in relation to the Pelagian heresy, as illustrating the necessity of grace to assist man's free-will, and notably by St. Jerome, Doctor (*Adv. Pelag.*) St. Augustine, Doctor (*De Grat. et Lib. Arb.* 9), and St. Prosper (*De Lib. Arbit. ad Ruffin.* xi.), but they all give it a general interpretation, as illustrating a doctrine affecting every man alike, so that in absolute strictness their testimony does not help to decide the question either way, save so far as their silence makes against the Ultramontane gloss, which, in truth, cannot be traced to any earlier writer than Pope Pelagius II. in his First Letter in 586 to the Bishops of Istria, who, in their reply, denied the truth of his interpretation and of the inference drawn from it. Pope Agatho revived it in 680, and it reappears in the Summa of St. Thomas Aquinas (Secunda Secundæ, 1–10) in the thirteenth century. Of twenty patristic citations made by Bellarmine in its favour, all are quoted as from Popes, and eighteen of the twenty are from the False Decretals.

ST. JOHN xxi. 15–17.

ST. GREGORY NAZIANZEN, Doctor.—"Do you not receive repentant David, whose gift of prophecy repentance saved? Nor the great Peter, when he suffered somewhat from human weakness in the matter of the Lord's Passion? But Jesus received him, and by the threefold questioning and confession, healed the threefold denial."—*Orat.* xxxix. for Epiphany.

ST. AMBROSE, Doctor.—"It was said to him thrice, 'Feed My sheep,' as though he had covered his sin by his exceeding love. . . . Finally, some have said that the triple question as to his love was put, because the denial had been triple, that the profession of love, repeated as often, might blot out the fall of the triple denial."—*Apol. David.* i. ix. 50.

"Thus the threefold answer vouched for his love, or else blotted out the error of the threefold denial."—*De Obit. Theodos.* 19.

ST. EPIPHANIUS, Doctor.—" He became then a strong rock of the building and a foundation of the house of God, when he had denied, and had turned again, and was found by the Lord, and was counted worthy to hear 'Feed My sheep' and **'Feed My lambs,'** and again 'Feed My sheep,' for Christ, in saying this, led us to the conversion of repentance."

ST. AUGUSTINE, Doctor.—" A threefold confession is rendered for the threefold denial, lest the tongue should serve love less than it had served fear, and lest impending death should seem to have drawn out more words than present life. Let it be the duty of love to feed the Lord's flock, as it had been the token of fear to deny the Shepherd."—*Tract. in Evang. Joann.* cxxiii. 5.

"Fitly, after the resurrection, the Lord committed His sheep to Peter himself to be fed. Not that he was the only one amongst the disciples who attained the feeding of the Lord's sheep, but when Christ speaks to one, unity is recommended, and to Peter first, because Peter is first of the Apostles. . . . Be not sad, Apostle, answer once, answer twice, answer thrice. Let confession conquer thrice in love, as presumption was conquered thrice in fear. That must be thrice loosed which thou hadst thrice bound."—*Serm.* ccxcv. 4, in *Nat. SS. Petr. et Paul.*

"Christ saith this a second and third time, that love might thrice confess what fear had thrice denied. . . . What was entrusted to Peter, what was enjoined to Peter, not Peter only, but the other Apostles also, heard, held, retained; and especially the Apostle Paul, his fellow in martyrdom and festival. They heard these things, and handed them down for us to hear. We feed you, and are fed together with you. . . . Therefore the Lord entrusted his sheep to us, in that He entrusted them to Peter. . . . The Lord commended the sheep to us. We are His sheep. We are His sheep along with you, because we are Christians. I have already said it, we feed and are fed."—*Serm.* ccxcvi. 3, 5, 17, *in Nat. SS. Pet. et Paul.*

ST. CYRIL OF ALEXANDRIA, Doctor.—" By this triple confession of blessed Peter, his sin, consisting of a triple denial, was done away, and by the words of our Lord, 'Feed My sheep,' a renewal, as it were, of the apostleship already bestowed on him is understood to take place, taking away the shame of his after fall, and taking from him the cowardice of human frailty.—*Comm. in Evang. Joann.* xxi.

ST. BASIL THE GREAT, Doctor.—" And we are taught this by

CHAP. II.] LEGAL EVIDENCE OF LITURGIES, ETC. 85

Christ Himself, when He was appointing Peter as shepherd of the Church after Himself; for He saith, 'Peter, lovest thou Me more than these? Feed My sheep;' giving equal authority to all shepherds and teachers thenceforward. And the proof of this is that all bind and loose exactly as he did."—*Const. Morast.* xxii. 5.

VENERABLE BEDE.—"That which was said to Peter, 'Feed My sheep,' was, in truth, said to them all. For the other Apostles were the same that Peter was; but the first place is given to Peter, that the unity of the Church may be commended. They were all shepherds; but the flock is shown to be one, which was then fed by all the Apostles with one mind, and since that time is fed by their successors with a common care."—*Hom. in Vigil. Petr. et Pauli.*

Two facts come out very clearly in these citations. First, that the Fathers regard the commission of feeding the sheep to be not a special privilege of Peter, but given jointly to all the Apostles; and next, that what is peculiar to Peter here in their mind, is that he was the only Apostle amongst the eleven who had forfeited his rank and authority, and that we have in this place his restoration to the position which they had held without interruption. And here, consequently, another maxim of the Canon Law applies exactly:—

"The renewal of a privilege confers no new right, nor does it even confirm an old one [so as to be a fresh grant], but merely maintains whatever held good at first."—*Decretal. Greg.* IX. lib. ii. tit. xxx. 4.

Accordingly, St. Peter is merely reinstated in whatever position he had acquired in right of the grant in St. Matt. xvi., 18, 19.

It remains to say a few words on one clause of this grant, which has been hitherto passed over in this inquiry. The assumption made up to this point is that the words, "I will give unto thee the keys of the kingdom of heaven," are fully glossed by the succeeding words, "Whatsoever thou shalt bind on earth," &c., and denote the same power of remitting and retaining sins which all the other Apostles received, but no more. And this is the general opinion of the more eminent Fathers. A few examples will suffice in evidence:—

ORIGEN.—"What, are the keys of the kingdom of heaven given by **the Lord** to Peter only? And shall no other of the blessed receive them? But if this promise, 'I will give thee the keys of the kingdom **of heaven,**' be common to **others** also, so likewise are all the things that **are** recorded before and after this as spoken to Peter."—*Comm. in St. Matt.* xvi.

ST. CYPRIAN, Doctor.—"**Our Lord,** Whose precepts **and** commands we are bound to observe, when settling the honour **of** a bishop and the constitution of His Church, speaketh the Gospel, and saith to Peter, 'And I say unto thee. . . . And I will give thee the keys of the kingdom of heaven,' &c. Thence, through the changes of times **and** successions, **the** ordination of bishops and **the** constitution of the **Church is carried down, so that** the Church is **set** up on the bishops, **and every act of the Church is controlled by these** same superiors."—*Epist.* xxvii.

ST. AMBROSE, **Doctor.**—"Therefore the Lord gave the Apostles **that** which previously **was** part of His own judicial authority. . . . **Hear Him** saying: 'I will give thee the keys of the kingdom of heaven,' &c. What is said to Peter is said to the **Apostles.**"—*Comm. in Psalm* xxxviii. 37.

ST. HILARY OF POITIERS, Doctor.—"**Ye holy** and blessed ones [Apostles], who through the merit of your faith received the keys of the kingdom of heaven, and obtained the right of binding and loosing in heaven and **in earth.**"—*De Trinitate,* vi. 33.

ST. GAUDENTIUS OF BRESCIA.—"All the Apostles, when **Christ** rises, receive **the** keys *in* **Peter; nay, rather,** they receive **the keys of** the kingdom of heaven *with* Peter, when he saith to them, '**Receive the Holy Ghost,' &c.**"—*Serm.* xvi.

ST. AUGUSTINE, Doctor.—"**The** Lord Jesus, as you know, chose before **His Passion His** disciples, **whom** He named Apostles. Amongst **them Peter,** almost always alone, was permitted **to be** the representative person of the whole Church. Because of **that** personification **of the whole** Church, which he alone supported, it was his **to** hear, '**I will give thee** the keys of the kingdom of heaven.' It **was not one** man who received these, but the Unity of the Church . . . . **when it** was said to him, 'I will give *thee*' that **which was given to all.**"—*Serm.* ccxcv. **2,** *in **Nat.** SS. Pet. et Paul.*

ST. LEO THE GREAT, Pope and Doctor.—"Because of that which **is said** to most blessed Peter, 'I will give **thee** the keys,' &c., the right of this power has passed to all the other Apostles also, and the appointment of this decree has descended to all the princes of the Church; but it is not without **reason** that what is intimated **to all is** intrusted **to one.** For it is assigned to Peter singly, because the person of **Peter represents** all rulers of the Church."—*Serm.* iii. cap. **3.**

Nevertheless, some very few (as St. Cyril of **Jerusalem**) note the **absence of** this particular **clause** from the two cognate grants made to the Apostles collectively (St. Matt. xviii. 18; St. John xx. 23), and urge that some special distinction must be intended, some peculiar privilege, belonging to St. Peter alone. And though Roman Catholics are barred from advocating this view, because the general consent of the Fathers is against it, no such restriction binds non-Romans, who are at liberty to take that which is the more devout and reverent line, that no saying of our Lord is mere surplusage, and without a special force of its own. But when we look for an early interpretation which gives to St. Peter more than the common power of binding and loosing, none is to be found save that of Tertullian, namely, that St. Peter first put the key into the lock, and opened the door of faith to both Jews and Gentiles.

Thus, an examination of the glosses of the Fathers on the three texts alleged for the Petrine privilege results in one of two issues. Either there was no such privilege, as distinguished from the joint powers of the Apostolate, conferred on St. Peter at all; or else—and this is the better way—his special privilege was limited to preaching the first Pentecostal sermon, and afterwards converting Cornelius—events which are absolutely incapable of repetition : even God Himself (if it be lawful to say so) not being able to recall the past, so that no one else, after St. Peter had once done these two things, could be the *first* to teach Jews or Gentiles ; just as no Pope can follow St. Peter in being *first* to confess Christ. No other distinction is named by the ancient Fathers, is claimed by St. Peter himself (Acts xv. 7), or is discoverable in Holy Writ. And, consequently, if this be the privilege of Peter, it did not merely die with him, but was possible for even himself to exercise not more than twice in his lifetime, so that it is absolutely incommunicable and intransmissible, and incapable of serving as a precedent for any claim whatsoever based on alleged succession to his authority and primacy. If it could be strained to mean anything, it would be that each Pope must needs start as a missionary pioneer to some country or nation which had not yet received the Gospel. But no Pope has ever done so. With this collapse of the alleged evidence, the whole case for the divine character of the Roman privilege is really gone, and no mind trained in the investigation of testimony, and free from overpowering bias, can do other than dismiss it. But there are various other pleas adduced in its support, one of which, as foremost among them, must now be considered. It is the fact that several titles of honour, dignity, and priority are bestowed on St. Peter in many ancient Christian writings, which are said to imply his unapproachable and pre-eminent authority over the other Apostles. Such epithets are "first of the leaders" (πρωτοκορύφαιος); "first in place" (πρωτοστάτης); "chief ruler" (προεξάρχων); "president" (πρόεδρος); "captain" (ἀρχηγός); "prince," "head," and many similar ones.

Now, what these epithets (none of which, by-the-by, is found till the fourth century) *prove* is the high estimation in which the ancient Church held St. Peter, and the fact that it believed him to enjoy some priority amongst the Apostles. They would be important evidence against any attempt to maintain that, owing to St. Peter's fall and denial, he had, in the belief of early Christians, forfeited his office irreparably (as a strict Novatian might have taught), and had been looked on with a suspicion extending not merely to his rank, but to his teaching, such as we know to have existed against St. Paul.

What they do *not* prove, nor even seem to prove, is the divine grant of supreme jurisdiction. For they are not authoritative titles, either found in Holy Scripture, or conferred by conciliar decree. The fact that nothing in the smallest degree resembling even the least exalted of them is discoverable in the New Testament deprives them of the mark of revelation; the fact that they are not common to the whole Church, leaves them without that of universal consent. They bestow nothing, and they define nothing. But what we are in search of is an express bestowal of exceptional privilege, as divinely revealed and clearly defined. The matter may be illustrated thus. The title " Great *or* Grand Duke" in modern Europe means one of two things, either sovereign authority, as in the case of the Grand Dukes of Baden, Saxe-Weimar, Oldenburg, Hesse, and the two Mecklenburgs, or else membership of the Russian Imperial family.

But the celebrated Duke of Wellington was and is known as the "Great Duke," and is frequently so described in English literature, notably in the Laureate's funeral ode. Let us suppose the case of a remote successor of his in the dukedom claiming this epithet as hereditary, and as conferring sovereign power, imperial rank, or even precedence over all other English Dukes. How would it be treated? Not by a denial of the fact that the epithet was applied to the first Duke of Wellington, nor yet by an attempt to explain away the epithet itself as a mere piece of rhetoric—rather admitting its entire fitness—but by examining the original patent of the dukedom, in order to ascertain if a clause embodying this particular distinction were part of it. And on its absence being certified, it would be at once ruled that however deserved the epithet might be, it was not conferred by any authority capable of bestowing either civil power or social precedence, and must therefore be regarded as a mere personal token of popular admiration, conferring no rights whatever on its subject. Nor would the case for the claim to sovereign rank be mended by advancing proof that the first Duke of Wellington was Prime Minister of the Crown for part of his life, and Commander-in-Chief for a much longer period. For it would have to be shown, in the first place, that these posts connoted irresponsibility to any superior; and in the next, that the patents which bestowed them made them hereditary, and not merely personal. But in St. Peter's case we have the original divine patent, in which no clause of superiority or transmissibility occurs, and no expressions of individual human respect can read an additional title, article, or section into it.

In the second place, the great majority of these epithets occur in documents of the Eastern Church, which has never at any time admitted the Roman claims of supremacy,

and which therefore obviously puts no such interpretation **on its** own language. The Western titles of St. Peter are **fewer** and far less imposing. And thirdly, not only are equally strong phrases used concerning St. **John,** and yet more forcible ones concerning St. James, but nearly every one of these special ones is applied to St. Paul as well as to St. Peter; so that even in the modern Roman Church they are grouped together as "Princes of the Apostles."[1] So, too, when the full heraldic titles of an English Duke are set forth, he is described as the "High, Puissant, and **most** Noble Prince"—words which scarcely seem to allow **of** rivalry, but which are common to every Peer of the same grade; while all Dukes have to yield precedence to a mere Baron who happens to be Lord Chancellor, President of the Council, or Lord Privy Seal.

The investigation of the "Privilege of Peter," so far as the three most ancient and important sources of testimony, Holy Scripture, early Liturgies, and the comments of the Fathers on the Petrine texts in the Gospels are concerned, thus results, to say the very least, in failure to establish it.

What remains now is rather to find if absolutely conclusive disproof be discoverable; but that part of the inquiry belongs to the domain of Church history, notably as regards the Councils.

---

[1] St. John is described by St. Chrysostom as the "pillar of all the Churches throughout the world, who hath the keys of the kingdom of heaven" (*Hom. in St. Johann.*), while St. Paul is called "the type of the world," "the light of the Churches," "the basis of the faith," "the pillar and ground of the truth." St. James, **yet** more strongly, is called by the Clementines, "bishop of bishops"; by the Recognitions, i. 68, "prince **of** bishops;" **by** Rufinus, *Hist. Eccl.* i. 1, "bishop of the Apostles;" and by Hesychius, **a** priest of Jerusalem, quoted by Photius, "chief captain of the New Jerusalem," "leader of the priests," "prince [exarch] of the Apostles," "summit of the heights," &c.

CHAPTER III.

LEGAL EVIDENCE OF CONCILIAR DECREES.

THE third stage of the inquiry into the authenticity of the Petrine claim of privilege, already pursued through Holy Scripture and the chief early glosses thereupon—that concerned with its historical aspect, and, first, the canons and decrees of the Councils—must now be entered on. And it should be borne in mind that the number, the variety, and the distribution of these Councils over a vast period of time, make it certain that the "privilege of Peter," from its intimate bearing on disciplinary questions, must needs occupy a considerable and prominent place in them, if it be so much as a fact of history, to say nothing of being a fundamental dogma of Christianity.

The Acts of the Councils, that is to say, the record of their proceedings from their convocation till their dispersion, also throw very much light upon the discussion; but the consideration of that part of the evidence must be postponed for the present, and only the actual decrees and canons are as yet to be cited.

Now, let us inquire into the authority of the Councils as recognised in the Church of Rome. First comes the eleventh clause of the Creed of Pius IV. :—

"I likewise undoubtingly receive and profess all other things delivered, defined, and declared by the Sacred Canons and General Councils, and especially by the Holy Council of Trent; and I condemn, reject, and anathematize all things contrary thereto."

Next, the profession of St. Gregory the Great, embodied in the Canon Law, *Decret.* i. dist. xv. 2 :—

"I acknowledge that I receive and venerate, as I do the Four Gospels, the Four Councils, to wit, the Nicene . . . also the

Constantinopolitan . . . the first of Ephesus . . . that of Chalcedon moreover, . . . I embrace them with entire devotion, I guard them with perfect approval, because on them, as on a squared stone, the building of the Holy Faith rises."

Thirdly, the solemn profession made by every Pope at his consecration, which in the *Liber Diurnus*, as cited by the Canon Law, *Decret.* i. dist. xvi. 8, is thus worded :—

"The eight Holy General Councils—that is, Nice first, Constantinople second, Ephesus third, Chalcedon fourth, Constantinople fifth and sixth, Nice seventh, and Constantinople eighth—I profess with mouth and heart to be kept unaltered in a single tittle [*usque ad unum apicem immutilata servari*], to account them worthy of equal honour and veneration, to follow in every respect whatsoever they promulgated or decreed, and to condemn whatsoever they condemned."

1. The very ancient body of **rules known as** the Canons of the Apostles knows not of any officer higher than bishops save the **primate or "first bishop"** of each nation (ἔθνους), and is thus earlier than the institution of provincial archbishops or metropolitans. This "first bishop," albeit the chief single authority, whose consent is to be sought by the others, must himself do nothing against their consent. No further appeal is provided. The whole Canon (xxxiii.) merits citation, because of its remarkably explicit testimony to that primitive independence of national Churches which is the peculiar object of Ultramontane hostility :—

"It is fit that the bishops of each nation should recognise their Primate [τὸν ἐν αὐτοῖς πρῶτον] and treat him as Head, and do nothing of moment without his assent; for each bishop should manage those concerns alone which pertain to his own diocese and its dependent regions. But neither let him [the Primate] do aught without the assent of all; for so shall there be concord, and God shall be glorified through the Lord in the Holy Spirit."

2. The Councils of Ancyra, Neocæsarea, and Arles I., all earlier than Nicæa, are silent.

3. The Council of Laodicea recognises the authority of metropolitans (*Can.* xii.), but specifies nothing higher or more central in character.

4. The first General Council of Nicæa, A.D. 325, con-

tains an important piece of evidence. In settling the claims of the see of Alexandria, it decrees (*Can.* vi.):—

"Let the ancient customs prevail in Egypt, and Libya, and Pentapolis, that the Bishop of Alexandria should have authority over all these, since this is the accustomed practice for the Bishop in Rome also; and similarly in Antioch and the other eparchies [*i.e.* primatial sees of the first class] let the precedence be preserved to the Churches."

There is a very ancient Latin version of this Canon, confirmed by Rufinus (*Hist. Eccl.* xi. 6), which explains that its meaning was that the Patriarch of Alexandria should have the same authority over all Egypt, Libya, and Pentapolis as the Pope of Rome had over the "suburbicarian" Churches of his province; that is to say, those of Central and Southern Italy, with the islands of Sicily, Sardinia, and Corsica; a limitation which shows that no universal jurisdiction was then attributed to the see of St. Peter, but only a province far exceeded in extent, population, wealth, and importance by several others at the time, except in so far as it contained the late capital of the Empire.

5. The Council of Antioch, A.D. 341, in its ninth Canon, forbids appeals to be carried further ($\pi\epsilon\rho\alpha\iota\tau\epsilon\rho\omega$) than the provincial synod assembled under the metropolitan.

6. The Council of Sardica, A.D. 347, seems to allow an appeal to the Pope under certain specified circumstances. Its third alleged Canon runs:—

"If in any province a bishop have a dispute with a brother bishop, let neither of them call in a bishop from another province as arbiter; but if any bishop be cast in any suit, and think his case good, so that the judgment ought to be reviewed, if it please you, let us honour the memory of St. Peter the Apostle, and let those who have tried the cause write to Julius, Bishop of Rome, that if needful he may provide for a rehearing of the cause by the bishops nearest to the province, and send arbiters; or if it cannot be established that the matter needs reversal, then what has been decided is not to be rescinded, but the existing state of things is to be confirmed."

Canon iv. provides that a bishop, deposed by a local synod, and appealing to Rome, shall not have his see filled up till the Pope has confirmed the sentence.

Canon v. empowers the Pope either to commit the rehearing to the bishops of the neighbouring province, or to send a legate of his own to rehear the cause.

Assuming, for the moment, the genuineness of these decrees, which are the basis of the whole appellate jurisdiction of the Roman Church, the following remarks have to be made: (1.) These Canons of Sardica, passed by an exclusively Western assembly, were never received by the Eastern Church. (2.) The specification of the name of Pope Julius makes it at least doubtful whether this was not a personal privilege which died with him, as there is no provision for securing the same right to his successors. (3.) The privilege, such as it is, has stringent limits, and does not grant any initiative whatever to the Pope, who must await a direct application to himself; no applicant save a bishop is contemplated; nor even he, unless when condemned by a synod. (4.) The terms of the Canon, inclusive of the reference to St. Peter, are such as to show that the Fathers of the Council were making a voluntary concession, which they were quite at liberty to withhold, not complying with a duty divinely imposed upon them.

No satisfactory evidence exists for the authenticity of these canons, and there is much reason for suspecting them to be a sheer fabrication at Rome. For no hint of their existence occurs till they were falsely alleged in 419 as Nicene canons by the Papal Legate at Carthage, while the African Bishops contented themselves with disproving that one fiction, but evidently knew nothing else whatever about them, not being able to assign them even to Sardica, obviously because they had never heard of them before; whereas the invariable rule of the time was to send the acts and canons of synods of more than provincial character round to all the great Churches for approval; so that the Sardican canons, if genuine at all, must have been known at Carthage, at any rate by 424, after attention there had been drawn to them five years previously, and a consequent search made, supposing no earlier information to have been accessible, as there must have been, since

Aratus of Carthage was at Sardica; and would have brought back any canons. What is more, there is entire silence on this head in the Acts of Constantinople in 381, and of Chalcedon in 451, albeit both dealing with the question of appellate jurisdiction; nor does St. Athanasius refer to these canons. And though St. Augustine's silence may be explained away on the ground that he mixes up the Council of Sardica with the seceding Arian synod of Philippopolis, no such excuse accounts for the equal silence of SS. Basil and Epiphanius, and of the three great ecclesiastical historians of the time, Socrates, Sozomen, and Theodoret, none of whom know of any Sardican document except the synodical epistle. Seeing that the canons, if genuine, altered for the West the system of appeals which had prevailed in the Church up to that time, based as it was on the rule of the civil code that all cases should be ended where they originated, their legal and historical importance is such that this unbroken silence is nearly unaccountable. Nor is any example known of their having been avowedly acted on anywhere in the West; precisely where the canons of the Council must have been known and in many provincial archives, whereas they are cited only in Papal missives to Churches whose bishops were not at Sardica. And as their Nicene character was alleged for the *fourth* time so late as 484 by Felix II. in his dispute with Acacius of Constantinople, it is obvious that this persistence in one falsehood makes the presence of another more likely. No one at Rome could have honestly believed them to be Nicene, because they expressly name Pope Julius, who did not begin to sit till 337, twelve years after the Council of Nice (a few Latin MSS. have *Silvester* here, an obviously fraudulent correction). The policy of urging them as canons of a great Council like Sardica, when it proved impossible to gain credit for them as Nicene, is so evident that its not being adopted prompts a suspicion that they were well known at Rome not to be decrees of any council whatever, so that any strict inquiry must tend to the same result, and that being so, it was more politic to keep up the Nicene claim. No Greek text is known earlier than the sixth century, and a very suspicious circumstance marks the three oldest Latin texts, the *Prisca*, that of Dionysius Exiguus, and the true Isidore. These, as a rule, give independent and various translations of all Greek canons, but they agree verbally for the so-called Sardican canons. The inference is that there was never a Greek original at all, but only a Latin forgery. If so, the whole fabric of Papal appeals falls, for it has no other basis. Indeed, the non-Sardican origin of these canons has been strongly asserted of late by a learned Italian theologian, Aloysius Vincenzi, in his treatise, "De Hebræorum et Christianorum Sacra Monarchia," Vatican Press, 1875, who places them considerably later, and inclines to think them African.

7. The Council of Gangra, held between 325 and 380, which enacted twenty-one disciplinary canons, received by the whole Church, is silent.

8. The second General Council—that of Constantinople in 381—supplies some very important items of evidence. Although it has always been received as œcumenical, it was not attended by any Western bishops, nor was the Pope so much as represented by any deputy, although the Roman Church is bound by the decrees which were passed. The second canon of the Council forbids all bishops to go beyond their own borders, or to interfere in other dioceses; and confirms the privileges allowed to the Patriarchs of Alexandria and Antioch by the Council of Nicæa, besides further enacting that the affairs of the Asian, Pontic, and Thracian dioceses shall be administered by their own bishops only, and that the synod of each province shall administer the affairs of the province; which is a virtual repeal of the alleged Canons of Sardica. Canon iii. enacts that the Bishop of Constantinople shall have precedence of honour next after the Bishop of Rome, because Constantinople is New Rome; an argument of no weight whatever, if the precedence of Rome were due to religious, not civil and political, reasons. What this canon consequently proves that in whatsoever sense Rome was first amongst

Catholic sees, in that same sense Constantinople was second. But on the Ultramontane theory, the Roman position is absolutely unique, and incapable of parallel, so that it could have no second, because every other see is equally subject to its authority.

9. Nine Councils, presided over by various Popes, were held in Rome in the fourth century; but only one canon is relevant, the first of those enacted by the Synod in 386 under Pope Siricius, for the restoration of ecclesiastical discipline in Africa, and it merely forbids the consecration of a bishop without the knowledge of the Roman Patriarch. Nothing is said as to his consent.

10. In a Council of the whole African Church held at Carthage in 418, Faustinus, Bishop of Potenza, one of the legates of the Popes Zosimus and Boniface I., claimed that the right of appeal to Rome, given by the Sardican Canons cited above, which he alleged to be Canons of the Council of Nicæa, should be allowed by the African Church. Alypius, Bishop of Tagaste, immediately challenged their authenticity, as he had never seen them in any copy of the Nicene Canons, and proposed that envoys should be sent to Alexandria, Antioch, and Constantinople to verify the fact. This was at first rejected, as tending to cast a doubt on the Pope's integrity, though subsequently acted upon; and it was then proposed to write to him to examine the question for himself; but this was not carried out. Then the genuine Nicene Canons were read, as also those of previous African Councils, and reaffirmed. Next, the case of Apiarius, a deposed and excommunicated priest, who had appealed to Rome and had been re-admitted to communion by Pope Zosimus, was considered anew on the grounds alleged by Faustinus, and was settled by letting the matter stand over till the canons had been verified, and by enacting a new Canon (cxxv.) forbidding all appeals beyond sea, or to any authority save African Councils and Primates, under pain of excommunication throughout Africa; and, finally, the Council sent a synodical letter to Pope Boniface by two legates, complaining of his conduct

in reinstating Apiarius, disputing the genuineness of the canons alleged by Faustinus, and telling the Pope in the plainest language that nothing should make them tolerate his conduct, or suffer such insolence (*typhum superbiæ*) at the hand of his emissaries, a protest virtually aimed at himself, who had commissioned and despatched them. One of the signatories of this epistle was St. Augustine.

Another Council, also held at Carthage, five years later, in 424, had this business of Apiarius before it again. He had been a second time deposed for immorality, and had got another Pope—Celestine I.—to rehabilitate him, and to send him back to Africa with Bishop Faustinus to obtain his reinstatement there. But his guilt was proved at the Council by his own confession, and his degradation confirmed. Hereupon the Fathers wrote to Pope Celestine, telling him that they had ascertained that the alleged Nicene Canons were not of that Council at all; that the Pope had transgressed the genuine Nicene Canons by interfering in another province; and that they could find no authority for his undertaking to send legates to them or any other Churches, so that they begged him to refrain from doing so in future, for fear the Church should suffer through pride and ambition: and added that they were quite competent, with the aid of the Holy Spirit, to manage their own affairs on the spot, better than he, with less local knowledge, could do for them at Rome; ending by telling him that they had had quite enough of Faustinus, and wanted no more of him.

11. The third General Council, that of Ephesus in 431, was held in consequence of the failure of Pope Celestine to check the heresy of Nestorius by condemning it in a merely local Roman Synod, and by threatening him with excommunication and deposition in case he refused to retract. No practical impression was made on Nestorius or the bishops of his party thereby, and the Pope joined in a petition to the Emperor to convoke a General Council as the only means of settling the dispute; while Nestorius himself was duly invited to attend in his episcopal capacity,

and to take his seat, although the time prescribed by the **Pope for** his retractation had long expired. The Council was presided over by St. Cyril of Alexandria, the most powerful prelate of his time, and two of its canons have an important bearing on subsequent events. They **are**: Canon vii., which enacts the penalty of deposition against any bishop or priest innovating on or varying the Nicene Creed; and Canon viii., which, after disallowing the claim of the Patriarch of Antioch **to ordain in Cyprus**, unless **he** could **prove such** to have **been the ancient** usage, enacts that **in all other** dioceses **and** provinces **no** bishop shall **invade any province** which **was not from the** beginning **under his jurisdiction or that** of his predecessors:—

" And if any should so occupy one, or forcibly subject it to himself, let him make personal restitution, lest the statutes of the Fathers should be violated, *and lest the pride of power should creep in under the pretext of a sacred office*, and thus we might unknowingly and gradually *lose that freedom* which Jesus Christ our Lord and Saviour of all men obtained for us with His precious **blood, and bestowed** upon us."

12. The fourth General Council, that of Chalcedon, **A.D.** 451, has more than one disproof of the Petrine claims in its decrees. Its ninth Canon, on ecclesiastical appeals (of which Canon xvii. is little more than a reiteration), directs litigants to apply to the diocesan bishop. If he, or any other bishop, be himself one of the parties to the suit, it is to be carried before the provincial synod. If a metropolitan be one of the parties concerned, the exarch, or primate of the region, is to take cognisance of the case; and, in the last resort, the Patriarch of the imperial city of Constantinople is to decide as final arbiter. The Canon **seems** to **apply to** the whole Church, in which case it means that appeals were now made to lie from Rome itself to Constantinople; but it cannot possibly mean less than that **no** appeal lay from Constantinople to Rome, nor than the formal reversal of the Sardican Canons, even on the assumption that they are genuine. But the decrees of this General Council also contain what is perhaps the

weightiest item of synodical testimony as yet adduced. In Canon xxviii. the Council decreed as follows:—

"In all respects following the definitions of the holy Fathers, and acknowledging the Canon of the 150 God-beloved bishops which has just been read, we likewise make the same definition and decree concerning the precedence of the most holy Church of Constantinople, or New Rome. For the Fathers with good reason bestowed precedency on the chair of Old Rome, *because it was the imperial city* (διὰ τὸ βασιλεύειν τὴν πόλιν ἐκείνην), and the 150 God-beloved bishops, moved by the same view, conferred equal precedence on the most holy throne of New Rome, rightly judging that the city honoured with the empire and the senate should enjoy the same precedence as Rome, the old seat of empire, and should be magnified as it was in ecclesiastical matters also, being second after it."

And the Canon then proceeds to confer on the Patriarch of Constantinople the right of ordaining all the metropolitans of Asia, Pontus, Thrace, and the bishops in barbarous regions; a fact which proves that not mere honorary dignity, but substantial authority, was included in the "precedence" specified. The Roman legates refused to be present when the Canon was passed, and demanded another session of the Council to abrogate it, producing a forged version of the sixth Canon of Nicæa, in which the words, "The Roman see hath always had the primacy," had been interpolated, and alleging besides that force had been used to compel the bishops to sign the Canon. The Conciliar Judges, however, after hearing the objections, ruled that the alleged Canon of Nicæa was unauthentic; that the Roman Bishop had merely a priority of honour, but that the Patriarch of Constantinople was his equal in all solid privileges; and after the assembled bishops had publicly denied that they acted under compulsion, decided that the Canon must stand.

The then Pope, St. Leo the Great, resisted this Canon always, and even professed to annul it, yet on the purely technical grounds that it conflicted with the sixth Nicene Canon, which gave the second place to Alexandria, and trenched besides on the rights of many metropolitans (*Epist.* lxxix.), not on its contradiction of the privilege of Peter, but he was unable to prevent its execution, or to affect its validity. There is no question at all as to its entire genuineness, as to its being a mere gloss upon and expansion of Canon iii. of Constantinople I., or as to the formality with which it was discussed in the Council, so that it is fully enforced on Roman Catholic acceptance by the three Roman professions of adherence to *all* decrees, without exception, of the General Councils, cited above. And thus we are faced by one or other of the following conclusions. Either the Council, in holding that the Roman primacy is a mere human and ecclesiastical dignity, conferred by the Church, and not a divine and inalienable privilege, was wrong on the point of fact, or it was right. If it was wrong (apart from the objection that then the whole fabric of Conciliar authority falls, as no Council has ever been more authoritative, or more definitely acknowledged by the Roman Church itself), then, since its dogmatic decrees are allowed to be the standard of orthodoxy, and yet as it must have erred in dogma if the Roman primacy be matter of faith, the conclusion is, that the said primacy is at best not matter of dogmatic faith, but only of historical fact; and so the Canon supplies proof that the Church of the fifth century did not hold the Papal claim to be of divine origin or theological obligation. On the other hand, if the Council was right on the point of fact, there is nothing left to be said in favour of even the historical character of the alleged Petrine privilege.

There is no difficulty in bringing the matter to a decisive test. If the allegation of the Council be true, that the civil position of Rome was the sole cause of its ecclesiastical primacy, then the same principle will be found to affect the precedence of other great sees. On the other hand, if the Ultramontane contention be true, then the rival principle will be seen at work, and the sees will be found to rank according to the dignity of their founders or the august character of their traditions. It is not questioned that it was regarded as a high distinction for any see to be entitled to the epithet of Apostolic, and to count an

Apostle as its first originator, if not as its earliest bishop (just as it is a feather in the cap of a school or a society in modern England to be of Royal foundation), but the strong practical good sense which marked the organization of the early Church was not likely to sacrifice convenience to sentiment.

Accordingly, although Jerusalem had the highest claim of all in point of origin, having been founded as a Church by Christ Himself, and organized as a diocese under St. James by the whole College of Apostles, as Hegesippus, cited by Eusebius (*Hist. Eccl.*, ii. 23), records for us, yet in consequence of its political insignificance, notably after the substitution of Ælia Capitolina for it under Hadrian, it was at first a mere suffraganate of the Metropolitan of Cæsarea, himself subject to the Patriarch of Antioch—a rank comparable to that of Sodor and Man amongst English sees. It was not till the Council of Nicæa that the Bishop of Jerusalem was given a certain honorary precedence, because of the august memories attached to his see, but even then saving all the rights of his metropolitan over him (*Can.* vii.), and not till the Council of Chalcedon in 451 did Juvenal, forty-fourth Bishop of Jerusalem, obtain the elevation of his see to the Patriarchal rank which it has ever since held, though always last in order of the five chief sees, and narrowest in area of jurisdiction. On the other hand, Alexandria, which never claimed any higher ecclesiastical title than that of the "Evangelical See," as founded by St. Mark, was the second city of the Roman Empire, and so was placed next to Rome ecclesiastically also, first informally *de facto*, and then formally *de jure* by the Council of Nicæa. Similarly, Antioch, the third great see of Christendom, was the third city of the Empire (Joseph., *Bell. Jud.*, iii. 3), but although it had a more illustrious origin as a diocese than Alexandria, as having been not only undoubtedly founded by Apostles, but alleged to have been for seven years the see of St. Peter himself, it never attained precedence over the more important capital of Egypt. And

Ephesus, though Apostolic by at least two claims, through St. Paul and St. John, never rose to higher rank than that of exarchate or primacy. In truth, no Pauline see (unless we account Rome such) was ever placed in the first rank, and many which St. Paul founded continued as mere suffraganates of cities greater in civil importance.[1]

St. Cyprian gives as the reason for the precedence of Rome over Carthage, that it was a larger and more important city:—

"Plainly because Rome ought to precede Carthage by reason of its size (*pro magnitudine sui*), Novatus committed greater and graver offences there. He who made a deacon here against the Church, made a bishop there."—*Ep.* xlix. *ad Cornel. Papam.*

---

[1] Here is the place to mention a linguistic ambiguity of which Roman controversialists have not been slow to avail themselves. The Latin language, unlike Greek, English, French, and German, has no definite article, no words such as *a* and *the*, to express the difference between that which is definite and that which is indefinite, and the context alone gives any clue to the distinction, but cannot always do so. Consequently, if we have Rome entitled *Sedes Apostolica* by an ancient Latin writer, it need mean no more than "*an* Apostolic See," one of the many dioceses founded by an Apostle. But they now invariably translate it as "*the* Apostolic See," implying a monopoly of that title and any attendant privileges. But in fact the epithet was common to many such Churches in early times. Thus Tertullian says: "Cast a glance over the Apostolic Churches, in which the very thrones of the Apostles are still pre-eminent in their places . . . Achaia is very near you, in which you find Corinth . . . you have Philippi . . . you have the Thessalonians. Since you are able to cross to Asia, you find Ephesus. Since, moreover, you are close upon Italy, you have Rome."—*De Præscript. Hæres.* xxxvi. Not only so, but St. Paulinus of Nola (†431) uses this phrase "*Sedes Apostolica*" to denote the rank of any bishop, even of comparatively unimportant sees. Thus, he applies it to Alypius of Tagaste (*Ep.* iii. 1) and to Victricius of Rouen (*Ep.* xviii. 6). We do get the definite article prefixed, and that by the Second General Council (Constantinople), but the Church so distinguished is Antioch, described by the Fathers as "*the* most ancient and truly Apostolical Church, in Antioch of Syria" (τῆς δὲ πρεσβυτάτης καὶ ὄντως ἀποστολικῆς ἐκκλησίας τῆς ἐν Ἀντιοχείᾳ τῆς Συρίας).—Theodoret, *H. E.* v. 9.

The principle had, in fact, been laid down by the Council of Antioch (A.D. 341) more than a century earlier than Chalcedon, in its ninth Canon :—

> "It is fit that the bishops in every province should know that the bishop presiding in the chief city [*metropolis*] is to have superintendence of the whole province, because all people who have business come together from all quarters to the chief city : for which reason it has seemed good that he should have precedence in honour also, and that the other bishops should do nothing important without him, but only such things as concern each one's diocese and its dependencies, adhering to the ancient rule of our fathers."

This Canon seems to give the best explanation of a very obscure sentence in St. Irenæus, on which Ultramontanes lay great stress: a passage where the Greek is lost, and the very barbarous Latin translation alone is extant. It runs thus :—

> "For it is necessary that every Church should come together to this [Roman] Church, because of its preferable [*or* more powerful] principality (*Ad hanc enim ecclesiam, propter potiorem* [*al. potentiorem*] *principalitatem, necesse est omnem convenire ecclesiam*)."—*Adv. Hær.* III. iii. 2.

In the absence of the original text, it cannot be said what stood there, and so the passage does not satisfy the two primary requirements of Canon law, as being either the original document or free from ambiguity. The Ultramontane gloss is that the words imply superior authority as of divine right. A second view, based on a conjectural restoration of the Greek text, as having had the word ἀρχαιότητα for *principalitatem*, and on the fact that the word *principalis* is used elsewhere in the Latin version to mean first in order of *time*, is that St. Irenæus refers here to the superior antiquity of the Roman Church, confessedly the oldest in the West. This interpretation, however, does not accord with the phrase "*convenire ad*," whose only possible meaning in Latin is "assemble at," whereas if "agree with" were intended, as Ultramontanes assert, the phrase used would be "*convenire cum*," followed by the ablative "*hac ecclesiâ.*" Moreover, part of the context, generally overloooked, is decisive for the first meaning, stating as it does that " In this Church the tradition derived from the Apostles is maintained by the faithful from all quarters (*undique*)." This shows that it was not any peculiar privilege vesting in the Roman see or Bishop which served to safeguard doctrine there, but the fact of the great concourse at Rome from all parts of the Empire, enabling local traditions to be compared, sifted, and checked there, as they could be nowhere else.[1] But the simplest and most obvious interpretation is to take the Councils of Antioch and Chalcedon as our guides, and so to understand the reference to be to the position of Rome as the capital city of the Empire, and thus as possessing in a pre-eminent degree the qualities of civil precedence and of habitual resort of a great concourse of visitors. As a fact, the Eastern part of the Roman Empire was so much more populous and prosperous than the West at this time, that no Western city, except Milan, was thought of sufficient importance to be made the head of a greater province or exarchate, such as Cæsarea, Ephesus, and Heraclea, themselves inferior to the Patriarchal sees, were in the East. And Milan remained absolutely independent of Rome till 571, nor was it effectually brought under Papal authority

---

[1] And we have got, besides, a probable clue to the original words for "*convenire ad*" supplied by that ninth canon of the Council of Antioch in 341, which enacts that the Bishop of the chief city in each eparchy is to hold the first place, and to have charge of the concerns of the entire eparchy, " because all persons who have business come together in the chief city from all quarters," where the Greek is διὰ τὸ ἐν τῇ μητροπόλει πανταχόθεν συντρέχειν πάντας τοὺς τὰ πράγματά ἔχοντας; while it is further stated that this is not a new enactment, but " according to the old rule which governed our fathers." This view is confirmed by the language of a Greek MS. Synodicon, printed by Cardinal Mai : " Formerly, in Old Rome, there was a confluence of business matters, and on this account all people flocked thither (συνέτρεχον) . . . . for which reason the distinction of precedency came to the throne of Rome." *Spicilegium Romanum*, viii. Præf. p. xxvi.

till St. Gregory the Great availed himself of a vacancy in the see at a very troubled time (592) to interfere in its concerns and to send a legate thither.

Thus the evidence of Church history amply justifies the Fathers of Chalcedon, and proves that they were right in alleging that the political supremacy of Rome as the capital of the Empire, making it the natural centre of all business affairs, and the chief resort of travellers from all quarters, made it also the most convenient centre for that great missionary organization, whose battle was emphatically fought in the large towns, as the now significant word "pagan," once meaning "rustic," or "villager," teaches us. And down to the middle of the third century all the extant evidence shows that the primacy was held to reside in the Church of Rome, not in its *Bishop*, who derived his importance from the see, not *vice versa*. St. Clement, for example, writes to the Corinthians in the name of the Roman Church, not in his own.

It may not be inappropriate to remark that in the French Church, although the titular dignity of "Primate of all the Gauls" is still reserved to the Archbishop of Lyons, yet the virtual primacy has long been in the hands of the Archbishop of Paris, albeit that capital was only a suffragan see of the Province of Sens until 1622, when it was raised to metropolitan rank.

13. Twelve Roman Synods were held under various Popes during the fifth century. The only relevant decrees are the deposition of Nestorius by the Council of 430 under Pope Celestine, disregarded, as we have seen, by the Council of Ephesus; the sentence of the Synod of 445 under Leo the Great, restoring Celidonius, Bishop of Besançon, who had been synodically deposed by his metropolitan, St. Hilary of Arles, and by St. Germanus of Auxerre, and excommunicating the former for insisting on his metropolitical rights and denying the Pope's title to hear the appeal, on the merits of which Leo was in truth entirely deceived by the appellant—but St. Hilary's resistance, never retracted, has not prevented him from being

a Saint and Doctor of the Roman Church; the fifth Canon of the Synod of 465, forbidding a bishop to name his successor—a virtual repudiation of the devolution from St. Peter to Linus; the condemnation of Acacius of Constantinople and Peter of Alexandria by Felix III. in 484, which, instead of being received in the East, was met by a retaliatory excommunication of the Pope, and caused a schism of thirty-five years, healed at last by a compromise; and the famous Synod of 496 under Pope Gelasius, in which apocryphal books were condemned, the accredited Councils acknowledged, and the writings of certain Fathers, inclusive of SS. Cyprian, Basil, and Augustine, declared entirely orthodox; thus cutting off objections to much of the evidence marshalled hitherto against the Petrine privilege. There was also a definition of the limits of his ecclesiastical and secular powers given by the Pope in this Council, ending with the words: "It is the duty of Pontiffs to obey the imperial ordinances in all things temporal." Ten other local Councils were held in this century, at Turin, Milevis, Zella or Telepa, Riez, Orange I., Vaison I., Arles II., Angers, Tours I., and Vannes. All they yield is that at Turin in 401 the Council adjudged the primacy of Narbonne for life to Proculus of Marseilles, though bishop in another province, decreeing that after his death the new Primate should be one of the bishops of the province of Narbonne; and that the dispute between the Archbishops of Arles and Vienne, who both claimed the primacy of Viennese Gaul, should be settled by giving the metropolitanate to whichever claimant could prove his see to be the civil capital of the province—another item of evidence in favour of Canon xxviii. of Chalcedon—while no hint of reference to the Pope as arbiter occurs; and that at Zella in 418, where the letter of Pope Siricius drafted in the Roman synod of 386 was read, and an exception was allowed (in accordance therewith) in the Roman Church to the fourth Nicene canon, requiring three bishops to consecrate another.

14. There is a curious piece of evidence at the begin-

ning of the sixth century, which looks at first as though making for the Papal claims, but which proves all the more against them because of the peculiar circumstances.

The Bishops of Italy, excepting the northern portions within the provinces of Milan and Grado or Aquileia, have always been zealous upholders of the Papal claims—indeed the most so of any section of the episcopate, till the comparatively modern development of bishops *in partibus* as a class. The Pope, as their immediate superior, exercising direct practical jurisdiction over them, has necessarily been a more important personage in their eyes, and been treated by them with a profounder deference, than is the case in other parts of the Latin obedience; and consequently, while acts of submission on their part prove very little, any display of independence proves a great deal. It happened that Pope Symmachus, who sat from 498 to 514, was accused of very grave crimes before Theodoric the Ostrogoth, who compelled the reluctant bishops of the suburbicarian provinces of Italy to hold a council to try the Pope. Symmachus himself had the good sense to see that nothing else could possibly clear him, and accordingly a synod of seventy-six bishops was convened at Rome in 501, known in history as the Synodus Palmaris.[1] It displayed the utmost unwillingness to assume any judicial authority whatever, and several of the prelates expressed their opinion that, as the Pope's inferiors, they were not competent to try him at all, while some went further, and at least implied that only God could decide a cause wherein so august a personage was the defendant. But although they studiously avoided using the legal forms of a trial, still, in order to rehabilitate the Pope, they were obliged to embody their acquittal in the shape of a decree, in which they empowered him to administer the sacraments in all churches attached to his see, and recommended the faithful to receive the Holy Communion at his hands, in token

---

[1] From the palm-ornamentation of the porch of St. Peter's, where it was held.

that the strife was now ended, and his innocence established;[1] whereby, despite their reclamation, they proved that it was in their power to have forbidden him to administer the sacraments and the laity to receive them from him, and so that even as a mere local synod, with no pretensions to œcumenicity, they collectively were the Pope's superiors. Symmachus had been acquitted by another Council of 116 bishops in the previous year, but as the forms of a regular trial were evaded then also, that acquittal affords no evidence as to his accountability to a local synod, and it might be explained as no more than a public and official vote of confidence, which, however gratifying and morally influential, could have no canonically legal force in respect of one of his exalted rank. The importance of this synod, as disproving the Gallican theory, that although the Pope is accountable and inferior to the rare and exceptional tribunal of a General Council, nothing less may take cognisance of his acts, or presume to judge him, cannot be overrated.

The sixth century was an era of Councils in the Churches of Gaul and Spain, held for doctrinal and disciplinary purposes, and at once so numerous, and dealing with so large a number of important and even vital topics, that it is all but impossible to believe that if the Papal claims had been

---

[1] The crucial words of the decree run thus: "Quibus allegatis cum Dei nostri obtestatione decernimus . . . . ut Symmachus Papa, sedis apostolicæ præsul . . . . sit immunis et liber, et Christianæ plebi, sine aliqua de objectis oblatione, in omnibus ecclesiis suis ad jus sedis suæ pertinentibus tradat divina mysteria; qui a eum ob impugnatorum suorum impetitionem propter superius designatas causa obligari non potuisse cognovimus. Unde secundum principalia præcepta, quæ nostræ hoc tribuunt potestati, ei quidquid ecclesiastici intra sacram urbem Romam vel foris juris est reformamus, totamque causam Dei judicio reservantes, universos hortamur ut sacram communionem, sicut res postulat, ab eo percipiant." The assertion of authority over the Pope, the exercise of that authority in the form of a synodical decree, and the subject-matter of the decree itself, are all too clear and explicit to permit of being explained away or even effectively minimised.

then recognised as valid in Western Christendom, there should not be a large mass of evidence forthcoming on their behalf. These Councils were as follows:—In **France,** Agde, Arles (two); Autun, Auvergne (two); **Auxerre,** Carpentras, Epaon, Lyons (three); Mâcon (three); Narbonne, Orange (two); Orleans (five); Paris (three); Tours; and Vaison; **in Spain,** Barcelona **(two)**; Braga (two); Gerona, Huesca, **Lerida,** Saragossa, Seville, Tarragona, Toledo (three); Valencia (two); total, forty-three synods. In all these there is but *one* reference, direct or indirect, to the Pope in any capacity, and that is the fourth Canon of Vaison II. in 529 (at which only twelve bishops were present), enjoining the commemoration of the Pope's name, to be prayed for at every Mass; **which** incidentally proves that it was not inserted in the **Gallican Missal** till then, but was absent, as in all the oldest Liturgies except the local **Roman one, so that even the bare Primacy was not** formally recognised in Gaul at that time, for the local metropolitan's name must have occupied the first place of commemoration at Mass. There are many Canons, moreover, practically inconsistent **with the latter system,** of which a single example will suffice—the first Canon of the Second Council of Lyons in 567, **which** decrees that if a dispute arise between two bishops of the same province, the matter **is to** be settled **by their** metropolitan and his comprovincials; but if **the disputants** should be of different provinces, **then** the two metropolitans **are** jointly to try the case, and their sentence **is to be final.** The importance of this Canon is in showing that the great province of Lyons, the principal see of all Gaul, did **not then** accept or recognise the Canons of **Sardica, on which** the whole **system** of Papal appeals **is based, for there is no** provision **for any ulterior** appeal.

And the object for which **the Second Council of Orange** was convoked **in** 529 **was to** examine and ratify **certain** articles and capitula **on** the subject of Semi-Pelagianism, which Pope Felix IV. had compiled at the request of St. Cæsarius of Arles **to** aid him in some local controversies on the subject. This fact shows that the Papal origin and sanction of the document in question did not suffice to give it currency and authority in the Churches of Gaul. Moreover, in its decree the Council does not so much as name the Pope as author or sanctioner of the articles in question, but recommends them solely as expressing the opinions of the "ancient Fathers," since they were, in fact, mainly taken from St. Augustine.

The fifth General Council at Constantinople in 553 supplies an important piece of evidence. The Council had before it a proposal to condemn, in confirmation of an edict of Justinian I. in 547, certain writings of Theodore of Mopsuestia, Theodoret of Cyrus, and Ibas of Edessa, technically known as the "Three Chapters." Pope Vigilius at first had refused assent to the edict of 547, and even declined to communicate with the bishops who had signed it. But in 551 he issued a treatise entitled *Judicatum*, in which he recanted this first opinion, and condemned the Three Chapters himself in a Synod of seventy Bishops. Hereupon, he was promptly excommunicated by Facundus, Pontianus, and other African bishops, and by the Bishops of Illyricum, as well as strongly censured by Rusticus and Sebastian, deacons of his own Roman Church, while even the Emperor was almost equally angry because of a saving clause in the *Judicatum*, limiting its censures to what was disallowed by the Council of Chalcedon. While the Council of Constantinople was debating the "Three Chapters," the Pope changed his mind again, and sent a formal decree or "*constitutum*" to be read in the session, wherein, although rejecting the tenets of Theodore of Mopsuestia, he revoked his censure of Theodoret and Ibas, forbade the condemnation of the Three Chapters, and denied the lawfulness of anathematizing the dead. But the Council refused to permit this letter to be so much as read, proceeded to condemn the Three Chapters in despite of the Pope's advocacy, and struck his name out of the diptychs or registers of the Church—a virtual act of excommunication—as a punishment for his contumacy. When its decrees were issued, Vigilius recanted once more, and, pleading the *Retractations* of St. Augustine as a precedent, approved the Council, and condemned the Three Chapters afresh, in which he was followed by his successors Pelagius I., John III., Benedict I., Pelagius II., and St. Gregory the Great. Whether we look to the contemptuous disregard of the Pope exhibited by the Œcumenical Council, or to his own helpless vacillations on the doctrinal issue at stake, the result is equally unfavourable to the Petrine claims.

Ten Roman Councils were held in the sixth century. Only two are relevant besides the Synodus Palmaris already cited. In 531 a Synod was held to discuss the appeal of Stephen of Larissa, Metropolitan of Thessaly, who had been deposed by Epiphanius of Constantinople. It is not known how the matter ended, but the plea set up by Stephen was that his see belonged in fact to the Roman Patriarchate, and not to that of Constantinople, and so the question was purely one of ecclesiastical geography, pertaining to an old dispute as to the whole vast province of Eastern Illyricum, claimed by the Popes from Damasus onward as part of their jurisdiction, and placed under a Papal Vicar, a new office, marking a first Roman encroachment. In 595, John of Chalcedon, a priest who had appealed from the Patriarch of Constantinople, was absolved.

The seventh century also had several Councils held in Gaul and Spain during its course, namely, Autun, Châlons-sur-Saône, Paris, Rheims, and Rouen, in the former country; Braga, Egara, Seville, Toledo (fourteen), in the latter: a total of twenty-two. All they yield on inquiry are—(1) that the fifth Council of Paris, in 615, decrees that on the death of any bishop, the vacancy shall be filled up by the election of a fit person by the clergy and laity of the diocese, to be confirmed by the metropolitan and his comprovincials; and enacts that any other method of appointment shall, in accordance with the ancient Canons, be absolutely void, even if the person be consecrated. There is no provision for appeal to Rome, much less for giving the Pope any voice in **the election**. (2.) A similar but briefer Canon was passed at Châlons in 649. (3.) The second Council of Seville, in 618, rules that in case of a dispute between bishops as to their jurisdiction over parishes and churches, thirty years' prescription is to confer full rights, "for this both the edicts and secular princes enjoin and the authority of Roman prelates has decreed." (4.) The third Canon of the fourth Council of Toledo, in 633, enacts that a general [national] Council of Spain shall be held yearly, if any question of the faith arise, or any matter affecting the Church **at** large; but that if nothing of such importance **be forthcoming**, it shall suffice **to** hold the several provincial synods **independently**, whenever the metropolitans shall appoint, **and the** judgments of **those** synods, whether general or provincial, shall be bind**ing** and final, for all causes brought before them. (5.) The sixth Canon of this same Council, in regulating the controversy as to trine and single immersion in baptism, quotes the opinion of St. Gregory the Great in these terms: " Therefore Gregory of blessed memory, Pontiff of the Roman Church, who not merely adorned the regions of Italy, **but** taught the Churches also with his doctrine, when the most holy Bishop Leander inquired of him which practice should be followed **in** this diversity in Spain, writes back to him, saying thus amongst other matters:" [Here follows **a** quotation, declaring that both usages are valid and **per**missible.] " Wherefore . . . . **since an** opinion is given by so great a man [*tanto viro*] that both are right and to **be** accounted blameless in the Church of God . . . **let us** hold to single baptism." Here it **is the** personal eminence of St. Gregory as a private doctor, not his official **character as Pope**, which **is cited as** weighty in deciding the controversy. (6.) The fourteenth Council of Toledo, in 684, assembled to give local confirmation in Spain to the decrees of Constantinople against the Apollinarians and Monothelites, having been "invited" by Pope Leo **II. to** do so, and the Council explained that there were two reasons for not having earlier complied with the invitation, namely, that a General Council of Spain had been held just before the Pope's letter arrived, and had been dissolved, while the severity of an unusually cold and stormy winter made it highly inconvenient to reassemble, but that the decrees had been carefully studied in each diocese, and approved, so that now they were ready to content the Pope, by giving clear proof of their orthodoxy in affirmatory Canons. There is not a word in their language which implies any uneasiness lest they should seem insufficiently deferential to the Pope, but only lest their submission to and agreement with the Œcumenical Council should be doubted because of the delay. A Council at Rome, under Pope Agatho, in 678, decreed the reinstatement of Wilfrid, Bishop of York, who complained of having been unjustly deposed, and of his diocese being divided into three sees against his will. But the sentence was disregarded by the civil and ecclesiastical authorities in England, who, some years later, actually renewed his deposition, and never retracted the partition of his diocese, but even carved a fourth see out of it. This is the sum of the local conciliar evidence furnished by the seventh century; but an incomparably weightier testimony has yet to be adduced, that of the sixth General Council, the last of the undisputed Œcumenical Synods of the Church Catholic.

That Council was held in 681 for the condemnation of the Monothelite heresy, and the legates of Pope Agatho took the lead in calling for that condemnation, and in vindicating the orthodox Catholic doctrine, bringing with them letters to the Emperor from the Pope and a Council of Western bishops who had assembled at Rome in 679. The result was that in the several sessions judgment was pronounced in these terms:—

(*a.*) Sess. xiii.—"It has been demanded that sentence shall be pronounced on the epistles of Sergius, *Honorius*, and Sophronius, which were read in the preceding session. The Holy Council said : According to the promise which was made by us to your Splendour, we, taking into consideration the dogmatic epistles which were written by Sergius, Patriarch of the Imperial City, both to Cyrus, who was then Bishop of Phasis, and also to Honorius, Pope of Old Rome, and likewise the epistle in reply from him, that is, Honorius, to the aforesaid Sergius, and finding them to be in all respects alien from Apostolic doctrine and from the definitions of the sacred synods, and of all the Fathers of repute, but following the false doctrines of the heretics, we wholly reject them, and pronounce them accursed as hurtful to souls. . . . . With these we have provided that *Honorius, who was Pope of Old Rome, be cast out of the Holy Catholic Church of God and be anathematized,* because we have found by the writings which he addressed to Sergius, that he followed his opinion in all respects and affirmed his impious tenets."

(*b.*) "Having examined the letters of Sergius of Constantinople to Cyrus, and the answer **of** Honorius to Sergius, and having found them to be repugnant **to the** doctrine **of** the Apostles, and to the opinion of all the **Fathers; in** execrating their impious dogmas, we judge that their **very names** ought to be banished from the Holy Church of God ; **we declare** them to be smitten with anathema ; and **together with** them, *we judge that Honorius, formerly Pope of Old Rome, be anathematized, since we find in his letters to Sergius that he follows in all respects his error and authorises his impious doctrine.*"

(*c.*) Sess. xvi.—" Anathema to Theodore the heretic, anathema to Sergius the heretic, anathema to Cyrus the heretic, anathema to *Honorius the heretic,* anathema to Pyrrhus the heretic.'

(*d.*) Sess. xvii.—" But since there has never, from the beginning, ceased to be an inventor of evil, who found the serpent to help him, and thereby brought poisoned death on mankind, and so finding suitable tools for his own purpose,—we mean Theodorus . . . . and also *Honorius,* who was Pope of Old Rome."

These **decrees** were signed, without any objection being raised, by the legates of Pope Agatho and **by all the** hundred and sixty-five bishops present.

This sentence on a Pope as a heretic, pronounced by a General Council, is such a deadly blow to the whole fabric of the Papal claims, as negativing at once the doctrines **of** Papal supremacy and infallibility, that the most desperate efforts have been made by Roman controversialists to elude **or** minimise its evidence. It is unnecessary to set down all these shifts and evasions here, it will suffice to name such of **them** as would be to the point if they could be proved.

1. Baronius alleges that the insertion of Honorius's name is an interpolation and forgery.

2. Honorius was really orthodox, and was condemned by the Council in error.

3. Honorius was condemned only in his capacity as a private doctor, as he did not put forth his letter to Sergius in his official capacity, nor intend to teach *ex cathedrâ* by it.

4. The fault for which Honorius was condemned was not heresy, but apathetic negligence in suppressing the heresy of others.

It may be observed, in the first place, that these four excuses are not *supplementary* to each other, so as to be separate pleas or parts which can be combined into one successful defence. Each of them *excludes* the other three, and is incompatible with them, so that the controversialist who selects any one of them in defence of Honorius must deny the truth of the three remaining pleas, and if he attempt to urge more than one of them simultaneously, he must contradict himself. Thus, it is plainly inconsistent to declare the decrees of the Council to be *forged*, and also to say that, although *genuine*, they were passed in error on the point of the Pope's orthodoxy. One of these two pleas might be true by itself, but they cannot both be true at the same time. As a fact, the four pleas are all false.

Not only was there no suspicion or whisper of interpolation in the Acts or decrees of the Council during the nine hundred years which elapsed between the publication of its decrees in 681, and that of the first volume of the *Ecclesiastical History* of Baronius in 1588; but the most explicit and authoritative acceptance of those decrees by the local Church of Rome itself is attested by irrefragable documentary proof. First, the anathema against Honorius does not rest for evidence on the Acts of the Council only. It is expressly repeated in the letter of the Council to the Emperor, and in its other letter to Pope Agatho, and all these three documents were duly signed by the Papal legates. Next, Pope Leo II., Agatho's successor, wrote to the Emperor, on May 7, 683, a formal letter, in which he says, amidst much else: "We likewise *anathematize* the inventors of the new error; that is, Theodore . . . Sergius . . . and also *Honorius*, who did not keep this

Apostolic Church pure with doctrine of Apostolic tradition, but endeavoured to overthrow the unspotted faith by his profane betrayal." Thirdly, this same Pope renewed this anathema in his letter to the Spanish bishops, inviting them to accept synodically the decrees of the Council, in which he tells them that Honorius is damned to all eternity. Fourthly, the two synods, at Nicæa in 787 and Constantinople in 869, reckoned by the Latin Church as the seventh and eighth General Councils—of which the latter, held against Photius, and entirely under Roman influence, is rejected by the Greeks—renew the condemnation of Honorius. The following citation of the Acts of this pseudo-Œcumenical Council of Constantinople is from the account by Anastasius Bibliothecarius, a Roman historian and divine, who was present during the sessions: "We anathematize, moreover, Theodore, who was Bishop of Pharan, and Sergius, and Pyrrhus, and Paul, and Peter, impious bishops of the Church of Constantinople; and together with them Honorius of Rome, together with Cyrus of Alexandria; and also Macarius of Antioch, and his disciple Stephen, who, following the doctrines of Apollinaris of evil fame, and also of Eutyches and Severus, the impious heresiarchs, taught that the Flesh of God was animated by a rational and intellectual soul devoid of operation and will, with mutilated senses, and in both without reasoning faculty." Fifthly, a formal Profession of Faith, to be made by each Pope at his coronation, was inserted in the *Liber Diurnus*, itself drawn up, as is believed, by Pope Gregory II., one clause of which, in condemnation of heresies, mentions Honorius by name, along with Sergius, Pyrrhus, and others, with the special remark that he "added fuel (*fomentum*) to their corrupt statements." Sixthly, in the office of the Roman Breviary for June 28, the feast of St. Leo II., the name of Pope Honorius was included for some centuries in the lessons of the second nocturn, amongst those Monothelite heretics who were condemned by the sixth General Council. The lesson has been falsified, ever since about the middle of the sixteenth century, by omitting Honorius's name; but the older editions, when not actually mutilated with a knife, exhibit it still.[1] Seventhly, a letter of Pope Hadrian II., formally drafted in a Council at Rome in 868, was read in the so-called eighth General Council of 869, in which he lays down very strong assertions as to the privileges of the Roman See, stating that as a rule no Pope can be tried by his inferiors; that the only ground on which he may be lawfully resisted is that of heresy; and that the posthumous condemnation of Honorius by the sixth General Council rests on that ground, and must needs have been preceded by permission from the then Pope to the assembled patriarchs and bishops to moot the question at all. This very claim, intended to exalt the privilege of Peter, establishes two facts, that in Pope Hadrian's mind Honorius was really and justly condemned as a heretic, and that the previous assent of Pope Agatho to the condemnation was brought by his legates to the Council. The question of the *truth* of the charge, and of the official character of the letter of Honorius on which it was based, will be considered when that part of the evidence against the Petrine claims is reached which consists of acts of the Popes themselves; but it is not relevant here, since the present issue is limited to the evidence of the Councils. And as all the undisputed General Councils have been cited, each of which contributes its quota of testimony against the alleged "privilege of Peter," while more than one hundred local ones in the first seven centuries, to say the least, fail to support it, it will suffice to close this part of the discussion here; but one additional citation, albeit of minor importance, may not be superfluous. It is the first ground of objection raised by the Gallican Church in the "Caroline Books," written by order of Charlemagne, at the close of the eighth century (790), against the sanction of the cultus of images by the quasi-General

---

[1] It occurs, for example, in a Venetian edition of 1523 in the writer's possession, and he has seen it in one of 1559.

Second Council of Nicæa in 787. That ground was, that this Council of Nicæa was a merely Eastern synod, as no Western bishops were present *except the Pope by his legates*, and therefore was not œcumenical nor binding, and the Council of Frankfort in 794 rejected and condemned it by **Canon ii.** Moreover, it compelled Pope **Hadrian I.** to retract his confirmation of the Nicene decrees, and to pronounce them heretical. The French and German bishops held out for at least five centuries before recognising this second Council of Nice.

Later synods, exclusively Western (except that of Ferrara-Florence, to be considered subsequently), obviously have not the same value as evidence of Catholic consent; and many of them, held under directly Roman influence, and even in the august city itself, might be readily quoted as showing how the Petrine claims were gradually advanced, where little resistance was likely, or even possible. But this very fact increases the weight of any adverse testimony discoverable in them, and such testimony is very far indeed from being absent. It will suffice to quote the decisions of five of the most important—those of Rome in 963; of Sutri in 1046; of Pisa in 1409; of Constance in 1415; and of Basle, which sat from 1431 to 1443. The first of these deposed Pope John XII. for simony, adultery, and other grievous crimes; the second, convened to examine the conflicting claims of three rival Popes—Benedict IX., Silvester III., and Gregory VI.—condemned Silvester as an impostor, degraded him from holy orders, imprisoned him for life, and compelled the abdication of the two others, one of whom must have been the lawful claimant. The words used of Benedict by Pope Victor **III. are that** he, being Roman Pontiff, gave judgment for his own deposition (*ipse, Romanus Pontifex, se judicaverit deponendum*); and of Gregory VI., almost similarly, "I judge that I am to be removed from the Roman bishopric" (*a Romano episcopatu judico me submovendum*). These turns of phrase are important, as they exclude the plea of voluntary resignation, and show that submission to the sentence of the Council, in order to mitigate its severity, is the truest version of the transaction.

Neither of these Councils professed to be Œcumenical. They were no more than local Italian Synods, and yet their depositions of the Popes in question have always been counted valid.

The Council of Pisa, one of the largest ever assembled, met to adjudicate upon the conflicting claims of the rival Popes, **Gregory XII.** and Benedict XIII., one of whom, at least, must have been the true Pontiff. It summoned them to appear before it, convoked as it was under the authority of the two parties in the College of Cardinals which severally adhered to each of the claimants; and after declaring them contumacious for absence and non-representation by proctors, formally withdrew from the recognition of both or either of them, declared in its fourteenth session that it, as representing the Catholic Church, had right of cognisance in the matter, and jurisdiction, as the highest authority on earth; and formally deposed, condemned, and excommunicated both Benedict XIII. and Gregory XII., as schismatics, heretics, and perjurers, electing in their stead Peter of Candia, Archbishop of Milan, under the title of Alexander V., who was duly crowned.

The Council of Constance had before it the renewed claims of the two Popes deposed at Pisa (for the validity of that Council's proceedings was contested then and since), and also those of the actually reigning Pope, Balthasar Cossa, Pope John XXIII., who presided at its opening. His notorious immorality caused several heavy indictments to be brought against him before the Synod, which, in its fourth session, declared itself an Œcumenical Council, deriving its authority directly from Christ Himself—a power which every one, including the Pope, was bound to obey in all matters regarding the Faith, the removal of schism, and the reformation of the Church in its head and members. It further pronounced null and void any censures or processes which the Pope might direct against the members of the Council. In the twelfth session John

XXIII. was finally deposed, and declared incapable of re-election; while the counts upon which he was condemned were of such a scandalous nature that they were not published along with the sentence. He is described in the **secret** articles as "an obstinate heretic" and "a notorious simoniac"; and in the twelfth session as "a devil incarnate."[1] The claims of Benedict and Gregory were disallowed, and in the forty-first session Cardinal Colonna was elected Pope under the title of Martin V.

The Council of **Basle held** forty-five sessions. Of these the first twenty-five were received by the Gallican Church, and, indeed, by the entire West, for they **were** acknowledged by Pope Eugenius IV., and his legates continued **to** take part in them; but the whole are now rejected **by** the Ultramontane school. Of course it has no Eastern recognition whatever. Its value for the present inquiry, therefore, must not rest so much on its disputed claims, as on its historical record of a great body of ecclesiastical opinion in the fifteenth century; since, as Cardinal Manning notes, when quoting it to support the dogma of the Immaculate Conception:—"And if the Council of Basle be not general, yet it represents the mind of the Episcopate of the Universal Church."—(*Sermons on Eccl.* **Subjects**, p. 129. Duffy, **1863.**) **It** was convoked by Martin V., who died just after its meeting, and it came, almost at once, into conflict with **his successor,** Eugenius IV. **Amongst the** decrees in the acknowledged sessions are **the reiteration of** the claim of the Council of Constance to be supreme over **all** persons, including the Pope; that if the Pope disobey it, **or any** other General Council, he is to be put to penance; that General Councils are alone infallible, because they are the Church itself, whereas the Pope, though the chief minister of the Church, is not above the whole mystical body, since **that** body cannot err in matters of faith, whereas experience teaches that the Pope can so err; **that** the Church, as the mystical body, has several times de-

---

[1] Von der Hardt. *Magn. Conc. Constant.*, **pars II.**

posed Popes when convicted of error in matters of faith, whereas no Pope has ever pretended to excommunicate the Church as a body; that the Council warned and required Pope Eugenius IV. to revoke his decree for its dissolution, and to appear before it in person or by proxy within three months; that the Pope should not be permitted to create any cardinals during the sitting of the Council, and that any such creation should be null and void; that no person should be excused from attending the Council on the plea of any oath or promise made to the Pope, all such pledges being declared not binding; that the claim put forward by the Bishop of Tarentum that the Pope alone possesses the right of appointing the time, place, and celebration of Councils, could not be sustained, since, if the Pope attempted to dissolve a lawfully convoked Council, he would thereby become an abetter and renewer of schism; that if any Pope neglected to call a Council once in ten years, as decreed at Constance, the right to do so would devolve on the bishops, without any obligation to ask his permission; that the legates whom Pope Eugenius was willing to send in 1433 to preside over the Council in his name be refused admission, because claiming powers inconsistent with his own; that he be required to revoke within sixty days his plan for transferring the Council from Basle, upon pain of being pronounced contumacious; and that his right of reservation and of reversion to ecclesiastical preferments be restricted to the local Roman diocese and its immediate dependencies. All these decrees were made within the twenty-five acknowledged and received sessions. Amongst those made in the latter and disputed sessions are, one directing that all causes ecclesiastical should be decided on the spot, and that no appeal to the Pope, to the exclusion of the Ordinary, should be allowed; that Pope Eugenius be pronounced contumacious, be suspended from his office, and all his acts be accounted null and void; that it is a Catholic verity that a General Council has authority over the Pope as well as over all others; that, once lawfully convoked, it cannot be dissolved, transferred, or prorogued by the Pope's authority against its consent, and that whoso resists these verities is to be regarded as a heretic; while in 1439 the Council declared Eugenius IV. deposed, and elected Amadeus, Duke of Savoy, Pope as Felix V., but this choice was not universally nor favourably recognised.

The most important facts in the history of these later Councils are the depositions of Popes effected at Pisa and Constance, with the elections of Alexander V. and Martin V. in the room of the deprived Pontiffs. This was, in fact, a revolution which for a time overthrew the autocratic Papacy and turned it into a constitutional government, with the supreme power transferred from the Pope to the whole body of the Church. But the speedy abeyance into which the law enacted at Constance for the periodical assemblage of councils fell enabled the Popes to recover their lost ground, and revive their supremacy.

It is obvious that if the "privilege of Peter," as affirmed in the Vatican Council, be a divinely revealed verity, and the Pope be in truth the Head of the Church, his inferiors could not possibly sit in judgment upon him, nor could the body, without committing suicide, cut off its own head. Therefore, if the attitude taken up by the Councils were heterodox and unjustifiable, we should find their nominees to the Papacy rejected as pretenders, schismatics, and heretics, and their acts disallowed as null and void.

Precisely so in English history, the whole Parliamentary annals of England under the Commonwealth are now a legal blank. The trial and condemnation of Charles I. are regarded as illegally done; the reign of Oliver Cromwell, politically important as it was, and the statutes of his Parliaments, many of them wise and salutary, and anticipatory (as in the union of Scotland and Ireland into one realm with England) of much later legislation, are simply ignored; the regnal years of Charles II. are counted from the day of his father's execution: and no Acts of Parliament nor decisions of the law-courts between 1641 and

1660 can be cited as of authority, or as having the smallest legal validity. But no such disavowal of Pisa and Constance exists in ecclesiastical history, and the claims of Alexander V. and Martin V. to be true Pontiffs and successors of St. Peter have never been disputed; albeit their title depends wholly on the validity of the deposition of their predecessors, which created the vacancies in their favour. Had there been any such collapse of the opposition at Pisa and Constance as that which left Eugenius IV. ultimately victor over the Council of Basle, we should have merely proof that modern Ultramontanism was not then universally received, but none that it was not in the right, and entitled to be so received; but the triumph of Pisa and Constance over Papal resistance is decisive of the controversy, and refutes the Vatican decrees of 1870.

CHAPTER IV.

LEGAL EVIDENCE OF ACTS, CONCILIAR, PAPAL, AND PATRISTIC.

HAVING established the thesis that the evidence of Holy Scripture, of the ancient Liturgies, of such Fathers as furnish glosses on the three Gospel texts which are the key of the Ultramontane position, and of the decrees and canons of a long series of Councils down to the beginning of the Reformation, is all adverse to the "Privilege of Peter;" it is now time to pass to the next part of the inquiry, namely, the incidental evidence supplied by the proceedings (as distinguished from the canons) of Councils, and by acts and language of Popes themselves, of canonized Saints, and other eminent persons, as to the extent of Papal authority. Here, too, it is to be distinctly remembered that any negative examples are very much more to the point than positive ones can be. This proposition may strike persons unfamiliar with the rules of evidence as being unfair, for they may naturally suppose that at least equal weight should be given to the facts which make in favour of Papal supremacy, and to those which make against it. That would be perfectly true if the claim made for the Popes were simply that in virtue of their office they held the most prominent position in the early Church, and often exercised a preponderating influence in ecclesiastical affairs. Occasional proofs of their being unable to secure their ends or enforce their authority would establish no more against this view than the failure of many English Acts of Parliament to effect their object, or to obtain popular recognition and obedience, establishes against the general proposition that England is habitually governed by laws enacted in and by Parliament. Yet, in truth, no dispute exists so far, and were nothing further demanded on behalf of the Popes, the controversy would die out for want of materials. But the claim is that of an original and indefeasible Divine right of direct sovereignty and jurisdiction, both in matters of faith and of discipline, exercised from the first by the Popes, and acknowledged by the whole Catholic Church. Every instance which makes against these pretensions is a flaw in the case, and is like a gap in a pedigree by which right of ownership to a title and estate is sought to be established. And if several such flaws and gaps be discoverable, they settle something further: for they not merely disprove the claim of special *privilege*, but make it impossible to sustain the Supremacy as matter of *prescription*, and as having thus such ancient and universal consent on its side as to raise a strong presumption in favour of primitive Christendom having ranked it as a Church ordinance, equally with Infant Baptism and Sunday observance, for which no express Divine sanction is recorded. And any evidence which tends to show that the power of the Roman See did, in fact, become greater in the lapse of time, and gradually overpower resistance, at once helps to show its purely human character. For a divinely bestowed authority is always strongest at first, growing weaker in popular regard as the memory of the original grant is weakened, which the instances of Moses and of the Apostles sufficiently prove; whereas a human authority, continually reinforced, often tends to grow, as the power of the French kings grew from Louis XI. to Louis XIV., and as the power of the House of Commons has grown in England from the Restoration to the present day. It is quite true, as observed more than once already, that the argument from prescription, the opinion that the Papal power *grew* into what it now is, by gradual exercise and extension, from natural, political, and ecclesiastical causes, and was not the same from the beginning, is rejected as heretical by the accredited Roman doctrine of to-day, which insists that there is a Divine charter of privilege, and nothing less, for the Papacy. Nevertheless, in practice, Roman controversialists professedly appeal to the evidence of history, in order to show that in point of fact the privilege of Peter was acknowledged and submitted to by the Universal Church from the first, and having induced acceptance of this as matter of history, then allege that only a Divine institution could have wielded such authority; and thus history is the ladder by which they climb up to the heights of Vaticanism. Let us test a few of the rungs.

SECOND CENTURY.—1. The earliest instance to the point is during the pontificate of Pope St. Anicetus, who sat from A.D. 157 to 168.

At that time St. Polycarp of Smyrna visited the imperial city, and had a discussion with the Pope on the date for the due observance of Easter, whether it should be kept on the 14th of Nisan, regardless of the day of the week, or always on a Sunday: a controversy which, trivial as it may now perhaps appear, was regarded as of great importance by the early Church, and was in debate for some centuries. Eusebius tells us, citing a lost treatise of St. Irenæus, that—

"when the Blessed Polycarp was staying at Rome, in the time of Anicetus, . . . they were speedily at peace with one another, not caring to dispute on this head: for Anicetus could not persuade (οὔτε πεῖσαι ἐδύνατο) Polycarp not to observe that which he had always done together with John, our Lord's disciple, and the other Apostles, with whom he had been conversant, nor on the other hand did Polycarp persuade (ἔπεισε) Anicetus to his observance, who said that he was bound to maintain the custom of the Elders before him. And this being so, they joined in communion with one another, and in the Church Anicetus conceded to Polycarp, doubtless by way of respect, the celebration of the Eucharist, and they departed in peace from one another; the whole Church—of those who observed [the custom] and of those who observed not—being at peace."—*Hist. Eccl.* v. 24.

Three things are to be observed here: first, that the same word is used of the Pope's endeavour to convince St. Polycarp and of St. Polycarp's endeavour to convince the Pope. Each tries to *persuade*, neither attempts to *order*. Next, when it comes to quoting authorities, it is St. Polycarp who urges Apostolic precedent and example, namely, St. John and the remaining Apostles; whereas St. Anicetus does not say a word about St. Peter or any special privilege of his own office, but alleges merely the custom of the "Elders" (πρεσβυτέρων) who preceded himself. Thirdly, instead of treating St. Polycarp's opposition as a ground of condemnation, he confers on him the very highest mark of distinction possible in that age from one Bishop to another; whereas his plain duty was, had this opposition been a piece of insubordination to a divinely chartered ruler, to check it at once, lest the example should be contagious, as it indeed proved to be.

2. The second instance concerns the very same dispute, only that now Victor I. (A.D. 193-202)—a Pontiff of a very different temper from St. Anicetus, with all the fierce intolerance of his African origin—immediately on the receipt of a letter on behalf of the Asiatic Churches to the Roman Church from Polycrates, Bishop of Ephesus, in which was alleged the precept and example of St. Philip, St. John, St. Polycarp, and several others in favour of observing Easter on the 14th Nisan, issued letters in which he declared all the Asiatic Churches heterodox and excommunicate. Hereupon the other Bishops of the Church, instead of submissively recognising the sentence, issued contrary *orders* to himself (ἀντιπαρακελεύοντο δῆτα αὐτῷ), bidding him rather think of peace, and of neighbourly union and charity, and used expressions " handling him very severely" (πληκτικώτερον καθαπτομένων τοῦ Βίκτορος). Amongst the remonstrants was St. Irenæus, who, acknowledging that Victor was only continuing the use he had received from his predecessors, writes thus: " And those presbyters who governed before Soter that Church over which you now preside, I mean Anicetus, and Pius, and Hyginus, with Telesphorus, and Xystus, neither observed it [the 14th Nisan] themselves, nor did they permit their successors to observe it." He then goes on to add that they did not count this a ground of

dissension from the Quartodeciman Churches,[1] but remained in union with them, and then cites the anecdote of SS. Anicetus and Polycarp quoted above.—(Euseb. *Hist. Eccl.* v. 24.)

Here is to be observed that obviously Pope Victor **did** not cite St. Peter's authority and example as his **warrant,** since, had he done so, St. Irenæus would have gone further back than Anicetus in his disproof. He merely refers **to** the five deceased Popes as *presbyters*, using the same **word** which Anicetus himself had used thirty **years** earlier of his predecessors, and thus shows incidentally that the **claim** of Apostolic rank and Petrine privilege for the Popes **had** not yet been advanced at the beginning of the third century, and that the Pope, even on a point of discipline **whereon** all Christendom subsequently **agreed** with his view, could not get his way, nor avoid sharp censure for trying to get it.

THIRD CENTURY.—3. The next examples **are of much** less evidential value, as the whole of their facts are derived from treatises by Tertullian after his secession **to the** Montanist **sect.**

a. Either Pope Victor or his successor Zephyrinus (A.D. 202 to 219) issued a decree allowing adulterers and **fornicators,** who had fulfilled a term of penance, to be absolved and restored to Church fellowship, which excited Tertullian's ire, as in his mind contrary to the moral teaching of Scripture : and he argues this **question at** much length, using very harsh language to his assumed opponent—the upholder of the Papal decree—whom he styles the "psychic" or natural man. No valid inference can be drawn from Tertullian's opposition to the Pope at the time, as he was then a sectary; but it at least makes the Ultramontane **use** of his name as a witness for the Supremacy manifestly indefensible.[2] The **one** fact that we can **get**

---

[1] That is, such as celebrated Easter on the day corresponding to the Jewish 14th Nisan, and not necessarily on a Sunday.

[2] This use of Tertullian as a witness for the Papacy is due to his applying the titles "Pontifex Maximus" and "Bishop of Bishops" to

K

from his statement, as he does not give us the actual text of the Papal decree, is that the argument of its supporters was that the grant to St. Peter of the power of the Keys and of binding and loosing passed to the whole Church, and to all Churches akin to Peter, and thus that relaxation of penalties for sin was competent to the Christian clergy. This shows that no specific claim was then made on behalf of the Roman Church as having greater authority than other sees, otherwise Tertullian would have argued that point: whereas in fact the plea he does urge is, as already cited under another heading, that St. Peter's power of the Keys meant nothing but his taking the lead in the admission of Jews and Gentiles into the Church, and in relaxing part, while retaining another part, of the Mosaic Law—actions in themselves incapable of repetition, and therefore constituting no transmissible precedent.—(*De Pudicitiâ*, i. xxi.)

b. There is one passage in Tertullian (*Adv. Praxeam*, i.) which illustrates the value of appeal to the Pope in matters of doctrine. Tertullian alleges that the Bishop of Rome (probably Victor) had acknowledged the orthodoxy and mission of the Montanist prophets, and had admitted their Phrygian Churches to communion; but that the heresiarch Praxeas, founder of the Patripassians, had slandered them to the Pope, and by insisting on the authority of his predecessors in the Roman See had persuaded him

---

the Pope in this same treatise. Yet not only does the context show that he is speaking in fierce irony, as might be gathered from his choosing a then exclusively pagan title of office to describe the Pope, branding him thereby as no better than a heathen; but the Popes themselves did not adopt the style of Pontifex Maximus till the episcopate of Paul II. (1464-1471); nor, indeed, was it dropped even by the Christian Emperors till after the death of Justin I. in 527, since he is named PONT. MAX. in an inscription found at Capo d'Istria or Justinopolis, thus refuting the current statement that Gratian († 383) was the last Augustus to bear it. So, too, the title of "Bishop of Bishops" was not arrogated till the reign of Gregory VII. Had these two titles really been in use in Tertullian's day, they would not have suddenly disappeared, to be revived so recently.

to expel them, while suffering Praxeas himself to propagate his own far more seriously heretical tenets. Either way the Pope favoured heresy, seemingly from sheer ignorance.

4. The piece of evidence next in order is one of the most remarkable on record. It is the powerful indictment against Popes Zephyrinus and Callistus in the ninth book of the *Philosophumena*, discovered in MS. in 1842, and now ascribed, by the consent of most scholars of repute, whether Catholic or Protestant, to St. Hippolytus the martyr, Bishop of Portus († *circa* A.D. 250). It is unnecessary to enter here into the question of the justice or reasonableness of his charges, which have been disputed with great learning and ingenuity by Dr. Von Döllinger in his *Hippolytus und Kallistus*; as the only point at issue now is what kind of language a Saint of the third century regarded as applicable to the Pope, without having thereby forfeited the respect and honour of several Popes for at least four centuries more, because of having used such language. He accuses Callistus, then, of having abetted the heresy of Noëtus, of having bribed Zephyrinus, a covetous and ignorant man, to aid him in so doing, of having perverted the heresiarch Sabellius himself, when he had been nearly turned from his errors by the influence of Hippolytus, and when Callistus had it in his power to have completed the conversion; of having swindled the depositors in a bank he set up with his master's money; of having been sentenced to scourging and to penal servitude in the mines, and, after his release, of having obtained ecclesiastical office from Zephyrinus by flattery, being still a knave and impostor; of having denied the Trinity and taught Sabellianism, although he excommunicated Sabellius; and of having set up a school of moral theology, heretical in its tendency, and contrary to the teaching of the Catholic Church.

There is much ground for believing that these terrible charges are mainly due to overpowering polemical bias, as St. Hippolytus was a stern rigorist, and Callistus inclined to the more gentle view of discipline which has generally prevailed in the Church. But if the Papacy had been regarded then as the peculiarly sacred and unique institution which it is now alleged to be, no one, and least of all a great saint and theologian, could have dared to speak in such terms of two Popes of Rome without incurring the severest penalties for treason and blasphemy. And this case is considerably strengthened, if Dr. Von Döllinger's highly probable view be accepted, that Hippolytus not only withdrew from the communion of Callistus, but was actually consecrated as rival Pope of Rome, and yet met with no condemnation from the Church.

5. St. Cyprian († 258) is the next in order to be summoned as a witness, and all the more important one, since he is constantly cited by the Ultramontanes as yielding material evidence in favour of the Petrine privilege. Let us cite first the chief passages on which that evidence is alleged to rest:—

(*a*) "We know that, giving a chart [*rationem*] to all who sail hence [to Rome] that they may sail without any offence, we have exhorted them to acknowledge and hold to the root and womb[1] of the Catholic Church."—*Ep.* xiv. *ad Cornelium Papam.*

(*b*) "Cornelius was made Bishop of Rome . . . when the place of Fabian, that is, the place of Peter, and the grade of the Sacerdotal Chair, was vacant."—*Ep.* lii. *ad Antonianum.*

(*c*) "Peter, however, on whom the Church was built by the same Lord, speaking singly for all, and with the voice of the Church, said 'Lord, to whom shall we go?' &c. . . . They are bold enough to sail and to bring letters from schismatics and heretics to the Chair of Peter and to the principal Church, and do not think that they are those Romans whose faith is lauded in the preaching of the Apostle, to whom false belief (*perfidia*) can have no access."—*Ep.* lv. *ad Corn. Pap.*

(*d*) Allegorising the martyrdom of the seven Maccabee children with their mother, St. Cyprian says: "With the seven children is clearly associated their mother also, their origin and root, who subsequently begat seven Churches, she herself having been first and alone founded

---

[1] *Matrix.* This word is used by Tertullian to describe the older Apostolic Churches which sent out missionaries to found new ones, and he calls Corinth, Ephesus, Antioch, Philippi, &c., *matrices et origines fidei.*—(*De Præscript. Hæret.* **21.**)

on Peter by the voice of the Lord."—*De Exhort. Martyr. ad Fortunatum.*

(*e*) "Therefore it behoves you [Pope Stephen] to write a very copious letter to our fellow-bishops appointed in Gaul, not to permit any longer that Marcian [Bishop of Arles] . . . shall insult our assembly. . . . Let letters be directed by you to the province and to the people abiding at Arles, by which Marcian being excommunicated, another may be substituted in his room."—*Ep.* lxvi. *ad Stephanum Papam.*

(*f*) "Upon him [Peter] being one, He builds His Church, and commits His sheep to be fed . . . and the Primacy is given to Peter, that it might be shown that the Church is one and the Chair one."—*De Unitat. Eccl.* 4.

(*g*) "He who opposes and resists the Church, who forsakes the Chair of Peter, upon which the Church is built, can he trust that he is in the Church?"—*De Unitat. Eccl.* 4.

The very force and explicitness of these various passages (to which several others less strong individually, but of cumulative weight, could readily be added) make them of prime value in the inquiry, because they prove for us, by a comparison with other passages, exactly how much they practically meant, and we have the still more cogent evidence of what St. Cyprian *did*, by which to test the intention and scope of what he *said*.

This is a touchstone which has to be applied constantly throughout the Roman controversy, as it very frequently happens that language which, taken by itself, seems to make very strongly for the Papal claims, is not only much diluted and qualified by other utterances of the very same persons, but is shown to be the mere complimentary diction of polite official etiquette, not really signifying much more than the ending of a modern letter with the words "Your most obedient servant" does, which may be used by a peer to a tradesman with whom he is corresponding.

The first thing to be noted, then, in St. Cyprian's writings is that several of his letters, twelve in all, are addressed to Popes Cornelius, Lucius, and Stephen, and in every one of them he writes on terms of perfect equality, never once styling the Pope by any title implying superiority to himself. His phrases are "brother," "colleague," "fellow-presbyter," "bishop," and "fellow-bishop;" **while he** criticizes and advises as one quite on a level with **his** correspondent.

And Pope Cornelius, in turn, when twice writing to St. Cyprian, similarly addresses him as his brother and equal, using no terms of superiority; whereas the clergy of the Roman Church, writing to St. Cyprian during a vacancy of the Popedom, call **him "most** blessed **and** glorious Pope" (*Ep.* xxxi.); just **as St.** Augustine, nearly two centuries later, is styled "supreme pontiff of Christ" and "most blessed Pope."—(*Ep. Paulini* xxxii. inter *Epp. Aug.*; *Ep. St. Hieron.* lxxv. *ibid.*) [1]

Next, St. Cyprian speaks in several places of the equality and independence of all Bishops, as **also** of all Apostles. A few citations will suffice to show this:—

(*h*) "For neither did Peter, whom the Lord chose, and upon whom He built His Church, when Paul disputed with him afterwards about circumcision, claim aught for himself insolently, or arrogantly assume it, *so as to assert that he held the Primacy*, and had a right to be obeyed by his juniors and successors."—*Ep.* lxxi. *ad Quintum.*

(*i*) "There is **one** Episcopate, a part of which is held by each [bishop] in joint **tenure** (*cujus a singulis in solidum pars tenetur*)."— *De Unitat. Eccl.*

(*j*) "No one **of us** sets himself up as Bishop of bishops, **or by** despotic intimidation forces his colleagues to the necessity of obedience, seeing that every bishop, according to the permission of his liberty and power, has his own right of judgment (*proprium arbitrium*), and can no more be judged by another than he can judge that other himself."— *Speech at Council of Carthage.*

(*k*) "Undoubtedly the other **Apostles** also were what Peter was, endowed with equal **partnership both of honour and of** power; but the beginning is **made from unity, that the Church of** Christ may be shown to be one."—*De Unitat. Eccl.*

---

[1] It will suffice to say here, once for all, **that this** mode of addressing the Pope **as a mere equal and** "fellow-minister" (συλλειτουργός) is common **in the early Church.** So St. Athanasius speaks of Pope Damasus (*Ep. ad Afr.*); Marcellus of Ancyra to Pope Julius I. (St. Epiph. *Cont. Hær.* 72); **St.** Cyril of Alexandria to Celestine I.; some Eastern Bishops **to** Liberius (Socr. *E. H.* iv. 12); and so, too, the Councils of Sardica, Constantinople, and Ephesus, in their letters to Popes Julius, Damasus, and Celestine I. The word "brother" is used by the Synods of Carthage, of Antioch, and Arles I.

These two sets of citations must be taken as qualifying one another seriously, and, if no further evidence existed, they would have to be treated as mutually destructive, and incapable of being adduced on either side of the controversy. But there is further evidence, and of a very cogent kind. In the first place, most of the passages which refer to the Chair of St. Peter at Rome, and to the duty of adherence thereto, were written in view of the Novatian schism in the local Church of Rome itself, which began in 251 by the surreptitious consecration of Novatian as Anti-Pope, who founded a rival communion in the imperial city, which did not die out for two hundred years. And their obvious meaning is, not that communion with the Roman see is the test of orthodoxy and Catholic fellowship for all Christians, but that communion with Pope Cornelius, and not with his rival Novatian, was the test of Catholicity for Christians at Rome just then.—(*Ep.* lv. *ad Antonianum.*) Just so, an American bishop might write to English clergymen warning them against the Bishops of the so-called " Reformed Episcopal Church," and explaining that communion with the see of Canterbury was the test of Church fellowship in England recognised by the American Episcopate. But that would not imply the subjection of the American Bishops themselves to that see. And during a vacancy in the see of Rome, St. Cyprian actually sent letters and legates to the Church there to check the schism.—(*Epp.* xlv., xlvi., xlvii.) Next—and here is the chief evidence in the matter—St. Cyprian and the whole African Church, following the rigorist view, refused to admit the validity of heretical baptism, and re-baptized sectaries who conformed to the Church; whereas Pope St. Stephen and the Roman Church adhered to the older and milder precedent of admission with prayer and imposition of hands. And so high did the controversy run, that the Pope excommunicated St. Cyprian and the African Church for refusal to accept his ruling. The Acts of the Council of Carthage in 255 are still extant, at which eighty-seven bishops were present, following up the similar proceedings of a synod of seventy-one bishops, apparently held earlier in the same year, and unanimously rejecting the letter of Pope Stephen, although enforced with a threat of excommunication, wherein he condemned the ruling of that earlier synod. St. Cyprian, in opening the proceedings, explained that he did not mean to excommunicate any one who did not take his view, as no one bishop had a right to force the conscience or restrict the authority of another; and we have a summary of the speeches made by no fewer than eighty-three of the bishops present, only one of whom so much as condescends to refer to Pope Stephen's letter. In a letter to Pompeius (lxxiv.), St. Cyprian, commenting on St. Stephen's acts and language, speaks of the Pope's "error," his championing the cause of heretics against Christians and the Church of God, his haughty, irrelevant, and self-contradictory writings, his ignorance and inexperience, his adoption of lies (*mendacia*), his betrayal of the truth and faith. It is very doubtful whether St. Cyprian did not die out of communion with Rome, and it is quite certain that neither he nor the African Church made any change in their discipline at this time, nor was there any alteration till after the deaths of both Cyprian and Cornelius; so that if any reconciliation and withdrawal of the excommunication did take place, it was without any submission on St. Cyprian's part. Nevertheless, the highest liturgical honour which the Roman Church can bestow has been conferred on him; for his name occurs not merely in the Kalendar and the Breviary, but is commemorated in the Canon of every Mass, immediately after the Preface, along with the Blessed Virgin, the Apostles, five early Popes, including St. Cornelius himself, and St. Laurence, with five others.

6. St. Cyprian sent information of all these proceedings to St. Firmilian, Bishop of Cæsarea in Cappadocia, who replied in a letter extant in St. Cyprian's works, from which some extracts will now be given.

In the preamble of the letter (sect. 2), he compares Stephen to Judas Iscariot, and then censures his "audacity and insolence;" charges him (sect. 6) with departing from the unity of the Catholic Church, and thereby with defaming the blessed Apostles Peter and Paul, and in sect. 17 adds :—

> "And in this respect I am justly indignant at the open and manifest folly of Stephen, that he who boasts so of the place of his bishopric, and contends that he holds the succession of **Peter**, on whom the foundations of the Church were laid, should bring in many **other** rocks, and erect new buildings of many Churches, whilst defending **with** his authority that there is baptism there. . . . Nor does he understand that the truth of the Christian rock **is** overshadowed, and in **some** measure abolished, **by him who so betrays and deserts unity.**"

Then, apostrophizing Stephen **himself,** St. Firmilian continues (sect. 23, 24) :—

> "But indeed thou art worse than all heretics . . . for what strifes and dissensions hast thou caused throughout the Churches of the whole world! What a mass of sin hast thou heaped up for thyself, when thou hast cut thyself off from so many flocks! For thou hast cut off thyself. Do not deceive thyself; for he is really the schismatic who has made himself an apostate from the communion of ecclesiastical unity. For whilst thou thinkest that all can be excommunicated **by** thee, thou hast excommunicated thyself alone from all."

And after some more censure, he adds at the close of **the** letter, that the **Pope** had denounced St. Cyprian as "a **false** Christ, a false apostle, and **a** deceitful worker;" a verdict in which Stephen has not **been** sustained, though the Church at large has agreed that **he** was right **on the** main question at issue between him **and the Churches of** Africa. There is **no reason** to suppose that St. Firmilian died in communion with Rome, and a letter of **St.** Dionysius **of** Alexandria is extant which implies the contrary. Nevertheless, he is accounted amongst the saints, and his resistance to the Roman Pontiff has not been held to affect his position.

There is a further point to be considered in estimating the value of this evidence: which **is,** that the African Church not only had not any Apostolic See within its own limits, but actually looked to Rome as its Mother Church, from which it had itself received the Gospel (Tertull. *De Præscript. Hær.* 36), and to which it was therefore bound by very close and peculiar ties. Nevertheless, no idea whatever of the duty of submission to the Roman chair seems to have crossed the mind of any African prelate of that day; for there was not even a minority, however small, in that Council of eighty-seven bishops to uphold Pope Stephen's view. And it is noticeable too, whereas this instance, in A.D. 255, is the first clear evidence we have of a Pope styling himself the successor of St. Peter, there is indirect proof that he did not allege any Petrine privilege or authority on his own part as the reason why his opinion should be followed. Imperious as his conduct undoubtedly was, it was yet based on the appeal to ancient precedent, not on his own indefeasible right to be judge of the controversy; since, had he put forward any such claim, it would have been necessarily mentioned and argued against in the Council and in the very copious letters extant on the subject in St. Cyprian's works. A stride forward is visible, a clear and evident proof of *growth* in the Papal authority and demands is obtained; but the two notions of heirship to St. Peter and primacy of jurisdiction over the whole Church were not even yet coupled together as cause and effect, so that the latter must belong to a later age, and be no part of the original privilege of the Roman See. It must, at best, be a right of prescription and custom; but this view is repudiated by Rome herself, who thus destroys her only canonical plea.

One part of St. Cyprian's evidence in favour of the Papal claims, however, has not yet been discussed, namely, the letter in which he urges Pope Stephen to write to the Church of Arles, in order to secure the excommunication and deposition of Marcian. This is explained by Ultramontanes as though St. Cyprian's request were that the Pope, in virtue of his supreme authority, should issue an edict against Marcian, which should serve as the warrant in distant Gaul for his deprivation. The obvious reply to this assertion is that no example of deprivation on the sole authority of the Pope occurs for a long time after. But it is unquestionable that the fact of a Western bishop being declared excommunicate by the occupant of the oldest, most dignified, and most powerful see in Western Christendom could not do other than strengthen the hands of his opponents, and weaken his own position, so as to make it far easier to depose him. In our own day, and in civil affairs, a diplomatic remonstrance from London, Berlin, or St. Petersburg to some minor potentate, say the King of Greece, or the Prince of Bulgaria, would carry great weight, without at all implying the relation of sovereign and vassal between the parties. But we are **not left** even to such a consideration as this: for, curiously enough, the very next Epistle in St. Cyprian's works is a Synodal letter addressed by him to the clergy **and** people of Leon, Astorga, and Merida, in Spain (as far removed from his immediate jurisdiction as Arles from the Pope's), in reply to an application they had made to him as to the best way of dealing with the apostate bishops, Basilides and Martial, who held certificates from the pagan State of having done sacrifice to idols. He gives his full sanction and approval, with that of his Provincial Synod, to what they had done in deposing the offenders, and electing other bishops in their room. He acknowledges Felix and Sabinus as the **true** bishops instead of Basilides and Martial, and, what **is** much more to the point, remarks that Basilides, by going to Rome and deceiving Pope Stephen, utterly ignorant of all the facts, and by persuading him to *canvass*[1] for the restoration of the deprived prelates to their bishoprics (not, be it observed, to *enjoin* it), had merely increased his guilt by adding fraud and misrepresentation **to** his previous **crimes**; while, as regards Pope Stephen himself, his **decision** was inherently unsound, as contradicting a canon enacted by his predecessor Cornelius, with the assent of all contemporary bishops, to the effect that men who had sinned in this way, though admissible to penance and communion, could never be restored to clerical rank.—(*Ep.* lxviii.)

---

[1] *Ut exambiret.*

This is a very remarkable comment on the first clearly authenticated instance of spiritual appeal from a local tribunal to Rome, that (1) the wrong side triumphed there; (2) and did so against the plain Canon law of the case; (3) that an appeal was made to Carthage against the decision at Rome; and (4) that the Pope's sentence was set aside at once, and without argument, as bad and invalid, both in Africa and Spain.

Finally, the latter clause of (b) is rejected by Rigalt and Fell as a gloss which has crept into St. Cyprian's text, while two of the strongest passages alleged from St. Cyprian in favour of Papal supremacy, cited above as though genuine, and disproved on their merits, are, in fact, forgeries and interpolations of a very recent date. They are the quotations (f) and (g). These are absent from forty-five extant MSS., of which eight are in the Vatican Library, and two are more than a thousand years old; as also from every printed edition of St. Cyprian between 1471 and 1563, ten in number, not counting re-impressions, and from citations made of the context by Pope Calixtus II., about 1120, &c. They first appear in the edition of St. Cyprian published by Paul Manutius in 1563, and were consequently omitted by Baluze in his standard edition. But he died while the work was passing through the press, and the Benedictine editors who succeeded him cancelled the leaf, and restored the forgeries, alleging that the words had appeared in all the French editions for 150 years previously, but retaining the note of Baluze as a witness against this fraud. This is far from an exceptional casualty, as will be shown under a separate heading at a future time.[1]

---

[1] These spurious passages of St. Cyprian have been replaced in the text by F. Hurter, S.J., in his *Sanctorum Patrum Opuscula Selecta*, and are cited as genuine by Mr. Allnatt in his *Cathedra Petri*. Their frequent recourse to literary falsification, of which examples will be given later, is itself one of the very strongest arguments against Ultramontanes. Did they themselves believe in the adequacy of the genuine evidence, they would not manufacture forgeries. As a question of dates, the instance given above may be illustrated by a case tried in

7. The next testimony of importance is the case of Paul of Samosata, Bishop of Antioch, charged with heresy and various other offences, and brought to trial in his own city, A.D. 264. The **first** Council which assembled to try him, although the Metropolitan of Cæsarea, **the** Bishop of Jerusalem, and St. Gregory Thaumaturgus were all present, was presided over by that very St. Firmilian whom Pope Stephen had excommunicated, and who had spoken so very forcibly against his doctrine and conduct: a fact which shows how little weight the Papal censure had carried with **it. Paul made a** feigned submission, **but on** its hollowness being detected, a second Council was convoked at Antioch, over which St. Firmilian again presided; while a third was convoked in 269, and the presidency once more offered to **St.** Firmilian, then very aged, who died before he could respond to the invitation.—(Hefele, *Concilienges*. I. ii. 9.) Paul was now deposed and excommunicated, and Domnus, son of Demetrian, a former Bishop of Antioch, elected in his room; while a Synodal Letter, stating what **had** occurred, was addressed to the Popes of Rome and Alexandria. Nevertheless, Paul—herein setting an example faithfully copied by Dr. Colenso sixteen hundred years later—retained possession of the episcopal residence and other temporalities of the see, relying on the favour of Queen Zenobia. The clergy and people appealed to the heathen Emperor Aurelian, as supreme **magistrate in civil** affairs, to adjudicate on the question of **property, and he** decided that the person to whom the Bishops **of** Italy and **Rome** (note the order) should address letters of recogni-

---

Edinburgh **in** June, 1878. A man claimed a debt, and produced an account-book, which he said had been kept regularly from 1866, as would appear from its continuous entries, in proof. Lord Young, the presiding judge, holding the book up to the light, discovered the watermark of 1874 on one of the pages, whereupon the plaintiff's counsel threw up his brief and abandoned the case. An Ultramontane might have argued that the book was an accurate reproduction of the earlier account, not forthcoming, no doubt, but whose disappearance could be satisfactorily explained.

tion should be held **the true** occupant of **the** see, and retain its temporalities. And, accordingly, Paul was expelled by sentence of a civil tribunal.—(Euseb. *Hist. Eccl.* vii. 27–30.)

Here there are some points to be noticed. The Synodal Epistle, still partly extant in Eusebius, makes no further reference to the Pope of Rome than as sending him information, but it does say that the clergy of Antioch had appealed to Maximus **of** Alexandria to come to their assistance. No thought of appeal to Rome seems to have occurred to them, and when the Roman Bishop, in conjunction with those of Italy in general, is appointed to settle the question of fact, it is by the act of a pagan civil ruler, not by the free choice of any ecclesiastical body, **far less** by the spontaneous exercise of an indefeasible right on **his own** part. It has been seriously argued, even by Fleury, that the Emperor's nomination proves that the very Pagans knew communion with the Roman Church to be the test of true Christians. Surely it proves nothing but his notion that persons living at such a distance from Antioch as did the Italian Bishops would probably be more dispassionate arbiters than the Eastern prelates, who had been personally engaged in the controversy. As to the alleged test, the history of SS. Cyprian and Firmilian, just given, refutes it.

FOURTH CENTURY.—Before proceeding to instance special cases which serve as evidence in the matter of privilege during the fourth century, it is desirable to prefix a few remarks on the general polity of the Christian body after the conversion of Constantine the Great.

It **is,** then, matter **of** familiar **knowledge that the** Church **copied** the civil **organization of the Empire in** several important particulars, **and** notably in the manner of parcelling **out** its jurisdictions. The names of exarchate, province, **diocese, metropolis, had all a civil** meaning and application **before they** were employed **as** ecclesiastical terms in nearly **the** same sense, and the Imperial method of ascending appeals, from **the local** to the regionary authorities, had also its ecclesiastical counterpart. But there are three differences between the two, so marked and deliberate, that they cannot fail to strike any one who institutes a dispassionate comparison between them. First, in the civil hierarchy, all rank, authority, and jurisdiction culminated in one supreme head, the Emperor. The Augustus was at once the fountain of honour, of justice, and of power. The greatest magistrates exercised their functions in his name, and were appointed, transferred, or dismissed at his pleasure; there lay an appeal to his personal and final judgment from the most exalted tribunals in the Empire. Resistance to his edicts was high treason, and independence could be acquired by no process short of rebellion, enabling a successful general either to depose his sovereign and usurp the very throne of the Cæsars itself, or at any rate to rend a province or two for a time from the unity of the Empire, and set up there as a rival wearer of the purple.

No parallel to this meets us in the ecclesiastical sphere for many centuries, and the idea of the Empire and the Papacy co-existing as similar, nay, as co-ordinate, powers, the two swords of the Gospel, the sun and moon of the firmament, is a creation of the Hildebrandine era, when it becomes a commonplace.

While the Empire was still Pagan, the magistrates who enforced or connived at persecutions of the Christians were fully aware of this much at least of Church polity, that the Bishop was the person to aim at if they desired to seize the local chief of the illicit religion. And they also knew perfectly well that the Christians of Rome formed the most important and teeming group in the whole body, so that a special prominence attached to their superior; an item of knowledge which accounts for the numerous martyrdoms of early Popes, even after stern historical criticism has retrenched all the names before St. Fabian regarding which no sufficient evidence is producible on that head.

Nevertheless, in all the records preserved to us of the jealous suspicion with which the State watched every detail of Christian usage, no hint is discoverable that this particular charge was ever made, that the Nazarene body acknowledged the sway of a human sovereign other than the Augustus. No question seems ever to have been put to any Pope, such as that which the Procurator of Judæa put to the Master: "Art Thou a king, then?" No such reply as: "My kingdom is not of this world"—curiously inappropriate as it would have been in the mouths of the later Pontiffs, from the Donation of Pippin till the fall of the Temporal Power in 1870—ever appears to have been made on the part of any Pope. Nor does any Christian apologist of early times labour the point, and attempt to allay the apprehension of treason against the Government which an institution like the later Papacy must necessarily have aroused; especially when it is borne in mind that the Roman authorities were quite familiar with just such an office as existing amongst the Jewish community, vested in the Patriarch long settled at Tiberias, who was acknowledged as spiritual head by all the Jews of the Empire, enjoying a revenue levied upon the whole Dispersion, and exercising direct jurisdiction over the most remote synagogues through the means of his legates *a latere*.

Next, the supreme tribunal, devised for legislative and judicial purposes by the Christian body, is wholly inconsistent in theory and in actual working with an absolute ecclesiastical monarchy of any sort. The Synod or Council differed in more than one noticeable point from the Roman Senate and the Jewish Sanhedrin.

It was unlike both these bodies, in that its sessions were intermittent and occasional, summoned for emergencies alone, instead of its being a permanently constituted organization. It was yet more unlike them in its distinctive principle of local representation, which makes it the true parent of the modern Parliament. It is true that the members took their seat in virtue of a certain ecclesiastical rank, but not if that rank were dissociated from actual office in the very district whence they came as delegates. The mere fact of episcopal consecration, or even of past services in an episcopal capacity, did not confer a vote. For that privilege it was necessary to be in actual possession and administration of a diocese; and the special function which each Bishop was expected to discharge from his place in the assembly was to attest, in matter of doctrine, the historical belief current in his diocese; and in matter of discipline to express the conclusions at which he had arrived by conference with his presbyters in their local synod. And thirdly, whereas the Senate never left Rome, nor the Sanhedrin Jerusalem, Church Councils might, and did, meet anywhere.

Such a theory and method as this is fundamentally incompatible with a despotism, which knows nothing of representative assemblies with free right of deliberating and voting. The very clumsiness of this machinery for all executive purposes—a fault inseparable from Parliamentary government—which must have been obvious from the very first, shows that only a conception of the constitution and functions of the Church altogether unlike the Papal one was present to the mind of ancient Christendom. No true despotism has genuine Parliaments. France did not acquire them till after the Restoration, Russia has not got them even now: the specious imitation which has recently been set up in Turkey is as delusive as the Roman Senate, once a free assembly, became when it did but dutifully register the edicts of the Emperor.

Now, if the Christian Synod had been a body in permanent session at Rome, it might be possible to regard it as being the Pope's executive ministry, employed, indeed, in deliberations, but only on such topics as he chose to submit to the members, as a Louis XIV. may have consulted his ministers. Or, without going so far, it might have led up at least to the conclusion that Rome was to Christendom what Jerusalem was to Judaism, and that the Roman See collectively, not merely in the person of its Bishop, exercised as of right a paramount influence in the Catholic Church. But the dispersive franchise, the variable rendezvous, the intermittent session, the equality of voice, the finality of decision, which are the peculiar marks of the Council in its perfected form, all denote an authority not merely independent of, but superior to, the Papacy. For it is a maxim of common sense and expediency, as well as of law, that it is superfluous to employ more force or agents than absolutely necessary to secure a given result: *Frustra fit per plures quod fieri potest per pauciores.* There is no trace whatsoever discoverable in the Gospels of any consultative function amongst the first disciples. Even the Apostles themselves never once appear as in any case a Privy Council or Cabinet to assist their King. They are His mere servants, nearer to His Person, indeed, than the remainder, admitted to more intimate intercourse, favoured with more explicit teaching, endowed, it may be, with greater spiritual gifts. But neither their advice nor their approval is ever asked. They have but to hear and to obey.[1] Contrariwise, no sooner does the Ascension take place, than the consultative and executive Christian assembly shows itself in full session and operation, busied with the task of providing a successor to the seat in the Apostolic College vacated by the fall and suicide of Judas Iscariot (Acts i. 15–26). Clearly, if St. Peter had received the plenitude of teaching and ruling power as Vicar of Christ, in a special sense and degree unshared by the remaining Apostles, we should find Christ's own method still pursued; and Peter, while confessing, it may be, his own unspeakable inferiority to Him whose Vicegerent he had become, would have claimed and exercised exactly Christ's authority, just as a Regent does regal power in the absence of the king. He would, in truth, have had no choice in the

---

[1] Even apart from the issue argued here as to the Councils, the practical working of the Roman Church down to 1870 testifies against Papal supremacy and infallibility. For though a mere Pontifical Brief, of a private or local character, could be issued by the Pope singly, yet an *ex-cathedrâ* Bull, addressed to the Latin Church generally, required for validity the previous consultation and adhesion of the majority of the Cardinals. This fact is given full expression, for instance, in the Bull of Paul III. convoking the Council of Trent, wherein he says that he is conscious of his own weakness and inability to deal with the heavy burden before him, and so has acted with the advice and consent of his venerable brothers, the Cardinals of the Holy Roman Church.

matter, and no plea of humility or unfitness could have excused him from discharging an office to which he had been divinely appointed, and from nominating the new Apostle at once, on his own separate responsibility.

What St. Peter did not, and therefore, **it** may fairly be said, could not do, is consequently not open to any one claiming to be his heir, successor, and representative to do either; a conclusion which not merely settles the question of the superiority of the Church over the Pope, but at once disproves his right to nominate to vacant bishoprics, a privilege which has perhaps wrought more mischief to Latin Christendom than any other arrogated by the Papacy.

Thus, to all persons gifted with legal or historical instinct, **the** mere fact of Councils being held at all is completely subversive of the "Privilege of Peter;" but, as there is a majority which does not possess either of these qualifications for judging of the question, it becomes necessary to adduce the specific disproofs which reinforce this general refutation.

Foremost amongst these, and meeting us almost at the outset of the fourth century, is the peculiar ecclesiastical position assigned to the Christian Emperors by the voluntary cession, nay, at the pressing solicitation, of the clergy, and not by spontaneous usurpation on the part of the State. Three hundred years of Cæsarism had not been without the effect of making a servile temper prevail in every class of society, and amongst the clerical body scarcely less than in civil, legal, and military circles. And, accordingly, when the Episcopate found that mighty power which had long been the implacable foe of Christianity suddenly transformed into a friend by the conversion of Constantine the Great, the reaction was too much **for** it, and it hastened, with too eager precipitation in allying itself to imperialism, to barter away the inherent spiritual freedom of the Church for **the** temporal advantages of Establishment. The like phenomenon is visible on a smaller scale in the adulation with which the Anglican clergy, already demoralised by nearly a century of the Tudor tyranny, greeted the accession of James I., in their joy at finding that he had no mind to favour the Presbyterianism in which he had been reared; but they had the advantage of receiving their chastisement somewhat sooner, in the overthrow of their polity as a consequence of their identification of Church interests with the unconstitutional action of Charles I. The vengeance which fell upon the ancient Church was nearly as swift, far more dangerous, and a great deal more permanent, in the shape of that Arianism which found its surest bulwark and strongest champions in the Imperial palace, or in those episcopal courtiers with whom the influence of the Augustus filled more than half the sees of Christendom. That a fatal Byzantinism, more destructive of all spiritual vitality than the extremest Erastian teaching of modern times, must have inevitably resulted from the subservience of the clergy to the Emperors, had it been persevered in, scarcely admits of question. And it may, therefore, be cheerfully conceded that the rise of the Papacy served as its corrective in the West, and was the less of two evils. But what the fact of this Cæsarism establishes is that no idea of a double personal allegiance, pulling different ways, seems for a moment to have crossed the mind of the ecclesiastical body; for, in truth, the Roman Pontiff was at first, and for a long time, as deep in the mire of servility as any one else. When the Emperors became Arian, or, as in Julian's case, reverted to Paganism itself, the bishops and clergy were, of course, aware then of a conflict of duties; yet that conflict did not consist in the rival claims of two sovereigns, a spiritual and a temporal emperor (as it did later, during the struggle between Gregory VII. and Henry IV.), but in the choice between a creed and a person, between the faith of Nicæa and obedience to Cæsar's will. It would have been absolutely impossible, had an authority existed in the Christian Church of the fourth century at all analogous to the mediæval Papacy, for such ecclesiastical powers to have been lodged in the hands of the Emperors as history records them to have wielded. At the very least, some evidence of protest at so momentous a change, or else some concordat whereby the Roman Pontiff ceded some of his inherent rights to the civil power, would be producible, had the " Privilege of Peter " been a recognised, not to say a predominant, factor in the Church system of the time ; but nothing of the sort is discoverable by the minutest investigation.

On the contrary, the earlier conciliar history of the Church is curiously explicit in traversing certain claims put forward by later Popes as inalienable privileges of the Roman chair. Thus, Leo X., in the Lateran Synod of 1516, lays down that " It is manifestly established that the Roman Pontiff for the time being, as having authority over all Councils, has alone the full power of convoking, transferring, dissolving Councils" (*Conc. Lat. Sess.* xi.). Nor was this a new claim at that time. It had been advanced as early as A.D. 785 by Hadrian I., who affirmed that "by the Lord's command, and the merits of blessed Peter the Apostle, and by manifold decrees of holy Canons and venerable Fathers, the peculiar authority and personal power of assembling synods is delivered to the Pope" (Hadr. I., *ap.* Bin. *Concil.* v. 565). And a similar assertion is perhaps found yet earlier in a letter ascribed to Pelagius II. (*Ep.* viii.) in A.D. 587, whose authenticity is, however, denied by Launoi.

As there is no question at all that precisely this right of convoking, proroguing, and dissolving a mere diocesan synod did belong to each bishop in his own diocese, it follows, as a matter of course, that if the Pope's relation to the whole Church be analogous to that of each Ordinary within each local jurisdiction, and he be supreme and general Ordinary, he must be found to have exercised from the first this power over all Councils which were more than mere diocesan or provincial assemblies. And, by parity of reasoning, every instance producible that he did not, in fact, convoke or direct such Councils goes so far to disprove, not merely this one special claim, but the whole alleged " Privilege of Peter."

It is true that the first introduction of the Emperor as a permanent factor in religious controversy lies at the door of the Donatists, who besought Constantine to send judges from Gaul to Africa to decide between them and Cæcilian (Optat. Milev. *De Schism. Donat.*); an application to which the Emperor acceded in a letter he addressed on the subject to Pope Melchiades (or Miltiades) preserved to us by Eusebius (*Hist. Eccl.* x. 5), which says that he had ordered Cæcilian to sail to Rome with ten bishops of his own side and ten of the accusing party, there to be heard by Melchiades himself, along with three colleagues nominated by the Emperor; namely, Reticius, Bishop of Autun, Maternus of Cologne, and Marinus of Arles.[1]

The decision of this Synod, which acquitted Cæcilian and condemned Donatus, was at once forwarded to the Emperor for approval and confirmation; and thus it appears that though, as just observed, the Donatists began the system of appeal to the State, there was entire acquiescence on the Catholic part, and the Pope himself readily obeyed the Imperial mandate as to the convening of the Synod, the nomination of its members, and the conduct of the dispute whereof cognisance was taken.

In the next year, 314, as the decision of the Synod of Rome had done little or nothing to allay the schism—a fact in itself incidentally proving that the Pope's share in the matter gave no finality to the proceedings in the minds of the disputants—Constantine, again appealed to, summoned Bishops from every part of the empire to meet in another Council at Arles, which was then in fact, though not technically, a General Council (Euseb. *ubi supra*),[2] and at the least did fairly represent Western Christendom. This Council was not only summoned by Constantine, but there seems reason to believe that he may have named its president, the Bishop of the see, that Marinus

---

[1] Bishop Hefele (*Conciliengeschichte*, I. iii. 13) alleges that Constantine in this letter expresses displeasure at being called in as arbiter at all; but no phrase of the sort occurs in it.

[2] St. Augustine calls it "*plenarium Ecclesiæ Universæ concilium*" (*Epist.* xliii.), but perhaps is speaking of Western Christendom only.

who had already taken part in the Roman Synod of the previous year. His signature stands first in the letter of the Council, and precedes that of the four Papal Legates sent by Pope Sylvester—(Mansi, *Concil.* ii. 469, 476). The letter itself, addressed to the Pope in order that he might on its receipt take measures for the publication of its decrees throughout his jurisdiction, is not couched **in** particularly submissive **terms.** It begins thus: "Marinus and the assembly of Bishops who **were gathered in the** town of Arles, to our most holy brother, the **Lord** Sylvester. **We** signify to **you,** dear brother [*caritati **tuæ***], what we have decreed in joint council, that all may know what they **are** henceforth to observe"—(Hefele, *ubi supra*).

Although Donatus was condemned a second time at Arles, his party appealed again from the sentence, and both he and Cæcilian appeared before the Emperor himself at Milan in 316, who gave judgment a third time in favour of the Catholics. That the schismatics should have resisted to the last is not surprising, but the really notable fact is the readiness of the Catholics to accept the sovereign's arbitration, instead of falling back on the two ecclesiastical decisions previously given.

But the chief interest of the inquiry naturally centres in the famous Œcumenical Council of Nicæa, which **is** not only the first ever held, and the most important for Christianity in its issues, but which has invariably been regarded as the most august and authoritative amongst even **General** Councils themselves. Every detail of its history **and** procedure has thus great weight in the establishment **of** precedents, and its testimony upon the matter now in hand is perfectly clear.

In the first place, then, the Council of Nicæa was convoked by the Emperor Constantine himself, and that, as it would appear, acting on the advice of his usual counsellor in ecclesiastical affairs, Hosius, Bishop of Cordova (Hefele, *Concilienges.* **II.** i. 22, 24). The question is raised whether he did this in his own name alone, or in concert with Pope Sylvester. Neither Eusebius nor any of the more ancient documents hints at any participation of Sylvester. But Pope Damasus, if the *Liber Pontificalis* ascribed to him be his, asserts the matter in its first chapter;[1] and it is certain that the sixth General Council in 680 said—but three centuries too late to be evidence—that "Constantine, ever Augustus, and the venerable Sylvester convened the great and conspicuous Synod at Nicæa"—(Hardouin, iii. 1417). It is likely enough that the Pope, as chief Bishop of the West, was communicated with beforehand by the Emperor, but a phrase used by Rufinus deprives even this concession of practical significance, for he says (*H. E.* i. 1) that the Emperor summoned the Council "at the advice of the priests" (*ex sententiâ sacerdotum*), without implying particular reference to any one personage; and it is therefore highly improbable that the two names were coupled in the letter of summons, even in the relative order of the citation given above. For there is not only the mere absence of precise documentary proof, which might perhaps be taken as balancing the arguments on both sides, but such a proceeding on the Emperor's part directly contradicts the course he is known to have pursued in convening the two previous Synods at Rome and Arles, in respect of which no doubt has ever been thrown on the single and independent character of his action. It would be necessary, in order to set aside this plain inference, to show that some great change had come over his own view of the situation, or else over Church policy or sentiment,

---

[1] A piece of evidence, erring by the mistake of being altogether too cogent, has been ingeniously manufactured out of a conjectural various reading of Valesius (ἐπίλεκτοι for ἐπίσκοποι) in the Synodal Letter of Pope Damasus to the Bishops of Illyria, in Theodoret, *Hist. Eccl.* ii. 22. He is made to say that the "three hundred and eighteen Fathers were *selected* by the Bishop of Rome to deliberate at Nicæa." The fact is that if the word ἐπίλεκτοι, and not ἐπίσκοποι, be the true reading in the passage, it must needs run thus: "Our Fathers, three hundred and eighteen Bishops, and also the holy *delegates* of the Romans," *i.e.*, denoting that the Papal legates at Nicæa were *priests* only, and not Bishops.

during the interval between 313 and 325, but no trace of the sort is discoverable.

Next, the solemn session of the Council was opened by the Emperor, and not by any of the Bishops present. Constantine acted as honorary president at first, and then ceded his place to the ecclesiastical " presidents "—(Euseb. *Vit. Const.* iii. 12, 13). Accordingly, Pope Stephen V. speaks of the Emperor as having in fact presided at Nicæa (Hardouin, v. 1119).

Thirdly, the actual ecclesiastical presidency was undoubtedly held by Hosius, Bishop of Cordova. The question here arises whether he held this rank *ex officio* as legate of the Pope, or on any other ground. In favour of the former opinion is this solitary testimony of Gelasius of Cyzicus, a writer of the fifth century, who compiled a history of the Council :—" And Hosius was the representative (ἐπέχων καὶ τὸν τόπον) of the Bishop of Rome, and he was present at the Council of Nicæa, with the two Roman priests, Vitus and Vincentius."

Bishop Hefele, in the Introduction to his *History of the Councils*, lays great stress on this passage, and treats it as practically decisive of the controversy. But, in the body of the work, where he has occasion to cite this same Gelasius on other points, he rejects his testimony as worthless. Thus, speaking of an alleged collection of minutes of a disputation held at Nicæa between some heathen philosophers and Christian Bishops, inserted by Gelasius in his history, he describes them as spurious and apocryphal, and adds that there is no evidence of Gelasius or any one else having seen or used the Synodal Acts of Nicæa, and again, that " he admitted things which were improbable and evidently false "—(*Concilienges.* II. ii. 23).

Once more, Hefele sets aside the evidence of Gelasius as of no value when alleging that the Emperor took part for several months in the Episcopal sessions, and states that this error has arisen from confusing the preliminary meetings, at which Constantine was not present, with the later deliberations, in which he did share—(II. ii. 29).

It so happens that a piece of evidence does exist which decides the controversy. Those who are acquainted with the documentary history of the Nicene Council are aware that the lists of the signatures which have come down to us vary considerably, and bear marks of error and interpolation on the part of copyists. However, Zoëga discovered a list in an ancient Coptic manuscript, whose enumeration appears on the whole the most authentic yet produced, and it has therefore served as a means of interpreting and reconciling those formerly known to exist. Cardinal Pitra has reprinted it in full—(*Spicilegium Solesmense*, vol. i. pp. 513-528). In this the three earliest signatures are thus expressed, agreeing substantially with Mansi's text (II. 692, 697):—" From Spain, **Hosius, of the** city of Cordova: 'I believe thus as is written above.' Vito and Innocentius, Priests: 'We have signed for **our** Bishop, who is **Bishop of Rome; he believes thus as** is written above.'"

Clearly, then, Hosius signed for himself and for no one else. Had he **been** Papal Legate, or even held the Pope's proxy, that fact would have necessarily been stated in his signature as being for himself and the Pope jointly; while the terms of the real legatine signatures plainly show that the two Roman priests were quite unaware of any partner or **superior** in their commission, but signed for the Pope on their own independent responsibility, which is the view of Eusebius, himself a member of the Council, who observes:—" The Prelate of the Imperial City was absent through old age, but his Presbyters were present, and *filled his place*"—(*Vit. Const.* iii. 7). Of course, it may be **freely** admitted that the place occupied by the Roman **signatures, as next to that** of the president himself, does **so far attest** the priority of **rank** accorded to the See which they represented; but it **is to** be noted, as tending to attenuate **even this** evidence, that the known order of rank amongst the provinces is not observed in the list, inasmuch as though Alexandria does come first after the legatine signatures, yet the **Thebaïd,** Libya, Palestine, and Phœnicia are interposed between it and the third Patriarchal See, that of Antioch. If fuller confirmation were required of the view thus set out, it is to be found in the detail respecting the Council of Sardica in 347, preserved for us by St. Athanasius, who tells us (*Apol.* ii. 50) that Hosius of Cordova signed its Acts first, **and** then Julius of Rome, through his legates Archidamus and Philoxenus, thereby clearly distinguishing the nature of the several signatures.

That debate being thus settled, it may be pointed out that **the** humble ecclesiastical **rank of** the Papal legates serves to accentuate another fact which seems to have been overlooked in this connexion, namely, that the Pope had at that time no such control or superiority over any other Bishop as to empower him to send a man of that rank as his mere envoy. The legates of later days have usually been Cardinals (after Cardinals were raised to their anomalous princely rank in the Latin hierarchy, from having been the mere parish priests of certain churches in the city of Rome), Archbishops, or at least Bishops of some distinction. And a Pope of modern times who chose to despatch an officer of the **kind** would have hundreds of such personages at hand, as **his** dependents, to choose from at his discretion.

It cannot be supposed for a moment that Pope Sylvester wished, even had he dared, to cast any slight on the Emperor or on the Council by sending delegates of inferior rank to sit and vote with their ecclesiastical superiors on a footing of equality; far less that he meant **to** insinuate that a priest holding a Papal commission ranked, in virtue thereof, above the Episcopal order; but simply that he had no other kind of envoy at his disposal; all Bishops, however obscure their sees or their persons, being for Synodal purposes his colleagues and equals in power, though inferior in rank of precedence and in general influence; just as the premier Duke and the junior Baron are each other's *peers* in the English House of Lords, whatever dissimilarity may exist in their social consideration.

Lastly, as regards the **formal confirmation of the** Acts of the Council, this **too** was the work of Constantine alone, **and** no hint of any special share **in the** transaction being allotted to the Pope appears in ancient records—(Euseb. *Vit. Const.* iii. 17–19; Socrat. *H. E.* i. 9). But it may be added here, in anticipation of an argument often adduced from the Ultramontane side, that as the object **of all** plenary Councils, whether Œcumenical or not, as **dis**-tinguished from **the** mere local scope of diocesan or even provincial canons and decrees, was **to** attest the consent and bind the practice of all Christendom, it was the invariable usage to send round the Acts to all Bishops who **had** not been present **or represented,** and especially to **such** as occupied Patriarchal and Exarchal **sees,** that their assent and influence might corroborate the proceedings of **the Council.** For it must **be steadily borne in** mind that the mere **enactment of canons by a Council of** ancient **times did not at once** raise **them** to the rank of binding **ecclesiastical laws.** They were **at** best only in the **position** of a British Act of Parliament before receiving **the** Royal assent, while the Sovereign's veto was still a living reality. Only, instead of going specially to the Pope for ratification, the Fathers **of a** Council had, in English Parliamentary idiom, "**to** go to the country," and to apply to the dispersive Church in its several dioceses for approval of their proceedings; and not until this had been given so extensively as to amount to **a general acceptance** of the policy of the Council, could it claim the **title of** Œcumenical, and the obedience of the Christian commonwealth. That the approval of the Roman Pontiff, and **his** confirmation of the Acts and Canons of any plenary Council, would always **be** asked in this fashion, is a necessary consequence of this **method of action, and** it **is** also clear that the unequalled position **of his See in** Western Christendom, giving it a degree of influence extending far beyond its strict Patriarchal boundaries, **would have** made disapproval on **his part a** serious **blow to the** general reception of any Conciliar acts, as he **might** very conceivably have secured their at least partial rejection in the West. But the Ultramontane fallacy lies in habitually **suppressing** the facts that confirmation in this sense does not mean validating that which otherwise would be without force, but signifying adhesion to the Conciliar definitions, thereby strengthening their position; and that appeal for confirmation of exactly the same kind was equally made to all the other Patriarchs and prelates of the Church. A case in point, already cited, serves to illustrate this position; namely, that Pope Leo **II. invited** the Spanish Bishops **to give** local confirmation to the decrees of the Sixth General Council held in 681, and that the **Fourteenth** Council of Toledo in 684 explained that adequate reasons had impeded earlier compliance with the message, but that those Canons had been in the meanwhile carefully studied and approved in the several diocesan synods of Spain, and that the national Council then being held was ready to pass confirmatory decrees. Thus it is evident that some degree of full ratification was still lacking to these decrees of Constantinople, even after they had received Papal approval, till the mind of the Spanish Church had been ascertained, albeit a mere outlying and not very prominent factor at that time in Western Christendom. Indeed, one of the items of evidence cited by Hefele when striving to maintain the Papal assent as an essential of œcumenicity, although itself unauthentic, as he admits (*Concilienges. Einleit.* vi. 1), namely, that five documents, dating from the fifth century, mention a solemn approval of the Acts of Nicæa given by Pope Sylvester and a Roman Synod of **275** Bishops, shows at once that the idea present to the minds of the authors of those documents, whoever they may have been, was not a ratification made by the Pope singly, but **a** local conciliar acceptance by that Western portion of the Church wherein the Roman Pontiff held undisputedly the first place of rank and influence.

It is thus clear that all the facts concerning the **First** General Council, regarding which contemporary evidence and documents are producible, are altogether incompatible with any supremacy of the Roman See; and, although much ingenuity has been exhibited on the part of Ultramontane apologists in constructing an argument out of such unpromising materials, yet even a slight examination shows it to be made up of hypotheses, glosses, and inferences, not of solid events of history.

The next piece of evidence which the fourth century yields is one of those anomalies that are more difficult to reconcile with Curialist theories than even an explicit rejection of Roman claims would be. The Synod of ninety-seven Bishops, chiefly Arian or semi-Arian, which met at Antioch in 341, and which had as its almost openly avowed aim the ruin of St. Athanasius, had no Western prelates, nor any legates from Rome, present at its deliberations, but was encouraged by the sympathy and attendance of the Arian Emperor Constantius.

The Bishops of this Synod sent a letter which cannot be styled other than one of defiance to Pope Julius, in which, after admitting the high repute in which the Roman See was held, as having been a school of the Apostles, and from the first a centre of piety (though even that, they said, was due to its Eastern teachers), they declared it to be unjust that they should be placed in a secondary position, on the ground that they were surpassed in importance and numbers by the Roman Church, seeing that they, in their turn, were superior in merit and resolution, and they offered Julius the choice of peace and communion if he would assent to their decrees, threatening him with excommunication if he refused such compliance—(Sozom. *Hist. Eccl.* iii. 8). So far, no case is made out against the Petrine claims, any more than by the very similar conduct and language of the Oriental Bishops who seceded to Philippopolis from the Council of Sardica six years later; for it may be most reasonably urged in reply that these remonstrants were Arian heretics, and that it is no wonder, seeing that they struck at the Deity of the Lord Himself, they should have also impeached the rights of His Vicar. But here is the real difficulty. This Council of Antioch enacted twenty-five excellent disciplinary Canons; which were rejected by Pope Innocent I. about sixty years later as the work of heretics, but, nevertheless, were recognised as being of such value that they were practically adopted into the general code of the Church, and were finally confirmed as part of that code by the Œcumenical Council of Chalcedon, **since** which time they have been embodied in the **code of the** Roman Church itself. This fact, whose importance **in the** controversy scarcely appears to have received adequate recognition, entirely refutes the claim that Papal confirmation is necessary to the reception of Canons, with all the more force because that claim was first advanced by Pope Julius himself in his reply to the very Epistle from the Synod of Antioch just cited. He alleged therein that "the eccle**siastical** law enjoined that the Churches should not enact Canons without the assent of the Bishop of Rome"—(Socrates, *H. E.* ii. 17); an assertion for which **no docu**mentary proof is forthcoming, and which, therefore, is probably only his way of glossing the principle of dispersive ratification just explained. Nevertheless, it was precisely this Council, whose lawful character he steadily refused to admit, whose Canons, albeit rejected again by one of his successors, made their **way into** such general acceptance that the Council of Chalcedon did not hesitate to give them that authority *de jure* which they already enjoyed *de facto*, so that their subsequent status shows that not merely does the want of Papal confirmation fail to annul a Canon, but that express and reiterated Papal **rejection has** proved insufficient for that purpose.

The next weighty piece of evidence which the fourth century has to show is the fall of **Pope** Liberius in 357, when he not only signed (under **severe pressure** indeed, and as St. Jerome tells us, *Chron.* A.D. 357, through weariness of exile) the Arian creed of the third Council of Sirmium, but also anathematized St. Athanasius; an additional incident which destroys the plea sometimes adduced by Ultramontanes in mitigation, that the creed was patient of **an** orthodox interpretation, and was signed by Liberius in that sense only. It is curious to read the gentle, forgiving, and compassionate language in which St. Athanasius himself speaks of this fall, dwelling in preference on the Pope's earlier confessorship (*Ad Solitar.*),[1] and then contrast it with the burning indignation of St. Hilary of Poitiers. After setting down the text of the letter addressed by Liberius to the Eastern prelates and clergy, wherein that Pope says that "it pleased God to let him know that Athanasius had been justly condemned, and that he had consequently expelled him from communion, and refused to receive his letters," St. Hilary, on reaching the place where Liberius speaks of the Sirmian creed as Catholic, interjects a note thus—["This is the Arian perfidy. This is *my* note, not the apostate's. What follows is by Liberius."] What does follow is the sentence: "This I have willingly received;" whereon St. Hilary again interjects—["I say Anathema to thee, Liberius, and to thy accomplices."] And after setting down a few words more of the letter, the Saint breaks out a third time—["Anathema to thee again, and yet a third time, renegade[2] Liberius"], using similar language yet a fourth time at the close of another letter of Liberius, which he has preserved for us—(St. Hilar. *Oper. Hist. Frag.* vi.)

The importance of this unhappy event lies in its illustration of the failure of the orthodoxy, no less than of the teaching power, claimed for the Roman Pontiff, as also of the manner in which a great Saint and doctor could speak of that personage. So heavy a blow does this fact deal, not merely to the Ultramontane view of the Papacy, but even to the more moderate opinion of the minimising school, that strenuous efforts have been made to set aside

---

[1] It is noticeable that nothing in the language of St. Athanasius points to any consciousness of the destructive shock to the very fabric of Christianity itself necessarily involved in the heresy of the Supreme Teacher of Christendom.

[2] "*Prævaricator.*" St. Hilary himself explains the word elsewhere: "Nos prævaricatores eos existimamus qui susceptam fidem et cognitionem Dei adeptam relinquunt."—*In. Ps.* cxviii. 15, 11.

its evidence. And, accordingly, even such a temperate writer as Hefele deserts history for special pleading when having to deal with it, and endeavours to establish alike the spuriousness of the *Fragments* of St. Hilary (including the letters of Liberius embedded in them) and the substantial orthodoxy of Liberius (*Concilienges.* I. v. 81).[1]

As regards the question of the Pope's actual complicity in heresy, the following is part of the ancient evidence:—

a. St. Athanasius himself cites for us the words **which** Constantius **addressed to** Liberius, explaining the **necessary** result of signature : " Be persuaded and sign against Athanasius, for whoso signs against him thereby embraces with **us the** Arian cause."

b. The Arian Philostorgius (*Epit.* iv. 3) says that both Liberius and Hosius wrote openly against the term *Homoousius*, and against Athanasius himself.

c. Sozomen (*Hist. Eccl.* iv. 15) says that Constantius forced Liberius to declare, in presence of the Eastern Bishops and the Court clergy, that the Son is not consubstantial with the Father.

d. St. Jerome (*Chron.* A.D. 357) says : " Liberius, tædio victus exilii, et in *hæreticam pravitatem* subscribens, Romam quasi victor intravit."

e. The martyrologies of Beda and Hrabanus **Maurus**, speaking of St. Eusebius of Rome, an alleged confessor in the Arian troubles, say : " The birthday of St. Eusebius ... who fulfilled his confession under the Arian Emperor Constantine, through the machinations of the Bishop

---

[1] It is **not** unworthy of remark that Hosius, Bishop of Cordova, who **also** signed one of the Sirmian creeds, though he did not commit the further sin of anathematizing St. Athanasius, and though he bitterly repented his fall, has never been allowed the title of Saint, despite his former eminent piety and services ; whereas the far less distinguished and more guilty Liberius is so reckoned, in virtue of his Popedom. Another point is worthy of mention, that the index to the Paris edition of St. Athanasius (1627) supplies references to the commendatory notices alone concerning Liberius, and gives no direction to the passages where his fall is mentioned.

Liberius, *alike a heretic;*" words substantially found also in the martyrology of Ado, as they once were in the Roman Breviary, from which they were struck out in the sixteenth century, when many other falsifications, all making for the Papal claims, were introduced by Cardinals Baronius and Bellarmine.[1]

As regards the authenticity of St. Hilary's *Fragments*, Bishop Hefele himself, and Stilting the Bollandist, a peculiarly unscrupulous writer, are the only persons who have called it in question; and on the other side are reckoned such Roman Catholic names as Natalis Alexander, Tillemont, Fleury, Dupin, Ceillier, Montfaucon, Coustant, Möhler, Döllinger, Renouf, and Cardinal Newman, not to speak of the entire consensus of Protestant scholars. The objection may therefore be dismissed as having no ground save the inconvenience of acknowledging the facts.

The year 378 supplies a leading example of the manner in which a request from Rome to the civil power, and a cession made in answer to that request, laid the foundation of a jurisdiction later alleged to have been derived by unbroken transmission and divine right from the Prince of the Apostles. After Damasus, by a liberal use of rioting and massacre, had wrested the Popedom from his competitor Ursicinus, the partisans of the latter, who had good reason to question the legality of the tenure of Damasus, made constant appeals for protection to the secular tribunals. Those who sided with Damasus convened a Synod, which drafted a letter to the Emperors Gratian and Valentinian, asking that, inasmuch as they had already given sentence in favour of Damasus and banished his opponents, they would continue to support him, and that by issuing orders to the provincial Bishops either to refer cases affecting the Ursicinists to judges named by the Pope, or else to despatch the suits for decision at Rome itself, should he prefer that course. The Synod urges, as a ground for extending this

---

[1] Cf. Janus, *The Pope and the Council;* Gratry, *Lettres à Mgr. Déchamps.*

favour to Pope Damasus, that he had shown his personal loyalty by submitting his own claim to the Popedom to the decision of the Imperial tribunal, and they alleged that Pope Sylvester had done the same towards Constantine, following the example of St. Paul in his appeal to Cæsar (Mansi, *Concil.*). Gratian accordingly issued an edict, enacting that persons condemned by the Pope, or by any Catholic Synod, and refusing to submit, should thereupon be tried by the metropolitans of the province, or else be compelled to appear at Rome, if summoned thither, and, lastly, be tried by judges whom the Pope should appoint. It will be seen later how a similar grant, of even wider scope, was obtained by another Pope in the following century, but the whole history of this proceeding points to the creation of an entirely new jurisdiction, not the maintenance and sanction of one previously acknowledged and exercised.[1]

The next salient piece of evidence hostile to the Petrine Claims is, however, legally regarded, of far more consequence. It lies in the history of the Second General Council, held at Constantinople in 381. Not even such pleas as apologetic ingenuity has framed in support of the Papal character of the Nicene Synod can be adduced in this instance. The Council itself is of the very highest historical and theological importance; and it is enough to say on this head that on the one hand it is the Creed then recast and amplified which has ever since been regarded as the Christian symbol of highest and widest authority; and on the other, that from the close of its deliberations, Arianism, which had not only maintained itself up to that time within the bosom of the Catholic Church, but had once or twice almost ousted the true flock from the visible fold, was formed, in Cardinal Newman's words, "into a sect exterior to the Catholic Church; and taking refuge among the Barbarian invaders of the Empire, is merged amongst those external enemies of Christianity, whose his-

---

[1] Hardouin, *Conc.* I. 840-843.

tory cannot be regarded as strictly ecclesiastical"—(*History of the Arians*, third edition, p. 405).

In the first place, then, the Second General Council was summoned by the Emperor Theodosius alone. For though the letter of convocation is no longer extant, yet the Synodical letter of the Council itself to the Emperor, which does survive, acknowledges that it was assembled by his command, and asks for confirmation of its acts. And no allegation of any share in the measure can be fairly made on behalf of another; for though Baronius does indeed, in his wonted fashion, assert that the Council assembled in virtue of a Synodal letter from Pope Damasus to Theodosius, extant in Theodoret, *H. E.* v. 9, yet Hefele shows that this refers to a second and minor Synod held in 382 (*Concilienges.* I. vii. 95).

Next, as Theodosius was only co-Emperor with Gratian, who retained the Western part of the Empire as his own domain, the writs of summons ran only in the East, and no strictly Western bishop appears to have been summoned, certainly not the Pope, who was present neither in person nor by legates.

Thirdly, the first president chosen by the Council was Meletius, Patriarch of Antioch, who was repudiated and excommunicated by the Roman Church, which recognised his competitor Paulinus as rightful Bishop of the See. And what emphasizes yet more this entire disregard for the judgment of the Roman Pontiff is that Timothy of Alexandria, albeit superior in precedence to Meletius, did not preside, although present at the Council soon after its sessions opened (Hefele, *ubi supra*). Meletius held the presidency undisputedly till his death, when he was succeeded by Gregory of Nazianzus during his brief tenure of the Patriarchate of Constantinople, and then by Nectarius, next occupant of that dignity; a point of some importance, as marking the deposition of Alexandria from the second rank amongst the Sees of Christendom, which it had held up to that time, and the substitution of Constantinople for it, on purely civil grounds; a change more formally embodied in the third canon of this Council, which thus contains in germ the substance of the more famous twenty-eighth canon of Chalcedon seventy years later.

The Acts of the Council were confirmed by Theodosius alone, and no other sanction is hinted at as necessary by the bishops in the Synodal letter, wherein they say to the Emperor: "In obedience to your letters, we met together at Constantinople .... We pray you now, of your goodness, to confirm by a letter of your Piety the decision of the Synod, that as you have honoured the Church by your letters of convocation, you would thus seal its decisions." There is not merely this negative testimony to the lack of Papal confirmation, but the positive fact that the Roman legates at Chalcedon, when lodging their protest against the twenty-eighth canon of that Council, and confronted when so doing with the cognate third canon of Constantinople, declared that no Constantinopolitan canons were recognised at Rome; while Leo the Great himself, writing to Anatolius of Constantinople, tells him that the document in question was never brought by his predecessors to the knowledge of the Apostolic See (*Epist.* cvi.); and in another letter to the Empress Pulcheria he goes much further, and says—apparently referring to this Council, as well as to that of Chalcedon:—

"The consents of bishops conflicting with the rules of the holy canons enacted at Nicæa, we, in conjunction with your Faithful Piety, make void, and by the authority of blessed Peter the Apostle further quash by a general definition; obeying in all ecclesiastical causes those laws which the Holy Ghost enacted through the three hundred and eighteen bishops to be peacefully observed by all priests; so that if even a much larger number were to decree something different from what they enacted, it should be regarded with no respect, if in any particular divergent from the constitution of the aforesaid."—(*Ep.* lxxix.)

No testimony can be clearer than this to the express rejection of the Constantinopolitan canons by Rome; the only point in St. Leo's letter to be touched on in this place. More than forty years later Felix III. omits Constantinople from the General Councils in his letter to the monks of

Constantinople and **Bithynia** in 485, naming only Nicæa, Ephesus, and Chalcedon; nor does Gelasius I. accord it any more recognition. Every one of the marks of authenticity on modern Roman principles is thus wanting to the Constantinopolitan Synod, and yet it **is neither rejected,** like the Councils of Sirmium and Ariminum, nor just allowed to slide into, as it were, and mingle with, the general mass of authoritative conciliar matter, like those of Laodicea and Gangra, but is reckoned now by **both East and West as a true Œcumenical Council,** and was confessed as such by Popes Vigilius (537–555), Pelagius II. 578–590), and Gregory the Great (590–604). We have two distinct statements, however, from the last-named Pontiff, which show the different estimation in which he held the disciplinary and the dogmatic enactments of the Council. **He** says, on the one hand: "The Roman Church up to the **present** does **not possess, and never** has received, the Canons **or Acts of** that Synod, but has received it in this respect, as **regards its definition** against Macedonius" —(*Epist.* vii. 34). But in another place, now embodied in the Canon Law, St. Gregory says also:—

"As the four books of the Holy Gospel, so I confess that I receive and revere the four Councils: to wit, the Nicene, **wherein the perverse doctrine of Arius is destroyed**; the Constantinopolitan likewise, wherein the error **of** Eunomius and Macedonius **is refuted**; the first Ephesian, wherein the impiety of Nestorius is judged; the Chalcedonian further, wherein **the** false teaching of Eutyches and Dioscorus is rejected, I embrace with **entire** devotion, I maintain with **the** fullest approbation, because on these rises **the** structure of **the Holy** Faith, as on a squared stone, and therein consists the rule of **life and** conduct for every **one.**"—(*Epist.* lib. i. *Regest.* 24. Cited *Decret.* pars i. dist. xv. 2.)

There will be something further to say on this subject when treating of the fifth century, but at present it is sufficient to concentrate attention on the remarkable disproof of the supreme ecclesiastical authority or even influence of the Roman See supplied by the fact that a Council, which not only had not any Papal sanction at the first, but which encountered positive rejection at Rome for nearly two centuries, should have forced its way to the very highest rank and prescription, and be classed now and for thirteen centuries past amongst the paramount title-deeds of the Catholic Church.

A minor controversy, arising out of the fourth canon of this same Council, though of far less crucial importance, may be cited as showing the imperfect hold which Rome had at that time even on the West. It declared the nullity of the consecration of Maximus the Cynic as Patriarch of Constantinople, and of all orders conferred by him in his episcopal character. With this view Pope Damasus agreed, addressing to Ascholius of Thessalonica two letters against the claims of Maximus. But a number of Latin bishops, including St. Ambrose, took the opposite view, and held a Synod in 381, in which they declared themselves in favour of Maximus, rejecting the title of St. Gregory Nazianzen and of his successor Nectarius; a difference not allayed till the Emperor interfered by sending commissaries to Rome to attest the truth of the Acts of a Greek Synod held at Constantinople in 382, which affirmed the legitimacy of the election of Nectarius, to whom the Pope then gave his adhesion, as seemingly did all the Western Bishops. This disregard of Damasus's judgment in the matter exhibited by St. Ambrose and his colleagues in Synod is a matter of which no doubt exists, as we have the Saint's own letter to the Emperor Theodosius (*Ep*. xiii.), in which he puts forward the arguments on behalf of Maximus, and proposes as the solution of the difficulty, not an appeal to the Pope, but a joint Synod of Eastern and Western Bishops, inasmuch as a case concerned with the appointment of the Bishop of so important a See as that of Constantinople was a matter which affected the interests of the whole Church, and ought therefore not to be decided by a mere part of Christendom acting separately. And there is one clause of this letter which is of the highest value, as showing the true character of that appeal of St. Athanasius to Pope Julius which is incessantly cited by Ultramontanes, in despite of the history of Liberius, as proving the recognition even then of the supremacy of the Roman Pontiff as teacher and judge of the Church universal. St. Ambrose brings in, as a mere illustration of that course of a fair hearing in a Synod of Eastern and Western Bishops, which he thinks should have been taken with Maximus, this remark: [He would have had a right to this], "even if no Council had been summoned, according to the law and custom of our predecessors, just as Athanasius of holy memory, and a little while ago Peter, both of them Bishops of the Church of Alexandria, and several of the Easterns did, so that it was evident that they had recourse to the judgment of the Church of Rome, Italy, and the entire West." It was thus not the sentence of a single prelate, however august his see, which St. Athanasius sought in his appeal, but the moral support of one geographical half of Christendom. Another phrase in the same letter explains what amount of interference on the part of the West in the affairs of Eastern Christendom was thought reasonable by St. Ambrose: "We do not claim a prior right to judge (*prærogativam examinis*); but there ought to be concurrence and a joint decision."

And in a Council held in the next year, 382, at Constantinople by a large number of the same Bishops as had sat in the Œcumenical Council of 381, the Eastern Bishops, explaining, in a synodical letter to Pope Damasus and other Western Bishops in Synod at Rome, their action in the matter of filling the Sees of Constantinople and Antioch, peremptorily set aside, as an unjustifiable intrusion, forbidden by the Nicene Canons, the attempt of the West to have a voice in these elections; while they also incidentally use a phrase contradictory of another Roman claim, speaking as they do of "the Church in Jerusalem, the Mother of all Churches"—(Theodoret. *H. E.* v. 9). This letter, explicit as it was in repudiating not merely jurisdiction, but even interposition, from Rome, was nevertheless admitted by the Roman Council to which it was addressed, instead of being treated as a flagrant act of schismatic revolt.

This account of the testimonies in the fourth century against the Petrine claims, then just beginning to be consolidated and put forward by such Popes as Damasus and Siricius,[1] may fitly close with two circumstances, in themselves of no great importance, but interesting for the great name to which they belong; namely, that St. John Chrysostom was ordained in 381 as reader by Meletius of Antioch, at that time excommunicated by Rome, and as Priest in 386 by Flavian of Antioch, also disavowed by Rome as a schismatic; but neither of these facts was held to disqualify him from elevation to the Patriarchate of Constantinople, to which he was consecrated by Theophilus of Alexandria in 398.

---

[1] This Pope issued in 386 the first authentic papal Decretal, addressed to Himerius, Bishop of Tarragona, in reply to a letter from that prelate to Pope Damasus, consulting him on various doubtful points of usage in matters of church discipline. The Pope's reply is that of an authoritative superior, who expects that the Roman usages are to be submissively followed everywhere, and in fact he directs Himerius to communicate the rescript to all the Spanish Churches. This is a distinct step forward, though the same claim appears in germ as early as Pope Stephen I.'s dispute with the Church of Carthage.

CHAPTER V.

LACK OF PROOF FOR ST. PETER'S EPISCOPATE AT ROME.

THUS the four great sources of historical appeal, to wit, the wording of the ancient Liturgies; the glosses of the early Fathers and Doctors of the Church on the alleged Petrine charter in the Gospels; the Canons of all the most important Synods ever held in the Church before the era of the Reformation, including every one of the true Œcumenical Councils, and the acts of these same Synods, those of Popes, and of eminent Fathers, are all clear in their disproof of claims made for the divine supremacy and infallibility of the occupant of the Roman See, even on the assumption that he is, in virtue of that position, the successor and heir of St. Peter himself—an assumption by no means adequately sustainable.

For, in point of fact, we have no right to make any such assumption at all. The contention on the Ultramontane part, it must be incessantly repeated, is twofold: that the Papal claims are of the nature of *privilege*, and that privilege one *divinely* revealed. It has been shown already that Roman Canon law hedges every claim of privilege round with the most stringent requirements of documentary and illustrative proof, and within the narrowest limits of interpretation and exercise; and also that the tokens of *revelation* which it requires in all other cases are the express letter of Holy Scripture, and—in some instances *or*—the unanimous tradition of the Church Universal. Dreams, visions, miracles, may be, and often are, alleged as ground enough for the canonization of a departed believer, or for the licensing of some popular devotion, but not for the establishment of any doctrine as an integral part of the

Catholic faith, much **less in proof of** such a strictly legal claim as that of privilege, **which** from its very nature cannot grow and develop as a prescriptive right often may do, but must always remain within its original limits, unless a fresh grant can be adduced. Thus, for example, **an** English nobleman whose ancestor had been created **a** simple baron, might gradually become, from the antiquity and alliances of his family, from wealthy marriages and inheritances, **and** from a succession of able and distinguished holders **of** the title, a personage and head of a house of much greater social importance **than** many persons of far higher rank in the **peerage. But** that fact **would not** *make* him a duke, marquis, **earl,** or even viscount, **unless a** fresh patent from the Crown conferring that additional dignity, with its attendant privileges, were issued. He could never *grow* into a duke, though he might grow into being a millionaire, or the chief personage in his county. And, similarly, no proof from Church history of vast powers actually exercised by the Popes, nor the clearest evidence of still larger claims having been habitually advanced by themselves or others on their behalf, is a single step towards establishing the existence of a *privilege*. It is ample, **and more** than ample, testimony for the growth of a *prescriptive* right, **but** that form of claim is specifically rejected and declared heretical as a tenet by the Vatican decrees, which teach that there **has** been no increase or "ripening" of the authority wielded **by the** earliest Pontiffs, whose primacy was, they say, **a** supremacy from the very first.[1] Of their own choice the Popes have elected to rest their case on the "privilege of Peter"; and even were

---

[1] "We renew the definition **of** the General Council of Florence, that the Holy Apostolic See and the Roman Pontiff hold the primacy **over** the whole world, and that the Roman Pontiff himself is the successor of blessed Peter, Prince of the Apostles, and the true Vicar **of** Christ and Head **of the** whole Church, and father and teacher of all Christians, and **that full** power was given to him in blessed Peter by the Lord Jesus Christ of feeding, ruling, and **governing,** the Church Universal."—*Decret. Conc. Vatic. de Ecclesia.*

not the evidence already adduced fatally adverse to the existence of any such privilege—saving that honourable priority in missionary work amongst Jews and Gentiles which is the peculiar and inalienable glory of Simon Bar-Jona—there are two huge gaps in the further testimony, which make the production of a continuous chain of proof quite impossible. These gaps are the lack of proof that St. Peter was ever Bishop of Rome, and that having received authority to transmit his peculiar privilege, whatever it was, to his successors in that office, he did in fact do so.

Let us take these points in order. It is plain, as regards the first of them, that Holy Scripture is absolutely and ominously silent,—nay, that it contains very strongly adverse presumptive evidence. Not merely is there nothing positive to connect St. Peter personally with the city of Rome, as has already been mentioned, except the one ambiguous and disputed reference to Babylon in his first Epistle, but there are certain negative statements which are scarcely reconcilable on any hypothesis with the Ultramontane assertion that St. Peter did actually sit as Bishop of Rome for twenty-five years, dying there as a martyr by crucifixion on the very same day, June 29, A.D. 67, as that on which St. Paul was beheaded. The first difficulty is that St. Peter appears as still residing at Jerusalem in A.D. 52, the date of the Council described in Acts xv. 6-30, and considerably later as being at Antioch (Gal. ii. 11), which does not give time for the five-and-twenty years required, necessarily beginning in A.D. 41 or 42. It is possible, of course, that these appearances at Jerusalem and Antioch *may* have been brief missionary journeys back to the East from Rome, but that is mere conjectural hypothesis, not Scriptural proof; as also is a modern theory, that St. Peter and the whole infant Roman Church founded by him in A.D. 44, were included in the expulsion of the Jews from Rome by Claudius in A.D. 52, that some of these Christians returned in 57, and also St. Peter himself to die in 69, a year or two after St. Paul's martyrdom, and twenty-five years after his own first visit.—(Mr. E. B. Birks, in the *Academy*, September 15, 1877.) This is a bold and ingenious guess, but contradicts much of the scanty evidence which we have remaining, and notably the silence of St. Paul and the Acts as to the first and second points, which could scarcely have been omitted, as will be noted presently.[1] The second difficulty has been stated already, that whereas Rome was the chief of Gentile Churches, St. Peter's jurisdiction was after a time divinely restricted to the Church of the Circumcision (Gal. ii. 7, 8, 9), and could not, so far as we are entitled to judge, be thenceforward exercised over any Gentile Church, unless St. Peter had survived the separate existence of Jewish Christianity, instead of being overlived by it for at least fifty years. Thirdly, the Epistle of St. Paul to the Romans, in the opinion of the best critics, was written about A.D. 57 or 58. The note prefixed to it in the Douai Version assigns it to about the twenty-fourth year after the Ascension, that is to say, A.D. 55. But this Epistle is entirely silent as to the presence of St. Peter or of any other Apostle at Rome then or previously. St. Paul expresses his longing to impart unto them a certain "spiritual gift, to the end that they

---

[1] As the purport of the Acts is to record the genesis and development of the primeval Christian Church, and to give all the really important facts thereof, it follows that even if the tradition which brings St. Peter to Rome in A.D., 42 or 44, be true, that event cannot have been of any special significance, marking a fresh departure in Church history. He can have effected nothing more than the constitution of a synagogue of Christian Jews at Rome, this not being a sufficiently notable circumstance to require mention as a fresh missionary campaign and victory. The fact that the Second Epistle of St. Peter is amongst the disputed books of the New Testament, and that St. Jerome, whose warm attachment to the Church of Rome makes certain that the opinion of that Church would weigh much with him, is one of those who doubt its genuineness (*De Vir. Illust.* i.), is strong presumptive evidence against St. Peter having been at Rome when it was written. For if he had been there, the local Church must needs have been in a position to say whether he had or had not addressed such an Epistle thence to the whole Catholic Church ; and this single attestation would have ended the controversy. Clearly nothing more was known at Rome than elsewhere on the point.

may be established" (Rom. i. 11)—words which most probably and reasonably denote his purpose to administer *Confirmation* to them, as SS. Peter and John had done to the Samaritans—a grace (τι χάρισμα πνευματικόν is the phrase employed) then bestowed by Apostolic hands alone, and incidentally proving that, as just said, no Apostle had yet reached the imperial city. Next, he declares his readiness (Rom. i. 15) to preach the Gospel at Rome exactly as he had done elsewhere, and adds that it was his custom not to preach in any place where another preacher had been before him "lest I should build upon another man's foundation" (xv. 20)—that this was a fixed principle with St. Paul appears from another passage, where he says: "Having hope, when your faith is increased, that we shall be enlarged by you *according to our rule* abundantly, to preach the Gospel in the regions beyond you, and not to boast in another man's line of things made ready to our hand" (2 Cor. x. 15, 16); demands their obedience to himself on the ground of his rank as "the Apostle of the Gentiles" (Rom. i. 5, 6, 7; xi. 13); and while sending greetings to various individuals, families, and even whole congregations in the city (Rom. xvi. 3–16), is entirely mute as to any central or presiding authority amongst them, such as the bishops and elders referred to in other Epistles, albeit Andronicus and Junias, "of note amongst the Apostles" (xvi. 7), are named as residing there, most probably as prisoners. This absence of all mention of any regular Church officers and organization is alone enough to disprove the hypothesis that there was already a settled Church of Rome founded by St. Peter in A.D. 42. The narrative in the last chapter of the Acts brings the chronology down some years further, as far as A.D. 61, but the account of St. Paul's arrival at Rome contains no hint that St. Peter came or sent to him, and actually tells us that the chiefs of the Jewish community there had no more certain acquaintance with the new sect than that "everywhere it is spoken against" (Acts xxviii. 22)—a degree of ignorance altogether inexplicable if the great preacher on the Day of Pentecost had been settled amongst them as a missionary for nearly twenty years. Nor does the negative evidence cease here. Four, perhaps five, of St. Paul's Epistles seem to have been written during his confinement at Rome—namely, Colossians, Ephesians, Philippians, Philemon, and 2 Timothy, bringing the date down to the very eve of the Apostle's martyrdom ("For I am now ready to be offered, and the time of my departure is at hand"—2 Tim. iv. 6), A.D. 65 or 66, but there is still the same absolute silence regarding St. Peter, though St. Paul sends greetings to the Philippians from "all the saints" at Rome (Phil. iv. 22). He mentions in Colossians that his "*only* fellow-workers" are his messengers to them, Tychicus and Onesimus, together with Aristarchus, Marcus, Jesus called Justus, Epaphras, Luke, and Demas—Coloss. iv. 7, 9–15; and in 2 Timothy, "only Luke" is left (2 Tim. iv. 11); for which reason he asks that Mark may be brought by Timothy to Rome as a worker. The entire unconsciousness which this chain of evidence, from A.D. 58 to 65, displays on St. Paul's part of a fact of such first-rate importance to Christianity as St. Peter's presence at Rome as the long-settled chief of the Christian community there, and in fact as head of all Christendom, must on any hypothesis have been, requires that the proof which outweighs such accumulated negative testimony shall be copious, explicit, and cogent. As a fact, it is so scanty, vague, and uncertain, that many eminent scholars have refused to believe that St. Peter was ever so much as even a visitor at Rome; but in this they may be suspected of controversial prejudice and bias.

The whole of the extant evidence on the subject will now be set down, and an attempt made to appraise its value:—

1. ST. IGNATIUS († *circa* 107).—" I do not, like Peter and Paul, issue commandments unto you."—*Epistle to the Romans*, iv.

2. ST. DIONYSIUS OF CORINTH (*circa* 165).—" Therefore, you also have by such admonition joined in close union [the Churches] that were planted by Peter and Paul, that of the Romans and that of the

Corinthians: for both of them went to our Corinth, and taught us in the same way as they taught you when they went to Italy, and having taught you, they suffered martyrdom at the same time."—*Epistle to the Roman Church.*

3. ST. IRENÆUS († 202).—(*a.*) "Peter and Paul were preaching at Rome, and laying the foundation of the Church."—*Cont. Hæres.* III. i. 1. (*b.*) "Indicating that tradition derived from the Apostles, of the very great, very ancient, and universally known Church, founded and organised at Rome by the two most glorious Apostles, Peter and Paul."—*Cont. Hæres.* III. iii. 2. (*c.*) "The blessed Apostles, then, having founded and built up the Church, committed into the hands of Linus the office of the Episcopate. Of this Linus, Paul makes mention in the Epistles to Timothy. To him succeeded Anacletus, and after him, in the third place from the Apostles, Clement was assigned the bishopric."—*Cont. Hær.* iii. 3.[1]

4. CAIUS, a learned Roman presbyter (*circa* 200), cited by Eusebius, and conjectured, not without probability, to be indeed St. Hippolytus.[2] "But I can show the trophies of the Apostles. For, if you go to the Vatican, or to the Ostian Road, you will find the trophies of those

---

[1] The historical value of this testimony of St. Irenæus is much weakened by a passage in an earlier part of his great work, where he asserts that all the elders who knew St. John testify that Our Lord's ministry lasted from His thirtieth year till He was between forty and fifty (II. xxii. 5); that is, for more than ten years; whereas we have certain fixed chronological data in the Gospels to disprove this view: for the Baptist's ministry began in the fifteenth year of Tiberius Cæsar (A.D. 28; or, if that reign be counted from the association of Tiberius with Augustus in the Empire, A.D. 26) and preceded that of Christ. But Pontius Pilate was appointed Procurator of Judea in A.D. 25, and recalled in A.D. 34, and as his government covered the whole period of Our Lord's public ministry, the furthest possible range is seven clear years, which would make Our Lord still under forty at His death, which is fixed by other data to A.D. 30. And the received view of the Roman Church is that A.D. 29 is the true date, following the statements of Tertullian, St. Clement of Alexandria, Julius Africanus, and Lactantius, thereby rejecting the testimony of St. Irenæus on a point where he must certainly have had more evidence to guide him than in his chronology of the Popes; for although he obtained the latter in mature life, and almost certainly at Rome itself, yet it is clear that the documents there, a very little later, did not agree with his statement.

[2] Professor Gwynn, however, appears to have proved by investigation of the "Heads against Caius," that they are distinct persons.

who have laid the foundation of the Church."[1]—Euseb. *Hist. Eccl.* ii. 25.

5. TERTULLIAN († *circa* 218).—(*a.*) "The Church of Rome, in like manner, makes Clement to have been ordained by Peter."—*De Præscr. Hær.* 32. (*b.*) "Happy Church [of Rome], in which Apostles poured forth their teaching with their blood ; where Peter is made equal to the Passion of the Lord, where Paul is crowned with the departure of John [the Baptist]."—*De Præscr. Hær.* 36. (*c.*) "The Romans . . . . to whom both Peter and Paul left the Gospel, sealed with their blood."—*Adv. Marcion.* II. iv. 5.

6. ST. CLEMENT OF ALEXANDRIA († *circa* 220) is cited by Eusebius (see later) as mentioning St. Peter's visit to Rome to contend with Simon Magus.

7. ST. CYPRIAN (A.D. 250).—"Cornelius was made bishop . . . . when the place of Fabian, that is, the place of Peter, and the grade of the sacerdotal chair, was vacant."

8. *Fragment of the* "PSEUDO-HIPPOLYTUS" (*circa* 250, but in truth a late forgery, borrowed from Origen, see below).—"Peter preached the Gospel in Pontus, and Galatia, and Cappadocia, and Bithynia, and Italy, and Asia, and was afterwards crucified by Nero in Rome, with his head downwards, and he had himself desired to suffer in that manner."—*On the Twelve Apostles.*

9. ORIGEN († 254).—"Peter seems to have preached to the Jews of the Dispersion throughout Pontus, Galatia, Bithynia, Cappadocia and Asia, who also, coming at last to Rome, was crucified with his head downwards, having of himself requested to suffer in this manner." —*Comm. in Genesin,* iii., ap. Euseb. *Eccl. Hist.* iii. 1.

10. ARNOBIUS († 307).—"In Rome itself . . . . they have hastened to give up their ancestral customs, and to join themselves to Christian truth, for they had seen the chariot of Simon Magus and his fiery car blown into pieces by the mouth of Peter."—*Adv. Gentes,* ii. 12.

11. ST. PETER OF ALEXANDRIA († 311).—"Thus Peter, the first of the Apostles, having been often arrested and cast into prison, and treated with ignominy, was last of all crucified at Rome."—*Epist. Canon.* Can. ix.

12. LACTANTIUS (320).—"His Apostles were dispersed throughout all the earth to preach the Gospel . . . . and during twenty-five years, and until the beginning of the reign of the Emperor Nero, they occupied themselves in laying the foundation of the Church in every

---

[1] There is an ambiguity here, for the terms "trophy," or "martyrium," are often applied to churches dedicated to the memory of Saints, without implying that their bodies were buried there. Cf. Euseb. *Vit. Const.* lvii.–ix. ; so St. Chrysost. *Hom.* xxvii. in 2 Cor. ; St. August., *Sermons* 296 and 322.

city and province. And while **Nero** reigned, the Apostle Peter came to Rome, and, through the power of God committed unto him, wrought certain miracles, **and, by turning** many to **the** true faith, built up a faithful and steadfast temple to the Lord. When Nero heard of these things . . . . he crucified Peter and slew Paul."—*De Mort. Persecut.* ii.

13. *Apostolical Constitutions.*—" And **Simon** [Magus] meeting **me**, Peter, first at Cæsarea Stratonis . . . . there being with me . . . . Nicetus and Aquila, brethren of Clement, the bishop and **citizen of** Rome, **who was the** disciple of Paul, our fellow-apostle and **fellow-helper** in **the** Gospel, **I** thrice discoursed before them with him . . . . and **when I** had overcome him . . . . I drove him away into Italy. Now, when he was at Rome, he commanded that the people should **bring me** also by force into the theatre, and promised that he would **fly in the** air, and when all the people were in suspense at this, I prayed **by myself."** **Then** follows the legend of Simon Magus's fall. *Apost.* **Const. vi.** 9. "**Of** the Church of the **Romans**, Linus, son of Claudia, was the first [Bishop], ordained **by Paul ; and** Clemens, after Linus's death, the second, ordained by me, **Peter**."—vii. 46.

14. *Clementine Homilies.*—" Simon, who . . . . was set apart **to be the foundation** of the Church, **and for this end** was by Jesus Himself, with His truthful **mouth**, named Peter . . . . having come **as far as Rome** . . . . by violence exchanged this present existence for life. But **about that** time, when he was about to die, the brethren being assembled together, he suddenly seized my hand, and rose up, and said in presence **of the** Church : ' Hear me, brethren and fellow-servants . . . . I lay **hands** on this Clement **as** your Bishop, and **to** him I intrust my chair of discourse. . . . . I communicate to **him** the power of binding **and** loosing, so that with respect to everything which he shall ordain on the earth, it shall be decreed in the **heavens.'"** —*Epistle to St. James*, i. and ii.

This is the *whole* of the ante-Nicene evidence now extant ; for though there **is an** obscure reference to St. Peter's martyrdom in the **Muratorian** fragment, it throws no light on the question.[1] And it will be observed that out of the *nineteen* passages of which it consists, *six* mention only St. Peter's martyrdom at **Rome**, saying nothing whatever of any relation of his to the Church of that city ; *three* mention the legend of his contest with Simon Magus as the single interesting fact of his Roman sojourn ;

---

[1] " Sicut et semote passionem Petri evidenter declarat [Lucas], sed et profectionem **Pauli** ab-urbe ad Spaniam profisciscentis." Here St. Paul's connexion with Rome is implied, but not St. Peter's.

five name St. Paul in terms of absolute equality with St. Peter in their relation to Rome, but do not define that relation in any way, while one of these five makes Linus, the first Pope, St. Paul's nominee ; *one* speaks of St. Peter as having been a worker of miracles and a successful preacher at Rome, which *one* somewhat vaguely describes as his place or see (*locus Petri*); and just *three* speak of him as having ordained Clement as bishop; while there is only *one* of these three which plainly states in express terms his having been himself bishop there, and as having appointed Clement as his heir and successor, clothed with all his own authority. But that one is in the apocryphal *Clementine Homilies*, condemned by Pope Gelasius in the Roman Council of 496, and ever since rejected by the Roman Church as the forgery of heretics. And even it is preceded, only a few lines earlier, by the dedication professing to be from Pope Clement to the Apostle James :—
" Clement to James, the lord and the bishop of bishops, who rules Jerusalem, the Holy Church of the Hebrews, and the Churches everywhere excellently founded by the providence of God, with the elders and deacons, and the rest of the brethren, peace be always"; so that if the authenticity of the document were satisfactorily proved, it would follow that the Pope, albeit the successor of St. Peter, was subordinate to the Apostle St. James, as head of the Church of the Circumcision, and, in right of his see at Jerusalem, head also of all other Churches throughout the world. As regards the two other testimonies to St. Clement's ordination by St. Peter, the modern Roman Church, by counting St. Linus first and St. Clement third in order of succession, implicitly rejects them, leaving itself thus no ante-Nicene witness except St. Irenæus (3 c.), from whom however, it has departed, as will be seen (and that at least so far back as fifteen hundred years ago), in two crucial particulars, and thus has destroyed with its own hand its one solitary appeal.

And it is further to be observed that the *Apostolical Constitutions* contradict the *Clementine Homilies* (and indeed themselves also) on two important historical issues, for they represent St. Peter as calling Clement already Bishop of Rome, before his own journey thither, and St. Paul's disciple, not his.

Finally, in that which is the clearest item of the testimony adduced, that of St. Dionysius of Corinth, that eminent saint declares that the joint relation of St. Peter and St. Paul to Rome was exactly the same as that which they both bore to Corinth, which Church they had united in planting and organizing. But we learn from the Acts, and from the Epistles to the Corinthians, that St. Paul was the original evangelizer and chief ecclesiastical authority in the Corinthian Church, though St. Peter's influence there is expressly recognised also (1 Cor. i. 12; iii. 22), while not so much as the vaguest tradition points to either Apostle as ever having been locally Bishop there.

Consequently, no tittle of proof is derivable from the fairly copious remains of the ecclesiastical literature of the first three centuries, that St. Peter was ever Bishop of Rome, or that he transmitted the peculiar privilege of supremacy and infallibility to his successors in the see. Yet, given the manifest importance of the event, historically and doctrinally, on Ultramontane grounds, it must have been mentioned, more or less explicitly, by the writers cited above, and by others also, if it were true in fact. And if it be urged that the destruction of early Christian literature has been so widespread that there may once have been abundant proofs of the matter in dispute, now lost to us, the reply is conclusive, that in questions of privilege, by Canon law, the document to prove it must be produced, and cannot be merely guessed at as having possibly existed; while, on the other hand, it is equally conceivable that the additional testimony, were it extant, would be unfavourable to the Petrine claims. The documents we still possess are adequate to convince any mind not biassed by controversial prejudice that St. Peter ended his career at Rome, and by martyrdom, especially as no competing tradition exists, and to make it at least highly probable that he had some share in preaching the Gospel amongst its teeming myriads, as also in building up the infant community. There is, moreover, in much likelihood, a residuum of truth in the story of his contest with Simon Magus (though not at Rome, for the oldest **form of the legend** places its scene in Asia), but more than this **cannot be** extracted from the ante-Nicene era, save by **relying on the** one document which the Roman Church **has formally repudiated**. As we come lower down, **the statements do get** more precise, **but** it has to be borne **in mind, on the** one hand, that historical testimony to **matters of fact** decreases rapidly in value **as** it recedes further **from** contemporaneous evidence, and, on the other, **that even mere** opinions upon **such** events as would go to increase the dignity and influence **of** any place, corporation, or person, have always a tendency to grow, to solidify, and to be put forward as ascertained facts by those chiefly concerned, without any deliberate intention to deceive, but from the natural working of interested bias.

In the Nicene **era** itself the only witness of importance **is** Eusebius(† *circa* 338), and great as were his abilities, vast as was his learning, and unique as are his services to Christian literature, the fact remains that he is a singularly untrustworthy writer, who may be compared to Burnet for habitual and **even wilful** inaccuracy, and who therefore cannot, in face of the many **errors** which have been **detected** in his narrative, **be** accepted as conclusive upon **any** point resting on his unsupported statements. Such is **the** judgment of critics like Scaliger. What Eusebius has to tell us is:

(*a*.) "That immediately under the reign of Claudius [*i.e.* A.D. 42] by the benign and gracious providence of God, Peter, that mighty and great Apostle, who by his courage took the lead of all the rest, was conducted to Rome against this pest of mankind [Simon Magus]. . . . So greatly did the splendour of piety enlighten the minds of Peter's hearers . . . that they persevered . . . to solicit Mark, **as** the companion of Peter, whose Gospel we have, that he should leave them a record **in** writing of the doctrine thus communicated by word of mouth. . . . This account is given by Clement in the sixth book of his *Institutions*,[1] whose testimony is corroborated also by that of Papias, Bishop of Hierapolis. But Peter makes mention of Mark in the first Epistle, which he is also said to have composed at the same city of Rome, and that he shows this fact by calling that city, with an unusual figure of speech, Babylon."—*Hist. Eccl.* ii. 14, 15.

(*b.*) "The same author [Philo], in the reign of Claudius, is also said to have had familiar conversation with Peter at Rome, whilst he was preaching the Gospel to the inhabitants of that city. Nor is this at all improbable."—*Hist. Eccl.* ii. 17.

(*c.*) "Nero was led on in his rage to slaughter the Apostles: Paul is therefore said to have been beheaded at Rome, and Peter to have been crucified under him. And this account is confirmed by the fact that the names of Peter and Paul still remain in the cemeteries of that city even to this day."—*Hist. Eccl.* ii. 25.

(*d.*) "After the martyrdom of Paul and Peter, Linus was the first that received the episcopate at Rome."—*Hist. Eccl.* iii. 2.

(*e.*) "During this time [Trajan's reign] Clement was yet Bishop of the Romans, who was also the third that held the episcopate there after Paul and Peter, Linus being the first and Anacletus next in order."—*Hist. Eccl.* iii. 21.

(*f.*) "After Evaristus had completed the eighth year as Bishop of Rome, he was succeeded in the episcopate by Alexander, the sixth in succession from Peter and Paul."—*Hist. Eccl.* iv. 1.

These six passages leave the episcopate of St. Peter as indeterminate as the ante-Nicene citations do. Their one support to the Ultramontane view is the statement (*a*) that St. Peter was at Rome as early as the beginning (second year) of the reign of Claudius, which would, no doubt, give time for the five-and-twenty years' session at Rome afterwards ascribed to him. But Pagi, in his note on Baronius under A.D. 43, shows that this opinion of Eusebius contradicts the chronology of the Acts (according to which St. Peter remained in Judæa and Syria till after the death of Herod Agrippa I., in the *fourth* year of Claudius); the express statement of Lactantius that St. Peter did not arrive in Rome till Nero's reign; the date in the *Paschal Chronicle* (which declares that the Apostles did not break up their College at Jerusalem until after the Council there in the *sixth* year of Claudius); and the utter silence of all ancient

---

[1] Ὑποτυπωσέων, not extant.

writers as to the double journey of St. Peter to Rome involved by it.

There remains, however, another testimony, going under the name of Eusebius, which is the real basis of the Ultramontane claim. In St. Jerome's Latin version of the *Chronicon* of that author, under the year 40, we read as follows: " Peter the Apostle, after he had first founded the Church of Antioch, is sent to Rome, and preaching the Gospel there, he abode as bishop for twenty-five years." This agrees with the independent Armenian version, except that the latter gives *twenty* years, but when counted up there are twenty-seven. The Syriac epitome, however, gives twenty-five years. But the Greek of George Syncellus disagrees with the Latin in several particulars, and runs thus: " Peter, the chief, having first founded the Church at Antioch, departs to Rome, preaching the Gospel, and this same person, after being first of the Church at Antioch, presided also over that of Rome until his death."

There are two or three things to be considered in estimating the value of these entries. First of all, that a chronicle, being intended as a book of frequent reference, is specially liable to alteration by copyists, who constantly add in matter which they think ought to be entered under the several years, and even bring the annals down to their own date; next, the discrepancies just cited; and, thirdly, the entire silence of Eusebius in his own more detailed history on the points here added, all which make it tolerably certain that we have here an interpolation of an unknown scribe at some unascertained, though doubtless early, date. And Pagi, following Baluze, both of them eminent Roman Catholic scholars, suggests that the notion of the twenty-five years' session of St. Peter arose from a hasty inference drawn from the passage of Lactantius above cited—where, however, these twenty-five years are counted from the first dispersion of all the Apostles on their missionary journeys until the reign of Nero, and have no special reference to St. Peter. In the genuine narrative of Eusebius it is to be noted that St. Paul's name twice precedes that of St. Peter, and their authority at Rome is said to be jointly exercised. And it is a curious fact, mentioned by Baronius and cited by Valesius in his notes to Eusebius, that on the most ancient seals of the Roman Church, whenever SS. Peter and Paul are engraved, the right hand, or place of honour, is given to St. Paul. There is a remarkable gloss on this fact by Cardinal St. Peter Damiani († 1072), explaining it thus: that whereas Jerusalem might rightfully seem the primary see of Christendom, and yet has but the fifth place, while Rome is first; this is because Christ is equally Head of all Churches, and not of one alone, and thus St. Peter's privilege, in his own see, gains priority for Rome. But St. Paul is like Christ, in presiding over all Churches, not over one only, and thus he is given a higher place than St. Peter when they are depicted together.—(*De Picturis Principum Apostolorum.*)

There is one obvious consideration which has nevertheless been too little regarded in this controversy. It is that the scattered and as yet clearly unorganized and unofficered Christian assemblies in Rome, to which St. Paul wrote his Epistle, must, in all human probability, have mainly consisted of those very Jewish pilgrims—"strangers of Rome" (Acts ii. 10)—who were converted by St. Peter's sermon on the Day of Pentecost, and who would most naturally make a household word of the great Apostle's name, and regard him as in truth the founder of their faith and that of the little congregation of proselytes whom they gathered round them by their informal preaching when they returned, and all the more because no Apostolic teacher reached them for many years after. This memory would, of course, be quickened in the minds of the elder converts when the Apostle visited the city at the close of his life, and his death amongst them would lead, by a most natural process, to their boasting that they were honoured above all other Churches by the presence of the two greatest Apostles, the heads of the Circumcision and of the Uncircumcision, both as being their founders, and as having won the crowns of martyrdom in their midst. This is quite enough to account for every one of the early references to St. Peter's share in the foundation of the Roman Church, even if a more exhaustive reason, to be stated presently, were not producible.[1]

It is not till the post-Nicene era that the episcopate of St. Peter at Rome is clearly alleged as matter of fact, and the first to do so is Optatus of Milevis († after 386), who is a great deal more sure of the details than any of the writers of the three previous centuries. His words are: "Thou canst not deny that thou knowest that in the city of Rome the episcopal chair was first bestowed (*collatam*) on Peter, wherein Peter, head of all the Apostles, sat. ... Therefore Peter was the first to sit in that one chair, which is first in gifts, to whom succeeded Linus, Clement succeeded Linus, Anacletus Clement."—(*De Schism. Donat.* ii. 2, 3.).

But his younger contemporary, St. Epiphanius († 403), does not know the story in this form. In his statement the equality of the two Apostles is still affirmed, as in the earliest of the ante-Nicene writers, thus: " In Rome Peter and Paul were also the first Apostles and also bishops; then came Linus, then Cletus, then Clement, the contemporary of Peter and Paul, of whom Paul makes mention in his Epistle to the Romans. . . . However, the succession of the bishops in Rome was in the following order: Peter and Paul, Linus and Cletus, Clement, &c." And, in contradiction to the assured certainty of Optatus, St. Epiphanius states expressly that we have no accurate knowledge (οὐ πάνυ σαφῶς ἴσμεν) as to the succession, since there is conflicting documentary evidence as to its order and origin.— (*Hær.* xxvii. 6.)

---

[1] It is noticeable that Cardinal Baronius uses substantially this very same line of argument to disprove the tradition that St. Peter personally founded the Church of Antioch. He says: "When we allege that the See of Antioch was founded or erected by Peter, that is not to be understood as meaning that Peter first preached the Gospel there, for that was done by the disciples, who were driven from Jerusalem after the death of Stephen." And he goes on to say that what St. Peter really did for Antioch was to bestow precedency on it, for which a visit from himself was needless.—*Ann.* 39, xvi.

Rufinus of Aquileia († 410)—one of the most learned and famous scholars of his time—makes a further statement which is fatal, if correct, to the theory of inheritance from St. Peter. He says, in his preface to the *Clementine Recognitions*, "Linus and Cletus were, in truth, bishops in the city of Rome before Clement, *but in Peter's lifetime* (*superstite Petro*), that is, they discharged the episcopal care, and he fulfilled the apostolic office." This view, it is to be observed, denies implicitly that St. Peter, albeit resident at Rome, had any specific and local relation to its see (any more than St. Paul had to Ephesus or Colosse), continuing to act in his general and delocalised apostolic capacity, while the two earliest Popes were not his successors, but merely his ordinees and contemporaries, bearing the same relation to him as Titus did to St. Paul, and, of course, not enjoying his privilege during his lifetime.

Another very important fact in this connexion is the date assigned to the pontificate of St. Linus by the very ancient Liberian and other catalogues of Roman bishops, by Anastasius the Librarian, and by the older Breviaries, which agree in stating that Linus sat in Nero's reign, from the consulate of Saturninus and Scipio (A.D. 56) till that of Capito and Rufus (A.D. 67), twelve years. Two lists of Popes, published by Mabillon (*De Re Diplomaticâ* and *Vetera Analecta*), severally assign to Linus a pontificate of eleven years three months and twelve days, and of twelve years five months and twelve days; while Eutychius of Alexandria says (*Ann.* sect. 336) that "Linus was Patriarch of Rome after Peter, and died when he had held that dignity for twelve years; and he was the first Patriarch of Rome;" and the Chronicle of Nicephorus has the entry; "Peter the Apostle, *two years;*[1] Linus, *twelve years.*" Here, then, is a consensus of authorities, according to some of which Linus was Pope of Rome during twelve years of St. Peter's life, for A.D. 67 is the most probable

---

[1] Probably a mere scribe's error, ETHB for ETHKB, as there s other Byzantine authority for twenty-two years' session.

year of the Apostle's martyrdom. And hence, if these data could be fully relied on, it would be as nearly as possible proved to demonstration that St. Peter either never held the local see of Rome, or that he divested himself of it in favour of St. Linus. In the first case, the Papal claim of special heirship breaks down, and Rome merely stands on the footing of any other city where an Apostle nominated the first bishop; and, in the second case, it is clear that St. Linus, albeit Pope, never enjoyed the "privilege of Peter," in virtue of that office, so that the two things are separable and need not be united. It is noticeable, as previously remarked, that the *Apostolical Constitutions* represent St. Linus as predeceasing St. Peter. And though the *Chronicle* of Eusebius counts the twelve years of Linus from the death of St. Peter, in contradiction to the explicit consular date mentioned above, yet it will be noticed on examination that there is some mistake in the computation of the regnal years of the Emperors just at this place, which seriously weakens its value as testimony, seeming to point either to corruption of the text, or to carelessness on the author's own part. The least that can be said on a survey of the whole evidence, and of the many attempts made from the days of Pearson and Dodwell to Lipsius in our own time to clear up the chronological difficulty, is that a formidable gap exists here in the links of proof for the descent of the Petrine privilege, and that no means of adequately filling it up are known to exist.

It is St. Jerome († 420) who first collects into one body the scattered notices of St. Peter from Eusebius and elsewhere, and gives currency to the story of his twenty-five years' session at Rome, thus: "Simon Peter . . . in the second year of the Emperor Claudius, went to Rome to overcome Simon Magus, and there occupied the sacerdotal chair for twenty-five years, until the last year of Nero."—(*De Viris Illustribus*, i.)

No doubt this was the popular view at Rome in the time of Pope Damasus, and St. Jerome most probably got it from the archivists there. But that it represents a late and growing tradition appears not only from the reasons already mentioned for discrediting it, but from the still more remarkable fact that in the fifth chapter of this very book, devoted to an account of St. Paul, St. Jerome is entirely silent as to St. Paul's having had any share whatever in the foundation or the ecclesiastical government of the Church of Rome, contenting himself with mentioning the Apostle's imprisonments and martyrdom there. This shows that already there was a tendency at Rome to thrust St. Paul into the background, and so far to contradict, if not to falsify, the testimony of all the earlier records, including the New Testament itself. And so serious an omission in one part of the narrative justifies the belief that there has been as serious an accretion in the other part; even if the long distance of St. Jerome himself from the era he is here illustrating did not, by the unvarying laws of historical criticism, make his testimony of much less account than that of the numerous writers who preceded him, and knew nothing of this story, unheard of, so far as extant records permit us to say, for three centuries and a half after the date with which it concerns itself.

Later on, the assertions regarding St. Peter's session, pontificate, and supremacy come thick and fast, but of course have no evidential value whatever; and it must again be pointed out that nothing in the citations above, which practically contain the *whole* of the relevant extant testimony, is valid to prove, in the *legal* fashion required by Canon law for establishing a legal claim of privilege, the fact of St. Peter having ever been Bishop of Rome in any sense not equally true of St. Paul, or having attached any specific grant or privilege to that see.

For (*a*.) no trustworthy document, within six generations of St. Peter's death, is producible, plainly alleging him to have been Bishop of Rome in the received meaning of that phrase, or to have endowed that see in any special manner.

(*b*.) The wording of such evidence as is actually tendered is obscure, doubtful, and contradictory.

(*c.*) A strict and literal construction of its matter leaves **no** ground available for even a primacy of honour, not to say a supremacy of jurisdiction.

(*d.*) There is no allusion at all to St. Peter in the Catacombs of Rome earlier than the third century, and none to his Roman bishopric till the fourth century; and none of any date ascribing the foundation of the Roman Church to him.

But if the case be so in respect of St. Peter himself, much more **does the evidence break down** which is tendered on behalf of **his** successors. It should be **enough, at** the very outset, to allege, as barring every claim **of the** sort, two of **the** leading maxims of Canon law in questions of privilege already stated, namely, that a privilege, if personal, follows the *person*, not the *office*, and dies with the person named in it; as, also, that a privilege may not be extended to any other person than the original grantee, because of identity or similarity of reason, unless such person be **actually or** constructively named in it.

Now, in the three Gospel texts on which the whole claim of privilege is avowedly **rested** as constituting the Petrine charter, the gifts **and** power bestowed, whatever they may have been, are personal and individual only in the form of grant: "*Thou* art Peter . . . . I will **give** to *thee* the keys . . . . whatsoever *thou* shalt bind . . . . I have prayed for *thee*, that *thy* faith fail not . . . . and when *thou* art converted, strengthen *thy* brethren . . . . Lovest *thou* me? Feed [*thou*] My sheep . . . . Follow *thou* Me;"—and contain no clause whatsoever which can be construed into a right of transmission; **whereas in** the three other Scriptural charters of privilege, **severally** given to Abraham, as head of the children of promise; to Aaron, as High Priest; and to David, **as** King of Israel, such transmission and devolution by hereditary descent is expressly named and provided **for**. St. Peter's charter may therefore be compared—let it be as comprehensive as possible in his own case—to a Crown patent conferring a great office of state, such as a viceroyalty or chief-justiceship, held at most for life; and the charters of Abraham, Aaron, and David, to patents of peerage transmissible to descendants. What St. Peter did not receive he could not give, and no document conferring on him the right to give is producible, or has even so much as been thought to have ever existed. Hence it is, as mentioned already, that Tertullian actually denies that even the right of binding and loosing sins could be lawfully exercised by the Church, because the **gift of** binding and loosing had been bestowed on Peter *personally*, not upon the Church in general, and therefore must refer **to those** acts which are peculiar to Peter, and done by him once for all, such as his unlocking the doors of the heavenly kingdom by baptism, in which the loosing and binding of sins takes place, his binding Ananias and loosing the lame man, and his loosing and binding severally those parts of the **Mosaic Law** which were to be repealed or retained— (*De Pudicitiâ*, xxi.). **Of course** the answer to Tertullian's argument is that **the** power of binding and loosing sins **was bestowed not on Peter** singly, but on all the Apostles —a fact he omits—but his reasoning as to those parts **of** the Petrine charter which are not paralleled in the Gospels is perfectly sound **Canon** law.

However, **a** rebutting plea may be entered to this effect. It is true that there is no power of devolution **or transmission** conferred on St. Peter by the express terms of his **charter.** But the Gospels are confessedly not exhaustive narratives, and we have no precise record of the many things which Christ taught the **Apostles** during the Great Forty Days, some of which, beyond all reasonable doubt, they carried out in such institutions as Confirmation, Ordination, and the like, which **are also** absent from the Gospels. It is not unreasonable, therefore, to suppose **that** an additional clause, empowering St. Peter to transmit his **privilege,** was amongst these supplementary **revelations,** and **his** testimony in the matter, as an inspired Apostle, would be **as** conclusive as the recorded words of Christ Himself.

Very good. But where is this testimony of St. Peter to

be found? Not in the **Acts of the** Apostles, not in either of his own Epistles, not even by tradition in any one of the apocryphal writings ascribed to him. There is not so much as a presumable guess as to whether he ever made a grant of the kind verbally or in writing, much less as to the actual form of words or acts by which it was expressed. Once more, the first and fundamental maxim of Canon law bars the plea, for the document cannot be produced. If producible, it ought to contain, **in** clear and manifest terms, at least three clauses :—

(*a*.) **A** statement that **not** only **had his restriction** to the Church of the Circumcision been a mere temporary **arrangement** for private convenience, **but that** his own **original charter** had **been** subsequently enlarged by Christ, **so as** to enable him to transmit and bequeath it.

(*b*.) That he, in virtue of these fresh powers, attached the chief Apostolate, as distinguished from, and in addition to, the mere diocesan Episcopate, to the See of Rome, when taking his place there, to the exclusion of Jerusalem, Antioch, and all other cities and places in which he had exercised his functions, **so** barring any claims on **their** behalf.

(*c*.) That he constituted the Bishops of Rome his heirs and successors **in** the plenitude of his authority, **giving** them jurisdiction over all the Apostles who might survive him, and **over** all Churches founded by them throughout the world.

Less than this will not sustain the claims now made, nor in any degree satisfy the requirements of Canon law, but no **jot** of it has ever been even thought to exist.

Nor **is** the difficulty fully stated **yet.** Even were it possible to surmount this obstacle, another **at once** presents **itself.** An historical claim must prove every step, and much of the doctrine and usage of ancient Christendom is defended by some of the very earliest writers, such as St. Irenæus and Tertullian, by appeal to the traditions of the several Churches, and the carefully preserved records of **the** Episcopal succession from **the** Apostles. **It** might be assumed that in Rome, the greatest city and most important see of the ancient Church, and also a centre of learning in a lettered age, these records would be so accurately kept as to be models of precise notation and trustworthy evidence. But, in point of fact, there is great confusion and obscurity as to the order, names, and dates of the earliest Popes. The following *eleven*, or rather *twelve*, rival views have come down from remote antiquity :—

1. The Apostles, *in their lifetime*, made Linus Bishop of Rome, to whom Anacletus succeeded, and then Clement.—S. Irenæus, *Adv. Hær.* iii. 3.

2. Clement is already Bishop of Rome, and presumably ordained by St. Paul, *before* St. Peter goes thither.—*Apostolical Constitutions*, vi. 8.

3. Clement is ordained as Bishop of Rome by St. Peter soon before his own death.—*Clementine Homilies* and Tertullian, *De Præscript. Hæret.* 32.

4. Linus is first Bishop of Rome, *after the death* of the Apostles Peter and Paul, Anacletus second, and Clement third.—Eutychius Alexandr.; Eusebius, *Hist. Eccl.* iii. 21.

5. Linus, first Bishop of Rome, is ordained by St. Paul : Clement, second Bishop, after the death of Linus, ordained by St. Peter.—*Apostolical Constitutions*, vii. 46.

6 and 6*a*. SS. Peter and Paul were jointly first Apostles and Bishops of Rome; then Linus, next Cletus, and then Clement, it being uncertain whether Clement was ordained bishop by the Apostles in the lifetime of Linus and Cletus, and kept in reserve without a see, to do occasional duty at Rome during the absence of the Apostles on missionary journeys, or ordained by St. Cletus after their deaths, there being historical statements both ways.—St. Epiphanius, *Adv. Hæres.* xxvii. 6.

7. Linus and Cletus, first and second Bishops of Rome, predeceased St. Peter, himself never Bishop of Rome, but merely an Apostle residing there, who then ordained Clement in the third place.—Rufinus, *Præf. in Recogn. Clem.*

8. Linus was first bishop, Clement second, and Cletus or Anacletus third, according to the current Latin opinion in St. Jerome's day, though St. Jerome himself makes Clement fourth in order.—St. Hieron. *De Viris Illustribus* 15. St. August. *Epist.* liii. *ad Generosum.* Optat. Milev. *De Schism. Donat.* ii. 2.

9. Cletus and Anacletus (or Anencletus) are two distinct persons, so that the order is, Peter, Linus, Cletus, Clement, Anacletus.—*Roman Breviary.*

10. **Linus was *elected*** by the people after **St.** Peter's death, and followed in order by Cletus, Anacletus, and Clement.— Anonymous author of the metrical *Five Books against Marcion*, bk. iii. (probably **St. Victorinus of** Pettau, † 303.[1])

11. Peter, Linus, Clement, Cletus, Anacletus.—*Liberian Catalogue*, A.D. 354.

In this catalogue, drawn up at Rome itself under the Pope whose name it bears, the consular date for the death of St. Linus fixes **it in A.D.** 67. The two lists in Eusebius (the *Chronicon* and the *Ecclesiastical History*) make it A.D. 79; and these three authorities severally fix the death of St. Clement in A.D. 76, 94, and 100.

Besides all this amount of irreconcilable variation, concentrated within the brief space of at most thirty-three years, there is yet another most weighty fact to be mentioned, which is that although the tradition runs that SS. Peter and Paul were martyred on the same *day* of the same *month*, yet there is said to have been an interval of a whole year between their deaths,[2] and St. Peter was **the** *first* to die.[3] This circumstance is not mentioned **very** early, **but it is in** chief possession—there being less precise statement **the**

---

[1] Other opinions are that Victorinus of Marseilles or Victorinus Afer is the writer, but no certainty exists on the subject.

[2] Prudentius, *Peristeph.* xii. 5; S. August. *Serm.* xxviii.; Arator, ii. 12.

[3] "*Prima* Petrum rapuit sententia legibus Neronis.'—Prudent. *Perist.* xii. 11.

other way,[1]—and also it is a detail extremely unlikely to be added later ; whereas the superior dramatic effectiveness of the simultaneous martyrdoms, celebrated as they are on the one day, most readily accounts for the omission of the interval between them, not for any purpose of fraud, but for greater picturesqueness and impressiveness in the narrative, if not indeed from simple mistake as to the matter of fact. Let us see what follows from these details, regarded legally, as to the claim of privilege.

First, then, the utter discrepancy of these eleven or twelve different accounts of the order of succession shows that no reliance whatever can be placed on the trustworthiness of the early Roman ecclesiastical records, from which St. Irenæus, Tertullian, Eusebius, Optatus, St. Jerome, St. Augustine, and the compilers of the Liberian Catalogue and of the original Roman Breviary, certainly; Rufinus, St. Epiphanius, and the compiler of the *Apostolical Constitutions*, most probably, obtained their information. If they could not settle such initial facts as to whether St. Peter is to be reckoned in, or left out of, the numerical account,[2] whether St. Clement was first, second, third, or fourth in succession from St. Peter, whether Cletus and Anacletus are two persons or one, or whether St. Linus and St. Cletus entered on their office before or after St. Peter's death, it follows that the value of their evidence for St. Peter himself having ever been Bishop of Rome, or having appointed any one to succeed him in his chair and privileges, is reduced to a mere nothing ; and yet no other testimony is offered us except this uncertain local tradition, accepted as true by writers at a distance from

---

[1] It derives some slight confirmation from the prior mention of St. Peter's martyrdom by St. Clement (*Ep. ad Corinth.* i. 5), seeing that more stress is laid on that of St. Paul, and if so, that is the witness of a contemporary.

[2] **Valesius notes :** "Irenæus and Eusebius say that Peter and Paul laid the first foundations of the Church of Rome, but they in no wise reckon them in the succession of the Bishops" (*eos in episcoporum ordine nequaquam recensent*). And again : "Eusebius never reckons the Apostles in the succession (*ordine*) of Bishops." In Euseb. *Hist. Eccl.* iii., 21.

Rome, who either did not verify their statements by personal examination of the documents, or found contradictory entries (as indeed St. Epiphanius expressly says he did) if they did verify them. And the order which has the largest amount of evidence, such as it is, has not been followed by the Roman Missal and Breviary.

Next, this very carelessness establishes a second fact, that the question was not **one of** very **great** importance in **the** mind of the early Church. **The exact** details **of the succession** at Rome, however **interesting** locally, **can have** been thus of no greater practical **significance to** the Christian **body** at large than those of **the** order **of the Bishops** at **Colosse or** Philippi. No stupendous powers, **no** unspeak**ably** august inheritance, could have been thought **to** depend **on** the regularity and indefeasibility of the Roman claim by orderly succession. And this uncertainty is all the more remarkable when contrasted with the perfectly accurate knowledge we have of the civil chronology of this very time, with the order and succession of the Roman Consuls, albeit then mere titular dignitaries, **of** no greater importance than a modern high sheriff.

Thirdly, if Linus and Cletus were appointed as Bishops of Rome, and predeceased St. Peter, it is clear that he did not divest himself of his "privilege" on their behalf, **so** that they were in that case **Popes** without enjoying any specific primacy in consequence—a conclusive proof that the privilege is not necessarily attached to the office. The **same** argument holds good if Linus **was** appointed Bishop during the lifetime of St. Peter, but survived him, because **even** in that case the Apostle must have separated the **see from** the privilege in his lifetime, and there is no proof that he provided for their reunion after his death. Again, if Linus was ordained by St. Paul—with whom alone one brief New Testament reference (2 Tim. iv. 21) connects him—he was Pope of Rome without having any claim whatever through St. Peter.

Fourthly, if St. Peter did indeed consecrate any one of the three, Linus, Cletus, or Clement, as Bishop of Rome, or as intended to succeed himself in any capacity, that very fact is fatal to his title to have ever been bishop of the local see of Rome himself, for the ancient Church knew nothing of coadjutor bishops, nor of a bishop resigning his see to another, nor yet of ordaining any one with right of succession. Accordingly, Pope Innocent I. († 417), in a letter to the Church of Constantinople, lays down that it was an unheard-of thing, never done by any of the Fathers, to ordain any one to occupy the place of another still living, no one having had power given him for that purpose (Soz. *Hist. Eccl.* viii. 26). And indeed the Council of Antioch in 341 had decreed, in its twenty-third canon, thus: "It is not lawful for a Bishop to appoint another as successor to himself, even if he be at the close of life; and if any such act be done, the appointment shall be void." It is scarcely probable that such a rule would have been laid down if the Council knew of the august precedent set by the Prince of the Apostles in the chief city of the world. And it is not easy to see how the Council could have helped knowing it, supposing it was a fact. The actual Canon law of the Roman Church itself is decisive on this head. It lays down that "The Pope cannot choose his successor, and if he did choose him, the election would be void. . . . The Pope is prohibited to choose his successor, not only by ecclesiastical law . . . but by the Divine and the natural law." And the reason assigned is twofold: Christ could and did appoint St. Peter thus, but Christ was Lord of the Church, and infallible; the Popes are mere stewards of the Church, and fallible.—Ferraris, *Prompta Bibliotheca*, s. v. "Papa," i. 1. A similar objection, by the by, refutes that part of the story which makes St. Peter to have been diocesan bishop of Antioch, and afterwards to have transferred his chair to Rome, for the Apostolical Canons, the General Councils of Nice and Chalcedon, the Synods of Antioch, Alexandria, Sardica, and Arles I., all severally condemn the migration and translation of bishops; and Popes Damasus and Leo the Great actually excommunicated all bishops who changed their sees, especially if to a greater and richer city.—(Theodoret, *H. E.* vii. ; Leo Magn. *Epist.* lxxxiv. 4.)

Fifthly, if St. Paul survived St. Peter by a whole twelvemonth, and they two were joint founders and rulers of the Roman Church, in that case, by all maxims of official succession, the whole Apostolic authority there must have been then concentrated in St. Paul's hands, and only he could bequeath it, if it were transmissible at all. The question of the order in which two people, A and B, who are each other's nearest heirs-at-law, or who inherit under each other's wills, happen to die, is often of great importance in the passage of property. For though A and B may be heirs to each other, either by kindred or by testament, it does not follow that X, the next heir of A, must be also the next heir to B, either at law or under a will. B has another heir of his own, Y. Now, in such a case as this, if A die first, B inherits, and Y inherits in turn at B's death. But if B die first, A inherits, and X takes it in turn from him, while Y gets nothing.[1] Apply this rule to the legal claim of privi-

---

[1] Curious cases of this nature come occasionally before the law courts. It is the rule of French jurisprudence that where two or more persons die at the same time by accident, as by fire or drowning, the presumption is that the person whose age and physical condition seemed to promise the greatest power of escape or endurance must be held to have survived ; while the English courts always rule that the deaths must be accounted simultaneous. A case of the sort (*re* Holden's Trusts) was decided by Vice-Chancellor Malins in May, 1878. The captain of the ship *Great Queensland* made his will in favour of his wife, and failing her, his daughter, and took them both to sea with him. The ship was lost, probably blown up by fire, and no tidings were ever heard of her. Hereupon a point of law arose. The executors could not tell who was next legatee, as that depended entirely on the order of the deaths. If the captain held out longest, his will failed by the deaths of his two legatees in his own lifetime, and he was practically intestate. If his wife survived her husband and child, then her family, to the exclusion of his relations, were the heirs. If the child lived longest, then her heirs, that is to say, the relations of both her father and her mother, were entitled to divide the estate. The court ruled that the deaths must be held to be simultaneous, and the legacies thus to have failed, so that only the captain's next heirs-at-law took anything, and those who claimed through the wife and child got

lege with which we are dealing. No Roman authority alleges any one of these three things : (*a*) that St. Paul was Pope, or inherited any Papal privileges from St. Peter, since he is not reckoned as Paul I., that Pope sitting from 757 to 767 ; (*b*) that any Pope inherited his primacy from or through St. Paul ; (*c*) that St. Paul was subject to any other successor of St. Peter during the twelvemonth which elapsed between their martyrdoms. Nevertheless, one of these three events must, on Roman principles, have happened if St. Paul did survive St. Peter, and the next Pope, whoever he was, succeeded either before or after the death of St. Paul. Here, then, is a flaw in the whole case, which effectually negatives the evidence for the Petrine privilege of the Popes. On the other hand, if SS. Peter and Paul died on the very same day, the presumption is that St. Peter, who suffered the lingering death of crucifixion, survived St. Paul, beheaded as a Roman citizen, and of course inherited any joint rights from him ; but this is just what the evidence contradicts.

There is only one even plausible solution of the difficulty as to the order of the early Papal succession, and even it does not get rid of all the contradictions just stated. It is that the same rule may have prevailed at Rome which we

---

nothing. A still more complicated case of the kind was decided by the House of Lords in 1860, that of Wing *v.* Angrave, arising out of the wreck of the *Dalhousie* in 1853. A husband and wife named Underwood, with three children, were swept away by the same wave, as attested by the only survivor of the wreck. They had left their property to their children, in the event of either dying in the other's lifetime, and in the event of those children all dying before reaching the age of twenty-one, to a Mr. Wing, as residuary legatee. He claimed under the two wills, but as there was no tittle of evidence as to which testator survived, it was held that Mr. Wing's claim was not made out, and that the deaths must be treated as simultaneous : so the estate went to their heirs-at-law, though no moral doubt was possible as to the truth of Wing's contention, that one of the two testators must have overlived the other, if by no more than an instant, and thus have produced the condition under which he claimed to inherit. These cases serve to illustrate the difference made in the transmission of an inheritance by the order of death amongst the transmitters.

have some reason to believe was put in force by St. Peter and St. Paul at Antioch, and by St. Paul and St. John at Ephesus, namely, that the Jewish Christians and Gentile Christians were at first organized as distinct Churches, under separate bishops, exercising simultaneous, yet independent jurisdiction,[1] and were merged in the next generation—with the one exception of the Church of Jerusalem, which was ruled by Jewish bishops till Hadrian's time [2]— into one Church under the *Gentile* bishop. In this case it is most probable that St. Peter and St. Paul, keeping still to the divinely appointed division of their labour, presided over two separate communities at Rome, the one attached exclusively to the Circumcision and the other to the Gentiles, whilst the earliest names on the roll of Roman Bishops are those of contemporaneous, not successive, Pontiffs, but with this inevitable conclusion, that when the separate Jewish Church merged, the whole body must have come under the government of the Gentile Pope, whose succession necessarily came through St. Paul, since the only thing St. Peter without doubt enjoyed separately from St. Paul, and might therefore have handed down to a third person (Cletus, say, or any other), was his jurisdiction over the Jewish Church at Rome, which, of course, died out when there was no longer such a Church existing. And the Pauline language of the Epistle of St. Clement—whether he were the "fellow-worker" named in Philippians iv. 3, of which no real proof is extant, or not—is weighty evidence, when coupled with the statement of *Apost. Const.* vi. 8, that his ordination was Pauline, rather than Petrine, according to the competing traditions of St. Epiphanius and Rufinus, in which case he is the particular link in the Pauline succession. However, the manner in which he speaks of the martyrdoms of SS. Peter and Paul (laying, by the by, very much more stress on the labours and eminence of the latter) implies that those events were comparatively distant at the date of his

---

[1] *Apost. Const.* vii. 46. Tillemont, *Mém. Eccl.* ii. 191.
[2] Euseb. *Hist. Eccl.* iv. 6 ; v. 12.

Letter to the Corinthians (*Ep.* I, cap. 5) although in the same generation, and thus seemingly disproves his own appointment by either of the Apostles to the see of Rome. But that the succession became exclusively Gentile very speedily admits of no question, and therefore the historical presumption is, that there is now no Petrine descent at all in the Roman chair, that line having died out within the first century: consequently no transmission of the Petrine privilege is so much as probable, even were the continued lack of the necessary legal proofs for establishing the claim waived as an objection. The opinion that there was a double episcopate at Rome in Apostolic times is not a modern one. Apart from the frequent mention of SS. Peter and Paul as jointly ruling there, the following notices are extant:—(*a*) In the ancient *Liber Pontificalis* or *Gesta Pontificum* it is said: "He [Peter] ordained two bishops, Linus and Cletus, that they might personally discharge all the priestly ministry for the people in the city of Rome, while Peter had leisure for prayer and for teaching the people in sermons." (*b*) St. Epiphanius says (*Hær.* xxvii. 6) that SS. Peter and Paul were first of all at Rome both Apostles and Bishops, and that it was reasonable that they should appoint others in their lifetime, because it was necessary for themselves to go on missionary journeys, and yet Rome could not be left without a bishop. The context leaves it very doubtful whether St. Epiphanius thought Linus and Cletus to have held office simultaneously or successively. (*c*) Rufinus states that Linus and Cletus were consecrated by St. Peter in his own lifetime, to discharge the Episcopal office, while he filled the Apostolic one. (*d*) Venerable Bede (*Vit. Abb. Weremuth.*) says: "The histories hand down that blessed Peter the Apostle appointed two bishops in order under him at Rome to govern the Church. . . ." The objection to this view is that no duality of bishops there is certainly known till the time of the Novatian schism, and that the Novatians did not appeal to such a precedent, as they would most probably have done, if possible. Venerable Bede is the first to state plainly that

St. Clement was ordained by St. Peter as his coadjutor with **right** of succession (*Hist. Eccl.* ii. 40), but that was a comparatively late usage, unknown even in the fourth century; for the co-existence of two bishops in one see is as explicitly condemned by ancient usage as translation, or as nomination of his successor by any bishop, even coadjutorship being unknown (St. Cypr. *Ep.* 52; Theod. *H. E.* ii. 17), the first unquestionable instance being St. Augustine's **co**adjutorship with Valerius of Hippo in 395, and that, as **he** confesses, contrary to Canon law (St. August. *Ep.* 110, *al.* 213); and thus, if the evidence of the Canons be against St. Peter's nomination of Linus, &c., it may be urged that it is equally valid against the joint episcopate of SS. Peter **and** Paul. The answer to this plea is the legal maxim, *Cessante ratione cessat ipsa lex.* There could be no valid reason for a double episcopate after the extinction of the Church of the Circumcision, but the convenience of such a plan while that Church still existed is obvious. Contrariwise, any objection which lies against translation **and coadjutorship** must have been always equally strong. **And the** proofs, given **above,** of the untrustworthiness of the Roman archives and traditions leave the silence of the **Novatians** but little weight as countervailing testimony.

And to the rejoinder that all this argument as to the failure of the Petrine succession **is** merely conjectural, the answer is, that **so also** is the **argument** for its continued existence: with this notable difference between the probability of the **two rival theories, that the** anti-Papal view has these three ascertained bases to go upon, that St. Peter was divinely restricted to the Church of the Circumcision, as **St.** Paul to that of the Gentiles; that St. Clement's diction **and** theology are demonstrably Pauline; and that the simultaneous session of Linus and Cletus is at least implied by three ancient authorities; besides the further merit that this view does offer a coherent and reasonable explanation of the confused and contradictory lists of early Roman bishops; whereas **the** Ultramontane view is nothing but a mere guess without any ground, and gives up the problem of the conflicting lists as insoluble. Consequently, the rebutting plea is legally much the stronger, and it is a legal question, involving the exercise of the widest and most formidable legal rights, with which we have to deal. The practical effect on the Petrine claims of the difficulties above enumerated may be judged by considering how the House of Lords would have to decide on a double claim to an ancient peerage and to a great office of State alleged to be inseparable from it (as the High Stewardship of England once went with the Earldom of Leicester), if the claimant put in ten conflicting pedigrees as evidence, from which it could not be gathered which of three persons in the direct line of descent was grandfather, son, or grandson, and whether there had or had not been two or more of the earliest peers of the line who had never held the official dignity. There could be no result possible save rejection of the claim as not proved.

CHAPTER VI.

DAWN OF THE PAPAL MONARCHY.

THE fifth century, itself the transitional period between the ancient and the modern world, more fitly here placed than at the later epoch of Charlemagne, was also the time when, from a variety of causes, chiefly political, the vague and indeterminate influence and priority of the Roman Pontiff began to be transformed into a monarchy over Western Christendom, at first partly constitutional, but gradually freeing itself from all checks save that of its own bureaucracy, and assuming the form of a despotism. The collapse of the Imperial authority in the West, as each puppet Emperor rose and fell at the bidding of some foreign ruler more powerful than he, the distance and relative weakness of the occupant of the Byzantine throne, the anarchy of society everywhere as the old order and civilisation was breaking up and the new deposits of alien races were slowly crystallizing into regular polities and kingdoms, made some central unifying and statical influence a prime necessity; and a variety of causes united to lift the Pope into the vacant seat. The modern Papacy is due to no Divine charter, no Imperial donation, not even to an inevitable theological development, but to a series of political accidents, so to speak, bearing a certain imperfect analogy to the process which in recent times has set Prussia in the chief place among the Great Powers of Europe. But in this chapter, as in its precursors, the aim will be not so much to exhibit proofs of the exercise of Papal authority, which have been even superabundantly dwelt on by Roman controversialists, as to record those protests in act or word which demonstrate that the Church at large was conscious that its rights were being steadily encroached on, and that no sacred charter, no immemorial prescription, could be truly alleged as the warrant for the new claims, almost as successfully, as they were persistently, put forward. It is necessary to repeat this warning, in order to escape the charge of unfair dealing with the evidence, certain to be brought by such as either do not fully understand or are unconvinced by our line of argument, and to point out that the matter is analogous to a pedigree lawsuit for a peerage and estates. It is no part of the task of the counsel who argues against the claimant to deal with the whole genealogy, and to discuss the career of each successor in the line. His work is done if he establish the existence of serious gaps and flaws, at any points in the course of descent, which disprove the title or even the legitimacy of the claimant. It is of no avail for such a claimant to prove the unbroken regularity of transmission for a dozen generations, if the marriage of his own father or grandfather be precisely the moot point on which his right of succession turns. And, in like manner, examples of wide and powerful influence exercised by the Popes, notably in the West, can be adduced by the hundred, but are rarely to the point, because they are in no respect differentiated from the action of other powerful bishops. A single illustration of this principle may serve once for all. Few arguments, then, have been more frequently urged by Ultramontane controversialists than the fact of the deposition of bishops by the Pope, as establishing his claim to be supreme ruler of the Church, and the source of all episcopal jurisdiction. But in the Acts of the Council of Chalcedon it is expressly stated that S. John Chrysostom, "going into Asia, deposed fifteen bishops and consecrated others in their stead."[1] Thus the matter sinks at once to the level of ordinary patriarchal jurisdiction, and is of no more avail as proof than the title of "Vicar of Christ," which, though now

---

[1] Ἰωάννης δεκάπεντε ἐπισκόπους καθεῖλεν, ἀπελθὼν ἐν Ἀσίᾳ, καὶ ἐχειροτόνησεν ἄλλους ἀντ' αὐτῶν.—*Conc. Chalced.* Act II.

restricted by Latin Christendom to the Pope, was formerly a title common to all bishops,[1] and its modern limitation was made matter of protest even in the Council of Trent.

The first important event in the Church history of the fifth century which illustrates this ambiguity is the appeal made to the Roman **Pontiff**, Innocent I., by St. John Chrysostom, Patriarch of Constantinople, when the conspiracy against him, begun and matured through the vindictive malice of the Empress Eudoxia, was running its course. It is unnecessary here to describe in detail the circumstances which ended in St. Chrysostom's exile and death, or Innocent's honourable share in defending his cause, which proved very useful to the prestige of Rome; but two incidents, which have been used by Baronius and Bellarmine as proving the supreme appellate jurisdiction of the Roman See, call for mention. In the first place, then, Theophilus, Patriarch of Alexandria, who was the principal tool of the Empress against St. Chrysostom, and who presided over the Synod of the Oak, in which sentence of deposition was passed against the aged saint, sent an envoy to Rome with a letter to Pope Innocent announcing the decree. Happily, Eusebius, a deacon of the Church of Constantinople, who chanced to be in Rome at the time, and knew something of the character of Theophilus, hearing of the matter, at once warned the Pope to be on his guard, and to wait for more information before returning an answer. Three days later a deputation of four bishops from Constantinople arrived in Rome, bringing three letters for Innocent: one from St. Chrysostom himself, another from forty prelates who adhered to him, and a third from the clergy of Constantinople.

As regards these events, the first-named, the notice sent by Theophilus, is not, even on the face of it, an appeal at all. It does not submit the sentence of the Synod of the Oak to the Pope, asking for his ratification, but simply

---

[1] S. Basil M., *Const. Monast.* 22; S. Ambros. *in* 1 Cor. xi., 10; *Quæst. V. et N. T.*, 127, in App. Opp. S. Aug.

acquaints him with it as a fact which it concerned him, as the other bishops of Christendom, to know. If Innocent, on his part, had happened to depose any bishop, especially one occupying an important see, it would have been just as much his duty to send notice of the fact to Theophilus, that he might give the necessary warning throughout his patriarchate, lest the condemned person might be inadvertently received to communion by any bishop or priest therein.

But the disproof supplied by St. Chrysostom's share in the transaction is more explicit than this. His letter is fortunately still extant, and a copy in Palladius[1] informs us that it was addressed not to Innocent singly, but also to Venerius of Milan and Chromatius of Aquileia, the two sees then next in rank to Rome in Western Christendom. And what he asks is not that the Pope, in virtue of his sovereignty, shall decide the cause and thereby end it, but that all the three bishops may jointly write, and declare by their authority all the acts of Theophilus and his faction, done in St. Chrysostom's absence, and when he did not refuse any fair trial, to be of no effect, but inherently null and void; that the censures of the Church may be fulminated against the offenders; and that Chrysostom and the bishops of his party may be restored to their sees. The next clause shows how this last was to be brought about; not by the mere issue of a Papal rescript, but by pressure being brought to bear on the Court of Byzantium to grant a new trial, under reasonable conditions and before an impartial tribunal, to which St. Chrysostom promises to submit. The Pope's reply to the Saint is lost; but Theodore, the Roman deacon, has preserved its substance for us, which is, briefly, that he intended to treat the decree of Theophilus as null and void, and recommended the summoning of a new Council of Eastern and Western bishops, such as could have no fault found with its consti-

---

[1] *Dial.* c. 2.

tution, **to try** the case afresh. His letter to Theophilus of Alexandria, however, is extant; and therein he bids him await the convening of another Synod, and therein argue his case on the lines of the Nicene canons and decrees, "which alone the Roman Church acknowledges since, if he could win his cause in that fashion, it would make the justice of his plea clear and indisputable.

No plainer admission is necessary that the Pope knew that the final decision **did not rest with** him; and that whatever right of interference **the comity** of the Church Universal might allow **to his eminent** rank, nothing like supreme authority was vested in his person.

And this practical abdication of claims **as of** right over **the** East comes all the more saliently forward when contrasted with the very large demands which the same Pope made almost simultaneously on some of the Western Churches. The vast diocese of Eastern Illyricum had been gradually brought under the Roman obedience, and had submitted to the visitatorial authority of four successive Pontiffs. In 414, some of its bishops, who had applied to Innocent earlier for guidance on some points **of** discipline, wrote to him a second time on the same topic, **not** having carried out his former directions. He replied very **austerely,** saying, " I had previously taken your doubts into consideration, and now I adjudge it to be an insult to the Apostolic See that any hesitation should have occurred in a matter referred to and decided by that See, *which is the head of all Churches.*[1] Again, writing in 415 to Exuperius, Bishop of

---

[1] Hardouin, *Conc.* i. 1015. It must suffice to say here, once for all, **that the** dealings of successive Popes with Eastern Illyricum were the chief means whereby precedents were created for the institution of Papal vicars or resident legates (the first of whom was Rufus of Thessalonica, appointed by Innocent), for evoking appeals before these vicars in their capacity as representatives of the Pope, and for transmitting all more important matters to Rome itself for final decision: all which steps for the advancement of the papal prerogative were taken in this province earlier than elsewhere; and, from local causes, with none of the checks and resistance which met the Popes in Africa and Gaul when encroaching on local rights.

Toulouse, he lays down the maxim that in all cases of difficulty and doubt or conflicting usage, it is the bounden duty of all Churches to resort to and abide by the decision of the Apostolic See, as the fountain head of genuine tradition.[1] And in a decretal addressed to Decentius of Gubbio in 414 he alleges that it is notorious that St. Peter and his successors alone constituted bishops and founded Churches in all the Gauls, in Spain, Africa, Sicily and the neighbouring islands; and that whatever is the local Church usage at Rome is therefore sufficient for the instruction of Decentius as to what he should do.

This claim, of which no whisper is discoverable earlier (though it is implied in the forged Epistles of St. Clement of Rome, included in the False Decretals), attests the gradual manufacture of a factitious tradition at Rome, and a very long stride forward in the Papal pretensions, being the first germ of the later assertion that Rome is the Mother, as well as the mistress, of all Churches. The Pope's own singular lapse of memory in the matter, if no harsher judgment be passed upon him, is shown by his entire omission of St. Paul as having had any share in building up Western Christendom, and by his claim over Gaul, whose evangelization was universally admitted in his time, as in ours, to be due to the Church of Smyrna, through the agency of St. Polycarp, whose envoys planted the Church of Lyons. And with reference to his assertion that the customs of the Roman Church should by right prevail as the rule at Gubbio and everywhere else, there is a special aptness in quoting the contemporary letter of St. Jerome to Evagrius or Evangelus:—

"If you look for authority, the whole world is greater than the City [of Rome]. Wherever a bishop is, whether at Rome or at Gubbio, at Constantinople or at Reggio, at Alexandria or at Thanis, he is of the same dignity and the same priesthood; the power of wealth or the lowness of poverty does not make a bishop higher or lower, but all are the successors of the Apostles. . . . But you say that at Rome a priest is ordained on the testimony of a deacon. Why do you quote

---

[1] Hardouin, *Conc.* i. 1003.

to me the custom of a single city? Why do you urge the small number [of the Roman deacons], as if it were amongst the laws of the Church?"

However, as Gubbio did lie within the limits of the Roman patriarchate, there is some palliation for Innocent's attitude towards its bishop. No such excuse can be alleged in favour of his dexterous transformation of an ordinary notice from the African Churches into a precedent of submission. The Synods of Carthage and of Milevis, held in 416 under the influence of St. Augustine, had formally condemned Pelagianism as a heresy, and sent the customary notice to the Pope, asking for his ratification of the decrees. This was not merely the usual, but the necessary, proceeding, according to the ecclesiastical laws of the time, that no part of the Christian commonwealth might appear to act apart from and independently of the others; only, such notice of conciliar proceedings was sent to every great Church, and was as much due from the Roman Pontiff, when any Synod had been held within his local jurisdiction, as from any other authority to him. But Innocent treated this customary act of comity as a special act of submission to the Roman See, in spite of the very clear, though complimentary, diplomatic language of the African missives, which ran in the following terms: The Fathers of Carthage say, "We have anathematized Pelagius and Cælestius .... Sir and Brother (*Domine Frater*), and have thought fit to inform you of it, that to the decrees of our mediocrity might be added the authority of the Apostolic See." And towards the close of their letter, less ambiguously, after mentioning the grounds of their decree, they add, "And even if it have seemed to your venerable self that Pelagius was rightly acquitted by the episcopal action in the East, yet this error and impiety, which has now so many abettors scattered everywhere, ought to be anathematized by the authority of the Apostolic See."[1]

---

[1] St. August. *Ep.* 175.

Here, then, amidst much polite deference of expression, is a very plain hint to the Pope that his judgment so far has been erroneous—(in point of fact, he had let Pelagius teach as he pleased in Rome itself for several years, so that the spread of the heresy was due to his negligence or ignorance, unchecked as it was till, removing from Rome about 412, Pelagius encountered St. Jerome in Palestine and Cælestius St. Augustine in Africa)—and a still plainer intimation of what his duty should lead him to do. There could, therefore, be no doubt in Innocent's mind as to the true character of the message. Nevertheless, in his reply, he adroitly assumes that they were consulting him in order to obtain his permission to validate their acts, and that they were now submitting their decision to his final approval. Some extracts from his two letters to Carthage and Milevis will best illustrate the matter:—

"You have acted in the true method, holding to the pattern of ancient tradition, and being mindful of Church discipline, in determining to refer the matter to our judgment, knowing what is due to the Apostolic See—seeing that all of us [Popes] set in this place desire to follow the Apostle himself—whence the episcopate itself and all the authority of its name has flowed. . . . But you have not thought fit to trample under foot those institutions of the Fathers which you guard with your priestly office, decreed by them not of human but of the Divine will, that whatever may be done in provinces, however separate or remote, they should not account concluded till it had come to the knowledge of this See, that every righteous finding might be established with its whole authority, and that all other Churches might thence take what they should teach, &c., just as all waters issue from their native fountain. . . . You have diligently and wisely consulted the sanctuary [*arcana*] of Apostolic honour (that honour, I say, to which, apart from its external manifestation, belongs the care of all the Churches) as to what opinion should be held on difficult matters, following therein the ancient rule, which, as you know, the whole world has always observed in respect of me. But I pass over all this, for I am sure it has not escaped your wisdom; for what was it which you decided by your action save that you knew that throughout all the provinces replies and questions always issue from the Apostolic fount? And especially as often as a question of faith is under discussion, I suppose that all our brethren and fellow-bishops ought not to refer save to Peter—that is, the author of their own name and dignity—as you, beloved, have now referred it: a thing which may be for the common profit of all Churches throughout the world."¹

What makes the audacity of these assertions more startling is the fact that the two letters from which they are extracted were addressed to the bishops of those very Mauretanian and Numidian Churches which in St. Cyprian's time had twice rejected by a unanimous conciliar vote and decree the judgment of Pope Stephen on a question of doctrine and discipline. Innocent, consequently, not only knew that his statements were false, but that all the recipients of his letters would know it too. Nevertheless he acted on a principle which has been all but invariably followed by his successors, that of making the very largest demands, far in advance of the rightful claims of his See, on the chance of their being allowed, in which case they would be all clear gain; while, even if rejected, the mere fact of having made them would serve so far as a precedent, that the demand next time would cease to arouse attention as a startling novelty, and the documents might also be utilised in places where the fact of their having been challenged and rejected could be passed over in silence, and it might be taken for granted that they had enjoyed their intended authority. At the risk of prolixity, it is desirable to cite some other letters of this Pope, albeit of much less importance, as helping to show the attitude he adopted, and its incompatibility with his own discharge of his high functions, assuming them to be all that he represented. One is a letter of consolation he addressed to St. Jerome when the Pelagians had burnt him out of his monastery at Bethlehem, and attacked the house of SS. Paula and Eustochium, towards the close of which the Pope says: "If you will lodge an open and manifest accusation against any persons, I will either appoint competent judges, or, if there be anything else prompter or more zealous which can be done by us, I will make no delay, beloved

---

¹ St. August. *Ep.* 181, 182.

son."[1] Here, knowing, as he must have done, St. Jerome's strong local attachment to the Roman See, exhibited long before in his conduct towards Pope Damasus, Innocent suggests to him the idea of bringing the cause out of the only jurisdiction which had a right to try it, that of the Bishop of Jerusalem, and to evoke it to Rome, before judges with no claim whatever. Another is his letter (sent, it would seem, by the same messenger) to John of Jerusalem himself, who was shrewdly suspected of knowing too much about the Pelagians' attack on St. Jerome, then in disfavour with him by reason of his conflict with the Origenists. This is couched in terms of dignified rebuke, well deserved, no doubt, though somewhat too much in the tone of a superior addressing his inferior, albeit the title "brother" is used; but there is not a word in it implying any canonical rights over the See of Jerusalem, or more than the duty of remonstrating against a grievous wrong which had been permitted, and seemingly not punished, by the very person whose care it should have been to preserve order. Taken together, these letters show a design to push covertly that which could not be demanded openly. A third letter, somewhat earlier in date, is in reply to one from St. Augustine and others, asking for information about the Pelagians in Rome, where the heresiarch had long resided. There is a variant in this letter of St. Augustine's, in one text of which we read, "We have heard that in the city of Rome, where he [Pelagius] lived a long time, there are persons who favour him for different reasons, some, because they assert that you have encouraged such teaching (*vos talia persuasisse perhibent*), more, because they do not believe that he holds such views at all." The other text, which is the Benedictine, reads, "Some, because he is alleged to have so persuaded them" (*quia eis talia persuasisse perhibetur*). Baronius, who follows the former of these readings, treats the clause as an example of heretical

---

[1] Baron. *Ann.* A.D. 416, xxxiii.

calumny, striving to prop itself on the support of the Apostolic See. The reply of **Innocent** is as follows:—

"Whether these [Pelagians] be in the city, as we know nothing about it, we can neither affirm nor deny it; and even if they be there, they have never had the boldness either to defend him when he has preached such doctrines, or to assert them in the presence of any of us, nor is it easy in such a crowded population to lay hold of **or** identify any person,"[1]

No apter comment could be made on his claim to **be the** ultimate referee and supreme teacher of all Christendom than this humiliating confession that he knew nothing **about** the principal heresy of his time, which had been growing and spreading at its will under his very eyes, in his own city of Rome. He may be acquitted of all connivance at it, but not of either being too ignorant of theology to recognise its bearing till he was instructed by the African prelates, or too remiss in discharging the duty of banishing all false doctrine from the limits of his diocese. It has been necessary to dwell at some length on the career of Innocent, because he is in truth the real founder **of the** Papal monarchy (though the greater personal eminence of Leo I. **has** caused that fact to be too much obscured), and it is in his language that we first find a direct **connexion** between the alleged Petrine succession **and the Primacy** of Christendom asserted, and the **claims of Rome based** directly on its being the See of Peter, **and** on Peter himself, not Christ, as being the prime source of all ecclesiastical jurisdiction: a view Innocent had put forward as early **as 414** in a letter to Alexander of Antioch, in which he alleges the dignity of that city **in the** Christian hierarchy to be solely due to its having been for a time St. Peter's See, and that it yielded to Rome only because St. Peter ended there what he did but begin at Antioch. "But," as Bower shrewdly observes, "if it be true, as Innocent pretends, that the See of Antioch owed its dignity to St. Peter, and not to the city, how will he account for its being

---

[1] Baron. *Ann.* **406,** xii.

ranked under that of Alexandria, which was neither founded nor had ever been honoured by that Apostle?"[1]

If these two great claims made by Innocent had been suffered to pass for any length of time unquestioned, doubtless they might have acquired prescription, but the African Churches met the demand by enacting in 418 the canon which stands as No. CXXV. in the *Codex Ecclesiæ Africanæ*, sentencing to excommunication all bishops, priests, and deacons who should appeal beyond seas, instead of contenting themselves with the decisions of African primates and councils; while the still larger claim was estopped by Canon XXVIII. of Chalcedon in 451.

But whereas Innocent had at any rate pronounced definitely against the Pelagian heresy, and approved the African decrees, his immediate successor, Zosimus, who attained the pontificate in 417, reversed this decision on the personal appeal of Cælestius, whose confession of faith, in which he denied original sin to be a doctrine of the Church, the Pope declared orthodox and Catholic, sending a letter thereupon to Aurelius of Carthage and the other African bishops, directing the accusers of Cælestius and Pelagius either to appear at Rome within a month to disprove the former's confession, or to let the matter drop finally, and in the meantime to abstain from all such "captious questionings and idle disputes" (*tendiculas quæstionum et inepta certamina*), calling on them to act thus in virtue of the authority of the Apostolic See.[2] He followed this letter up with another, in which he summarily acquitted Pelagius of all blame, nay, praised him highly, and sharply rebuked the African bishops for listening to such pests (*turbines Ecclesiæ vel procellæ*) as Heros and Lazarus, the Gallic bishops who had acted as the accusers of the two heresiarchs, and whom the Pope reviles in the coarsest language, declaring further that the Apostolic See had specially excommunicated them, but found no fault in the two accused, who up to that time, "though censured

---

[1] *Hist. of the Popes*, i. 143.   [2] Baron. *Ann.* 417. xix.

by unjust judges, have never been separated from our body nor from Catholic verity."[1]

St. Augustine was not the man to be put down by bluster of this sort, but at once procured the assembling of an African council of 214 bishops at Carthage in February 418, which unanimously renewed the condemnation of Pelagius and Cælestius, informing Zosimus that they adhered to the decision of his predecessor Innocent; while yet another council of 225 bishops—if it be not rather the same reassembled after prorogation—met in May of the same year, and again condemning the Pelagians, further enacted the canon against transmarine appeals just referred to, and obviously directed in opposition to the Roman claims.

Whether the Pope's action be regarded as that of the claimant to be the teacher, or as that of the claimant to be the ruler, of all Christendom, this episode is equally fatal to the pretensions of his See; for he was compelled by the force of public opinion, and still more by the terrors of an Imperial decree against the Pelagians, to retract his former decision, and to anathematize and excommunicate both Pelagius and Cælestius; though in the very letter containing his retractation he asserted that "the Popes inherited from St. Peter his divine authority, so that no one may challenge the Pope's decision."[2]

St. Augustine's comment on the matter, after this consummation had been reached, is curious. It was his desire, as that of all the leading theologians of his school, to hush up as far as possible the scandal of the Papal error, and to establish the influence of the Roman Chair, if for no other reason than that its great power made it the best available agency for putting pressure on the civil authority in the West in any ecclesiastical crisis. Accordingly he palliates the conduct of Zosimus, ascribing his acquittal of Cælestius not to approval of that teacher's doctrine as Catholic, but to his confidence in the professed willingness of Cælestius to condemn anything erroneous which might be found

---

[1] Baron. *Ann.* 417. xv.-xxxix.   [2] Ep. Mansi, iv. 366.

therein. And then he uses these words, which form a noteworthy comment on the infallibility dogma:—

"But if—which Heaven forbid (*quod absit*)—there was a decision at that time in the Roman Church concerning Cælestius or Pelagius, to the effect that their opinions, which Pope Innocent had condemned in and with them, were pronounced approved and tenable, the result of that would be to brand the stigma of apostasy (*prævaricationis*) on the Roman clergy."[1]

But, as precisely this very thing had happened, the Saint's censure remains.

The later struggle of Pope Zosimus with the African Church in the affair of Apiarius, in which he was again defeated, has been already discussed in a former chapter, wherein the canons of the Councils are examined;[2] nor was he more successful in an attempt to exercise jurisdiction over the bishops of Gaul, when he strove to set aside the decrees of the Council of Turin by adjudging the primacy of Gallia Narbonensis to Patroclus, Bishop of Arles, and endeavoured to depose or excommunicate Proculus, Bishop of Marseilles, who steadily resisted him, and held possession of his see in despite of the Papal edicts, being recognised till his death by the Bishops of Gaul and of Africa. In the course of this dispute Zosimus made one dangerous admission, in that he alleged that the metropolitan dignity and jurisdiction had been so unalterably annexed to the See of Arles by the decrees of the Fathers and councils that it was beyond even the power and authority of the Roman See to transfer them to any other; albeit in his own action he was contravening, as just remarked, the decrees of Turin. He died shortly after penning the letter which contains this statement.[3] It suffices here to say that the contest between Rome and Carthage continued under his

---

[1] *Ad. Boni.* ii. 5.   [2] Chap. iii.
[3] Bower, *Hist. of Popes*, i. 160. "Quod contra statuta Patrum et Sancti Trophimi reverentiam, qui primus Metropolitanus Arelatensis civitatis ex hac sede directus est, concedere, vel mutare, *ne hujus quidem sedis possit auctoritas.*"—Zos. *Epist. ad Episc. Vienn. et Narbon.*, ap. Baronium, *Ann.* 417, xlviii.

successors Boniface I.[1] and Celestine I. The heads of the letter addressed by the Council of Carthage in 424 to Pope Celestine have already been summarised (*u. s.*); but one of its clauses is such a peremptory challenge of the whole later theory of Papal supremacy and infallibility, and of the actual wording of the Vatican decrees,[2] that it deserves a verbal citation. After repudiating the notion that any special privilege of the Roman Church, entitling it to interfere with other Churches, existed at all, or could be pressed without violating the Nicene canons, the Fathers add that these Nicene canons, providing for the trial of spiritual causes within each province without further appeal, were most wisely and righteously drafted:

"especially because permission was given to every one who found fault with any judgment of the arbiters (*cogniterum*) to appeal to the councils of his province, or even to a general council, *unless perchance there be somebody who can believe that our God might possibly inspire any one single person with the power of righteous judgment, and deny it to countless priests assembled in council.*"

---

[1] Boniface I. is one of those very questionable links in the chain of Roman succession which make its canonical regularity most doubtful. There was a double election, and his competitor, Eulalius, Archdeacon of Rome, was actually proclaimed and throned in due form as Pope. Symmachus, Prætorian Prefect of Rome, reported to the Emperor Honorius that the latter was the valid election. Boniface attempted, like Damasus, to force his way in by help of a mob, and that in the teeth of an Imperial edict declaring that he was the intruding claimant. He appealed, and pending the rehearing, the Emperor decreed that neither candidate should enter Rome, and that Achilles, Bishop of Spoleto, should perform all episcopal functions there in the meanwhile. Eulalius, who seems not to have known of this decree, which even the Prefect had not received, transgressed its provisions by entering the city as Pope. He and his unarmed friends were speedily assailed by an armed mob of Boniface's faction; but the Emperor held him accountable for the riot, and decreed his expulsion and the recognition of Boniface as the true Pope. No trial on the merits ever took place; and the friends of Eulalius never accepted the Imperial decree as valid, nor would communicate with Boniface.—Baron. *Ann.* 419, xxxiii.-xlî.

"Romani Pontificis definitiones esse ex sese, *non autem ex consensu ecclesiæ*, irreformabiles."

And then they go on to point out the practical inconvenience of appeals beyond sea, as regards the production of witnesses; while, on the other hand, no former council which they had been able to find had ever empowered the Pope to send legates *a latere* to try cases on the spot.[1] And they close by implying very clearly that in commissioning his legate Faustinus to force on the African Church certain canons [of Sardica] as though Nicene canons, he was lending himself to what he certainly knew to be false; because when his predecessor Boniface had made the same attempt, envoys had been sent to him from Carthage, bearing authentic copies of the Nicene canons, attested by Cyril of Alexandria and Atticus of Constantinople, from whose archives they had been procured.

The next matter of importance to be considered is the assembling of the Third General Council at Ephesus in 431. As in the two preceding cases, it was by Imperial, not by Papal, fiat that it was convened. Theodosius II., on November 19, 430, addressed a circular letter in his own name and in that of his cousin, Valentinian III., Emperor of the West, to all metropolitans, bidding them assemble at Ephesus by Pentecost 431. He seems to have done this chiefly on the petition of Nestorius; and the very fact of this council being convened at all is an emphatic refutation of the Papal claims, simply because Nestorius, whose teaching was to be the subject of debate, had already been condemned and deposed by Pope Celestine, on August 11, 430, in a Council at Rome, accepted as the voice of the whole Western Church. Clearly, if a Papal sentence be final, there was no reason, and even no room, for a synod to reopen the matter, or so much as to affirm the Pope's decision. But no such claim appears in Celestine's own letter to the Council, in which he expressly says that the Divine commission to teach had come equally to all Bishops by hereditary right, that the command is a general

---

[1] "Nam ut aliqui tamquam tuæ sanctitatis latere mittantur, nulla invenimus Patrum synodo constitutum."

one, and to be executed by the joint and co-ordinate action of all.[1] Two incidents, however, mark the growth of Papal claims since the Council of Nicæa. In the first place, he sent two bishops, Arcadius and Projectus, together with Philip, a priest, as his legates; and next, they were expressly instructed, while giving a general support to Cyril of Alexandria, the president of the Council, to uphold in all things the authority of the Roman See.[2] Another able stroke of policy was that Celestine, albeit having his legates in attendance, entrusted to Cyril his own proxy, thereby making it arguable that it was in virtue of that proxy, and for no other reason, that Cyril presided. But this, albeit relied on by modern controversialists, failed of its alleged effect; not only because no power of being or of naming the president had ever been entrusted to the Pope, who thus could not delegate what he did not enjoy, and also because no instructions were given to the actual legates to treat Cyril as their chief in that sense, but further because Cyril happened to absent himself from some of the sessions, and on those occasions his place was filled by Juvenal of Jerusalem (not yet a patriarchal see), instead of by one of the Papal legates, who would have naturally occupied the presidency, as next in order, had Cyril sat merely as proxy for Celestine; though, without doubt, his holding the proxy did give him greater influence in the synod, as may be gathered from the brief references which Evagrius, Zonaras, and Photius make to the fact that he acted for Celestine as well as for himself. And it is just possible that it was this new precedent which led Gelasius of Cyzicus to assume that Hosius of Cordova held a similar proxy at Nicæa for Pope Sylvester.

That Nestorius and the bishops of his party were nevertheless summoned to take their seats in the Council shows that their ecclesiastical position was not held to be affected by the Roman decrees; but the Papal legates, by a brilliant stratagem, succeeded in more than recovering all the ground

---

[1] Mansi, *Conc.* iv. 1283. [2] Hardouin, *Conc.* i. 1347.

lost in this wise. Knowing Cyril's temper, and being assured that, so long as Nestorius was condemned somehow, the Egyptian patriarch would not scrutinise too minutely the terms in which this might be done, all three of them in concert alleged that they and the Council generally were merely executing the decree of Pope Celestine, which the legate Philip asserted to be in effect that of Peter, "Exarch and Head of the Apostles, Pillar and Foundation of the Church Catholic, ... who even to the present time ives and exercises these judicial powers in his successors."[1] However, the actual sentence of deposition had been passed upon Nestorius in quite different terms before the Roman legates arrived, and they did not assent thereto; while the synodical epistles of the Council to the Emperor and the Pope contain no such admissions: for in the former epistle all that is stated is that, as the Western Churches agree with the doctrine enunciated at Ephesus by the Eastern, the sentence pronounced may be taken as the common judgment of all the Christian world; and the Pope is told that "we commanded that the sentence which your Holiness pronounced should remain firm;" a phrase which necessarily implies their right of annulling it, had it pleased them so to do; while in neither letter is there any recognition of the legatine character in Cyril's person, but only in that of the three Roman envoys. And St. Cyril's own teaching on the Apostolic and episcopal offices is still extant in abundance, proving amply that he held no such views as those which the legate Philip had advanced, but regarded the Apostles

---

[1] Labbe, *Conc.* iii., *Conc. Eph.* Act. ii. col. 1147-1158. An Ultramontane argument has been based on a phrase which occurs more than once in these Acts, and is to the effect that the Fathers of the Council, jointly with the legates, admitted themselves to be merely "executing" the decree already finally pronounced by Celestine. As a fact, the phrase, when tested, proves to refer to the legates exclusively, and merely denotes their discharge of their legatine commission, for the verb ἐκβιβάζειν and the noun ἐκβιβασταὶ are used only by the legates when speaking of themselves, or by the Council in the same restricted sense.

as enjoying a parity of rank and authority, and himself as Celestine's equal and colleague, albeit lower in precedence, since occupying a less important see.[1]

Another circumstance, belonging to this same year 431, has an importance which must have been quite unobservable at that time, and indeed until the Jansenist controversy arose: namely, that Pope Celestine then addressed a letter to the Bishops of Gaul, urging them to uphold the **doctrines of St. Augustine** on grace and free-will, and to silence **all** opposition **thereto**. In order to make **quite clear what he** meant, he appended **to his letter nine articles, which** expressly maintain the **very tenets** condemned by the Bull *Unigenitus* of Clement **XI.** in 1713. This conflict of infallibilities is so direct and explicit, that an attempt has **been** made to evade it by denying Celestine's authorship of the articles in question; but the external evidence is too precise, seeing that they are ascribed to him by Dionysius Exiguus in his collection of decretals and canons made in the sixth century, by Petrus Diaconus in 519, and by Cresconius in his *Concordia Canonum* in the seventh century; and in fact they were never disputed till their authenticity became inconvenient.[2]

With the accession of Leo the Great to the Papal Chair a new era sets in. That eminent **man is** not only the first **to** formulate Papalism as the essential principle of **the** Church, derived by full devolution from St. Peter, but he occupies a remarkable place on two other grounds. He was, on the one hand, the first of the Popes who can be justly entitled a theologian (with the one possible exception of his predecessor Dionysius[3]), and who helped to teach Christendom, instead of having to borrow his instruction from outsiders, or to err grievously in default of such instruction,

---

[1] As there are copious citations to this effect from St. Cyril accumulated in Mr. Allies's *Church of England Cleared from the Charge of Schism*, 2nd edition, pp. 206-212, it is needless to reproduce them here.

[2] Dupin, *Bibl. Eccl.* iii. 2.   [3] See Routh, *Rell. Sac.* iii.

as was the case with too many of his predecessors. On the other hand, he was the innovator who began the usage of preaching to the people in Rome itself. We are not left to the merely negative evidence of his being the first Roman sermons now extant, for the historian Sozomen, whose narrative comes down to A.D. 439, the very year before Leo's accession, makes the following remarkable statement: "Neither the Bishop nor any other person teaches there [Rome] in church;"[1] a testimony confirmed by Cassiodorus,[2] whose familiarity with Roman customs shuts out the plea of error which might be alleged in the case of a foreigner like Sozomen. The bearing of these two facts on the claims of the Popes as supreme teachers of Christendom is very direct, because they establish jointly that in no intelligible sense whatever could Rome have been resorted to or regarded during the first four centuries of Christianity as a place of theological instruction. She had to accept the theology provided for her by the divines of more learned and philosophical Churches, instead of originating any teaching herself; and the pulpit was as silent as the pen throughout that long period within her walls.

On no hypothesis whatever that Rome was recognised as the teaching centre of ancient Christendom could such a state of things have existed. Even if the function of supreme teacher be limited to the sense in which the sovereign in Great Britain is the supreme legislator—that is, that the stamp of Papal assent gave validity and currency to all doctrinal teaching, which, without it, might indeed be true, but would still be only private and unauthoritative—yet in that case theologians would have as surely gravitated to Rome, if only to obtain this necessary certificate more quickly, as politicians gravitate to London, Paris, or Berlin if they desire to share in or influence legislation in England, France, or Germany; and a great school of divinity must inevitably have grown up at the feet of the infallible Pope. But down to the very present no such manifestation has been

---

[1] *Hist. Eccl.* vii. 19.   [2] *Hist. Tripart. Eccl.* ix. 39.

visible at Rome from the earliest period. Nothing like the famous School of Alexandria was formed there in ancient times; nothing like the reputation of Paris or of Oxford fell in the mediæval days to the lot of the University of Rome, which has never taken a respectable place amongst European seats of learning in all its centuries of existence, never trained one indigenous theologian of celebrity, nor sent out, as the two Universities just named habitually did, a supply of gifted scholars to supply the schools and pulpits of Latin Christendom. A broad fact of this kind, stretching over many centuries, affords far ampler disproof of the claim to universal teachership than any mere technical flaws in the plea itself, however serious and pregnant, can possibly do.

For more than twenty years previous to his elevation to the Papacy, Leo had been an active member of the Roman clergy, and was Archdeacon of Rome as early as 422. There can be no doubt at all of the manner in which the imperial character of Rome, transferred in idea to the ecclesiastical sphere, had seized on his imagination, nor how thoroughly he accepted the Petrine legend which the local patriotism and practised ingenuity of the urban clergy and lawyers, and the far-reaching ambition of successive Pontiffs, had steadily built up out of the scantiest and most uncertain materials. When we remember the entire good faith with which Charles I. and his principal adherents clung to the theory of the hereditary Divine right of kings, albeit a sheer invention of the sixteenth century, and contradicted by the whole tenour of English history previous to the Tudor tyranny, we shall have less difficulty in understanding how even Leo's masculine intellect could accept and steadily maintain the absolutist theory of Church government, especially as his practical turn of mind enabled him to see at once what a powerful instrument it must be in able hands for cementing a disintegrated and decaying society; and it can scarcely be matter of surprise that he never hesitated to avail himself of it. The one ground of regret is that the readiness to use both force and fraud in pushing the claims of the Roman See, which is the stigma of the later Papacy, is as manifest in Leo, despite his just right in some respects to the title of Saint, as it is in a Boniface VIII. or a Eugenius IV.

The first leading instance occurred early in his Pontificate. So far back as 416 Pope Zosimus, as mentioned above, had assigned the primacy of Narbonensian Gaul to the See of Arles. In 445 St. Hilary, then Archbishop of Arles, during a visitation of his province, deposed formally in synod Celidonius, Bishop of Besançon, as canonically disqualified from office, because he had married a widow, and had also, previous to his ordination, taken part in a criminal trial ending in a capital sentence, and thus had, in a sense, blood on his hands.

Celidonius went to Rome, and appealed in person to the Pope, on the plea that his diocese lay within the jurisdiction of Vienne, not of Arles; and Leo quashed in his favour the decree of Zosimus and the sentence of Hilary, restored him to his rank, received him to communion, and permitted him to perform episcopal functions in his presence; all before any formal rehearing of the case; and thus the Pope violated, as Dupin points out, Canon V. of Nicæa, Canon LV. of Elvira, Canon XVI. of Arles I., Canon VII. of Turin, Canon II. of Orange I., Canon VIII. of Arles II., and the decretal of Innocent I. to Victorinus. St. Hilary, on receiving the news, set out in his turn for Rome on foot, not, as he said himself publicly, to have the cause reheard on appeal, but to protest against Leo's interference, and arrived in the middle of winter. He at once charged the Pope with having decided against the merits of the case and in violation of ecclesiastical law; and the result was that, by an act of arbitrary violence hitherto unknown in Church history, he was thrown into a Roman prison by order of the Pope, who found that an easier process than to justify his own proceedings. St. Hilary, however, managed to escape, and returned to Arles, only to find Celidonius speedily reinstated at Besançon by the Pope, who

---

[1] *De Antiq. Eccl. Discip.* Diss. ii. p. 209.

treated the Saint's escape from prison as an abandonment of the suit and a disclaimer of Papal jurisdiction, and proceeded further to excommunicate St. Hilary, and to deprive the See of Arles of its jurisdiction over Viennese and Narbonensian Gaul, an act, which, as we have seen above, his predecessor Zosimus had declared to exceed the powers of the Roman Chair itself. And the only ground Leo alleges for this act, in his epistle to the Gallic bishops, is that St. Hilary "did not await the great moderation in judgment of the Prince of the Apostles, which he always exhibits through his vicars."[1]

No act at all parallel to this outrage on canonical rights in the person of an orthodox bishop of a great see had previously occurred, which could serve as a precedent. And it should not be forgotten that as yet the only provisions which made any sort of interference, other than merely diplomatic, feasible for the Pope, were the dubious canons of Sardica, which, however, were rejected by Africa and the East, and do not appear to have been put in ure anywhere in the West. But they had been fully adopted into the code of Roman Canon law; and accordingly, if Leo (who cites them, though not on the question of appeals, as Nicene canons, despite the then recent African exposure, in a letter to Theodosius II. in 449, Leon. *Epist.* xliii.) had chosen to fall back on them, and had caused the case of Hilary and Celidonius to be reheard at Arles, in accordance with them, it might arguably be pleaded that he was dealing with the matter on grounds of strict legality.[2] The only other right he could have conceivably enjoyed in respect of the case would have been in virtue of his patriarchal office. But herein a very weighty difference existed between the Eastern and the Western Churches.

---

[1] Baron. *Ann.* 445, xiv.
[2] Tillemont (*Mém.* xv. 74) hints that the reason why Leo did not fall back on the Sardican canons was because St. Hilary was not likely to know any more about their existence than the African bishops had done; another indirect argument for their being a forgery.

In the East the patriarchates were of very wide extent, geographically and jurisdictionally, and only a very few autocephalous Churches, such as that of Cyprus, were scattered here and there within their area. It was thus not easy for any Eastern prelate of the first rank to make encroachments on a large scale, because he could not do so without stirring up an equally powerful neighbour in defence of his imperilled privileges. But in the West, owing to the sparse population and the absence of large cities, only one patriarchate existed, as against the four Eastern ones, and it was restricted to the narrow area of the provinces of Central and Southern Italy (not even including Milan or Aquileia), together with the Islands of Sicily, Sardinia, and Corsica—that is to say, the "Suburbicarian Provinces," which under the Empire had been constituted the region subject to the authority of the Imperial Vicar, Prefect of the city of Rome.[1] Consequently Gaul, Spain, Germany, and Britain all lay outside the Pope's special jurisdiction, and might have seemed safe from his encroachments. But the very fact that he had no rival in office throughout the West, nor, indeed, any inferior of so much as approximately comparable rank save the Bishop of Milan, made it much easier for him to bring all the pressure of his unique position to bear on any of the Western diocesans, who, as comparatively isolated, and in no case holding more than exarchal rank, were much less able to fight their own battles, or to find any powerful ally, than the occupant of a menaced Oriental see. Nevertheless the Westerns could appeal to the then very recent canon of Ephesus, forbidding any prelate to usurp jurisdiction in a diocese or province which had not been from the very beginning subject to his see, and obliging him to restore it, in the event of any such encroachment having been made. This canon was of course perfectly familiar to Leo, nor can he be supposed ignorant of the narrow area of his own legal jurisdiction. And

---

[1] Dupin, *Antiq. Discip. Eccl.* I. ix.

accordingly, as has been shewn, he does not plead Canon law as his justification at all, but has recourse to a theory of "superabounding" jurisdiction inherent in himself as heir of St. Peter, empowering him to override all Church law in any emergency, though it permitted the ordinary routine to be guided in the usual fashion. It is impossible, however, to acquit him **even** on the ground of his belief in **this** theory, **because he** was making a new precedent **on this** occasion, and could not appeal to any previous exercise of similar authority on the part of either St. **Peter** himself or of any of his own predecessors in the Roman Chair. **St.** Hilary took his stand on the canons, and **refused to yield** to the pressure put upon him, **as** involving **a betrayal of** the rights he was bound to defend. And then Leo took the step which has branded his memory ever since, and is wholly incapable of palliation. He applied to the weak and dissolute Valentinian III. to bring the arm of the State to bear on a man whom he falsely represented not merely as a spiritual offender, but as a rebel against the civil power, and obtained the following Imperial rescript, addressed to Aëtius, then commander-in-chief in Gaul, whose **terms,** there can be **no** reasonable doubt, Leo dictated **himself,** and which **simply** swarms with falsehoods :—

"It is certain that the one and only safeguard **of** Us and Our Empire is in the favour of God Most High, towards meriting which Christian faith and our venerable religion mainly conduce. Whereas, therefore, the authority of a sacred Synod[1] hath confirmed the Primacy of the Apostolic See, the merit of St. Peter, who is the Prince of the Episcopal Choir (*corona*), and the dignity of the City of Rome, so that no presumption should attempt to do aught unpermitted by the authority **of** that See ; then only will the peace of the Churches be preserved, if the **whole** world (*universitas*) acknowledge its ruler. And whereas this **rule has** been hitherto inviolably observed, Hilary of Arles (as We learn from the faithful narrative of the venerable Leo, Pope of Rome) hath with **contumacious** daring presumed to attempt certain unlawful acts, and consequently an abominable disturbance has invaded the Transalpine Churches, as a recent example proves. For Hilary, who

---

[1] There is a careful absence of any specification. In fact, no such synod had ever existed so far, and Leo knew it.

is styled Bishop of Arles, without consulting the Pontiff of the Roman Church, but from his own rashness alone, has usurped and seized upon the ordinations of bishops which in no way belong to him ; for he removes some illegally, and has ordained others irregularly, against the wishes and remonstrances of the citizens. And as these bishops were not readily received by those who had not elected them, he collected an armed band, and in hostile fashion either laid siege to or breached by storm the defences of the walls, and installed by process of war into his see the man whose duty it would be to preach peace.[1]

"When these offences against the Imperial Majesty, and against the reverence due to the Apostolic See, had been investigated by order of the holy Pope of the City, a certain sentence was passed on him [Hilary] by reason of those whom he had unduly ordained. And that sentence would have been valid throughout Gaul, even without the Imperial sanction.[2] For what could fail to be lawful power over the Churches, if supported by the authority of so great a Pontiff? However, this motive has called Our attention also to the matter, lest it should be assumed possible for Hilary (whom nothing but the kindness of the amiable Pontiff suffers to bear still the name of bishop), or for any other person, to mix warfare up with Church questions, or to disobey the precepts of the Roman Pontiff. For by such outrages the Faith and the honour of Our Empire are violated. Nor do We urge this ground alone, which is a crime of the deepest dye, but, in order that not even the slightest disturbance may arise amongst the Churches, or religious discipline be in any respect relaxed, We decree by this perpetual edict that it shall not be lawful for the bishops of Gaul, or of the other provinces, contrary to ancient custom, to do aught without the authority of the venerable Pope of the Eternal City ; and whatsoever the authority of the Apostolic See has enacted, or may hereafter enact, shall be the law for all. So that if any bishop, summoned to trial before the Pope of Rome, shall neglect to attend, he shall be compelled to appearance by the governor of the province, in all respects regard being had to what privileges Our deified parents conferred on the Roman Church.[3] Wherefore your Illustrious and Eminent Magnificence is to cause what is enacted above to be observed in virtue of this present edict and law, and a fine of ten pounds [of gold] is to be at once levied on any judge who suffers Our commands to be disobeyed."[4]

---

[1] A second falsehood. No such acts were committed.

[2] A third falsehood, for the Bishops of Gaul declared the Pope's sentence canonically void.

[3] No evidence exists as to what is here intended. There is nothing of the kind amongst the acts of Constantius III. and Galla Placidia, the actual parents of Valentinian III., and the reference may just possibly be to the disputed rescript of Gratian, previously referred to.

[4] Baron. *Ann.* 445, ix. x.

This secular mandate of course secured the reinstatement of Celidonius; but St. Hilary did not yield a whit as to the rights of the matter, and though he had sought reconciliation with Leo by the means of legates whom he sent, yet he directed his envoys not to agree to any conditions involving breach of the canons, and of course they could obtain no others. A very interesting letter to St. **Hilary from Auxiliarius, Prefect of** Italy, whose mediation **he had** asked, is still extant in the Life of the Saint **by his pupil, St. Honoratus,** Bishop of Marseilles, **a brief extract from which is worth** citing, as highly **instructive**:—

"I have been conversing with the holy **Pope Leo.** . . . I never remember any conduct of your Blessedness **which was** stained with **the** disease of arrogance; but men take it impatiently **if** we speak as **we feel,** and Roman ears are more easily influenced by **soft** speeches; so if your Holiness can now and then stoop **to** that, you gain much and can lose nothing. Do me this favour, and dispel these slight clouds into fair weather by a trifling change of demeanour."

St. Hilary, **however, was too** high-minded to follow such advice, and died without making any submission whatever or acknowledging the validity of the Pope's conduct. **It** would seem, therefore, that **he** also died excommunicated; but such was **the force of his** personal holiness that he is nevertheless enrolled high **amongst the** Roman saints; nay, Leo himself speaks **of** him as "**Hilary of holy** memory," **in** a letter to the clergy of Arles on the **election of** his successor Ravennius in 449.[1]

It is impossible to lay too much **stress on this** nefarious transaction, which is the **true beginning of the** Papal usurpation over the Church, and **fitly** appears as the result **of** no Divine grant, but **of** the reckless edict **of** a dissolute secular tyrant, who closed **his** infamous career with the murder, by his **own** hand and sword, of the illustrious general Aëtius (the very person to whom the above rescript was addressed), and with **the** violation of a noble Roman matron, decoyed to his palace by a fraud, whose husband

---

[1] S. **Leon.** Ep. **xxxvi.**

avenged his wrongs by shedding the ravisher's blood.[1] This edict of Valentinian III., not the speech of Christ to Peter uttered at Cæsarea Philippi, is the charter of the modern Papacy; and it is in virtue of the powers conferred thereby that the Popes at once began to wield the power which they exercised for several centuries over France, Spain, Germany, and even Britain: though, as regards the last-named country, there was not even the show of civil right which might be and was pleaded in the remaining Western provinces, because Britain and Armorica, or Lesser Britain, had ceased to form part of the Empire in the year 409, when, finding that they received no military aid against their enemies, they threw off a yoke which could no longer justify itself by giving protection to its subjects. And the Emperor Honorius, instead of challenging their decision by the arbitrament of the sword or any other process, issued letters to the new States, in which he recognised their independence and abandoned all claims to sovereignty over them. Armorica, unable to defend itself for any length of time, speedily returned to its former allegiance, but Britain never again constituted a part of the Roman dominions, and consequently the edict of Valentinian was thirty-six years too late for validity within its limits.[2] It may, therefore, be classed with any English Act of Parliament in 1819 which might conceivably be urged as having authority in the United States, in despite of the Treaty of Versailles, whereby Great Britain acknowledged the independence of the revolted colonies on September 3rd, 1783. After this bold and unconstitutional stroke of policy, whereby Leo the Great succeeded in bringing the Churches of Gaul under the jurisdiction of the Roman Chair, the next matter of importance in his career, though it had only an indirect bearing on the Papal claims, had such disastrous and permanent influence on all

---

[1] Gibbon, c. xxxv. Another account ascribes his death to some soldiers of Aëtius.

[2] Gibbon, chap. xxxi.

Western Christendom as a precedent that it requires mention. Engaged in a struggle with the Manichees, though he put the Imperial laws in force against them, he contented himself with the penalty of perpetual exile for such as continued obstinate;[1] but when consulted by Turribius of Astorga about the Priscillianists, he gave a scarcely qualified approval to the execution of Priscillian himself and some of his companions, by order of the usurper Maximus, in 385, the first instance on record of death being imposed as the Christian penalty for theological error, and thus the primal germ of the Holy Inquisition. Leo's words are :—

"Our fathers, in whose time the wicked heresy broke out, took active measures throughout the world that the impious error might be expelled from the Church universal, at which time the secular princes also detested this sacrilegious madness to such a degree that they laid low its author, with several of his disciples, by the sword of the public laws. For they saw that every regard for personal character would be done away, every marriage bond would be loosed, and the laws of God and man be overthrown together, if men of this stamp were suffered to live anywhere while holding such opinions. And that strictness was long helpful to the mildness of the Church, which, being contented with such a judgment as priests can decree, shrinking from bloody penalties, is nevertheless aided by the severe laws of Christian princes, inasmuch as persons who dread capital punishment sometimes have recourse to a spiritual remedy."[2]

He omits to say that these "severe laws" were invariably enacted at the earnest solicitation of Christian bishops, so that the less said about the lenity of the Church in refraining from inflicting penalties which the laws, civil and ecclesiastical, did not empower the clergy to impose, the better.

Leo is far more honourably known as a theologian, for the leading part he took in the intricate controversies which arose out of the Eutychian heresy, itself in its inception and intent a mere recoil from Nestorianism. His writings on this subject, addressed to St. Flavian, Patri-

---

[1] Leon. Ep. viii.   [2] Leon. Ep. xv.

arch of Constantinople, and familiarly known as "the Tome of St. Leo," steer with much learning, devoutness, skill, and judgment, the middle and Catholic course between these opposing errors, and have ever since ranked very high amongst theological treatises; albeit the Pope contrived to weave his dominant idea of the Divine privileges of his See into the web of a document in no wise concerned with that controversy; an artifice wherein he had considerable experience, inasmuch as he had continuously done the same thing in every one of the frequent cases where his personal and official eminence had induced the bishops and clergy of the time to refer their manifold disputes to him for his advice, but which he was always careful to treat in his replies as the acts of subjects, humbly approaching a sovereign and infallible authority to learn its will. And the great depth and piety of his sermons, hardly below St. Augustine's, should not be forgotten.

The convocation of that assembly which is branded in ecclesiastical history as the "Robber Synod" of Ephesus, supplies the next item of evidence against the Petrine claims, for that gathering differs in one most important particular from nearly all the numerous heretical assemblies which formulated false doctrine. They were, for the most part, on the face of things, party gatherings, scarcely pretending to represent the whole Christian body, but taking care to collect the abettors of one particular school of opinion. But the Synod of Ephesus in 449 was intended to be an Œcumenical Council, to rank beside Nice, Constantinople, and that assembly which had already met at Ephesus in 431, and was attended by Papal legates. Consequently, all the circumstances attending its convocation and proceedings, till the tumults began which wrecked its character, are germane to the present inquiry, as attesting the persistence of the earlier methods.

The summons, then, was issued by the Emperor Theodosius II. by a circular letter to all the patriarchs and exarchs in the Eastern Empire, convening them to attend. Having no jurisdiction in the West, he could not himself do the like to the bishops there (though his colleague, Valentinian III., joined in issuing the summons), but he sent an invitation to Pope Leo, desiring his attendance. This the Pope declined, unless the Synod should be convened in some part of Italy, excusing himself on the double ground of serious pre-occupation and the **absence** of any precedent for the attendance of a Pope, **but** promising **to send his** legates to represent him. If **Leo** had been **less set** upon reading the "Privilege of **Peter**" into everything, he might have reflected that the **very facts** that up to this time no Pope had possessed any voice **whatever in** determining the place where a **General** Council should assemble, or had even been asked **to** preside over such an assembly, were entirely inconsistent with either privilege or prescription on behalf **of the See** of **Rome.**

The bold stand made at the Robber Synod by the three Roman legates in defence of the doctrine formulated by their superior in his **famous Tome,** and the shock which the murder of St. Flavian sent throughout the Christian world, did much **to** augment the position of Leo; and **as** St. Flavian, just before his murder, had appealed to **Leo** and a true General Council, the Pope seized the opportunity of a visit of Valentinian III. to Rome, and urged the Western Emperor to demand from his Eastern colleague the convocation of a new council, which the Pope, as extant letters of Valentinian III. **and the Empresses** Eudoxia and Placidia, obviously written **at** his dictation, clearly show, intended first as an instrument for extending over the Eastern Church the **same arbitrary powers** which **the** edict of 445 had lodged **in his** hands as regards the **West.** For the conditions they propose **are** that the council should be summoned within the confines of Italy, that it should be under the presidency of the Pope, and be conducted **in** such manner and form as should be prescribed by the Roman See.[1] But the letters do not

---

[1] Epp. S. **Leon.** ed. Cacciari, ii. pp. **203-208.** "Ἵνα ὁ μακαριώ-**τατος** ἐπίσκοπος τῆς Ῥωμαίων πόλεως, ᾧ τὴν ἱερωσύνην κατὰ πάντων

seem to have been very amicably received in the East; and an example of the most favourable view then held of the privileges of the Roman Chair is happily extant for us in an epistle from the famous Theodoret, Bishop of Cyrus, to Pope Leo, asking for his help against the enemies of Flavian, on the ground of his Primacy. "We hasten," he says, "to your Apostolic throne to obtain healing from you for the Church's wounds, for in all respects the Primacy is your fit place" (διὰ πάντα γὰρ ὑμῖν τὸ πρωτεύειν ἁρμόττει). If he had stopped short there, his testimony to the Petrine claims would have been invaluable; but he immediately goes on to recount the grounds of Rome's precedence, and they are in order as follows: It is the largest, most splendid, and most populous of cities, and the ruler of the world, which has even imposed its own name on all its subjects. It is eminent for the purity of its faith, as in the days of St. Paul, and even more so; and it possesses the tombs of Peter and Paul. "These," he says, "have made your throne most distinguished; this is the apex of your good things."[1] Not a word about the abiding privilege of Peter, Leo's constant text: and yet, as the letter was written for the express purpose of conciliating the Pope's goodwill, and was penned by a Byzantine Greek, it may safely be assumed that the writer went quite as far as he felt possible in the direction of respect and compliment, not to say flattery. Two other expressions of Theodoret's views may be briefly cited here. He states that St. Peter's confession was the basis and foundation of the Church;[2] and complaining to Flavian of Constantinople about the

---

ἡ ἀρχαιότης παρέσχε, χώραν καὶ εὐπορίαν ἔχειν περί τε τῆς πίστεως καὶ ἱερέων κρίνειν ... ἐπινεῦσαι οὐκ ἠρνησάμην τὸ πρὸς τὴν σὴν ἡμερότητα τὴν ἐμὴν αἴτησιν οἰκειῶσαι· ἵνα ὁ προλεχθεὶς ἱερεὺς, συναχθέντων ἐκ πάσης τῆς οἰκουμένης καὶ τῶν λοιπῶν ἱερέων ἐντὸς τῆς Ἰταλίας, παντὸς προκρίματος ἀποκινηθέντος, ἐξ ὑπαρχῆς τὴν στρεφομένην αἰτίαν πεφροντισμένῃ δοκιμασίᾳ διαγνούς, ἐξοίσῃ τὴν ἀπόφασιν ἣν ἡ πίστις καὶ ὁ τῆς ἀληθοῦς θειότητος λόγος ἀπαιτεῖ.

[1] S. Leon. Ep. i. 530. "Οὗτοι τὸν ὑμέτερον περιφανέστατον ἀπέφηναν θρόνον· οὗτος τῶν ἀγαθῶν τῶν ὑμετέρων ὁ κολοφών."

[2] Epist. lxxvii.

ambition of the Patriarch of Alexandria, the see of St. Mark, says that he pushes its claim every way, "though knowing perfectly that the great city of Antioch possesses the throne of mighty Peter, who was teacher of blessed Mark, and first and chief of the Apostolic choir."[1]

The Emperor Theodosius II. returned a formal refusal to the letters of Valentinian III. and the two Empresses about Easter, 450, declaring his own adherence to the decrees of the Robber Synod. He died at the end of July that same year, and was succeeded by his sister Pulcheria, who married Marcian, and had him associated with her on the Imperial throne. The new sovereigns, who were orthodox, at once opened friendly communications with the Pope, as also did Anatolius, St. Flavian's successor in the chair of Constantinople. But Leo, finding that their goodwill did not extend far enough to concede all the points which he had endeavoured to extort from Theodosius II., wrote to Marcian deprecating the assembling of the council at all, at any rate till a more convenient season, professedly on the ground that the ravages of war had so devastated the West that its bishops could not well leave their flocks at such a time.[2] However, no attention was paid to his desire, and Marcian issued in his own name and in that of Valentinian III. letters of summons to a General Council to be assembled at Nicæa, on September 1, 451. Hefele, following Arendt, endeavours to evade the difficulty of this direct rejection of the Pope's request by saying that the Emperor could not have got Leo's letter in time, seeing that the summons was issued in May, 451, and Leo's envoys did not leave Rome till early in June. Even if the dates here be allowed as proving the one point so raised, the real issue is untouched, because Marcian must have had the letters of Valentinian, Eudoxia, and Pulcheria to his predecessor, Theodosius II., in his possession as State papers, wherein Leo's desire to have the council in Italy, if at all, was clearly expressed. And thus the Fourth General

---

[1] Epist. lxxxvi.   [2] S. Leon. Ep. lxii.

Council of Chalcedon stands out in history as not merely summoned, like its precursors, by Imperial, not by Papal, mandate, but as having been convened in direct opposition to the Pope's express desire, without thereby losing its title to regularity and œcumenicity.

Nevertheless, Leo, seeing that there was no help for it, wrote both to Marcian and Pulcheria, complaining that his demand for either considerable delay or for an Italian council had been disregarded, but pledging himself to send legates as his representatives, and he excused himself from personally attending, on the ground of much occupation.[1]

To the Fathers of the Council itself, transferred to Chalcedon instead of Nicæa by Imperial orders, Leo wrote to much the same effect, saying that he had been invited to attend, but that the necessity of the time and precedents of the kind did not permit it. And though he does not venture to say that the Emperor asked him to preside, he does tell the Council "to account that I am presiding over the Synod in the persons of these brethren, Paschasinus and Lucentius, bishops, Boniface and Basil, priests, who have been commissioned by the Apostolic See."[2]

To the legates themselves he gave peremptory instructions :—

"You are not to suffer the regulations enacted by the holy Fathers to be violated by any rashness, upholding in all respects the dignity of Our person in your own, whom we have sent in Our place. And if any persons, relying on the splendour of their cities, should attempt usurpation of any kind, you are to resist it with fitting steadfastness."[3]

---

[1] Leon. Epp. lxxiii., lxxiv., and lxxv. Some texts of one of the two letters to Marcian contain a clause to the effect that Paschasinus of Lilybæum, the chief legate, should preside over the Council—"*Prædictum fratrem et coëpiscopum meum vice mea synodo debet præsidere*"—a demand in full agreement with Leo's views, but not undoubtedly authentic, as it is absent from other texts. However, Marcian had written to the Pope in 450 about a Council to be held "*te auctore,*" σοῦ αὐθεντοῦντος (St. Leon. Ep. i. 550)—words which *may* be so interpreted with a little pressure, but whose more obvious meaning is a courteous hint that his sanction was expected.

[2] S. Leon. Ep. lxxii.   [3] Baron. *Ann.* 451, cxxxix.

The meaning of this direction is quite clear. It was aimed at Canon III. of Constantinople in 381, giving that see the next place of honour after Rome (though in strictness not bestowing any substantial power along with that rank), and so far repealing, or at least modifying, Canon VI. of Nicæa, which puts Alexandria second and Antioch third, and is the "regulation" implied by the Pope. There was nothing to be feared from the elder patriarchates, but Constantinople was a formidable rival, and accordingly it was the settled policy of Rome to affect to regard it as a mere pretender to the highest rank, and as still in real dignity but a suffragan see, under the Metropolitan of Heraclea.

There was a special reason for endeavouring to depress Constantinople at this time. A then recent (421) decree of Theodosius II. had wrested the province of Eastern Illyricum from Rome and transferred it to Constantinople, thereby undoing the work of several Pontiffs, and that on the express ground that the new capital enjoyed all the prerogatives of elder Rome.[1] And Boniface I. had resisted this decree, chiefly on the ground that Constantinople was not even third in rank amongst the Churches, being inferior to Alexandria and Antioch in virtue of the canons. Until this contention could be fully established, the Papal hold on Illyricum was at least precarious.

But when the Council met, the eighteen Imperial Commissioners, as representing the Emperor, took the first place in the assembly; and the Roman legates were allowed to take precedence of all the prelates assembled; but Anatolius, Patriarch of Constantinople, was assigned the second place, according to the canon of 381 (against which proceeding the legates made no protest[2]), and those of Alexandria and Antioch were ranked tihrd and fourth.

---

[1] "Non absque scientia viri reverentissimi sacrosanctæ legis antistitis urbis Constantinopolitanæ (quæ Romæ veteris prærogativa lætatur)." —*Cod. Theodos.* XVI. ii. 45.

[2] Indeed, Paschasinus himself, when objecting to the order of precedence observed at the Robber Synod, when Flavian was put fifth,

But as Dioscorus, Patriarch of Alexandria, was the person chiefly accountable for the crimes of the Robber Synod, it was necessary to call him to account; and in the very first session the legate Paschasinus demanded that Dioscorus should be at once deprived of his seat and vote (mainly on the ground that he had held a synod without the permission of the Roman See, "a thing never done before, and not lawful:" a sufficiently bold remark, in view of the General Council of Constantinople in 381), or else the Roman legates would quit the assembly, in accordance with their instructions. No heed was paid to this threat, and the matter was gone into more regularly by the Imperial Commissioners, whom the Emperor's mandate had entrusted with all matters of strict law and judicial inquiry which might arise in the Council, with the proviso that they were to follow the canons, not the civil law, in their decisions.[1] The judicial examination resulted in what would be called by English law a "true bill" against Dioscorus, who was then removed from his place and put on his trial, but his accusers were obliged to withdraw also from their places as judges. At the end of the ensuing debate Paschasinus called for the final condemnation of Dioscorus, and this being acceded to, he skilfully worded it in the following terms:—

"Therefore Leo, the most holy Archbishop of Rome, doth by our mouths, and in behalf of the most holy Synod here present, and in union with the thrice blessed Apostle Peter, who is the rock and foundation of the Church Universal and the basis of the orthodox faith, declare that [Dioscorus] is deprived of the episcopal dignity and degraded from all sacerdotal rank and office."[2]

---

said, "*We* (the Roman legates) hold Anatolius to be first," which the Bishop of Cyzicus at once noted as proving their knowledge of the "Canons," *i.e.*, those of 381, which the Roman Church affected to ignore.

[1] Tillemont, *Mém.* xv. 646.

[2] Hefele, *Conciliengesch*, xi. 191; also St. Leo, *Ep. ad Episcop. Gall.* lxxxi. It is not unworthy of mention that the legates attempted to include amongst the grounds for deposing Dioscorus that he had excommunicated Pope Leo, but they could not secure the adoption of

So far the game was even. The Pope and his legates had lost two points, in being forced to accept a summons to a General Council which he had endeavoured to prevent, and in being refused permission to regulate the judicial management of the assembly. They had won two points, in that they received the actual ecclesiastical presidency, and had been suffered to word the condemnation of **Dioscorus** in terms which could readily be interpreted to mean anything which the legates might choose to read into them. The real struggle now began. The legates next called on the Council **to** accept the Tome of St. Leo absolutely, and on the express ground that, having been issued by the Universal Pope and representative **of St.** Peter, it was binding on the whole Church in virtue of such publication. They had reason to hope for success herein; for in the second session the Fathers, led by Cecropius of Sebastopolis and Florentius of Sardes, had expressed by acclamation their full **assent** and subscription to the Tome.[1]

But **the** Fathers of the Council were too shrewd to commit themselves formally in any such fashion. They accepted the Tome, indeed, but not till they had first carefully compared it with the decrees of the three previous General Councils and with the writings of the most eminent Greek divines, notably St. Cyril of Alexandria; and finding it conformable thereto, ratified it as orthodox, and took care to state in their records **how and** why they had done so; in marked contrast to the manner in which St. Cyril's own Letter to Nestorius had been accepted without any debate by the Council **of** Ephesus. Thus Anatolius of Constantinople says: "The Letter of the holy Archbishop Leo agrees with the Nicene Creed, with that **of** Constantinople, and with what was done at the Council **of** Ephesus under the holy Cyril, when Nestorius was

---

that count by the synod; and nevertheless Pope Nicolas I., writing to the Emperor Michael III., alleges that as the chief reason for his deposition, a perversion of the facts which Bellarmine has followed (*De Auctorit. Conc.* ii. 17).

[1] Mansi, *Conc.* vi. 594.

deposed. That is why I have assented to it, and I have willingly subscribed it." Maximus of Antioch says: "The Letter of the holy Archbishop Leo agrees with the Nicene exposition of faith, with that of Constantinople, and that of Ephesus, and I have subscribed it." And similarly, about 160 bishops expressed their assent in the like phrases; but what is most remarkable is, that the same admission was extracted from the Roman legates themselves, who stated by the voice of Paschasinus that the agreement of Leo's belief with that of the previous General Councils was the one ground for receiving his letter, thus: "It is clear that the faith of Pope Leo is the same as that of the Fathers of Nicæa and Constantinople, and that there is no difference. *That is the reason why the Pope's letter, which has restated this faith because of the heresy of Eutyches, has been received.*" Not only so, but the Acts also tell us that many of the Bishops present, feeling somewhat doubtful as to the orthodoxy of certain phrases in the Tome, exacted minute explanations from the legates, and declined to give in their adhesion till they had been satisfied, after an adjournment of the Council for five days to give time for quiet collation of Leo's teaching with Cyril's, a respite which they extended to seven days. What makes this point more curious is that the group which acted thus was chiefly composed of the prelates of that very diocese of Eastern Illyricum which was the bone of contention between Rome and Constantinople.[1] The legates lost far more by provoking this discussion than they had gained by their previous success, for they published to the world the fact that a Council (nay, each single member of the Council who chose, as many there actually did choose) had a right to sit in judgment on the writings of a Pope, and to accord approval or disapproval to them, instead of accepting them humbly as the voice of the one Vicar of

---

[1] Fleury, *Hist. Eccl.* vi. 400, 401. St. Leo himself admits that the reception of his Tome by the Council gave to it "supreme and infallible force," as having "confirmed it by universal inquiry, examination, discussion, and thereon consent and testimony."—*Ep.* cii.

Christ.[1] But a yet severer **check** awaited them. The legates had not interfered when the Imperial Commissioners placed the Patriarch of Constantinople next to them at the outset of the Council; yet it was their intention to essay **the** repeal of Canon III. of Constantinople, which assigned him that rank, and the fact that the acts and minutes **of** the Council were allowed to run in the joint names of the Pope and of the Council itself gave them hopes of success.

But in the fifteenth session Aëtius, Archdeacon **of** Constantinople, proposed that the Council should settle finally the position and rights of that Church. The Roman legates at once took alarm, and, declaring that they had no instruc-

---

[1] It is a favourite Ultramontane plea that the Council did, in fact, **so** accept the Tome, because of certain acclamations of "Peter hath spoken by Leo," which were uttered as it was read. But, apart from the objection that shouts are not canons or decrees, the Fathers of the Council added further: "The Apostles thus taught, Cyril thus taught, Leo and Cyril have taught alike." And what is yet more to the point, in the eleventh session, after the Imperial Commissioners had given a decision which pleased the Bishops, these said: "God gives judgment through you"—(Mansi, *Conc.* vii. 289); words of weighty import in connexion with their ruling on Canon XXVIII. The acclamations of the Council **of** Ephesus when Pope Celestine's letter in condemnation of Nestorius was read, usefully serve **to** illustrate and assess the value of those of Chalcedon. They were: "The Council thanks Celestine, the second Paul; Cyril, the second Paul; Celestine, defender of the Faith; Celestine, accordant **with** the Council. One Celestine, one Cyril, one faith in the whole Council, **one faith** throughout the world." Another point may be mentioned **here. St.** Gregory the Great, rebuking John the Faster for styling himself Œcumenical **Bishop,** wrote on the subject to the Patriarchs of Alexandria and **Antioch:** "This name 'Universal' was offered during the Council **of Chalcedon** to the Pontiff of the Apostolic See . . . but no one **of** my predecessors ever consented to use so profane a title." These words have been taken to mean either that the Council itself offered **the** title, or recognised it when offered. In fact, the title, "Œcumenical Archbishop and Patriarch," was applied to Leo unofficially only, by some private Alexandrian petitioners against Dioscorus, who were probably acute enough to guess what language would best secure the aid of the Roman legates, the chief of whom, in one of his speeches, described the Pope as "Archbishop of all the Churches."

tions from the Pope on the subject—which, as we have seen, was a little on this side of the truth—rose and left the Council. The absence, however, of five members from so large a body, even though now probably thinned by the departure of many Bishops, was less severely felt than they expected. Not one followed their example, or lent them his countenance; and the famous Canon XXVIII., reaffirming the secondary place of Constantinople, giving it, further, actual patriarchal jurisdiction, and declaring, what analytical comparison shows to be true, that the Roman primacy rests on no Divine charter or Petrine inheritance, but on a human grant from political reasons, was *unanimously* enacted, without so much as a debate being raised upon it; though several Bishops who did not oppose it refrained from attaching their signatures. The exact terms of its palmary clause merit fresh citation here:—"For the Fathers suitably bestowed precedency on the throne of Old Rome, because it was the Imperial city." Hereupon the legates returned to the Council, protested, demanded the revocation of the canon, and denounced it as a contempt of the Papal Chair and a violation of the Nicene canons; also alleging that it could not be the spontaneous expression of the Council's opinion, but must have been extorted by force. The Council declared, by acclamation, that it had voted freely, and reaffirmed the canon. Then the legates fell back on the alleged breach of canon law; and the Commissioners directed the evidence to be adduced. Paschasinus produced a falsified copy of the Nicene canons, containing these words in the beginning of the sixth: "The Roman Church hath always held the primacy." The genuine Greek texts were produced in reply, and proved to have no such words (still found only in the *Prisca* Latin version); though even if they had been there, that would not have affected the canon in debate, which still left Rome the first place, and did but state the grounds on which she had obtained it.[1] And no help could be secured from the only

---

[1] This forged canon is the only one ever textually adduced by the

persons whose interests seemed really at stake, the Bishops of the patriarchates of Alexandria and Antioch, who exhibited no jealousy for the privileges of those ancient Churches, probably seeing the insincerity of the patronage offered them as clearly as moderns can now do, and having good reason to expect that, did they yield to the voice of the tempter, they would find the little finger of Rome thicker than the loins of Constantinople. And the matter was finally summed up by the Imperial Commissioners, who said "Our interlocutory (διαλαλιά) has been confirmed by the whole Council."

The anger and indignation of Leo at this first serious defeat **he** had met in his hitherto triumphant career of aggression against the liberties and rights of Christendom, **and** at the flat denial of his favourite thesis by the decision of so vast and powerful an assembly, can scarcely be exaggerated.

It has been already mentioned[1] how he wrote to the Empress Pulcheria, declaring that he had quashed the canon, as inherently void, on the ground that it contravened what he chose to allege **as** the inviolable and irrefragable Nicene canons. His words in a similar letter to Anatolius of Constantinople are: "Those holy and venerable Fathers who in the city of Nice . . . enacted laws of ecclesiastical canons which will last to the end of the world . . . and if aught be attempted anywhere otherwise than as they decreed, it is quashed without delay."[2]

But sufficient attention has not been drawn **to his marked**

Popes in proof of their claims. Their rule was to appeal to "ancient **canons** and constitutions of the Fathers,' without specifying the particular clauses relied on; and when such allegations were not simply fictitious, they referred to mere local enactments of the diocesan synods of Rome.

[1] Chap. **iv.** p. 165.
[2] "Sancti illi et venerabiles Patres qui in urbe Nicæna . . . . mansuras usque in finem mundi leges ecclesiasticorum canonum condiderunt . . . . et si quid usquam aliter quam illi statuêre præsumitur, sine cunctatione cassatur."—*Leon. Ep.* lxxx.

bad faith in the matter, of a piece with his conduct at all times when his schemes of aggression were involved.

In the first place, he had himself boldly violated the fifth Nicene canon in receiving Celidonius of Besançon to communion before his condemnation by his metropolitan had been duly heard on appeal, and before any restoration in his own province; and no sacredness can be claimed for the sixth canon which does not also belong to the fifth. And even the sixth alleges for itself no higher ground than "old customs," not Divine mandates.[1] And he also knew that Canon IV. of Nice I. had been set aside in the Roman Church by his predecessor Siricius on his single responsibility.[2]

Next, he could not be unacquainted with that letter of his predecessor Julius I. in reply to Danius, Flacillus, and others of the Antiochene clergy who had written to him, wherein that Pope states very clearly that the Council of Nicæa had expressly provided for the possible future revision of the decrees of one Synod by another, and did not hold any to be final and irreversible. The crucial words are these:—

"Wherefore the Bishops who assembled in the great Synod at Nicæa not without God's counsel suffered that the decrees of that former Synod should be examined in another Synod, in order that they who were judges, having before their eyes a second future judgment, might make investigation with all carefulness, and those on whom judgment was passed might be persuaded that they had been condemned not by the hostility of their former judges, but on grounds of justice."[3]

Thirdly, Leo had himself fully accepted, as his predecessors had done, and as his own legates also did on this occasion, the alterations made by the Council of Constantinople in the Nicene Creed [4]—surely a matter of much graver import to Christendom and the Faith than a mere

---

[1] Τὰ ἀρχαῖα ἔθη κρατείτω.—*Can. Nic.* vi.
[2] See *ante*, chap. iii. sect. 13.
[3] Jul. Papa, ap. St. Athanas. *Apol.*
[4] Hardouin, i. 815.

question of honorary precedence amongst sees—and had thus barred his own plea of Nicene irreformability.[1]

Fourthly, writing to the Fathers of Chalcedon themselves, and assenting to their decrees on doctrine, while withholding his **assent** from Canon XXVIII., he alleges that it had been enacted under duresse (*extortis assentationibus*), a false statement, which was either gratuitous **on** his part or due to his being deceived by his legates, **but** which, at any rate, he did not retract.

Nevertheless, by asserting several times, as he does **in** his epistles, the lofty character **and claims** of Chalcedon **in** all matters of doctrine—the strongest **passage is** this, addressed to the Emperor Leo I.,

". . . . if you do not suffer the holy Synod of Chalcedon, which established the doctrine touching the Lord Christ's Incarnation, to be assailed by any attempt at repeal; because in that Council, assembled by the Holy Ghost, all things were so established by such full and perfect definitions *that nothing can be added or taken away* from that enactment (*regulæ*), which was promulgated by Divine Inspiration."[2]—

Leo in fact destroyed the plea **for the** divine character **of** the Roman primacy; for if that position be true, then Canon XXVIII. was not a mere ecclesiastical irregularity, but a doctrinal heresy, as denying what is **now that which** Leo tried to make it fourteen centuries sooner, the *articulus stantis vel cadentis Ecclesiæ Romanæ*, the Privilege of Peter divinely annexed to the Roman See. But if the Council **were** thus doctrinally orthodox, **and spoke by the** Holy

---

[1] It is worthy of mention in this connexion that his successor, Leo III. (795-816), was unable to prevent the general adoption of the *Filioque* clause in this Creed, which had been inserted therein by the Third Council of Toledo in 589. Despite a formal decree (*a nostra parte decernitur*) he issued against the interpolation, and his setting the standard text up publicly in Greek and Latin, the new form continued to establish itself soon in the Italian Churches, so that it was accepted even in the local Roman Church by 1014, when it was inserted in the *Ordo Romanus*; so the Pope was not "supreme Teacher" at that time.

[2] Leon. Ep. **cxv.**

Ghost, it either was not in error at all in enacting Canon XXVIII., or the error, if any, was not a doctrinal one; so that the primacy of the Pope is, on Leo the Great's showing, at best a mere question of history, on which error is trivial and unimportant, and in no sense touches the Faith. And it suffices here to say that, though Anatolius of Constantinople, undoubtedly through pressure put upon him by Marcian and Pulcheria (who had vainly endeavoured to obtain the Pope's consent to the new rule), wrote a very humble, but practically evasive, letter to Leo, excusing himself from any active share in enacting Canon XXVIII. of Chalcedon—an excuse which was not true—yet the canon itself remained unshaken by the Pope's refusal to acknowledge it,[1] and has continued ever since to regulate the order of the sees in the Oriental Church, no protest having ever been raised by Alexandria or Antioch. And it is scarcely premature to state here that Rome herself had formally and publicly to give in on the subject in that Synod of Constantinople in 859 which, rejected by the East, is counted by Rome, in whose interests and under whose influence it was held, as the Eighth General Council, and whose twenty-first canon begins thus:—

"We decree that none of the mighty ones of the world shall attempt to dishonour or attempt to remove from his own throne any of those who preside over the Patriarchal Sees, but to account them worthy of all respect and reverence, especially the most holy Pope of Old Rome, and next the Patriarch of Constantinople, afterwards those of Alexandria, Antioch, and Jerusalem."

---

[1] Baronius, indeed, alleges that Marcian revoked the Canon in an edict of 454, but Fleury (*H. E.* xxviii. 54) and Tillemont (*Mém.* xv. 731) agree that the law in question did but carry out the intentions of the Council, by abolishing certain "pragmatic sanctions," accorded by the State inconsistently with the ecclesiastical canons. And Liberatus of Carthage, who was one of the envoys to the Roman Church in 535, states expressly in his treatise on the Nestorian and Eutychian controversies, that what was thus "established by the Council continues to the present day, under the patronage of the Emperors, and despite the resistance of Rome."—(*Breviar. de Causa Nestorii et Eutychetis,* c. 13.)

These words, though followed immediately by language of servile deference to the Roman See, are in truth the formal refutation of Leo the Great's one plea against Canon XXVIII. of Chalcedon, and, by thus retrospectively affirming that Canon, are the epitaph on the grave of the Petrine legend which was dug by the Fourth Œcumenical Council.

The distinguished personal character of Leo the Great, his fearless orthodoxy, the eminent and patriotic services he had twice done to the city of Rome, by averting the attack of Alaric and mitigating that of Genseric, and the absence of any self-seeking, even in his all-embracing and otherwise unscrupulous ambition on behalf of his see and office, all tended to make the system of which he was in a large measure the creator durable in the West and transmissible to his successors. And it may fairly be doubted, entirely as his claims cover logically the largest demands made subsequently by a Hildebrand or an Innocent III., whether he really grasped the full meaning of his own statements and policy, or foresaw how readily the office of supreme guardian and interpreter of the Church's faith, laws, and ordinances, which he arrogated to himself, might glide, as it did glide, into an imperial autocracy, refusing to be bound by the laws it imposed on all others, ceasing to be the first servant of the law, and claiming to be its master, in the terms of those words of Innocent III., embodied in the Canon law: "Secundum plenitudinem potestatis de jure possumus supra jus dispensare."[1]

The weapon which Leo had forged against the liberties of the Gallican Churches was not long suffered to lie idle. Hilarus, his immediate successor in the Papal Chair, who had been his archdeacon, legate, and trusted pupil, wrote to Leontius, Archbishop of Arles, in November, 462, after a previous letter in January, which had signified his own election as Pope, complaining that no acknowledgment of its receipt had been sent, and declaring that, as it was neces-

---

[1] *Decret. Greg. IX.*, 8. iv.

sary that the discipline of the Church should be uniform everywhere, it was the duty of Leontius to take measures for that end, and to send a competent envoy to Rome, that the Pope might question him on all such matters as needed amendment, and send his directions accordingly.[1] He followed up this with a third letter in December, 462, addressed to Leontius and the Bishops of the provinces of Vienne, Lyons, Narbonne, and the Pennine Alps, directing them to hold a Synod every year for the purpose of enforcing Roman discipline (*præcepta Apostolica*), and of referring to the decision of the Papal Chair all the graver questions which might arise.[2] This is a very remarkable fact in ecclesiastical history, as showing the steady persistence with which the Popes held to the policy vainly attempted by Victor I. in the second century: that of making even the local usages of Rome binding in detail on all Churches. It is true that the scheme was never fully carried out, since even now the Tridentine Canons do not by any means all run in France; but it was never lost sight of, and remains the ideal theory of Ultramontanism to the present day. But even when thus acting, Hilarus made one slip by admitting the civil origin of the vast authority he claimed to wield: for in a letter consequent on a dispute as to jurisdiction between Leontius of Arles and Mamertus of Vienne, he says:—

"Nothing in the way of authority which has been conferred on our brother Leontius by my predecessor of holy memory can be abrogated; .... because you are to know that it has been decreed by the law of Christian princes [*i.e.*, the edict of Valentinian III.] that whatever the Pontiff of the Apostolic See has pronounced upon his own investigation to be done by the Churches and their rulers, for the peace of all the Lord's priests and the observance of discipline, in the removal of confusion, is to be reverently received and steadily complied with; nor can anything which is supported by ecclesiastical and royal ordinance be uprooted."[3]

This claim amounts to no less than the right of abro-

---

[1] Baronius, ***Ann.***, 462, §§ 3, 4. [2] *Ibid*, 462, § 9.
[3] *Ibid*. 464, § 7.

gating all local canons, and of reducing all synods short of General Councils to mere consultative assemblies, entitled to do no more than merely report to Rome the information they had collected, but it betrays its weakness in the very act of alleging its original Erastian warrant.

Another incident of this same Pope's reign **serves to** illustrate clearly a different form of encroachment; which **at** once betrays consciousness of its illegality on the part of those affected by it, and shows the difficulty of effectual resistance, even at that comparatively early date, on the part of feeble and disorganized local Churches against the most powerful **and** highly organized See in the world. Two difficulties had almost simultaneously risen in the Spanish Church. The Bishop of Calahorra, a suffragan of the Archbishop of Tarragona, had assumed metropolitical rights, and even ordained bishops to minor sees in his neighbourhood without the knowledge or consent of his superior; and the Provincial Synod of Barcelona had translated to that See, with the full assent of its clergy and laity, one Irenæus, a bishop of the province, whom the previous Bishop of Barcelona had from his deathbed recommended for the post. Some doubts being felt as to the compatibility of this proceeding with Canon XV. of Nicæa, the matter, by the advice of the civil governor, a personal friend of the Pope, was referred to Rome for decision, at the same time that the action taken against the encroaching Bishop of Calahorra was also notified. Ascanius of Tarragona, and all the other bishops of that province, **wrote** to the Pope, beginning thus :—

"Although there be no obligatory ecclesiastical discipline [binding **us to refer** this matter], yet in point of fact we felt that we ought to apply **to** that privilege of your See, in right whereof the single preaching of blessed Peter shone forth to enlighten all throughout the world, when he had received the keys of the kingdom after the resurrection of the Saviour; and the primacy (*principatus*) of His vicar is so eminent that it should be feared and loved by all; therefore we, firstly doing homage in your person to God, Whom you serve blamelessly, have recourse to the faith proclaimed by the Apostolic voice, seeking an answer from that quarter whence no directions **are** given erroneously or hastily, but all with true pontifical deliberation."

It is to be remembered, however, that in this letter the Pope was simply asked to approve something which had been already decided on and carried out by the local authority with sufficient precedents, and (as Tillemont remarks) that no promise of revoking such action in the event of Papal disapproval occurs. Hilarus, perhaps thinking such independence in action a dangerous omen, but imperfectly compensated by the complimentary terms of the synodical letter, decided the two causes inversely as regards their merits, as they appear to a dispassionate reader now. He revoked the translation of Irenæus in terms of severe rebuke to the Metropolitan and Synod of Tarragona, but entirely condoned the numerous offences of Silvanus of Calahorra, and even confirmed, in defiance of all precedent, his irregular consecrations and intrusions of bishops, on the plea of the calamities of the times, and of avoiding the appearance of harshness (words which Tillemont glosses as meaning that Silvanus was too powerful to be safely meddled with); albeit the deviation from the canons in the former case is at most a very doubtful point of ecclesiastical law, whereas Silvanus had openly violated numerous enactments of councils, and unquestionably incurred the penalty of deposition. It is true that the Pope went through the form of holding a Synod at Rome, which formulated these decrees; but no purely local Roman councils had ever so much as the shadow of independence, being mere courts of Papal registration. There is no record of the manner in which these decisions were received in Spain; but they are themselves a sufficiently incisive comment on the good faith of the Popes as custodians and administrators of the conciliar laws of the Church, and on the wisdom of the synodical epistle cited above.

Under Pope Simplicius, the successor of Hilarus, who sat from 468 to 483—an eventful period, which saw the downfall of the Western Empire—some further slight advances were made in pushing the Papal claims to universal jurisdiction, at any rate in the West: the most noteworthy instances being an intrusion on the metropolitan rights of the Bishop of Ravenna (whose province lay outside of those suburbicarian regions within which alone the Popes had up to that time exercised direct authority), and the appointment of a permanent legate in Spain. Simplicius made some attempts also to interfere in Eastern affairs ; but the anarchy which prevailed, both in Church and State, especially during the recrudescence of Monophysitism in Egypt, rendered all effort in this direction useless; and it was reserved for his successor, Felix III., to renew the struggle under somewhat more favourable conditions.

The Emperor Zeno, acting, as it would seem, with the **advice** of Acacius, Patriarch of Constantinople, a learned and able courtier-prelate and man of the world, issued in 482, shortly before the death of Pope Simplicius, the famous document known as the *Henoticon*, or " Act of Union," in order to allay those renewed quarrels between the Nestorian remnant, the Eutychians, and the Catholics, which had broken out afresh after the Council of Chalcedon. In itself more than patient of an orthodox interpretation, and honestly intended to bring about the peace of Christendom, the Henoticon was yet of a wholly lay and civil nature, and contained words which at least seemed to cast a slight on the decrees of Chalcedon ; and while citing with approval the Twelve Anathemas of St. Cyril of Alexandria against Nestorius, which had become in a sense the text-book of the Eutychians, it passed over in entire silence the Tome of St. Leo, the arsenal of their adversaries. For these reasons the Henoticon was exceedingly unpopular at Rome. The feeling of irritation was increased by the fact **that two** leaders of the heterodox party—Peter Mongus **and** Peter the Fuller, titular patriarchs of Alexandria and Antioch—had signed it, however dishonestly (for it was abhorred by the Eutychians generally), and were thereupon upheld by Acacius of Constantinople (who had previously been their principal opponent and denouncer) against the rival Catholic claimants of those two great Sees, and notably **John** Talaia of Alexandria, whose **deposition** had been procured because he had refused to notify his election to Constantinople, though doing so to Rome. **Talaia** appealed in person to Pope Simplicius, who sided strongly with him, and he carried on that appeal before the next Pope, Felix III. That Pontiff cited Acacius to appear before him at Rome, to stand **his trial at the** Papal tribunal, in **virtue of the power to bind and loose** conferred on the Apostle Peter and his successors; and **at** the same time issued a monition to the Emperor Zeno (wherein he alleged that St. Peter spoke in him, his Vicar, and Christ in St. Peter) to compel the attendance of Acacius "before the Apostle Peter and his episcopal brethren."[1]

This was a new departure, a plan for turning the appel**late** jurisdiction claimed **so far by** Rome into a direct **and coactive** jurisdiction; a bold attempt to extend the power of **Rome over the entire** East, for three out **of the** four Oriental patriarchates were **directly concerned in** the **controversy, as the fourth became a little later; and one** special motive was unquestionably **to effect a** practical repeal of that Canon XXVIII. of Chalcedon, which Leo **the** Great had pretended to quash, but which remained **the** undoubted **law** of Eastern Christendom, and gave **Con**stantinople **equal** privileges with Rome. The submission of Acacius to the citation would have been a confession of inferiority and subordination, and was therefore a stake well worth playing for. But before the Papal legates, Vitalis **and** Misenus, left Rome with the citation and monition, envoys from Cyril, archimandrite of the Acœmetæ, one of **the** enemies of Acacius **at** Constantinople, reached the **Pope with fresh accusations against the Patriarch. These** appeared of such importance that Felix delayed the action of the legates, directing **them to** confer directly with Cyril before delivering their credentials and other papers. This delay gave the Court timely warning, and the legates **were** arrested on **their** arrival at Abydos, and their papers seized. Cowed by **their** imprisonment, and worked on **by the**

---

[1] Hardouin, *Conc.* ii. 829–831.

Patriarch, the legates consented to hold public communion with him, with the legate of Peter Mongus, and with the **other** supporters of the Henoticon ; and on the news reaching Rome, the Pope convened a synod there of sixty-seven bishops, in which they were degraded and excommunicated, and the sentence was extended to Acacius himself, on the ground of that supreme Papal authority alleged to be acknowledged by the spurious prefix to the Sixth Canon of Nicæa, as glossing the Petrine charter of St. Matt. xvi. 18, which is also named in the **decree.**

Excommunications of great prelates were no novelties in ecclesiastical history, as the case of St. Athanasius, to cite **no** more, amply proves. But there are peculiarities in this sentence on Acacius which stamp it as diverse from all preceding ones, and as the most daring attempt yet made at innovation on the canon and statute law of the Church Catholic. As a rule, what had been meant hitherto by **an** excommunication of this kind was merely suspension **of** intercommunion. Bishop A, in issuing such a sentence in respect of Bishop B, did but notify publicly the fact that, until B had cleared himself of some charge by disproof or retractation, A could not hold communion with him or his adherents. That is to say, it was a protest, and a disclaimer of complicity, but little more. Contrariwise, the decree which Felix III. pronounced against Acacius declared **him** finally degraded from all sacerdotal and ministerial functions, and cut off for ever from the communion of the faithful.[1] In the next place, the trial **of a** Patriarch by any tribunal short of a General Council, such as had condemned Nestorius and Dioscorus, was a *casus omissus* in the ecclesiastical procedure of the time : just as modern English ecclesiastical law provides no means for trying a criminous archbishop. But Felix appears to have launched this sentence on his own single responsibility, as though he had been empowered to do so in virtue of some acknowledged canon or, at any rate, some universally received custom. It

---

[1] Hardouin, *u.s.*

is a moot point whether Acacius was condemned in the synod which deposed the two legates, and the evidence is rather against it, as may be seen in Hefele's attempt to prove the contrary. It is as follows: (1) The Pope alone signed the letter announcing the decree of deposition; (2) the Greeks made this a ground of objection, as showing that no synod had concurred; (3) Pope Gelasius, in replying to this objection, instead of alleging that a synod did unite in the condemnation, declares that the Pope had full power of acting alone in the matter (Gelas. *Ep. ad Episcop. Dardan.*). On the other side are the pleas that it was usual for the Pope to sign alone, and that the Greek objection was either that the Roman synod was not a General Council, or that, having been summoned for a different purpose—that of trying the peccant legates—it was not competent to enter on such a wholly different matter as the trial of the second Bishop of Christendom.[1] Hefele does not mention the one fatal objection, that the acknowledged canon law of the time never contemplated the trial of any bishop save in his own province, and by his own comprovincials, so that the interference of a wholly foreign synod, convened under a foreign prelate, however exalted in rank, had no judiciary status whatever. And further, the Pope acted on this occasion as a judge of first instance, not even falling back on his alleged right to hear all appeals, for no suit against Acacius had been instituted in the East, and there was thus no judge or judgment to appeal from. This objection was actually raised at Rome itself by some Orientals who were present when the sentence was promulged, and the reply they received was that in an Italian council the Pope was supreme, and that, as General Visitor of all Churches, he was entitled to decree all such sentences in his own name and on his own authority.[2] There had been a precedent, indeed, for the action of the Roman synod, assuming it to have had a share in the proceeding,

---

[1] Hefele, *Concilienges.* xii. 213.
[2] Pagi, Crit. in Baron. *Ann.* 485, § 5.

but not a very helpful one. It was the condemnation of St. Chrysostom by Theophilus of Alexandria and an Egyptian Council, to which the Saint refused to give heed, on the express ground that, being outside his province, they had no right to try him;[1] and he appealed from their sentence to a General Council, in which he was upheld by Pope Innocent I., who did not attempt to decide the matter by his own sole prerogative. Felix entrusted the formal documents of deposition to a secret envoy named Tutus, a Roman priest, who procured a monk to fasten the decree to the Patriarch's vestment at the gates of the cathedral. A riot ensued, in which some monks seem to have been killed by the Patriarch's friends, but he himself took no notice of their share in the transaction, addressing himself to Tutus alone, whom he induced, it is said by bribery, to communicate publicly with him, and thus a second time to discredit a Roman legation. As to the sentence itself, so far from regarding it and making any submission, he excommunicated and anathematized the Pope in turn, and expunged his name from the diptychs of the Church, an act in which he had the support and sympathy of almost every Oriental prelate, including even Andrew of Thessalonica, Papal Vicar for Eastern Illyricum, and thus began a schism which lasted thirty-five years. Acacius died in 489, and was succeeded in the chair of C P. by Fravitta, whose election was acceptable to the Pope, and who, indeed, seemed to justify that opinion by writing a complimentary letter to him as the representative of St. Peter's faith and primacy, and begging to be received into communion with him. But when Felix learnt that Fravitta had no intention of recognising the validity of the Papal sentence on Acacius by striking that prelate's name out of the diptychs, he refused the proffered reconciliation. Fravitta died in less than four months from his elevation, and was succeeded by Euphemius, a man of unquestioned and zealous orthodoxy, who went so far in his overtures for peace with Rome as to erase

---

[1] Pallad. *Dial.* 2.

the name of Peter Mongus from the diptychs, and to replace that of Felix. But the Pope preferred to continue the schism, by insisting on the erasure of the name of Acacius as excommunicate, and of Fravitta as not having been acknowledged by Rome, though there was no pretence of any doctrinal error on the part of Euphemius; and as this concession could not be made without yielding the whole matter in dispute, and acknowledging the Papal right to over-ride all ecclesiastical law, nothing could be done, and Felix died, as he had lived, the responsible author of the first great schism in the Catholic body; nominally as the champion of orthodox belief, but really as endeavouring to establish practically that monarchy over the Church Universal which had been theoretically sketched out by his predecessors Innocent and Leo.

The next successor of Felix III. in the Roman Chair, Gelasius I. (A.D. 492), took yet another step forward in the path of aggression, which had now become the normal course of every Pope, by sending no letters to the Patriarch of Constantinople announcing his accession to the Papacy, though such had been up to that time the unbroken usage. Gelasius declared, in reply to the remonstrances of Euphemius, who told him plainly that the name of Acacius could not be erased, that although all other Churches were bound in duty to send such missives to Rome, there was no reciprocal necessity in the matter, but it was merely a mark of Papal grace and favour to such prelates as deserved it by loyal communion with the Roman See, amongst whom Euphemius could not be reckoned until he abandoned the cause of Acacius, who, though confessedly no heretic himself, had become infected by communicating with such as were unquestionably heretical; no account being taken by the Pope of the fact that a formal abjuration of the heresies in question had preceded the act of communion.

In the following year Gelasius, availing himself of an embassy sent to the Emperor by Theodoric the Ostrogoth,

---

[1] Baron. *Ann.* 492, §§ 10-25.

King of Italy, despatched an encyclical letter to the Oriental bishops, and another letter to the Emperor singly, defending his action in the matter of Acacius from the constitutional objections raised by the Greeks against its legality. His reply is, first, that he had merely executed the decrees of Chalcedon against the Eutychians and all their **supporters**, an **act** which lay within the competency of **every** Christian bishop. Next, in meeting the objection that **Peter** Mongus had publicly renounced the Eutychian heresy **before** being received **into** communion **by** Acacius, **and was therefore** not legally and openly a **heretic**, whatever he might be secretly, he answers (in contradiction to his earlier plea) **that** Mongus, having been **bound by the sentence** of St. Peter, could not be loosed by any lesser **authority; and** as no sentence of absolution from Rome had preceded his reception to communion, that act was wholly invalid. And thirdly, he boldly challenges the count **that** Felix and himself had violated the canons, by alleging that the Greeks had no right to appeal to any canons whatever, having themselves violated all canon law by the mere fact of refusing obedience to the Primatial See. To it, he says, appeals lay open from all Christendom by canon law, whereas no appeal from it was recognised, for though it had a right to judge all, it could be judged by none, nor **could** any sentence it had once pronounced be set aside **by** any authority, but must simply be obeyed.[1]

The fact that the Pope nowhere **ventures to name** the canons which invested his See **with** these unbounded powers, shows that he was simply trading on the possible ignorance and certain weakness of many of those whom he addressed: for nothing is more indisputable than that no scrap or shred of evidence in support of such claims can be produced from the acts and canons of any early Council whatever; and what he meant by canons was no more than the *ex-parte* comments of his predecessors in the Papal Chair on Canon VI. of Nicæa, and the *ex-parte* claims and

---

[1] Baron. *Ann.* 493, §§ 13, **14**

declarations based on those comments. This comes out very clearly in a yet more startling document, the synodical letter he addressed to the bishops of Eastern Illyricum, who had shown some inclination to side with Constantinople in the dispute. He procured a declaration of Papal right from a Roman Synod of seventy bishops, alleging the charter of St. Matt. xvi. 18 as the sole ground of the Roman Primacy, apart from any synodical law or constitution whatever, and recognising only Alexandria and Antioch as Patriarchal Sees, because both connected, indirectly and directly, with the Apostle Peter.[1]

On this followed the epistle to the Illyrians, whose most salient propositions, separated from the charges against Acacius, set forth at much length, are these : (1) That the Pope has a right, as Universal Bishop, to try all cases of heresy by himself, without the aid or intervention of any council whatever ; (2) that the Holy See has power to revise and reverse all ecclesiastical sentences, to sit in final judgment on all Churches, and cannot have its decisions called in question by any one ; (3) that it has the power of reversing all conciliar decisions ; (4) that synods have no further use than that of giving greater publicity to sentences which in fact rested on Papal authority alone, itself having no limitation to its discretion in executing the laws of the Church ; (5) that the Roman Primacy is divine, and antecedent to all ecclesiastical legislation ; (6) nay, superior to it, in that no canons or conciliar decrees whatever can narrow that original jurisdiction, or are so much as valid for any purpose affecting the rights of the Roman See, unless with its express or implied sanction ; (7) that no power, secular or conciliar, can confer any rank in the Church, unless such as is acknowledged by the Pope, so that the decrees of Constantinople and Chalcedon, erecting the former city into a Patriarchate, were null and void, and it remained in right a mere suffraganate of the Exarch of Heraclea ; (8) that the Pope may use any means he

---

[1] Baron. *Ann.* 494, §§ 20, 21.

pleases for the suppression of any assumption of spiritual character in derogation of the Holy See, if the ordinary tribunals should prove insufficient for the purpose.[1]

Such was the position taken up by a Pope at the close of the fifth century, and it is clear that even the Vatican decrees themselves add almost nothing to so vast and wide-reaching a programme, in which the most daring assertion takes the place of proof, evidently regarded as entirely superfluous. Gregory VII. and Innocent III. did nothing to enlarge these claims—save in the one particular that Gelasius admitted the duty of Bishops to obey the Crown in temporal matters[2]—and did but translate them as far as possible into practical action. But no intelligent student of history will need any further proof of their untenability than the broad fact that it needed six more centuries of incessant struggle to bring them to bear even in the West, while their failure to affect the East has continued to the present day. And a canonist's conclusive answer to the plea that long acceptance by Western Christendom has established a prescription which legitimates and validates the Papal Claims is the contrary maxim of Canon Law : *Non firmatur tractu temporis quod de jure ab initio non subsistit.* (*Reg. Jur. lib. vi. Decretal.*)

---

[1] Hardouin, *Conc.* ii. 905-916.   [2] See *infra* p. 256.

CHAPTER VII.

LEGAL BREAKS IN THE CHAIN OF PRESCRIPTION.

It is a commonplace of history that the removal of the seat of empire from Rome to Constantinople had a considerable share in establishing the sway of the Popes over Western Europe. The rival of greatest power and dignity was withdrawn to a distance, instead of being actually or potentially upon the spot, and the occupant of the Papal chair was forced, even had he been unwilling, into the position of arbiter and guide in the troublous anarchy of the two centuries which followed the irruption of the Barbarians. And it was impossible for Constantine the Great to transfer the unequalled prestige and august memories of the "Eternal City" to the shores of the Bosphorus along with the Government offices and the shadowy Senate. All that remained behind was inherited by the dignitary whose possession of the ancient mistress of the world wore, almost from the moment of this change, the semblance of actual sovereignty; though it was not for more than eight centuries later (1198) that the Pope was even in theory King of Rome, or more than the Emperor's chief vassal within its walls.

But there is another, and in some respects more powerful, factor in the rapid development of Papal power during the period between the sixth and eighth centuries which has perhaps not attracted like notice from historians. It is this: the Empire was older than the Church, far more perfectly organized as an administrative system until a long time had elapsed, and covered for centuries a far wider area. It was in many respects a consummate piece of statecraft, it had all the arts of two civilisations at its back, and it had watched the growth and progress of the Church with a fear and suspicion which took shape, as all students know, in ten persecutions. This fear and suspicion were very far from disappearing with the conversion of the Empire, though their manifestation was then different from the rough methods of Valerian or Diocletian. It was still the care of statesmen to prevent the Church from growing too powerful, from becoming an *imperium in imperio*, able to disturb the symmetry of Government. And the traditions of a statecraft sharpened and polished by long centuries of political experience proved stronger in the East than the tentative and undeveloped priestcraft of the ecclesiastics who tried at any time to match themselves against it. But in the West, after the break-up of the Empire, all these conditions of the struggle between Church and State were precisely reversed. To understand the situation, there is nothing more helpful than to compare the map of Europe as it was at the close of the fourth century with its aspect in the sixth. At the former date the whole of what we now call Turkey, Greece, Roumania, Servia, Hungary, Germany south of the Danube, Italy, Switzerland, France, Spain, Portugal, and England, formed integral parts of a single realm, ruled by one monarch, or at most by two, who were viewed as colleagues rather than as rivals, and with one system of law current throughout. At the latter epoch this vast territory is broken up into a number of petty States under the rule of Gepidæ, Ostro-Goths, Suevi, Mœso-Goths, Franks, Burgundians, Alemanni, Huns, Thuringians, West-Goths, Longobards, Saxons, Heruli, and various minor tribes, owning some undefined submission to their more powerful neighbours, and suffered to share their spoils on those terms. Except for the general similarity of tribal customs amongst races of the same stock, there is little to represent uniformity of law; scarcely so much as the notion of international comity is noticeable; and each petty monarch takes the sword as the one principle of statecraft, whether for external defence or internal administration. Save in the one case of England, where the Teutonic invaders made a war of extirpation on the polity, ecclesiastical and civil, which they found there, deliberately wasting the cities and substituting a rude paganism for Christianity, the conquerors of the Empire were powerfully impressed by the strange civilisation with which they came in contact, and, though inevitably destroying much of it, yet retained such fragments as they were able to understand and assimilate. But as they naturally displaced the provincial officers, and set up their own governors, judges, &c., in their stead, the civil tradition was thoroughly broken; while the ecclesiastical body, being little, if at all, interfered with, continued to represent and transmit all that survived of the elder culture and law. The Church was everywhere similarly organized, with the powerful See of Rome as a common centre of appeal and assistance; and the clergy, however low their intellectual development may appear when tried by either an earlier or a later standard, were far more than a match, in all diplomacy, for their untutored victors, who had no conception of the contest in which they were engaged, being unfamiliar with any kind of power save that of open force with the strong hand. Consequently, when any fresh attempt at extending the authority of the Roman See over some Western Church was made, there was no such co-operation of the civil power in defence of the threatened liberties as always had to be reckoned with in schemes of aggression upon the East; for the barbarian kinglets neither comprehended the issues involved, nor, even had this been otherwise, could they have held their own for a moment against the trained diplomacy and the world-wide organization of the Roman Curia. And one most noteworthy result of this comparative weakness and superlative ignorance on the part of the lay authority everywhere in the West was, that the hierarchy was no longer content, as it had previously been, and as it has never ceased to be in Oriental Christendom, with dominion in the strictly spiritual sphere, but aimed steadily thenceforward at temporal supremacy also, at the subjugation of the laity to ecclesiastical law, to the extent of regarding even emperors and kings as but the chief civil officers of the

Church, who derived their commission from her consecration, and were removable at her pleasure for any failure in submissiveness.

It is this new departure which differentiates the fifth century from its predecessor; for, as we have seen, every claim afterwards put forward for the supreme authority of the Roman Chair over the whole Catholic Church in spiritual matters had been already formulated then in the most precise terms. But Gelasius I., the very Pontiff whose demands on behalf of his See were so high and far-reaching, **had admitted in the clearest language the duty of** submission on the part of the clergy to **the lay power in** civil matters.[1] And this is all the more **noticeable because** of **the** explicitness of his demands **for the** submission of the civil power in its turn to the clergy in all matters of religious doctrine.[2]

The fifth century came to a close while the two great bodies which composed the Catholic Church were divided by the schism due, in the first instance, to the ambition **of** Felix III., and more than persevered in by Gelasius I. The Pope who next succeeded, Anastatius II., was **a man** of milder **and** more equitable temper than either **of his** predecessors, and would gladly have made reasonable concessions to Constantinople, with the view of restoring unity. This retractation of the Leonine policy, already the accepted programme **of** the Roman Church, proved **so** distasteful

---

[1] "Si enim quantum ad ordinem pertinet disciplinæ, cognoscentes Imperium tibi superna dispositione collatum, legibus tuis ipsis quoque parent religionis antistites, ne vel in rebus mundanis exclusæ videantur obviare sententiæ; quo, rogo, **te** decet affectu **eis** obedire, qui pro erogandis venerabilibus sunt attributi **mysteriis?**" (Gelas. *Ep. ad Anastat. Imp.* ap. Baron. *Ann.* 494, iv.).

[2] "Nosti etenim, fili clementissime, quod licet præsideas humano generi dignitate, rerum tamen præsulibus divinarum devotus colla submittis, atque ab eis causas tuæ salutis expetis; inque sumendis cælestibus sacramentis, eisque (ut competit) disponendis, subdi te debere cognoscis religionis ordine, potius quam præesse. Nosti itaque **inter** hæc, ex illorum te pendere judicio, non illos ad tuam redigi velle voluntatem" (*Ibid.* iii.).

that great obscurity hangs over the whole abortive negotiation, and all that is certainly known is that the Pope sent a legation to the Emperor, consisting of two distinguished Bishops, Cresconius of Todi and Germanus of Capua, entrusted with a letter wherein—albeit the claims of the Roman Chair to sovereign rank in the Church in virtue of the Petrine privilege are stated in the opening paragraphs according to the fashion set by Leo the Great—phrases stand which imply at least a doubt of the finality of a Papal sentence, as necessarily binding in the other world. The Pope says :—

"Our predecessor Pope Felix and Acacius are both doubtless in that place where no one can fail to receive the meed of his deserts from so great a Judge. . . . The blessed Apostle counsels us not to venture to pass judgment on matters touching which none can judge better or more truly than God ; lest any should take on himself to act rashly in this respect ; and on that account the unity and peace of the Church might be destroyed. . . . We therefore beseech your Clemency that the name of Acacius may be specially passed over in silence, and seeing that he caused offence and scandal for many reasons to the Church, let him be passed over in compliance with this special appeal ; since, as we have said, the deserts of each member of the whole priestly body can in no wise escape that Judge who knows what should be meted out to each according to the account of his stewardship of his gifts, and to whom alone the thoughts are open."[1]

This is something very different from the earlier demand that the name of Acacius should be publicly erased from the diptychs of Constantinople, as a sinner of whose fate no doubt could be entertained, since lying under the Pontifical anathema. Nor did the placability of Anastatius stop here. The *Liber Pontificalis* tells us further that he consented to hold communion with Photinus, a deacon of Thessalonica, who had never broken off communion with Acacius, and that he even purposed the restoration of that Patriarch's name to the Western diptychs. Its testimony on this head has been denied by Ultramontane writers, but there are some convincing proofs that, whether these special acts are

---

[1] Baron. *Ann.* 497, iv.-v.

truly ascribed to Anastatius or not, they do not overpass his actual concessions; for in the letter already cited he, in fact, revokes the most salient clause of his predecessor's sentence on Acacius by acknowledging the validity of the sacraments and orders conferred by him, and that too in a paragraph wherein he says that the Emperor, whom God has appointed "His vicar on earth," is bound to take cognisance of such matters.[1] Baronius, while affecting to discredit the charges of the *Liber Pontificalis*, shows his own belief and feeling by observing (much as Platina had done a century earlier):—

"But if any one chooses to assert contentiously that Anastatius was too much inclined to restore the name of Acacius to the diptychs whence it had been erased, but was unable to accomplish it because anticipated by death; that is the very reason for admiring more and more God's providence towards the Roman Church, seeing that He withdrew from this life the stumbling Pontiff who presided over the Apostolic See, before he could carry out his designs, and that he was punished with death before he could be so much as tempted by Festus the envoy to sign the Henoticon of Zeno. For we know that it has often happened through the will of God, as the principal way whereby He is always wont to safeguard the integrity of the Catholic faith, that whoso was about to bring the Catholic purity of the Roman Church into peril has been cut off by a very sudden death."[2]

Anastatius did, in fact, die on November 17, 498, having sat just a week short of two years. How persistent was the feeling aroused against him in the Roman Church for preferring the peace of Christendom to the authority of his See may be gathered from the fact that Dante, without doubt representing the accepted tradition of his own day, depicts Anastatius as entombed in hell, because of his connexion with Photinus.[3]

The death of the Pope gave the signal for another of those sanguinary contests in the choice of a successor which had already stained the Roman annals. A hasty, but valid, election placed Cælius Symmachus, a convert from Paganism, and the candidate of the party which may be most

[1] Baron. *Ann.* 497, x.   [2] *Ibid.* xxviii.
[3] Dante, *Inferno*, Cant. xi. 4.

easily defined as the Ultramontane one, in the Papal Chair, and he was duly installed in the Basilica of Constantine. But the Senator Festus, leader of the section which desired peace with the East, procured on the same day the election of the Archpriest Laurentius, who was enthroned in Sta. Maria Maggiore. Civil strife, attended with pillage and slaughter, whose guilt seems attributable equally to the rival factions, immediately broke out, and continued till both agreed to submit the election to the arbitration of the Arian sovereign of Italy, Theodoric the Ostrogoth. The party of Symmachus assented with much reluctance to this appeal before a civil authority, but had no other practical course open to it. However, Theodoric confined himself strictly to the single question of the voting, declining any examination into the personal merits of the competitors, and ascertaining that the election of Symmachus was not only prior in point of time, but that he had received the actual majority of votes, promptly decided in his favour: nevertheless requiring that some security should be given against any future breach of the public peace in the event of a disputed election to the Papacy. Accordingly, the king issued a precept for the convention of a Synod to draw up regulations for future elections, to insure their orderliness and tranquillity. This was not altogether an innovation on his part. Pope Simplicius, aware of the factious temper of his flock, had applied to Basilius, Prætorian Prefect under King Odoacer, not to allow the electoral body to proceed to the choice of a Pope on the next vacancy unless in the presence and under the control of the Prefect himself. But when Simplicius died, the electors paid no attention to this provision, and even went so far as to give no notice to the civil magistrate, contrary to the usual custom. Basilius hereupon attended the electoral assembly, and remonstrated against its conduct, on the very sufficient ground that the far from unlikely disturbances which might accompany the discussion would probably spread to the State as well as to the Church, and that it was consequently the business of the civil authority to take due precautions against rioting Nor did he content himself with this remonstrance: for it seems certain that to his representations was due the remarkable law enacted by Odoacer, interfering for the first time with the management and control of Church property, which had till then been left absolutely in the hands of the clergy. It seems, however, that the diversion of these funds for the purposes of faction, and the consequent stirring up of public trouble, had become frequent and dangerous; so that the new law struck vigorously at the abuse by prohibiting all alienations of any kind of Church property, declaring all sales or contracts of the sort null and void, and the alienated property recoverable by the foundation to which it belonged, after any length of adverse possession. An anathema (it does not appear on what authority) was appended to the edict, which was received with much anger by those at whom it was levelled, but they were unable to make any effectual resistance so long as it continued in force.[1] The object of Theodoric was to abolish the evils of canvassing; and when the Synod assembled under the presidency of the new Pope, it consisted of seventy-three bishops, sixty-seven priests, and seven deacons. The following canons, proposed by the Pope, were enacted: (*a*) Any priest, deacon, or clerk, in the lifetime of a Pope, and without his assent, canvassing for the Papacy, making any promises, endeavouring to extort pledges, or joinimg in any caucuses, to secure an election, should be deposed and excommunicated. (*b*) Any one convicted of canvassing for the Papacy during the Pope's lifetime should be anathematized. (*c*) If the Pope should die too suddenly to allow of his personally making arrangements for the choice of his successor (*ut de sui electione successoris, ut supra placuit, non possit ante decernere*), the candidate with the majority of suffrages, if not disqualified by canvassing, should be consecrated. (*d*) Informers against violations of these canons, even if accomplices, should not only receive a free pardon, but be rewarded

---

[1] Baron. *Ann.* 483, x.-xv.

besides.[1] It is not unworthy of remark that the Anti-Pope Laurentius, accepting the decision of Theodoric, took his seat in this Synod, and withdrew at its close to the Bishopric of Nocera; so that no such doubt hangs over the claim of Symmachus to the Papacy as over that of Damasus or Boniface I.

The hostility of the party which had promoted the election of Laurentius was, however, not appeased by his voluntary cession, and in the year 500 the Pope was impeached before King Theodoric for various crimes, and notably as the cause of the violent disorders which had again broken out in Rome. Mention has been made in a former chapter of the remarkable precedent set when a mere local Italian Synod was compelled, in spite of its reclamations, to sit in judgment on the Pope;[2] but there are some curious details which merit notice here. First, the Senator Festus persuaded the king to repeat the precedent set by the Emperor Honorius at the time of the disputed election on the death of Pope Zosimus,[3] and to appoint an Episcopal Vicar as temporary administrator of the See of Rome, to the supersession of the Pope till he had been formally tried: and also to make the necessary preparations for the trial itself, besides performing all episcopal offices as though the See were vacant. Peter, Bishop of Altino, was accordingly nominated, with instructions, however, to exhibit all due respect to the Pope. Instead of doing so, Peter, on his arrival in Rome, at once suspended Symmachus from all his functions, without so much as granting him an interview, or hearing what defence he had to make. This misconduct greatly increased the disturbances at Rome, and obliged the king to come in person to appease the general discontent. It was then that Theodoric convened the Synod of 115 Italian Bishops which first assembled to try the Pope, who, in fact, personally called for the inquiry as

---

[1] Bruns, *Canones*, ii. 289.   [2] Chap. III. p. 109, note.
[3] Baron. *Ann.* 419, xxxiii.

the only effectual way of clearing himself. Theodoric withdrew to Ravenna, to make it clear that he did not intend to overawe the Synod, but absolutely refused the Pope's application for the dismissal of Peter of Altino from his office of sequestrator of the See, and for his own reinstatement before trial. The matter was not pressed after the king's refusal, and is thus a very weighty piece of evidence as to the degree of Papal authority at this date. Symmachus, however, took advantage of a riot, in which he was attacked by the bravos of the opposition party, to retract his consent to the jurisdiction of the Synod; so its members informed the king that the Pope had refused to comply with their summons, and that they did not know how to act, as there was no provision in ecclesiastical law for trying a Pope, especially before the **Bishops** under his own direct jurisdiction.[1] The king told them to decide any way they chose, provided their decision should make for the restoration of peace; and they availed themselves of this leniency to get rid of the whole difficulty by declaring themselves incompetent to decide the question at issue at all, further than by saying that in view of the rank and privileges of St. Peter, the Pope must be declared free from all human responsibility, be restored to all his functions and honours, and, in respect of the charges against him, be left to the judgment of God alone.[2] This was, however, very far from being a unanimous decision. It emanated from only seventy-two Bishops, all known **partisans of the** Pope. The minority of forty-three Bishops **lodged a formal** protest against the acquittal pronounced by what they termed the "Synod of the Incongruous Acquittal" (*Contra Synodum Absolutionis Incongruæ*), on **the threefold** ground that the majority consisted of persons **who had** come with a predetermination to acquit Symmachus, **whatever** the evidence might be; that his accusers had never been heard, so that no real trial had taken place which

---

[1] Hardouin, *Conc.* ii. 974.   [2] *Ibid.* p. 970.

could justify an acquittal; and that the Pope having four times refused, under various pretexts, to appear before his judges, though duly cited, merited condemnation on that ground alone, according to the usual course of law. Remarkable as this protest is, because coming from a body of prelates belonging to the Roman Patriarchate, who might naturally be expected to be submissive to their unquestionable superior, there is a yet more singular document connected with this abortive trial, which emanated from the Papal party. It is the counter-allegation put forward by Ennodius, then deacon and secretary of Symmachus, and afterwards Bishop of Pavia, to the effect that a Pope can be tried only by his own consent, and that, in fact, there never could be any sufficient reason for indicting him with a view to a trial, because one of the chief privileges attached to the Chair of Peter is that of *hereditary innocence;* so that every Pope is, in virtue of his office, a saint, and is either already pure and holy at the time of his election, or becomes so by reason of it. This bold proposition, revived some centuries later by Gregory VII., was far from passing unchallenged; but it was read before a Roman Synod in 503, and embodied by it in its Acts.[1] The motive for holding that Synod was that the Churches of Gaul, thoroughly subjugated as they had been to the Papal Chair by the Edict of Valentinian III., were startled at the news that the Pope was to be put on his trial, and sent a remonstrance to the Italian Bishops through Avitus, Archbishop of Vienne, declaring their opinion to be that the Pope could not be brought to trial by his Bishops, as he was head and chief of the Church Catholic, and they his subjects and inferiors.[2] Such doctrine was far too acceptable and useful at Rome to be left in an informal shape, and Symmachus convened a Synod of 218 Italian Bishops, who, besides accepting the thesis of Ennodius, further enacted that the Pope, as supreme judge in all ecclesiastical

---

[1] Hardouin, *Conc.* ii. pp. 983 *ff.*   [2] *Ibid.* p 981.

and spirtual causes, was responsible to God alone, and—**as** a kind of corollary—that no Bishop, however blameworthy, could be called to account by his own flock, and should not be bound to make any answer, even to a synodal impeachment, until he had first been restored to all property, dignity, or privileges of which his accusers might have deprived him. These canons were enforced by sentences of deposition for the clergy and excommunication for all others. In the previous year, 502, another Roman Synod had professed to repeal the law of Odoacer, **already** mentioned, against the alienation of Church property, though immediately re-enacting it in almost identical terms, and had thus added a virtual claim **of** absolute superiority over the State in all the temporal accidents of the Church **to the** far-reaching spiritual privileges now heaped, so far as **a** local Synod could do it, upon the occupant of the Roman Chair. Thus, although there is abundant evidence that a powerful minority regarded all this as an unwarrantable and dangerous innovation, nevertheless the net result of the troubles under Symmachus was a great increase in the prestige of the Papacy.

Meanwhile, Eastern Christianity was becoming disintegrated more rapidly than that of the West was crystallizing, and the prospect of an accommodation between Rome and Constantinople, already faint, was destroyed by an open breach between Pope Symmachus and the Emperor Anastatius, in which each charged the other with abetting heresy (truly enough so far as the Emperor was concerned); and the interchange of violent discourtesies—on the one hand, inclusive of withholding the usual letters of congratulation on the accession of a new Pope; on the other, a scarcely-veiled sentence of excommunication on the Emperor, as virtually involved in the condemnation of Acacius—did much to embitter the relations of East and West, but, singularly enough, in so doing further advanced the Papal cause. The reasons are as follows. Although Symmachus was an object of distrust and suspicion to the whole moderate school at Rome, and has never **been cleared of** some of the worst charges against him, notably that of selling holy orders,[1] nevertheless no doubt was seriously entertained of his adherence to the doctrinal decrees of Ephesus and Chalcedon. But his pontificate synchronized with a remarkable recrudescence of Eutychianism in the East, actively fostered by the Emperor Anastatius, who showed his hand first by sequestering the Patriarch Euphemius, a man of high character for devoutness and honesty, and then procuring his deposition by a packed Synod; in which he also caused the republication of the Henoticon of Zeno. Macedonius, the Patriarch appointed in the room of Euphemius, proved to be of like temper; and, refusing to reject the Council of Chalcedon at the Emperor's bidding, was arrested and sent into exile. And though even the Emperor failed to persuade or compel any Synod to depose a man so highly esteemed, Timotheus, treasurer of the Great Church, a mere Court lackey, was intruded in his room. His first act was to renounce communion with the Catholic Patriarchs of Antioch and Jerusalem, while sending letters of communion to the Eutychian Patriarch of Alexandria and other Bishops of that party. This precipitated the crisis; and the Catholics of Syria and Palestine, casting about for help in their peril, turned to Rome, known to be free from Monophysite leanings, and addressed a memorial to Pope Symmachus, imploring his assistance, having good reason to think that his personal quarrel with the Emperor would make him all the readier in supporting his own co-religionists. The wording of this memorial is very noteworthy, as showing, on the one hand, what language of deference was thought necessary for the propitiation of the Pope, and, on the other, what saving clauses are interwoven, in order not to make any such formal acknowledgment of Papal authority as might be inconveniently pressed at some future time. A few phrases will serve in illustration. First comes a preamble, in which

---

[1] Hefele, *Conc.* xiii. 220.

they cite the parables of the lost sheep and the lost drachma, and remark that far greater interests are now imperilled, affecting "three-fourths of the habitable world," though purchased with the precious Blood of the Lamb, "as the blessed Prince of the glorious Apostles, whose chair Christ, the Good Shepherd, hath entrusted to your Blessedness, hath taught." Then, reminding the Pope of St. Paul's vision calling him over to Macedonia, they ask him to hasten in like manner, as an affectionate father, to his sons, perishing in the gainsaying of Acacius, and deliver them—

"Since it is not the power of binding only which has been given you, but also that of loosing those long bound, after the pattern of your master. . . . For you are not ignorant of Satan's craft, since you are daily taught by your holy teacher Peter to feed the flock of Christ throughout the whole world, committed to you not to be constrained by force, but voluntarily ; you who with the most learned Paul cry to us your inferiors (*subjectis*) and say : 'Not for that we have dominion over your faith, but are helpers of your joy.'"

Next, defending themselves from the charge of heresy, and explaining the difficulties of their position, which made some intercourse with heretics inevitable, they claim his help as something which he is bound to give, not only on the general ground that only a hireling, and no true shepherd, would abandon sheep thus exposed to the wolf, but specially that he owed a debt of gratitude to the East, whence his own teachers, Peter and Paul, had been divinely sent. Then they say that if their calamity had been less serious, they would have come in person, instead of merely sending a letter. "We would have hastened to our spiritual physician that we might venerate (*adoraremus*) the passions of those good physicians, that is, Christ's glorious disciples, your teachers, and your own holy footsteps : that we might receive medicine for gainsaying, and loosing of bonds, and remission of sins from your holy mouth." A long profession of faith, in accordance with the decrees of Chalcedon, ends this dispirited appeal,

T

markedly unlike any earlier document we possess.[1] No record has been preserved of the Pope's reply, but his general policy in the East was that of a rigid exaction of the hardest terms of communion, so that it may fairly be assumed that the Oriental Bishops took but little by their motion. A revolution of an unexpected nature did far more, however, for the Papal claims than even the submissiveness of the Eastern hierarchy. The Emperor, pushing his support of Eutychianism still further, deposed Flavian of Antioch, and intruded the heresiarch Severus in his place, speedily afterwards depriving Elias of Jerusalem also. The Catholic remnant in the East seemed about to be crushed in a hopeless struggle against the Court, when Vitalian, military governor of Mæsia and Dardania, in the north of that great province of Eastern Illyricum which had always had close relations with Rome, raised the standard of revolt in the first of the religious wars which were to prove such a curse to Christendom, and marched upon Constantinople at the head of a powerful army before the Emperor had time to prepare for defence. Alarmed at the havoc already wrought by the invaders, Anastatius hastened to submit to the demands of Vitalian, which (undoubtedly suggested from Rome) were the recall of Macedonius and Flavian to their Sees, the restoration of all the deprived anti-Eutychian bishops, public confession of the Creed of Chalcedon, and the convocation of an Œcumenical Council, to which the Pope was to be specially invited, to inquire into the legality of the imperial decrees against the Catholics.[2] Just at this crisis Pope Symmachus died, and was succeeded in the Papal Chair by Hormisda; and little as the Emperor was inclined to fulfil his engagements, once the troops of Vitalian had withdrawn, he was obliged to open negotiations with the new Pope in order to keep

---

[1] Baron. *Ann.* 512, xlviii.-lxii. Baronius characteristically draws the conclusion that kissing the Pope's feet was at this time the usual mark of respect paid by bishops admitted to an audience at Rome.
[2] *Ibid.* 514, xl. xli.

up appearances. The letter, addressed "to the most holy and most religious Archbishop and Patriarch Hormisda," was despatched to Rome in January, 515, and the envoy who bore it also carried letters to the Pope from Vitalian (now lost), and from Dorotheus of Thessalonica, the latter of whom besought the Pope not to lose such an opportunity of healing the divisions of the Church. The Emperor's missive was far from cordial or conciliatory. He lays the blame of the cessation of intercourse between himself and Rome on the "stiffness" (*duritia*) of the late Pope, and curtly giving notice of his design to assemble a Council, invites Hormisda to attend in the character of a "mediator."[1] Dorotheus must have wounded Papal susceptibilities nearly as much by the address of his letter, wherein he styles Hormisda his "fellow-minister," and by at least implying, amidst deep professions of respect for the Chair of St. Peter, that Symmachus had been a mere intruder, and that only the regularity of the late election had availed to end the schism in the Roman Church itself.[2]

Hormisda was far from anxious to meet these advances, such as they were, and began by declining to give a definite answer till he should have more information, and with repeating the objection raised long before by Leo the Great, that there was no precedent for the presence of the Roman Pontiff at any Council outside Italy. But pressure from King Theodoric obliged him to give way in some degree, and on receipt of another letter from the Emperor, inviting him to a Council to be held at Heraclea, in Thrace, on July 15 that same year, he consented to send legates in his stead, not, however, to Heraclea itself, but to Constantinople. These legates were the Ultramontane Ennodius of Pavia, already named, Fortunatus of Todi, the priest Venantius, Vitalis, a deacon, and Hilarus, a notary. The instructions of the Pope to these envoys were very full, and aimed far more at increasing the prestige of his See

---

[1] Baron. *Ann.* 515, iv. v.   [2] *Ibid.* viii.-xi.

amongst the Easterns than at healing the divisions of Christendom. He bids them to accept any offer of lodging made them by the Greek Bishops, but not to eat or drink with them, nor even receive gifts of provisions from them, or anything except means of transit, until after the public act of joint communion. They are provided with answers beforehand to almost every proposal or question likely to come from the Emperor; they are told not to communicate with him at the altar till he has publicly declared that his doctrine is not only that of Chalcedon and the Tome of St. Leo, but that he accepts all the ordinances and teachings of the Holy See; on which condition they may hold out hopes of the Pope's attendance at the coming Council. If any petitions are lodged against Bishops for having rejected the Council of Chalcedon and the Tome, they are to receive them, but to reserve the hearing of the cause for the judgment of the Apostolic See, "that you may give hopes of a hearing, and yet our right of deciding the matter may be reserved." They are to refuse all intercourse with the Patriarch Timothy, and are particularly instructed, every time they have occasion to name the Pope to the Emperor, to speak of him as " your Father," giving his orders to a son bound to obedience.[1] To this document, of which only a few of the chief clauses are here cited, was added a schedule of the terms of peace to be imposed on the Emperor, now humbled by the sense of the insecurity of his throne because of the militant and insurgent temper of his Catholic subjects. These terms are as follows:—1. The Emperor is to send a circular letter to all Bishops, declaring his acceptance of the Council of Chalcedon and of the Tome of St. Leo. 2. The Fathers of the Council are to sign a like declaration, and to anathematize, not only Nestorius and Eutyches, with their followers, but also Acacius. 3. All persons exiled for any ecclesiastical reason are to be referred to the hearing of the Apostolic See,

---

[1] Baron. *Ann.* 515, xxiv.-xxxv.

which is to have full powers of inquiry and decision.
4. All persons expelled or exiled, who are known to have remained in communion with the Roman See, are to be at once restored as a matter of right. 5. All Bishops charged with the persecution of Catholics are to be reserved for the judgment of the Apostolic See.[1] The legates were entrusted at the same time with a letter from Hormisda to the Emperor, in which he says that though there is no precedent for a Pope complying with such an invitation to a Council as he had received, he is nevertheless not unwilling to take the matter into consideration, provided a pledge be given beforehand that the Council will decide in one specified way and no other.[2]

Anastatius, placed as he was between two fires, was ready to accept nearly all of these exorbitant demands, but there was one point of more serious importance to him than the others, on which he felt obliged to make a stand, lest he should fatally incense the people of Constantinople. That point was the erasure of the name of Acacius from the diptychs, and the recognition of the validity of the Papal sentence against him. The legates pleaded their precise instructions, of which this was in truth the principal item, as it would be a fatal blow to the privileges of Constantinople; and the negotiations broke off, so far as they were concerned. But the Emperor addressed another letter to the Pope for them to transmit, wherein, after professing his acceptance of the doctrine of Chalcedon, he declares that he could not venture on the erasure of Acacius from the diptychs on his own responsibility without great risk of tumult and bloodshed, and that, for his own part, he did not think it right to drive living men out of the Church on account of dead ones; but that he was ready to leave this question to the Council for settlement.[3] He followed up this letter with an embassy in the next year, sending two

---

[1] Baron. *Ann.* xxxvi.-xxxviii.
[2] *Ibid.* 515, xix.-xxiii. [3] *Ibid.* 516, viii.-xi.

laymen of high rank, Theopompus, Count of the Domestics, and Severianus, Count of the Imperial Consistory, with letters to the Pope and to the Roman Senate, in which he repeated his desire for peace, and asked that the question of Acacius might at least be postponed for the Council to decide. But his overtures were rejected with contumely by the Pope, partly, it would seem, on the pretext of the lay character of the ambassadors; and the original demands were repeated in all their stringency. But in the meanwhile, the Emperor's position had sensibly improved at home, by reason of the popularity he gained through standing firm in the matter of Acacius, and he had besides re-established his authority over Mæsia and Dardania, and had superseded Vitalian himself, whose secret understanding with the Pope had been scarcely doubtful. Accordingly, he saw no use in prosecuting the scheme of a Council, but dismissed the bishops already assembled at Heraclea, and countermanded such as were still on their way; whereupon the Roman legates withdrew from Constantinople.

The Pope was much blamed by all save his own immediate partisans for having thus made the hopes of reconciliation abortive, but a tactical error of the Emperor's gave him an excuse for making a fresh attempt on the liberties of the Eastern Churches. Anastatius determined to revenge himself on those Bishops of Illyricum who had abetted Vitalian's rising, and arrested four of them, including Alcyson of Nicopolis, Metropolitan of Epirus, who died in custody. His comprovincials immediately elected as his successor one John, an ardent partisan of Rome, who at once despatched a letter to the Pope, announcing his consecration, and declaring his adherence to all Papal teachings, including the condemnation of Acacius. A synodal letter from his comprovincials accompanied this private one, and Hormisda promptly replied, commending their zeal, warning them against any intercourse with heretics, and calling on them to redeem their professions of devotion to Rome by signing the document known as the Formulary of Hormisda, which shall be given a little later. And as Dorotheus of Thessalonica, Eparch of Eastern Illyricum, refused to break off communion with Constantinople, the Pope took a step in advance of any aggression on local rights yet essayed by Rome, by disregarding his official rank as Papal Vicar for that province, assuming in his stead direct metropolitical jurisdiction within its limits, ordaining Bishops to all vacant sees, and finally proceeding to excommunicate Dorotheus himself, exempting all his comprovincials from his authority, and even refusing them leave to hold official intercourse with him as their Primate, under pain of being themselves excommunicated.[1] But while thus punishing one whose sole offence had been tardiness in preferring Papal to Imperial commands, Hormisda re-opened negotiations with Anastatius, sending Ennodius of Pavia and Peregrinus of Misenum as legates in April, 517, to Constantinople, ostensibly with public letters only, addressed to the Emperor, the Patriarch, and the Bishops, with exhortations to orthodoxy and unity; but also with more private instructions to stir up cabals in the Roman interest at Constantinople, and to take measures in concert with the enemies of the Government, in case the Papal demands were not acceded to. The Court, which had private information throughout, allowed the legates to do as they pleased, and commit themselves fully to constructive treason, but then suddenly arrested and deported them, while the Emperor terminated the abortive negotiations in a far from undignified letter to the Pope, contrasting his arrogant and implacable temper with the example of the Saviour, and ending with the significant words: "We can bear with being insulted and made of no account; we cannot bear to receive orders."[2]

It seemed as if the Papal game had been played out in the East, but a fresh chance was given by the impolitic cruelties of Severus of Antioch, an anti-Catholic zealot, who

---

[1] Baron. *Ann.* 516, xliv.–xlvi.
[2] *Ibid. Ann.* 516, xlix. "Injuriari et annullari sustinere possumus, juberi non possumus."

fired the Catholic monasteries, and slaughtered as many as three hundred and fifty monks on a single occasion. An appeal to the Emperor against Severus, his own nominee, proved to be in vain, and accordingly the sufferers addressed themselves to the Pope and the Western Bishops in general for help and redress, undertaking on their part to anathematize all who had been condemned by the Apostolic See.[1] This document was signed by twenty-five Archimandrites, and one hundred and seventy priests and deacons. Hormisda, in his reply, tells them that all their sufferings are due to their having left the one true shepherd—namely, himself—but that affliction has brought them back to the degrees and mandates of the Apostolic See, though somewhat tardily, and that if they persevere in that course, and anathematize all whom Rome has condemned, he will extend his favour to them, and notably if they resist all commands of the secular authority in spiritual concerns, as the Temple priesthood did King Uzziah.[2]

The death of Anastatius in 518, and the accession of Justin I., an orthodox sovereign, changed the situation at Constantinople with much rapidity. The Patriarch and all the Court-prelates hastened to abjure Eutychianism, to revive the decrees of Chalcedon, and to restore the names of Euphemius, Macedonius, and Leo the Great to the diptychs. But although the doctrinal gulf between Rome and Constantinople was thus narrowed, the proceedings were not such as gave satisfaction to the former, for the Synod which assembled to ratify the change took no account whatever of Papal acts in its proceedings, and though restoring the name of Leo to the diptychs, placed it below those of Euphemius and Macedonius, both of whom had died excommunicated by the Pope for refusing to admit the validity of the sentence on Acacius. But the new Emperor was anxious to make peace with Rome, and Rome cared little for any restoration of orthodox teaching which

---

[1] Baron. *Ann.* liv.–lviii.   [2] *Ibid.* 518, iii.–xii.

did not include submission to her demands. Accordingly, when the Patriarch sent formal notice to the Pope of the Synod which had just been held, and of the restoration of his name, as well as that of his predecessor Leo, to the Constantinopolitan diptychs, asking him to send envoys to conclude the peace now begun, the Emperor sent Count Gratus with a letter to the same effect, and, what is more important, that officer bore also a private letter to the Pope from the Emperor's nephew, the famous Justinian, broadly hinting that the question of Acacius was to be decided in the Pope's sense, and asking him to come in person to Constantinople, or at least to send legates clothed with plenipotentiary powers, on that understanding.[1] A victory for the Papal Chair was thus a foregone conclusion, nor was any serious resistance to be expected from the Patriarch John, a man of facile and yielding temper. The Pope saw his advantage, and was far from cordial or encouraging in his reply. To the Emperor he briefly says that it is high time the Greek Bishops came to a better mind, and that he will send directions to them as to their conduct for the future, as also a Formulary to sign, on their reception of which his own policy will depend. To the Patriarch he is more explicit, and even less friendly; asking him how he can reconcile the discrepancy of accepting the decrees of Chalcedon, and yet continuing to uphold Acacius; and alleging that the necessary corollary of his having at last embraced the faith of blessed Peter is that he is bound to receive also all the judgments of the Apostolic See without any hesitation, and to set a good example to all the Oriental Bishops by being the first to sign the Formulary.[2]

The Pope then prepared to send a legation to the East, consisting of the Bishops Germanus and John, Blandus, a presbyter, and Felix and Dioscorus, deacons. They were given the most precise instructions not to hold communion,

---

[1] Baron. *Ann.* 518, lxxi.-lxxxi. "De nomine tantummodo Acacii vestræ Beatitudinis convenit audire consensum."
[2] *Ibid.* lxxviii.-lxxxi.

nor even to eat, with any one who did not first sign the Formulary; to insist on the erasure from the diptychs, not only of the name of Acacius, but of his successors, and that if it should be argued that two of these, Euphemius and Macedonius, were not only of unquestionable orthodoxy, but had even suffered as confessors for the faith of Chalcedon, they were to reply that they had no authority to vary one tittle from the text of the Formulary; and that if the Patriarch gave way on these points, then they were to require him to send a circular letter to all the bishops within his jurisdiction, urging them to follow his example.[1] The legates were also entrusted with a large number of letters to high civil personages, both men and women, urging them to do all in their power to bring about the desired result. The progress of the legates was almost a triumphal march through the cities they traversed on their way, and they procured signatures without difficulty to the Formulary, thereupon admitting the signatories to the Roman communion. At Constantinople itself they were received with high honours, and the Emperor desired them to hold a preliminary conference with the Patriarch, to settle the terms of union with him. They replied that the terms were already settled by the Pope, and that they were not empowered to alter them in any respect; and, in fact, the Patriarch made no difficulty as to the erasure of the name of Acacius, which had been the one point insisted on by the predecessors of Hormisda. But when the further demand was pressed that he should also anathematize his own orthodox predecessors, Euphemius and Macedonius, who had been all but martyrs for the decrees of Chalcedon, and whose sole offence had been the non-recognition of an uncanonical Papal judgment, John displayed unexpected firmness, and protested against the clause, as also against the far-reaching claims of jurisdiction with which it was accompanied, as making the Pope master of Christendom, and communion with him the one requisite for

---

[1] Baron. *Ann.* 519, iii.–vii.

salvation. The legates, however, would abate nothing, and the Emperor, whose own mind was made up for peace at any price, and who, as a grossly illiterate man, unable even to read or write, was quite incapable of estimating justly the principles at stake, first had the civil sanction of the Senate given to the Formulary, and then proceeded to extort the Patriarch's signature. He still held out, asking that, instead of signing the Formulary itself, he might be allowed to draft a letter of his own to the Pope to the same general effect, but varied in wording, to avoid the difficulties presented by a document drawn up in the Roman Chancery. There was a long discussion over this proposal, and a compromise was at last agreed on, that the Patriarch might prefix a letter to his signature, but was to sign absolutely. Accordingly, John, addressing Hormisda in the traditional form as his "brother and fellow-minister," astutely inserted two clauses in his letter which effectually barred the possibility of basing any future claims over Constantinople on the fact of his signature. The first of these runs thus :—

"I hold that the most holy Churches of God—that is, yours of Old Rome and this of New Rome—are one ; I define that it, the See of blessed Peter, and this, the seat of Imperial Government, are one."

The second clause went yet further, by implicitly reasserting Canon XXVIII. of Chalcedon, in these terms :—

"I assent to all the Acts of those four Councils, Nicæa, Constantinople, Ephesus, and Chalcedon, touching the confirmation of the Faith *and the constitution of the Church*, and I suffer no disturbance of their wise decisions, for I know that such as attempt to interfere with a single tittle of their decrees have fallen away from the Holy Catholic and Apostolic Church of God."[1]

At a Synod held in presence of the Roman legates, the Formulary was then accepted by the Emperor, his Court, the Patriarch and the clergy, and the names of Acacius, Fravitta, Euphemius, and Macedonius, as well as those of

---

[1] Baron. *Ann.* 519, xlviii.

the Emperors Zeno and Anastatius, were struck out of the diptychs; whereupon the legates declared the thirty-five years' schism at an end, and the Churches re-united; and that on the sole terms which Rome had demanded from the beginning—those of simple submission to her demands.

It is now time to give the text of this remarkable document in full, as the best comment on the preceding narration.

"The chief means of salvation is to keep the rule of the right faith, and to depart in no wise from the decrees of the Fathers. And forasmuch as the words of Our Lord Jesus Christ cannot be set aside when He said, 'Thou art Peter,' &c., these words are proved true by their results, since religion has always been preserved unspotted in the Apostolic See. Therefore, desiring not to be separated from its faith and hope, and following the decrees of the Fathers in all respects, we anathematize all heretics, especially the heretic Nestorius, formerly Bishop of the city of Constantinople, condemned in the Council of Ephesus by Celestine, Pope of the city of Rome, and by St. Cyril, Bishop of the city of Alexandria. Together with them anathematizing Eutyches and Dioscorus of Alexandria, condemned in the holy Council of Chalcedon, which we follow and embrace. Uniting with these the parricide [1] Timothy, surnamed Ælurus, and his disciple and follower, Peter or Acacius, who abode in the fellowship of their communion, because, since he mixed himself up with their communion, he merited a like sentence of condemnation with them. Likewise condemning Peter of Antioch, with his followers and those of the aforenamed. Wherefore we receive and approve all the letters of Pope Leo, which he wrote concerning the Christian religion. Whence, as we have said before, following the Apostolic See in all respects, and teaching all its decrees, I hope that I may merit to be in the one communion with you, that which the Apostolic See maintains, wherein is the whole and perfect steadfastness of the Christian religion; promising further that the names of such as are separated from the communion of the Catholic Church—that is, who do not agree in all respects with the Apostolic See—are not to be recited during the Holy Mysteries. I have subscribed this my profession with my own hand, and have presented it to thee, Hormisda, the holy and venerable Pope of Old Rome."

Justin was not content with procuring the submission of the capital to the new act of union, but proceeded to

---

[1] As an accomplice in the murder of his predecessor, the Patriarch St. Proterius.

force it on the East in general, with but little resistance anywhere, save from Dorotheus of Thessalonica, who had reason to know more of the aims and temper of Rome than most of the Oriental prelates, and who went so far as to snatch the Formulary out of the hands of the legate John, who had been specially despatched to him, and to tear it up publicly; an act at once followed by a riot, in which the legate nearly lost his life. The Pope demanded satisfaction, and that Dorotheus should be sent to be tried at Rome; but the Emperor contented himself with trying him at Constantinople, and suffered him, after a mere nominal penalty, to return to his see, on condition of his sending a formal legation of apology to Rome, which he did in 520, but without making any real concessions, and throwing all the blame on the legate—an excuse with which the Pope was forced to content himself.

At first sight it does not seem at all clear why the Emperor Justin should have exerted himself so actively to bring about the humiliation of the great communion of which he was the natural protector; though it is easy enough to understand the eagerness of the lately persecuted Eastern Catholics to obtain, at the price of what they never intended as practical concessions, the support of the orthodox and powerful Church of Rome against any fresh violence from the Eutychian party. But it is easy to come at the facts by looking a little forward into the history of Italy. Although King Theodoric was sole master of that country, and the Pope's position as his subject made that dignitary in a sense independent of the Emperor, and able to treat with him from a level impossible had he been his born subject instead; yet in the theory of the Byzantine Court the Italian sovereign was a mere removable viceroy of the Emperor, true monarch of the whole Roman dominion. And as Theodoric was an Arian in creed, and insisted on full toleration of his co-religionists, his sway was extremely distasteful to the Catholic zealots, whose centre of operations was at Rome; and there is sufficient proof that the bribe held out to the

Emperor Justin was that of material aid from the Pope in any attempt to recover the crown of Italy, provided he in turn would assist the Papal designs against the liberties of the Eastern Churches. But, willing as the Emperor had been to fulfil his part of the bargain, Hormisda was to learn the evil of having grasped at too much. Widespread refusal to accept that part of the Formulary which had required the condemnation of Euphemius and Macedonius began to manifest itself, the new Patriarch, Euphemius, John's successor, setting the example. There were tokens that to insist on this point might provoke a revolution perilous to the crown, perhaps to the life, of the Emperor; and accordingly both Justin and Justinian wrote to the Pope, entreating him to be content with the erasure of the name of Acacius alone, and telling him of the risks attending too rigid insistence on all the terms of the Formulary; and the Patriarch sent a similar memorial, accompanied with a magnificent present of altar-plate. Hormisda returned at first an absolute refusal to modify his demands, but, on the Emperor letting it be evident that he was ready now to side against Rome, changed his policy, and left it open to the Patriarch to receive into the Roman communion, as holding a proxy from himself, all who would anathematize Acacius and the Eutychian leaders.[1] The immediate result was that the Patriarch replaced the names of Euphemius and Macedonius on the diptychs, without any protest from Rome, and thus much of the ground so recently gained after nearly a century of steady effort was lost again. Shortly afterwards Hormisda died (August 6, 523), and was succeeded by John I. The short career of this Pontiff supplies the key to the relations between his predecessor and the Emperor, as will now be shown briefly. The Emperor Justin soon betook himself to an acrid persecution of his Arian subjects, and King Theodoric, who regarded himself as their natural champion, readily responded to an appeal they made to his good offices, and,

---

[1] Baron. *Ann.* 521, xxviii.–xxx.

after casting about for the most effectual mode of aiding them, bethought himself of sending the Pope as his ambassador to Constantinople, to remonstrate with the Emperor, and to obtain a cessation of the persecution. The means he employed to extort a consent was a threat of enacting an edict against the Catholics of Italy, if that against the Arians of the East were not abrogated by the Emperor—a piece of moral suasion which proved successful; and the Pope actually did set out for Constantinople, at the head of an embassy in which five other bishops and four senators of high rank were conjoined. He was received with extraordinary honours, and made no difficulty about communicating with any one save Timothy, the Eutychian Patriarch of Alexandria, so that a full retractation was in this way made of the constructive anathemas of the Formulary. John succeeded entirely in the mission with which he was entrusted, and procured toleration for his sovereign's clients with suspicious facility, as it seemed to Theodoric, for upon his return to Italy to give an account of his embassy, he was thrown into prison immediately after his interview with the king at Ravenna, and remained there until his death on May 18, 526. No explanation of this transaction is adequate, or even plausible, save that which ascribes the king's anger to the discovery of a wide-spread conspiracy for the re-annexation of Italy to the Empire, for an alleged share in which Boethius and Symmachus also suffered the penalty of death. That such a conspiracy was in fact on foot is more than probable; that the designs of the Byzantine Court were as Theodoric suspected admits of no doubt at all, for the wars of Belisarius proved it ere long; and the intercourse between Rome and Constantinople had been too intimate for a long time not to arouse the gravest distrust. A very important principle was introduced on the appointment of a successor to Pope John I. The king nominated Felix, a man of high character, to the Papal Chair on his own responsibility, in order to avoid the tumults and bloodshed only too likely to attend a disputed election, as the competitors were numerous and party spirit was running high. But all sides joined together against the royal choice, as an infringement of the liberty of election; and Theodoric agreed to a compromise, whereby the existing appointment was to hold good, but all future elections were to vest in the clergy and people of Rome, subject to the approval and confirmation of the Crown, which was to have the right of veto—an arrangement whose practical good sense is attested by its continuance, at any rate in theory, till the erection of the College of Cardinals into the electorate of the Popedom more than five hundred years afterwards. Theodoric died a few months after the accession of Felix IV., and was followed to the grave in the next year, 527, by the Emperor Justin. The removal of the Gothic king's strong hand was soon evident, for on the death of Pope Felix IV., in 530, there was a disputed election between Boniface and Dioscorus, who were both chosen and installed on the same day by their several adherents, whose actuating motive in both cases appears to have been open bribery. The death of Dioscorus within a few days left the victory with Boniface II., who first proceeded to excommunicate and curse the memory of his late competitor as a simoniac, and caused the sentence, after receiving a number of confirmatory signatures, to be laid up in the archives of the Roman Church: a proceeding reversed, however, by Agapetus, his near successor. His next step was to obtain a decree from his pliant Synod, empowering him to name his own successor, and he thereupon chose his deacon, Vigilius, for the reversion of the Chair. But neither the electors nor the State—represented by Queen Amalasuintha, daughter of Theodoric, and regent in the minority of her son, King Athalaric — proved content with this encroachment, and the Pope was compelled to revoke the new ordinance in a Synod held the next year (531), to burn it with his own hand in presence of the Senate, and to confess himself guilty of high treason (*Papa reum se confessus est majestatis*).[1]

---

[1] Anastas. Biblioth. ap. Baron. *Ann.* 531, ii.

The failure of the Formulary to exercise any practical influence in the East was illustrated in this Pontificate by one of the many disputes recorded between Rome and Constantinople in respect of jurisdiction over Eastern Illyricum. Stephen, Metropolitan of Larissa in Thessaly, within that eparchate, sent one of his suffragans to Rome, appealing against a sentence of deposition pronounced against him by Epiphanius, Patriarch of Constantinople, partly on the ground of the merits of the sentence itself, but also alleging that by the custom of his province the appeal lay to Rome, and not to Constantinople, even apart from the general right of the Pope to hear appeals from all quarters. It was easy for Stephen to show that the Popes from Damasus I. onwards had exercised or claimed jurisdiction there, and had appointed a succession of vicars; and the fact that the Bishops, whose complaints of the irregularity of his election had led to his fall, made their appeal to Constantinople, and not to Rome, was not likely to make their judgment weigh much with a Roman Pope and Synod. Accordingly, a decree was passed restoring Stephen to his see; but we have a letter from Pope Agapetus, four years later, complaining to the Emperor Justinian that Epiphanius had paid no attention to the Papal decision, but had consecrated one Achilles instead.[1]

Pope Boniface II. died in 532, and the scenes of bribery and corruption which had disgraced the election when he was chosen—his own share in which is almost proved by a decree then enacted by the Senate against any future offence of the sort—were repeated on a yet larger and more shameful scale during the vacancy of the see. In fact we have a letter from King Athalaric, addressed to Pope John II., stating that not only were the funds for the relief of the poor diverted to this purpose, but the very altar-vessels were put up to auction to supply means for the same object.[2] He made this charge on the complaint of the

---

[1] Baron. *Ann.* 535, lii.–liii.   [2] Cassiod. *Var.* ix. 15.

Advocate of the Roman Church, and the result was the enactment of a fresh decree from the king, affirming and amplifying the edict of 530, regulating the fees payable for the future at the election of any Pope, metropolitan, or bishop, ordering the new Pope, John II., to publish the decree itself in all churches subject to his jurisdiction, and enjoining the Prefect of Rome to have it engraved on marble tablets, and set up conspicuously in the vestibule of St. Peter's.[1] These proofs of the continuous bribery which prevailed in the local Church of Rome have a very important legal and theological bearing on the whole question of the Petrine claims, because the received Roman doctrine is that simony is not only mortal sin and sacrilege, but also heresy of the gravest kind; voiding, besides, all offices procured directly or indirectly through its means, and no length of prescription can ever cure this defect.[2] Consequently, every instance of the kind constitutes a flaw in the Papal succession, not only voiding the special Pontificate in which it occurs, but seriously weakening the evidence for the canonicity of any subsequent election where the result may have been affected by electors deriving their orders or title from a simoniacal Pope. Baronius, fully alive to the difficulty, assures us that the bribers never were elected, and that the suffrages always fell on men of blameless antecedents. But he neither offers any proof, nor explains the singular persistence of the candidates in a method which, on his showing, never succeeded.

A doctrinal dispute which had originated under Pope Hormisda, and was revived under John II., has equal value as a test of that part of the Papal claims which alleges that the Pope holds the office of supreme and infallible teacher, as well as ruler, of the Catholic Church. The question at issue was whether the expression "One of the Trinity suffered in the flesh" were orthodox or

---

[1] Cassiod. *Var.* ix. 16. [2] Ferraris, *Prompta Bibliotheca*, s.v. "Simonia."

heretical. Some Scythian monks who upheld the phrase were impeached as heretics, and appealed in 519 to the Pope's legates, then at Constantinople, who promptly gave judgment against them. They appealed to the Pope himself, sending four of their number as envoys to Rome, where they were very badly received; for not only did Hormisda confirm the sentence of his legates, but kept the envoys in virtual imprisonment for a twelvemonth, at the end of which they either made their escape or were expelled. In any case they contrived, before quitting Rome, to post up in several public places their confession of faith in twelve articles, to which as many anathemas were appended against all, without exception, who rejected them. The Pope was extremely indignant at this piece of audacious defiance, and addressed a letter on the subject to Possessor, an African Bishop, in which he complained against them in violent language as dishonest, crafty, disputatious, heterodox, intractable, and rebellious, with no compunction in setting up their own judgment against that of the Holy See, and added that he makes these charges in order that Possessor may give them the widest publicity throughout the East.[1] This was accordingly done, but only with the result that Maxentius, one of the inculpated monks, published a reply, denying the authenticity of the Pope's letter, as impossible to have proceeded from any Christian Bishop, and as a flagrantly heretical document: a view in which he was upheld by the great body of Oriental bishops, and by the African bishops also, headed by St. Fulgentius of Ruspe. So the matter rested until the controversy was kindled afresh in 533, in consequence of an edict of Justinian against all heretics, when it became a matter of practical importance to know which of the competing views brought its champions within purview of the law. Those who took the side which Hormisda had espoused sent two envoys to Rome to obtain a decree in their favour from

---

[1] Baron. *Ann.* 520, xvi.-xviii.

the new Pope, instructing them to plead that the point had been already ruled in their favour, and that it could not now be decided in the opposite way without great discredit to the Church of Rome, according to that saying of the Apostle, "If I build again the things which I destroyed, I make myself a transgressor."[1] Justinian, who held the other view, despatched two Bishops, Hypatius of Ephesus and Demetrius of Philippi, on a mission to Rome, bearing with them a long confession of his own belief, inclusive of the disputed tenet, and also a letter to the Pope telling him that this was the received doctrine of the whole Eastern Church, and desiring him to declare in answer that he received to his communion all who held that faith, and no others. The Pope heard both sides, but found himself in great difficulty, between the risk to the prestige of his Chair involved in condemning his predecessor's ruling, and the practical danger of setting himself against the powerful Emperor and the whole Eastern Church. He assembled the Roman clergy to discuss the questions, but they were so divided on the merits that no result could be attained in this wise; and he then applied for counsel to extern Churches, and notably to Ferrandus of Carthage, the first canonist of the day. Ferrandus promptly replied in favour of Justinian's view, and was supported therein by the chief contemporary theologians. Hereupon the Pope assembled his Synod anew, and formally approved the confession of Justinian, declaring that all who disputed it should be excommunicated. He sent notice of this judgment to the Emperor and to the Senate of Rome, specially warning the latter against holding communion with those monks at Constantinople (the Accemetæ) who upheld the doctrine of Hormisda.[2] This curious transaction has a further historical value, in that it enables us to appraise exactly the force of certain phrases of compliment addressed by Justinian to the Pope, which have

---

[1] Galat. ii. 18.   [2] Liberatus, *Breviar.* c. 24.

been relied on by Ultramontanes as establishing the acceptance of the Supremacy by the East in the sixth century. The most noteworthy of these expressions are embodied in the Code, and a few citations will be useful:—

"Justinian, victor, pious, fortunate, famous, triumphant, ever Augustus, to John, the most holy Archbishop and Patriarch of the noble city of Rome. Paying honour to the Apostolic See and to your Holiness, as always has been and is our desire, and honouring your Blessedness as a father, we hasten to bring to the knowledge of your Holiness all that pertains to the condition of the Churches, since it has always been our great aim to safeguard the unity of your Apostolic See and the position of the holy Churches of God which now prevails and abides securely without any disturbing trouble. Therefore we have been sedulous to subject and unite all the priests of the Orient throughout its whole extent to the See of your Holiness.[1] Whatever questions happen to be mooted at present, we have thought necessary to be brought to your Holiness's knowledge, however clear and unquestionable they may be, and though firmly held and taught by all the clergy in accordance with the doctrine of your Apostolic See; for we do not suffer that anything which is mooted, however clear and unquestionable, pertaining to the state of the Churches, should fail to be made known to your Holiness, as being the head of all the Churches. For, as we have said before, we are zealous for the increase of the honour and authority of your See in all respects."[2]

Nothing looks more precise than this pronouncement; and yet it is not merely balanced by the same title of "Head of all the Churches," applied in the same Code to the See of Constantinople,[3] and by the formal re-assertion in the *Novells* of the decrees of Constantinople and Chalcedon as to the rank and powers of the former city,[4] but this seeming act of submission is actually the preamble of the very confession of faith which Justinian forced on the Pope, compelling him to alter the ruling of the Roman Church on a

---

[1] This incidentally proves that the East had not been hitherto subject to the Roman See.
[2] *Cod. Justin.* lib. i. tit. 1.
[3] Ἡ ἐν Κωνσταντινουπόλει ἐκκλησία πασῶν τῶν ἄλλων ἐστὶ κεφαλή. —*Cod. Just.* I. ii. 24.
[4] *Novell.* cxxxi. 1, 2.

point of doctrine, in order to bring it into conformity with the teaching of the Eastern Church. There can be little doubt, however, that Justinian, whose plans for the re-annexation of Italy to the Empire were nearly ripe, was fully alive to the value of the Pope's alliance, and would spare no fair words which might help to secure it; while it equally suited the Pope's purpose to accept them as seriously meant, saying in his reply :—

> "Amongst the shining merits of your wisdom and goodness, most Christian Prince, one star sheds especial light, in that through love of the faith and desire of charity, you, instructed in Church discipline, maintain the reverence due to the Roman See, and subject all thereto, and lead unto its unity; . . . . which See the canons of the Fathers and the statutes of sovereigns declare to be truly Head of all the Churches, as the most honoured words of your piety furthe attest."[1]

John II. died in May, 535, and was peaceably succeeded by Agapetus, Archdeacon of Rome. His Pontificate, though one of the briefest in the annals of the Papacy, for he sat but ten months, was very eventful in its bearing on the consolidation of the Papal power. The first incident which calls for notice is his reply to the congratulatory letter sent him by Justinian, who asked him therein to confirm his predecessor's decision as to the proposition "One of the Trinity suffered," and to declare excommunicate such as rejected it. The new Pope complied, but told the Emperor that he did so because the doctrine was that of the Fathers, not because a layman was good enough to tell him what to teach.[2]

Justinian soon applied to him again, urging that the Arian bishops and clergy should be allowed, on conforming to the Catholic Church, to retain the ecclesiastical rank they had held in their sect; and further desired that he

---

[1] Baron, *Ann.* 534, xv.

[2] "Non quia laici auctoritatem prædicationis admittimus, sed quia studium fidei vestræ patrum nostrorum regulis conveniens confirmamus atque roboramus."—Baron. *Ann.* 535, xxxii.

would transfer the seat of the Papal Vicariate over Eastern Illyricum from Thessalonica to Justiniana Prima, a town which has long ago returned to its earlier name of Scupi (Σκοῦποι), being now known as Skopia or Ushkub.

In return for these concessions, the Emperor offered to reopen the case of Stephen of Larissa, deposed by the Patriarch Epiphanius, and to allow its rehearing, provided the Pope would send legates to the East for the purpose. The reply of Agapetus to the more important of these demands is of the highest evidential value, as explaining the true meaning of an appeal to the "Canons" on the part of the Roman Curia when any question of the prerogatives or discipline of the Holy See was mooted. The Pope declares the concession to be impossible, not merely on the ground of practical inexpediency, but that to admit heretics to ecclesiastical office would be an open breach of the "constitutions of the Fathers," a phrase which he glosses a little later as meaning "the public and synodal acts of the Apostolic See."[1] In point of fact, the conciliar authority is all but entirely in the opposite sense. The General Council at Nicæa had enacted in its eighth canon (according to its most probable interpretation) that conformists from the Cathari should retain their ecclesiastical rank. Canon LXVIII. of the African Code gives every Bishop the option of recognising Donatist Orders, and specially directs that notice of this enactment be sent to the Pope, as being merely the re-affirmation of the received usage of the African Churches. St. Augustine expressly states that a Roman Synod had decreed the admission of the Donatist clergy in their ecclesiastical rank: his indications fix it as that of 313 under Pope Melchiades.[2] The first Council of Orleans in 511 had enacted in its tenth canon that heretic ecclesiastics, on conforming, should be admissible to any grade at the Bishop's discretion, with a benedictory imposition of hands; while the

---

[1] Baron. *Ann.* 535, 1.   [2] *Lib. ad Bonifac.* c. 47.

whole evidence on the other side is Canon LI. of the Council of Elvira in 305, denying ordination to lay converts from heresy, and decreeing the deposition of clerical ones.

When the ground of the Pope's assertion is sought, none is discoverable save a decretal letter of his predecessor Innocent I. to Alexander, Patriarch of Antioch; wherein it is laid down that clerical converts from Arianism cannot be admitted as ecclesiastics, because, having lost through their heresy the gift of the Holy Spirit, which operates chiefly in ordination, they have no power of bestowing it. It is thus clear that the Popes treated the local constitutions and usages of their own See as being in fact laws of and for the Church Universal, and that such is the meaning to be put on any of their allegations of canons as making in their favour, when no such canons are to be found recorded in the Acts of the acknowledged Councils. Agapetus accepted the offer of the Emperor as to the case of Stephen of Larissa, complaining, however, of what had been done so far; but there is no record of the final settlement of the dispute. The victories of Belisarius over the Vandals in Africa led to a temporary revival of the Church there, almost crushed out as it had been by the long Arian persecution; and a synod of 217 bishops, assembled at Carthage in 534 under the Metropolitan Reparatus, sent a letter to Pope John II., in which they told him that their opinion was against permitting the conforming Arian clergy to retain their rank; but that they wished, before formally publishing this decision, to know what might be the usage or rule of the Roman Church on the matter, and that they would be glad of the Pope's advice, on the chance of his being able to give them a reply which they could generally approve and accept.[1] This letter had been designed for John II., but it fell to Agapetus to answer it, which he did

---

[1] "Potest enim Sedes Apostolica (quantum speramus) tale nobis interrogantibus dare responsum, quale nos approbare concorditer, explorata veritate, faciat."—Baron. *Ann.* 535, xxiii.

in a sense very different from that of the senders, treating it as an act of homage and duty to the Apostolic Primacy, and directing Reparatus to make the Papal rescript, refusing recognition to the Arian clergy, known to all within his jurisdiction, that no one might plead ignorance of the decision of the Apostolic See as to the meaning of the canons.[1]

A more important episode in the life of Agapetus was now at hand. Athalaric, the young King of Italy, died in 534, and the feeble Theodahat, nephew of Theodoric, on whom Queen Amalasuintha bestowed her hand, and whom she raised to the rank of king, rewarded her confidence by imprisoning and murdering her. This gave Justinian the opportunity for which he had been waiting. He at once declared war on Theodahat, and promptly attacked and subdued Dalmatia and Sicily. Theodahat, conscious that he was unprepared for successful resistance, determined to send the Pope on an embassy to Constantinople to make terms, directing him to say that, if his proposals were rejected, Rome should be destroyed, and the Senate and people be put to the sword. It is noticeable that the property of the Roman Church had been so squandered by successive simoniacal Popes, either by direct alienation or by mortgage, in order to pay for electioneering expenses, that Agapetus had to pawn the Church-plate to raise funds for his outfit; a fact which confutes the theory of Baronius, for it is obvious that the unsuccessful bribers could not have obtained control over the Papal revenues, and that the waste must be set down to the account of Popes themselves. His political mission to Constantinople came to nothing, but he was at once engaged in an important Church question. The Empress Theodora had procured the election of Anthimus, Bishop of Trebizond, to the vacant Patriarchal See, an appointment at once in the teeth of the canons against translations,

---

[1] Baron. *Ann.* 535, xxxvii.-xli.

and objectionable besides, because of the Eutychian tenets ascribed to him. Agapetus refused to communicate with Anthimus till he should publicly clear himself of the charge of Eutychianism, and added that he should in no case acknowledge him as lawful Patriarch. He stood out boldly against the threats of Justinian, bringing him round to his side at last, and securing the supersession of Anthimus, and the election of Mennas, Warden of St. Samson's Hospital, Constantinople, whom the Pope consecrated in his stead. Baronius cites this as a direct exercise of the Supremacy, in that Agapetus, as above all canons, deposed the first Bishop of the Eastern Church without the concurrence of a Council, though such concurrence was required by canon law.[1] But in truth there was no question of deposition at all, because Anthimus had no canonical claim to the see, as being invalidly chosen; and there is the incontestable evidence of the *Novells* of Justinian that Anthimus was also synodically condemned, and, further, that all the proceedings were civilly validated by an imperial decree.[2] As to the consecration of the new Patriarch by the Pope, Liberatus tells us expressly that it was by favour of the Emperor that the act took place.[3]

Agapetus died at Constantinople, in April 536, and Sylverius, son of Pope Hormisda, was nominated by Theodahat, and elected —it is said, under intimidation—by the clergy. The new Pope had an understanding with Belisarius, then preparing to advance on Rome, and actually succeeded in getting the people to rise against the weak Gothic garrison, and to invite the Imperial general to take possession of the city for his master, which he did on December 10, 536.[4] This might have given him a title to the goodwill of the conquerors, but a perfidious intrigue, long matured against him, was to avenge his treason to his own sovereign. Vigilius, deacon of the Roman Church, who had accompanied Pope Agapetus to Constantinople, continued there as resi-

---

[1] Baron. *Ann*. 536, xxxi.
[2] *Novell. Just*. xlii.
[3] *Breviar*. c. 21.
[4] Gibbon, c. 41.

dent nuncio or legate, and entered into a plot with the Empress Theodora for his own advancement to the Papacy with her aid, which he was to repay by declaring himself a Eutychian on his election. She provided him with seven hundred pounds of gold for the purpose of bribery, and also with letters to Belisarius and his wife Antonina, to secure their co-operation. He was too late to reach Rome before the election, and the question then was how to get rid of Sylverius. In the meanwhile Theodahat had been slain by a subject he had outraged, and Witiges, the new Gothic king, made a bold attempt to reconquer Rome. He was supported by a party within the city, and a correspondence was produced implicating Pope Sylverius in the plot. It is believed by most modern critics that the charge was falsely trumped up between Theodora and Antonina, and that Vigilius had procured the forgery. In any case, it appears that the Pope was brought before Belisarius and told that he might save his person and rank by promising to condemn the Council of Chalcedon, and to receive the Eutychians to communion. He steadfastly refused, and was at once stripped of the ensigns of his rank, without any trial, ecclesiastical or civil, and banished to Patara in Lycia. Hereupon Vigilius paid over to Belisarius two hundred pounds of gold, and the very next day the general convened the Roman clergy, informed them that the Pope was deposed, and procured the unresisted election of Vigilius in his room.

But the intruder was afraid to fulfil his part of the bargain by such an unpopular act as the public profession of Eutychianism in Rome itself; though committing himself fully to that heresy in letters to the Empress, and to the three Eutychian Patriarchs (Anthimus of Constantinople, Severus of Antioch, and Theodosius of Alexandria), whose authenticity, though of course denied by Baronius (mainly on the strength of a mendacious letter from Vigilius to Justinian, alleging that he had never held any belief save that of the Four General Councils and the Tome of St. Leo), is acknowledged by Pagi and by Fleury, who accept the contemporary statements of Liberatus, Victor Tunetanus, and Facundus. This was all a little too strong for Justinian, who sent Sylverius back to Rome, to wait the result of a formal trial, but Belisarius betrayed him into the hands of his rival, who deported him to the desolate island of Palmaria, where he was soon either starved to death or more directly assassinated.[1] Baronius invents a fresh election of Vigilius to the Papacy on the death of Sylverius, in order to avoid the serious gap his eighteen years of illegal occupancy makes in the Petrine succession; but this is rejected by Pagi and Papebroch, who hold, nevertheless, that the defect was cured by the subsequent recognition of Vigilius as Pope, not only at Rome, but by the Fifth General Council; but as the point was never mooted at the Council, this latter plea is of little weight, and the difficulty remains in full force.

The vacillations of Vigilius in the matter of the "Three Chapters" during the seven years that he was detained in Sicily and at Constantinople (from 547 to 554 inclusive), and the contemptuous treatment he met from the Fifth General Council, have been already referred to, and need not now be repeated; but they had one result not apparent on the surface—namely, that the willingness he exhibited to play fast and loose with the decrees and acts of Chalcedon had a perilous effect on nearly all the Western Churches, which were warmly attached to that Council. The Churches of Gaul, of the quasi-Patriarchate of Aquileia, of Illyricum, and of North Africa, either openly or virtually renounced communion with Rome, as having betrayed the faith and helped to throw a slur on the whole body of Christian doctrine, by condemning the Three Chapters which Chalcedon had accepted as orthodox. Vigilius closed his evil and contemptible career in 555, on his return journey from Constantinople to Rome. His successor, Pelagius I., who had been his ready tool, was like him thrust uncanonically

---

[1] Liberatus, c. 22; Procopius.

on the electors by Imperial power; so that the whole body of the Roman people and clergy refused to acknowledge or communicate with him, and he could not even secure the canonical minimum of three episcopal consecrators in all Italy, but had to substitute a mere presbyter in the third place.[1] So he found the great fabric of Papal prestige, so patiently built up by the Popes of the preceding century and a half, tottering before his very eyes, and threatening to fall at any moment. On the one hand, the independence and almost regal position of the Popes, which had been growing up by reason of the removal of the seat of Empire from Italy to Constantinople and had suffered little restraint at the hands of the Gothic kings, received a sudden check on the restoration of the Imperial power through the victories of Belisarius and Narses; and the Papacy was reduced politically to the level of the Patriarchate of Constantinople, and was actually treated as a post within the patronage of the Emperor.

Imperial interference with the election of a Pope began in the reign of Honorius, on the occasion of the contest in 418 between Boniface I. and Eulalius for the Papal chair, to which each had been elected and consecrated by rival factions. Boniface appealed to the Emperor, and procured his opponent's exile, and also the enactment of an Imperial law requiring a new election in the event of any dispute. This transaction served as a ground for much subsequent interference by the State in the concerns of the Roman Church; and during the reign of Justinian, as for some centuries after, the election of a Pope by the senate, clergy, and people of Rome was merely provisional until confirmed by the Emperor, without whose licence the consecration could not take place, nor could the Pope-elect lawfully exercise any rights or perform any duties of his office till such licence had been received.[2] On the other hand,

---

[1] *Liber Pontificalis*; Anastas. Bibliothec.

[2] However, Pelagius II. was elected without Imperial sanction during the Lombard siege of Rome in 577.

this subservience to the Byzantine Court was ill received by the bishops and clergy of the Western kingdoms beyond the limits of Imperial influence, and seriously weakened Papal authority and prestige. And not only did the Churches of Gaul renounce the communion of Pope Pelagius, as also those of Illyria and Africa, but even the Bishops of Northern Italy repudiated it, on the ground that the Pope, by accepting the decrees of Constantinople, had contradicted those of Chalcedon, and had committed himself to heresy. The Tuscan Bishops struck his name out of the Liturgy; those of Venetia and Istria erected the metropole of Aquileia into a Patriarchate,[1] to which they attached themselves, abandoning all connexion with Rome for a century and a half; and it was only the terror of the Lombard invasion which brought back the powerful dioceses of Milan and Ravenna to the Pope's communion. That was the position which Pelagius had to face. His mode of dealing with it was to throw himself on the civil power for assistance. He called on Narses, then Viceroy of Italy, to arrest the refractory bishops and send them to Constantinople for punishment, on the ground that separation from the Roman See is an act of schism which it is the duty of the State to punish as rebellion; but he could not obtain his request, and found his own spiritual pronouncements equally disregarded.

These events show that by the middle of the sixth century it had still proved impracticable to establish a prescription for the Papal claims and to enforce the two inferences from the Petrine succession of the Papacy (though that was by this time entirely undisputed), that the

---

[1] The title of Patriarch, still enjoyed by the Archbishop of Venice, is a survival from the schism of Aquileia; for the seat of that patriarchate was transferred to Grado on sanitary grounds within a few years, and the Lombard king Agilulf persuaded the Pope to set up a Catholic Bishop there with the title of patriarch, as a counterpoise to the schismatic prelate, which was accordingly done, and the rights of this new dignity were made over to the see of Venice by Nicolas V. in 1451.

Pope is the supreme teacher of Christendom, and that communion with him is an essential factor of Catholicity. The two next successors of Pelagius I.—John III. and Benedict I.—did not visibly alter the situation; but Pelagius II., who was chosen in 577, revived the Leonine attitude by protesting against the style of Œcumenical Patriarch assumed by John the Faster at Constantinople. He professed to annul the acts of a Synod at Constantinople, on the ground of that title having been used in the course of the proceedings and in the signature of its decree which acquitted Gregory of Antioch; he alleged that the universal primacy vesting in the Roman See gave it the sole and exclusive privilege of convoking and presiding over all great Church Councils; and he threatened to excommunicate John unless he divested himself of a title which even the Roman Pope, though supreme Patriarch over all, did not assume to himself. The Pope's action produced no effect at Constantinople, but it had some share in determining the attitude of his own successor in the Papal chair—Gregory the Great—to whose eminent qualities is due the rehabilitation of the Papacy, and the new start it was enabled to take on its road to spiritual despotism.

CHAPTER VIII.

THE FINAL COLLAPSE OF THE PAPAL SUCCESSION.

It has been sufficiently shown, that down to the pontificate of Gregory the Great it had proved impossible for the Popes to establish even so much as legal prescription in the very West itself for their asserted sovereignty over Christendom; while the whole tenor of Church history, specially as regards the General Councils, proves to demonstration that they could never get their possession of a Divine and imprescriptible charter of privilege acknowledged anywhere by entire Churches, persistently as they pressed it from the time of Leo the Great, and often as they seemed on the point of success. But the Papacy which Gregory bequeathed to his successors was a far more powerful factor in Christendom than that which he inherited had been. From the seventh till the fifteenth century Rome was as truly the centre of European policy in the civil, as well as in the religious, sphere as it had been when still the seat of the empire of the Cæsars; and the newer theory of its right to govern the nations of the world, or at the least to be looked up to by them as the most august and authoritative spot upon the earth, bade fair to be as influential as that memory of universal rule which went for so much in generating the original sovereign claim of the Pope, less as the alleged successor of St. Peter than as the chief personage in the city acknowledged as conqueror and capital of the world.

It is unnecessary to follow the course of the fortunes of the Roman See henceforth in the almost unbroken fashion required for the earlier stages of this inquiry. It will suffice to state broadly that the authority of the Popes grew steadily greater as it became more concentrated in the West, and as intercourse with the East became rarer and more difficult; and that after being advanced even further by the genius and daring of Nicolas I., Gregory VII., and Innocent III., it culminated in the Bull *Unam Sanctam* of Boniface VIII., which claims universal sovereignty as a *de fide* right of the Roman Pontiff. One very noticeable factor in the increasing veneration for Rome itself as the Holy City was the falling-off of pilgrimages to Jerusalem, owing to the enormous increase which the political changes of the times made in the cost, the toil, and also in the dangers of the journey. The city which could boast of the tombs of the two chief Apostles naturally succeeded to the virtually vacant place of honour and devotion, and became the goal of devout visitors, to so marked a degree that its very name has entered integrally into the words which signify "pilgrim" and "pilgrimage" in several Romance languages, such as the Spanish *romero* and *romeria*, the Portuguese *romiero*, the Italian *romeo*, the Old French *romipete* and *romieu*. The greater the stress laid on the immense power of the Papacy in mediæval Europe, the higher the claims put forward for the dignity and privileges of the Apostolic See, the weightier are all counter-balancing facts, the more fatal all interruptions of the new prescription. Moreover, if the Petrine privilege followed the papal dynasty, and it only, it is necessary to have trustworthy evidence of its regular transmission and devolution through a legitimate succession of Pontiffs. But the materials for the history of the early papacy are at once scanty and dubious. The principal authority for a large number of pontificates is the *Liber Pontificalis*, containing the lives of the popes from St. Peter to Nicolas I., and going under the name of Anastasius Bibliothecarius, a writer of the ninth century. But we have no clue as to the sources whence he drew his materials; and Ciampini, a scholar who published a critical essay on the *Liber Pontificalis* in 1688, rejects all but five of the lives as not being the work of Anastasius, but of several unknown authors,

x

of whose credibility there are no means of judging.[1] Nor does it appear that the defect can be made good by search in the Vatican archives, for the learned work of Mgr. Marini concerning that collection throws no light whatever on this matter, which is thus shrouded in total uncertainty.

And there is a yet graver consideration than all others behind. Let us assume for a moment, though in the teeth of all Scripture and history, that the doctrine of the Petrine privilege is true, that St. Peter was given infallible and sovereign jurisdiction over the whole Church Catholic, that he was Pope of Rome, that he conveyed his privileges indefeasibly to the Popes who succeeded him, and that the Successor of the Fisherman is the supreme ruler and teacher of Christians, the one Vicar of Christ on earth, whose single word is the "living voice of the Church," infallible and paramount. Even so, something further is essential: the Pope who claims these august prerogatives must be Pope *de jure* as well as *de facto*. Under the Roman Empire it did not matter by what title Cæsar wore the purple, whether he had made his way to the throne of the world by inheritance, by election, by successful rebellion, or by murder. So long as he could maintain himself on his dangerous throne, his legal rights were unimpeachable, his acts were all civilly valid, but not for a moment longer. Nothing in the least resembling the later doctrine of the Divine right of kings meets us in the whole of Roman imperial history; no parallel to English Jacobitism or French Legitimism can be found after the overthrow of any dynasty, even when such a regular transmission of the Empire as a dynasty implies does occur for a while. Contrariwise, it is an axiom of Latin theology and canon law that unlawful possession of the Papacy confers no rights whatever, and that all acts done by one who is Pope *de facto* without being also Pope *de jure* are null and void.

---

[1] *Examen Libri Pontificalis*, p. 107.

This nullity extends, of **course, to** the institution of **all** beneficiaries within the area of the quasi-Pope's domestic jurisdiction, and to the creations of Cardinals. That is to say, a false Pope may seriously affect the competency of the electoral body which will have to choose his successor. When the choice of the Popes lay **with** the clergy and people of the City of Rome, it is plain that if the majority of the clergy at any given time had not been canonically instituted, they were not competent electors in **the eye of** the law, and their nominee could acquire no rights **in virtue** of their votes. This is even plainer in the **case of** the College of Cardinals, as being composed of persons whose whole claim to their rank rests **on** their nomination by the Pope. They are not specially ordained, **as** bishops and priests are, who may be possessed of perfectly valid orders, and yet have no legal right to a particular benefice or see; and they have no shadow of claim to the red hat or to the electorate for the Papacy, unless the Pope who named them had full powers. And that is not by any means a matter at once satisfactorily ascertainable, for another maxim of Latin theology is that any doubt as to the rightful tenure of the Papal chair by any claimant is to be ruled against him, not for him, as is laid down expressly by Bellarmine, who says: "A doubtful Pope is accounted no-Pope."[1] This includes all cases of disputed elections, whenever there is not full proof of the valid election of the particular claimant who ultimately prevailed; for the mere fact of his having prevailed does not settle this preliminary question, as it is not pretended that the electors were infallible judges **of** that issue.[2] The cases of absolute nullity, admitting of

---

[1] Dubius Papa habetur pro non-Papa.—*De Concil.*, lib. ii. cap. 19, sect. xix.

[2] The mere fact of an anti-Pope claiming the Papacy does not make the title of the acknowledged Pope uncertain, but only when a reasonable doubt arises as to which candidate has been lawfully elected. What the thirty-nine anti-Popes who claimed the Papacy even before the inextricable confusion of the Great Schism do prove is that no

no dispute, are these: Intrusion by some external influence, without any election by the constituency; election by those only who are not qualified to elect; simony; and antecedent personal ineligibility of certain definite kinds, such as bastardy. The cases of highly probable nullity are those of heresy, whether manifest or secret, and whether previous to or after election to the Papacy.[1]

A few citations in proof of these positions must be set down in order to show that they are accepted principles of the Roman canon law, and not arbitrary cavils of hostile controversialists. The species of irregularity arising from some purely personal disqualification may be left out of account; because in point of fact its stringency has been so much impaired by incessant dispensations that it can scarcely be appealed to as admittedly effective. It may, however, be remarked that, as a dispensation from irregularity must always come from an authority superior to that of the irregular candidate for promotion to any ecclesiastical grade, and some forms of irregularity can be dispensed from by the Pope alone, it follows that when it is the Papacy itself which is vacant and to be filled, there can be no power lodged anywhere in the Roman Church to make an otherwise disqualified candidate eligible for that particular piece of promotion. For the College of Cardinals, though they enter upon the government of the Roman Church during the interval between the death of one Pope and the election of his successor, do not hold his prerogatives in commission, and cannot perform singly or conjointly any specifically Papal acts, as, for instance, the creation of cardinals or bishops, the confirmation of episcopal elections, or even the collation to benefices in the Pope's gift.[2]

Church is so lacking in the note of Unity as the local Roman Church. It has been the typical home of schism.

[1] Highly probable only, and not absolute; because, as the citations show, while there is a consensus of theologians and canonists on the subject, there is no express decree of canon law to the same effect.

[2] Ferraris, *Bibl. Canon.* s. v. "Cardinalis."

First, then, as to the question of forcible intrusion. This is governed by a maxim of Leo the Great, formally embodied in the canon law by the Lateran Council under Nicolas II. in 1059: "No line of argument permits that persons should be held for Bishops who have neither been elected by the clergy, nor desired by the laity, nor consecrated by the comprovincial Bishops with the assent of the Metropolitan."[1] The Lateran Council applies this to the case of the Papacy, explaining that, as there is no metropolitan superior over the Roman Church, the cardinal bishops are to be accounted as discharging that function in the election. The case before the Council was that of John, Bishop of Velletri, who had been forcibly imposed as Pope under the name of Benedict X. by the Count of Tusculum, on the death of Stephen X., without any election by the Roman clergy and people. And there is a decree of Nicolas II. cited by Gratian: "If any one be enthroned in the Apostolic See without accordant and canonical election by the Cardinals of the said Church, and thereafter by the religious clergy of lower grade, let him be accounted not Pope or Apostolic, but Apostate."[2] Of course, in a matter of the sort, these utterances must be taken as declaratory, not less than legislative; as retrospective, not less than prospective. They do not limit themselves to enacting that certain accessions to the Papacy shall be treated as void for the future, but lay down in general terms that they are inherently void.

It follows as a necessary corollary from these premises that none of the clergy appointed to benefices by such titular Popes can acquire electoral rights in virtue of such institution, unless some act of indemnity by a competent

---

[1] "Nulla ratio sinit ut inter episcopos habeantur, qui nec a clericis sunt electi, nec a plebibus expetiti, nec a comprovincialibus episcopis cum metropolitani judicio consecrati.'

[2] "Si quis Apostolicæ Sedi sine concordi et canonica electione Cardinalium ejusdem ecclesiæ, ac deinde sequentium clericorum religiosorum, inthronizatur; non Papa vel Apostolicus, sed Apostaticus habeatur."

authority be superadded; but from the nature of the case, no authority but a lawfully elected Pope is competent; and if at any time the whole clerical electorate, or a working majority of it, has been canonically vitiated, there can be no lawful after-election made, and no subsequent validation of the irregular tenure.

Nor is intrusion from without the only form of nullity in this class. It is a maxim of the canon law that violent and forcible entrance upon a benefice, though lawfully acquired, voids it: "By violent entry upon possession of a benefice every one loses, through that very act, the right he has thereto, and it becomes legally vacant."[1] This principle exactly applies to the celebrated case of the disputed election in A.D. 366, between Damasus and Ursicinus. We do not know, and are never likely to know, which of the two was canonically elected, if either; and it was Court influence, not any synodical finding, which decided the matter in favour of Damasus, whom the partisans of Ursicinus never acknowledged as lawful Pope. But it is certain that Damasus entered on his office by means of violent rioting and homicide, and that twice over, and thereby forfeited the very doubtful right he had acquired by an election posterior to that of Ursicinus.[2] And there are parallel cases later in the history of the Roman See.

Next comes the nullity due to simony. It is known to us from the epistles of St. Jerome that greed of money was a crying sin of the Roman clergy even in his day, so that it had to be dealt with by the civil law; and though the form their covetousness took then was that of endeavouring to extort deeds of gift and rich legacies from wealthy lay-folk, it was not long before simony became habitual; so that the civil power was obliged to interfere with enactments to check the notorious abuses attending every episcopal elec-

---

[1] "Per violentam ingressionem in possessionem beneficii perdit quis eo ipso jus, quod ad illut habet, et vacat ipso jure."—Ferraris, *Bibl. Canon*, s. v. "Beneficium," vii. 20.

[2] *Marcellini et Faustini Libellus*, inter opp. Sirmondi, vol. i.

tion, and above all, that to the Papal Chair itself. **Proof has been** given of this fact in the previous chapter, and **need not** be repeated. But a few citations of spiritual decrees on the subject will be pertinent:—

(*a*.) "If any Bishop, or Priest, **or Deacon obtains** this rank by money, let him be deposed, and his ordainer also, and be **altogether** cut off from communion, as Simon Magus was by Peter."[1]

(*b*.) "If any Bishop should ordain for money, and put to **sale a** grace which **cannot** be sold . . . let him who is convicted **of this** forfeit his **own rank**; and let him who is ordained get no advantage from the purchased ordination or promotion, but let him be expelled from the dignity or cure which he procured for money. And if any one act as go-between in such scandalous and illegal transactions, if he be a cleric, let him be degraded from his **rank**."[2]

(*c*.) "Every Bishop, Priest, **or Deacon, convicted of giving or re**ceiving ordination **for money, falls from the Priesthood**."[3]

(*d*.) "All crimes are **accounted as nothing** in comparison with the simoniacal heresy."[4]

"Ordinations performed for money . . . we decide to be null and void."[5]

(*e*.) "All simoniacal elections are void, even without any formal judicial sentence, and though the elected person may be wholly ignorant of the facts; unless it can be shown that the simony has proceeded from an enemy, in order to damage him. And every person simoniacally elected is bound to resign, and cannot obtain absolution till he has done so."[6]

(*f*.) "And, finally, the more **accredited opinion, that of** Pope Leo. IV., is that even penitence **does not avail for the recognition** of the orders of simoniacal clerks, **but that their deposition** is perpetual and irreparable."[7]

(*g*.) The Bull *Cum tum divino* of Julius II. pronounces **all** simoniacal elections to the Papacy void, and incapable of being validated by any recognition accorded to the Pope as chosen. And Gammarus, Auditor of the Rota, in his commentary on this Bull, alleges it to be so worded as to be retrospective in effect, fully voiding all such former elections.

---

[1] *Can. Apost.* xxx.
[2] Conc. Chalced. can. ii.
[3] Conc. II. Nicæn. *Epist. Tarasii Patriarch.*
[4] Paschalis Papa, apud Gratian, causa i. qu. 7.
[5] Can. v. of Roman Synod under Gregory VII. in 1078.
[6] Ferraris, *Bibl. Canon.* **s. v.** "Simonia," art. ii.
[7] Van Espen, *Jus Eccl.* **part.** ii. **sect.** iii. tit. xiii. cap. 6.

Heresy is the last form of nullity which we need consider; and in respect of the Pope may take three shapes: heresy before his election, heresy after his election, and heresy in his formal definition of doctrine. The rules which govern this flaw are as follows :—

(*a.*) "Every heretic, whether secret or manifest, incurs the greater excommunication, and also deposition, whether he be cleric or laic, Pope or Emperor."[1]

(*b.*) "As a dead man is not a man, so a Pope detected in heresy is not Pope; because he is *ipso facto* deposed."[2]

(*c.*) "The fifth opinion is therefore true, that a manifestly heretical Pope thereby ceases to be Pope, as he ceases to be a Christian, and a member of the body of the Church."[3]

As against the cavil that this is a purely hypothetical case, impossible of occurrence, and put forward only as an intellectual speculation (which Bellarmine would have us believe), stands the saving clause in the celebrated canon, "Si Papa" in the Decretum of Gratian, taken from the writings of St. Boniface of Mentz (the most papalising of early mediæval theologians), and claiming general irresponsibility for the Pope, however culpable in his acts. It lays down that there is one case in which the Pope may be called to account:

(*d.*) "In this event let no mortal presume to censure his faults, because he who is empowered to judge all is to be judged by none, unless he be detected erring from the faith."[4]

And, apart from the obvious fact that dry law does not provide for impossible cases, here is the significant comment of the greatest of all the mediæval Popes, Innocent III., appended by Pithou in his edition of the *Corpus Juris Canonici*:

---

[1] St. Raymond de Peñaforte, *Summa*, *Lit. de Hæres*.
[2] St. Augustin. Anconitan. *Summa*, qu. 5.
[3] Bellarmine, *De Rom. Pont.* ii. 30.
[4] *Decret. I.* xl. 6.

(*e*) "Faith is so especially necessary for me, in that while I have God as my Judge for other sins, I can be judged by the Church for that sin only which is committed against the Faith."[1]

Other canonists and divines who have laid down that heresy forfeits all Papal rank and privileges are Ulric of Strasburg, Hugo **of Ferrara,** Peter de Palude **(**Latin Patriarch of Jerusalem), **Johannes** Andreæ, William **of Ockham,** Antonio **de Rosellis, and** Cardinal Turrecremata.[2] **It is to** be noted, moreover, that no **saving** clause **occurs in any** of these decisions to the effect **that a Pope** who **repents of** his heresy, and retracts it, **is thereby** reinstated **without** further **process.** They speak **of the fall from the Popedom** as final **and** irreversible. All **these, however, touch** only the question **of** heresy after **reaching the Papal chair.** But the formidable Bull of Paul **IV.,** *Cum ex Apostolatûs Officio,* promulgated **in 1559** (besides **reaffirming** this same doctrine in its very first section, **wherein it** states that "the Roman Pontiff . . . **if he** be found erring from the **Faith,** can **be** convicted ;" **and also** reviving the above-quoted decree, "Si Papa," in its second section), takes **a yet wider** sweep, and imports a fresh element of uncertainty, **in addition to** the doubt whether the Pope at any given **time** may not be a secret **heretic,** and so a mere delusive **simulacrum,** all whose **acts are** inherently null. The **crucial** section runs thus :—

(*f*) "Adding that if it should at any time appear that any Bishop, even ranking as Archbishop, or Patriarch, or Primate, or Cardinal of the aforesaid Roman Church, or even, **as** already stated, Legate, or even the Roman Pontiff himself, previous to his promotion as Cardinal, or his election to be Roman Pontiff, has deviated from the Catholic Faith, or fallen into any heresy, his promotion, or his

---

[1] *Serm.* 2 *de Consecrat. Pontif.*
[2] See the citations in Renouf's *Condemnation of Pope Honorius;* and the admission of F. Ryder, that such has been a very common opinion held by very Roman theologians, "and that if a Pope could define heresy, in so defining, he would un-Pope himself."—*Contemporary Review,* Feb. 1879, p. 471.

election, even if by full agreement, and made by the unanimous assent of all the Cardinals, shall be null, void, and ineffective, nor shall it be capable of being styled or becoming valid or legitimate in any respect, in virtue of entrance on office, consecration, subsequent possession of authority and governing power, enthronement or homage as Roman Pontiff, or obedience paid to him in that character by all persons."

A further clause absolves all persons who have taken part in the election of any once erring, heretical, or schismatic person as Pope, from every oath and pledge of obedience they may have taken to him or to any others coming within purview of the Bull, directing them, contrariwise, to treat them as magicians, heathens, publicans, and heresiarchs, and to invoke the aid of the secular arm against them, and in favour of canonical claimants, without incurring any censures or penalties for such action.

Although this remarkable document has no retrospective character, and applies in its legal bearing only to cases arising after its publication, it has a far wider theological sweep. For it establishes as incontestable these two propositions, that Paul IV. and the thirty-two Cardinals whose signatures are attached to the Bull did not hold either that the Cardinals would be divinely guarded against making an invalid election, or that any such grace is inseparably bound up with the Papal office as to confer fitness and eligibility upon an otherwise disqualified candidate. And yet, if infallibility in matters of faith be an unvarying attribute of the Papacy, it is clear that antecedent and retracted error can be no more an obstacle to receiving that grace on election and consecration, than repented ante-baptismal sin is a bar to remission of sins in baptism. The Papal office and the Petrine privilege are thus asserted to be separable ; and as secret heresy, unknown to all the electors, and perhaps even forgotten by the candidate himself, is enough to disqualify, it follows that there is no warrant, on Ultramontane principles, for a valid election at any time, or for doing more than hope that the actual wearer of the tiara is Pope at all ; seeing that this Bull is an *ex-cathedrâ* pronouncement, and thus a binding law in the Roman Catholic Church.[1]

Examples of nullity of all these various kinds have been cited in preceding chapters of this volume—disputed elections more than once, intrusion and simony together in the case of Vigilius, heresy in those of Liberius and Zosimus, and so forth. But however serious these were as they occurred, and completely as they demonstrate that no divine exemption of the Roman Chair from the moral and legal vicissitudes which have affected other less eminent sees has been vouchsafed, they do not amount necessarily to entire solution of continuity in the Petrine succession, assuming that to be an historical and theological fact. It is always possible to contend that the intruded or self-deposed Popes must be looked on as simple blanks in the series, and their reigns as interregna, but that the normal condition of things was restored upon the next valid election, and that the canonically appointed Pope entered at once on the exercise of the lately dormant and now revived privilege of Peter. But the whole strength of this defence lies in the words "canonically appointed," and it will be established presently that there has been no canonical election to the Papacy probable for a thousand years past, or possible for about four hundred.

Personal depravity in a Pope, however gross and notorious, and though amongst the grounds which have several times justified depositions from the Papacy, is not in itself a cause of legal nullity. But its frequency [2] and enormity is a moral argument of the weightiest kind against that form of Ultramontanism which makes the Roman See,

---

[1] It can be seen in full in the Appendix of Père Gratry's *Lettres à Mgr. Déchamps*, both in the original edition and in the English translation.

[2] Gilbert Genebrard, Archbishop of Aix (1537-1597), in his *Chronologia Sacra*, sæc. x. iv. (Cologne, 1571), alleges that fifty Popes in a hundred and fifty years—that is, nearly one-fifth of the total number till the present time—were apostates rather than apostolic, and Baronius (*Ann.* 897) is no milder in his language.

and indeed the Pope singly, to be the whole Church in microcosm, or rather the energizing soul and vital principle of the Church. For it proves that the mark of Holiness, one of the Five Notes of the Church, has been conspicuously absent from the local Church of Rome.

The first signal disproof of the Papal claims in the period with which we are now to deal is the alleged reply of Dinoth, Abbat of Bangor-Iscoed, at the Synod of St. Augustine's Oak in 603 (a few months before the death of Gregory the Great), to the Roman missionaries who claimed the obedience of the British Churches in virtue of the Papal appointment of St. Augustine as Metropolitan :—

"Be it known to you, without any ambiguity, that we all and singly are obedient to the Pope of Rome and to every true and devout Christian, to love each in his own order with perfect charity, and to aid each one of them to become sons of God in word and deed. And I know not any other obedience than this due to him whom ye style Pope, nor that he has a claim and right to be Father of fathers. And the aforesaid obedience we are ready to yield at once to him and to every Christian. Further, we are under the jurisdiction of the Bishop of Caerleon-on-Usk, who is, under God, appointed to oversee us, and to make us keep the spiritual path."[1]

This remarkable speech is not unquestionably authentic, and is even rejected by scholars of note. But it is ancient, and even if a mediæval invention, it does not go beyond the actual facts of the repudiation of Augustine's mission and authority by the British Bishops, and their refusal to adopt any of his proposals, as recorded by Bæda (*Eccl. Hist. Ang.* i, ii. 2), which cannot, from their determined character and sweeping range, have been couched in very dissimilar language. As it stands, it goes even further than denial of the special supremacy claimed by the Popes over all Christendom, for it shows that they were not held by its author to possess so much as Patriarchal rights

---

[1] Haddan and Stubbs, *Councils and Ecclesiastical Documents*, vol. i. p. 123

over the entire West. And its value as a legal statement is enhanced by the absence of what would certainly have been forthcoming at a later date, namely, denunciation of such independence as heretical. St. Augustine of Canterbury, undoubted as is his piety, was not a man of large sympathy or broad mind; but was both narrow and intolerant of diversity from the customs in which he had been reared. Nevertheless, the only points of deviation between British and Roman usage upon which he endeavoured to enforce conformity to the latter were the computation of Easter and the ceremonial of baptism.[1] It is clear from this fact that then even at Rome itself it was not yet ruled doctrinally that denial of the Papal claims is heresy, for Augustine's temper makes it certain that otherwise he would not have failed to put the charge of disobedience towards the divinely privileged Head of the Catholic Church in the forefront of British sins against that Church, instead of giving that place to the mode of reckoning Easter. And the same remark holds good even of St. Wilfrid's language at the Council of Whitby in 664, impassionedly Roman as it was; for though he argued against the British computation of Easter as a mere local peculiarity, contrary to Catholic usage; as not being, as alleged, conformable to the practice of the Apostle St. John; and as opposed, in particular, to that of St. Peter, Prince of the Apostles, which he believed and asserted to be continuously observed in Rome; yet he rested his case not on the inherent right of the Pope to settle such matters for all Christendom, but on the supposed historical fact of unbroken tradition in Rome, derived from St. Peter, as to the true method of reckoning.[2]

But the leading case in the seventh century against the Papal claims is undoubtedly the *ex cathedrâ* definition of heresy by Pope Honorius I. Reference has already been made to the action of the Sixth General Council in formu-

---

[1] Bæda, *H. E.* ii. 2.   [2] Bæda, *H. E.* iii. 25.

lating his condemnation, and to its reiteration for many centuries; but the truth of the charge was not then proved, which shall now be done.

The Monothelite heresy, which first appears at the outset of the seventh century, is a sub-form of Monophysism, and is due to a well-meaning, but unwise, attempt to find some new terminology whereby the Monophysites might be induced to return to Catholic communion. The author of this attempt was Sergius, Patriarch of Constantinople, misled, it would seem, by a letter ascribed to his predecessor Mennas, about sixty years previous, and addressed to Pope Vigilius, in which it was said that our Lord had "one will and one life-giving energy or operation." He referred the expression to Theodore, Bishop of Pharan, who accepted it as orthodox, whereupon Sergius formally adopted it. Some years later, the Emperor Heraclius, desirous of ending the Monophysite controversy, which was politically dangerous to the Empire, conceived the plan of conciliating the Monophysites by means of Monothelite explanations (to be offered by the Catholics) of the sense to be put on the ascription of two natures to Christ. He consulted Cyrus, Bishop of Phasis, on the matter; and Cyrus in turn laid it before the Patriarch Sergius, whose reply was that the question of one or two operations had never been formally decided, but that various eminent Fathers had spoken of one operation only. This answer convinced Cyrus, who soon after became Patriarch of Alexandria, and committed himself publicly to Monothelism. The opposite side was maintained by St. Sophronius, who became Patriarch of Jerusalem in 633, and who had shortly before endeavoured to dissuade Cyrus from the course he was taking, and finding that impossible, went to Constantinople to consult Sergius, not knowing him to be the real author of the trouble. But he could get no better terms from him than a promise to let the controversy drop on both sides. But when St. Sophronius achieved his high rank, Sergius, feeling alarm at the influence he might exercise, wrote a long letter to Pope Honorius, setting forth his view of the controversy, and asking him to give his adhesion to himself and Cyrus, and against Sophronius. Thus the matter was public and official in the highest degree, being virtually an appeal from three out of the five Patriarchates to a fourth, and that the highest in dignity, to pronounce on a most serious theological controversy, wherein the whole reality of the Atonement was involved.

In the reply which Honorius sent, he committed himself definitely to the cardinal doctrine of Monothelism, saying, "We confess ONE WILL of our Lord Jesus Christ."[1] And he added, near the close of his letter, these further words, "These things your fraternity will preach with us, as we preach them in unanimity with you;"[2] thereby making common cause with Sergius, and identifying himself with his teaching. He replied as Pope, declaring what should be the teaching in the Western Church so far as he was concerned, and specifying that the same teaching ought to be followed in the East also. Accordingly, his Letters were dogmatic *ex cathedrâ* decrees; and they were explicitly heretical, for they were, in fact, not only appealed to by the Monothelites for half a century afterwards as their mainstay, but also formed the groundwork of the *Ecthesis* of the Emperor Heraclius, which embodied the crucial phrase already cited, and was condemned as "most impious" by Pope Martin I. in the First Council of Lateran in 649. It was expressly as "dogmatic epistles" that the letters of Honorius were condemned by the Sixth General Council, and ordered to be burnt as profane and hurtful to souls— the first example in ecclesiastical history of this kind of sentence (Labbe, *Conc.* vii. 978, 1006).[3]

---

[1] "Unde et *unam voluntatem* fatemur Domini nostri Jesu Christi."

[2] "Hæc nobiscum fraternitas vestra prædicet, sicut et nos ea vobiscum unanimiter prædicamus" (Hefele, *Conciliengesch.* b. vi. Append.).

[3] Full details of the long controversy here summarised will be found in Hefele, *Conciliengesch.* b. xvi.; and Mr. E. F. Willis's *Pope Honorius and the New Roman Dogma* (London, 1879) presents a convenient analysis of it, as well as a refutation of Pennacchi's apology

Ultramontane writers, either from having no sufficient knowledge of theology, or from a fixed determination to use what F. Gratry does not hesitate to qualify as "falsehoods" in defence of the figment of Papal infallibility, have not shrunk from saying not merely (with Hefele) what is conceivable enough, that Honorius had no intention of teaching heresy, being in truth neither logician nor theologian, and thus incompetent to meddle in an abstruse controversy, but that his epistles are "entirely orthodox."[1] Against this wild assertion it will suffice to quote part of one sentence from Bishop Hefele: "The affirmation that the Letters of Honorius are entirely orthodox is false."[2]

But the peculiarity of the case of Honorius is that it is equally destructive of the Ultramontane position, whatever view be taken of his theology. To establish his entire orthodoxy is of absolutely no help; because, in order to do so, it is necessary to reject the three General Councils (as counted in the Roman reckoning), of Constantinople in 681, Nicæa II. in 787, and Constantinople in 869, all of them attended by Papal legates, and formally confirmed by Popes Agatho, Hadrian I. and Hadrian II. themselves (instead of being rejected at Rome, as Canon XXVIII. of Chalcedon was by Leo the Great); in each of which Honorius was condemned by name as a heretic, and as a fautor of heresy, not for mere supineness. If he was orthodox, then they, in condemning him, were heterodox, as was also Leo II., who condemned Honorius anew thrice over —in a letter to the Emperor Constantine Pogonatus; in another to the Spanish Bishops (wherein he asserts the

---

for Honorius, addressed to the Vatican Council; while separate points are discussed in P. Gratry, *Lettres à Monseigneur Déchamps*, and in Mr. Le Page Renouf's *Condemnation of Pope Honorius*, and *The Case of Pope Honorius Reconsidered* (London: 1868-9).

[1] Manning, *The Vatican Council and its Definitions*, p. 223. London: 1870.

[2] "Die Behauptung . . . die Briefe des Honorius sind durchaus orthodox . . . ist falsch" (*Conciliengesch.* xvi.).

damnation of Honorius, "Æterna condemnatione mulctati sunt, id est, Theodorus . . . una cum Honorio"—Labbe, *Conc.* vii. 1456); and in a third to Erwiga, King of Spain,—and Gregory II., who is believed to have drafted that profession of faith contained in the *Liber Diurnus*, to be made by each Pope at his coronation, wherein Honorius is again specified as a heretic. And so, for the many centuries this profession was made, every Pope had to pledge himself to the assertion that Honorius had been bound by sentence of perpetual anathema, for having added fuel to the execrable and heretical dogma of Sergius and the other Monothelites.[1]

There is absolutely no escape from the dilemma of asserting either the heresy of Honorius, as a Pope undertaking to teach the Church Universal by formal dogmatic letters, or the heresy of all those General Councils and Popes that condemned him in the most explicit terms as a heretic. It is this fact of his condemnation, and on such grounds, whether true or false, which is the keystone of the whole matter. The most triumphant demonstration of his orthodoxy would but make matters worse for infallibilism, since, if he was an Athanasius, those other Popes have all fallen like Liberius. The Councils which formulated the several condemnations could not have believed in any tenure of a Petrine privilege which empowers the Popes to teach the Church Universal, and to be divinely guaranteed from error in doing so.

The next salient example of a flaw in the prescription for the Petrine claims belongs to the ninth century; and, though not of so startling a nature as the condemnation of Honorius, is nevertheless in some respects even more adverse to the theory of Papal sovereignty. For in the

---

[1] "Auctores vero novi hæretici dogmatis, Sergium . . . una cum Honorio, qui pravis eorum assertionibus fomentum impendit . . . cum omnibus hæreticis scriptis atque sequacibus, nexu perpetui anathematis devinxerunt" (*Liber Diurnus*, ed. De Rozière, pp. 194–201).

case of Honorius it may at least be said that the censures upon him proceeded from no authority inferior to that of General Councils and other Popes; and as the Gallican school has always held the subordination of the Popes to General Councils, while admitting the Papal monarchy so limited, there is room for a modified assertion of some Petrine privilege as annexed to the Papacy, albeit far short of personal infallibility. But the instance now to be cited does not leave room for even so much.

The controversy upon image-worship had been decided in Western Christendom, by the Caroline Books and by the Council of Frankfort, in a sense opposite to that of the Second Council of Nicæa. But it was still raging in the East; and the extreme champions of images in Constantinople strove to prevent the question from being reopened by the Emperor Michael II., who desired to abate some of the more extravagant abuses of the cult. They asserted that the State had no right of interference in such matters, and that the ultimate decision rested with the See of Rome, as the supreme Church of Christ on earth, in which Peter sat in the beginning; and moreover in a letter to Pope Paschal I. from Theodore the Studite, head of the party, that Pontiff is styled "Prince of all the priests of the Lord, supreme pastor of the Church, rock on which the Catholic Church is built, Peter himself, and unpolluted source of Divine truth," with other kindred expressions. But their value may be appraised by noting that in addressing the Patriarch of Jerusalem for the like purpose, the same Theodore assures him that he is really first of all the Patriarchs, though but fifth in nominal rank, and that the supreme patriarchal dignity must vest in his See.[1]

The Emperor, knowing that the Churches of Gaul, at any rate, were not in agreement with the Studite faction, sent an embassy to the Western Emperor, Ludwig the Pious, in 824, explaining his own standpoint as equally

---

[1] Baron. *Ann.* 818, i. ii.; 817, xx.

removed from the iconoclasm of 754 and the iconolatry of 787 (though he made no express mention of the Synods), and asking his assistance to get some satisfactory compromise arrived at; stating at the same time his intention of sending his envoys to Rome also, to undo the effect of the misrepresentations made there by the Studites. Ludwig consulted his clergy, then the most learned in Europe; and on their advice applied to Pope Eugenius II. to sanction a formal inquiry into the whole question of image-worship, to be conducted by a select commission of the most learned divines in France, who were to examine the Scriptures and the Fathers to ascertain the mind of the Church, with a view to a final settlement of the debate. The Pope assented, and the Commission met at Paris in November, 826, sending in its report not very long after.

This remarkable document opens with a formal censure of the letter of Pope Hadrian I. to Constantine VI. and Irene on behalf of image-worship; and, though approving his condemnation of the extreme iconoclasts, blames severely his permission of relative worship to images, his use of the term "holy" for them, and his ratification of the Nicene canons of 787. It rejects his patristic quotations as irrelevant and misleading; and charges him with having given great scandal to the faithful, and disparaged the Pontifical dignity, as well as the truth itself, and misunderstood, through sheer ignorance, the teaching of Gregory the Great, to which he had appealed in support of his own. They next proceed to deal in the same stringent fashion with the letters of Pope Gregory II.; and soon after add that their inquiries had convinced them of the great practical evils of the "pestilent superstition" of image-worship, which they viewed with much alarm, especially since the Popes, whose duty it was to keep others in the right path, had themselves strayed far from it. And they recommend the Emperor not to throw the blame of the condition of things on the Pope personally, seeing that there were others who might fairly bear the whole of it, and that without scandal to the Church; and seeing also that the Pope might be brought to a sounder mind by study of the extracts they had made from **the Holy Scriptures** and the Fathers, because his See itself is subject to the precepts of Scripture and of the Holy Catholic Fathers, and the Pope himself **cannot** be styled Universal unless he combats with all his might on behalf of the whole state of the Universal Church.[1] The Emperor Ludwig **took no** practical action upon **the** report, but **it remains as a** monument of the freedom with which a body of private divines in the ninth century, not even synodically assembled, held themselves at liberty to sit in judgment upon formal Papal utterances.

But the accession of a Pope of genius and high character, Nicolas I., a little later in the century (A.D. 858), nearly synchronizing with the appearance of the **False** Decretals, to which **he** was the first Pope to appeal **in evidence of his** claims (though there is proof that he knew nothing in 860 and 863 of their existence, **for** he then stated what is true, that the Decretal of Siricius is the oldest known. But he quotes them in 864 as genuine, necessarily aware of their fictitious character, as being absent from the Roman archives, where he alleged them **to** have been long preserved with honour),[2] more than won back all the influence and prestige which the Roman Chair had formerly enjoyed in the West; while the opportunity afforded in the East by the struggle between the partisans of the rival patriarchs of Constantinople, Ignatius and Photius, together with circumstances which

---

[1] Baron. *Ann.* 825, vii.-xx.; and more fully in Bouquet, *Hist. de France*, vi. 338-341. The anger of Baronius over this report is amusing.

[2] Mansi, *Conc.* xv. 695. See note at the end of this volume. It may be noted here that the very fact that it was thought expedient to **forge** these False Decretals, and to weave them into the Roman Canon **Law** (of which they still form an integral, large, and most important portion) is in itself ample proof that the claims made in and by them were known in Rome itself to be entirely unwarranted and fictitious. They would have been worse than superfluous, had genuine testimony been producible.

enabled the Pope to interfere in the newly converted kingdom of Bulgaria, gave him no little power in that part of Christendom also. Akin to Leo the Great and Innocent III. in mental vigour and in personal dignity of character, akin to Gregory the Great in love of justice and in administrative capacity, Nicolas I. was without bounds to his ambition for the aggrandisement of his See, and had no scruples as to the means he employed for making it the supreme arbiter of Christendom alike in the ecclesiastical and the temporal domain, a result he so nearly achieved that he stands out in history as the actual creator of that Papal monarchy which had been only vaguely planned by his most eminent predecessors, who, moreover, had scarcely dreamed of domination in the civil sphere over those sovereigns whose subjects they were, not only in the eye of the secular law, but by their own oath of allegiance at each accession to the Papacy, which they took down to the close of the twelfth century, when Innocent III. in 1198 declared himself independent Lord Paramount over all the Papal States, and was the first Pope-King. And as Constantinople was dwindling steadily in power, both civilly and religiously, from the advance of Islam in the East, and the consequent narrowing of the limits of the empire, as well as from the decay of Oriental Christianity, which made the three Patriarchates of Alexandria, Antioch, and Jerusalem mere shadows of their past, there was no possible rival, or even effectual check, left for Rome to fear. Had the tenet of the Petrine Privilege been true, we should find the long resistance to the Papal claims ended thenceforth, and the truth of all the contentions steadily put forward by the Popes from the time of Anastatius I. finally acknowledged. But the purely human nature of the vast and imposing edifice is disclosed by the fact that, when no competitor or restrainer was any more to be looked for, it was ruined as a tenable theory by internal dissensions and irregularities in Rome itself. Such local disturbances had been intermittent, it is true, in the

Roman Church for several centuries, but the evils were never sufficiently long-seated to be incurable. Not so in the period we have now to consider.

The first episode of importance is that connected with the name of Pope Formosus. He had been Bishop of Portus, and legate of Nicolas I. in Bulgaria, and was excommunicated by two synods under John VIII. for alleged misconduct in that capacity, as well as for other offences, and compelled to swear that he would never return to Rome, nor aspire to more than lay communion. The next Pope, Marinus, absolved him from both the excommunication and the oath, and restored him to his See, though still prohibiting his access to Rome itself. Some years later Formosus was elected Pope, though perhaps doubtfully, if a prior election had already chosen Sergius, a deacon of the Roman church, who was at the altar awaiting his solemn inauguration when the party of Formosus broke into the church and forced him away.[1] Formosus was then consecrated Pope, and held the dignity for five years. His next successor, Boniface VII., sat but fifteen days, and was followed in the Papacy by Stephen VI. He caused the corpse of Formosus to be disinterred, dressed in the pontifical robes, and put on trial before a synod for the alleged crime of usurping the Popedom, on the ground that he was canonically ineligible, because he was at the time Bishop of Portus, and because no bishop had ever been up to that date translated to the Papal Chair. He was condemned, stripped of his robes, three fingers cut from his hand, the mutilated corpse was flung into the Tiber, and all his ordinations were declared null and void. A rising against Stephen proved successful a few months later, and he was strangled in prison. His

---

[1] There is no doubt that this did happen to Sergius. But the undecided questions are whether it happened once or twice; and if once only, whether his successful competitor was Formosus, or John IX. at a later time.

successor, Romanus, is said by Platina to have annulled all his acts;[1] but though this is somewhat doubtful, there is no question that Theodore II., who came next, during his short reign of three weeks reversed all the proceedings against Formosus, declared all his ordinations and other acts legal and valid, and caused his body to be buried in the Vatican. John IX., the next Pope, was not content with this measure of atonement to the memory of Formosus, but convened a synod which formally annulled the acts of that held under Stephen VI., and ordered them to be burnt; and moreover all the ecclesiastics who had taken part in it were obliged to confess themselves guilty, and plead for pardon. There is a doubt whether this was not all reversed again, and the body of Formosus once more disinterred under Sergius III., a Pope of the opposite faction, but, on the whole, it is more probable that Sergius was the chief agent employed by Stephen VI. in the original outrage, long before his own accession to the Papacy.[2] The importance of this series of events is that they show how completely the Church of Rome was divided against itself, and in what direct contradiction its successive Popes and synods found themselves, at the close of the ninth century, thus preparing the way for the more fatal proceedings which soon followed. In 903, Christopher, a priest of the Roman Church, rose against Pope Leo V., a few weeks after his

---

[1] The words Platina adds to this statement are important: "Nil enim aliud hi pontificuli cogitabant, quam et nomen et dignitatem majorum suorum extinguere"—a charge identical with that made by Baronius against the pseudo-Popes of the Pornocracy (*Ann.* 908, iii.).

[2] Auxilius, the contemporary writer who tells us of the annulling and repetition of orders at this time (*ordinatio, exordinatio, et superordinatio*), says that if Stephen and Sergius were right, there had been a break of twenty years in the continuity of the Christian religion and sacraments in Italy, and that nothing short of a General Council could clear up the doubt as to the bishops and priests concerned (*De Ordinat. Formosi*, capp. xxviii. xl. apud Mabillon, *Vetera Analecta*, pp. 37, 39, Paris, 1723). But no such Council ever investigated the matter, and the religious confusion of Rome at that time has never been cured.

enthronement, threw him into prison, and intruded himself into the Papacy. He was in his turn overthrown and imprisoned by Sergius III., who intruded himself similarly, and whose character is painted in the blackest colours by the chroniclers of the time. It is at least certain that it was under his auspices that the infamous triad of courtesans, the two Theodoras and Marozia, obtained the influence which enabled them to dispose several times of the Papal crown. They, or Alberic of Spoleto, son of Marozia, nominated to the Papacy Anastatius III., Lando, John X., Leo VI., Stephen VII., John XI., Leo VII., Stephen VIII., Martin III., Agapetus II., and John XII., the last of whom, a mere boy at the time of his intrusion, was deposed for various atrocious crimes by a synod convened by the Emperor Otto I. in 963. This whole series, as Baronius declares, consisted of false pontiffs, having no right to their office, either by election or by subsequent assent of the electors, each of them eager to undo the acts of his predecessors, and choosing persons of the same evil stamp as themselves for the cardinalate and other dignities.[1] And the conclusion he most cleverly draws from the premisses, which he is far from concealing or minimising, is that the Divine favour and protection were conspicuously proved

---

[1] Baron., *Ann.* 897, iv.; 908, vi. vii.; 912, viii.—especially this last reference, which runs thus: "What was then the aspect of the holy Roman Church? How utterly foul, when harlots, at once most powerful and most vile, bore rule at Rome; at whose will sees were exchanged, bishops appointed, and what is awful and horrible to hear, their paramours were intruded as pseudo-Popes into the See of Peter, who are not set down in the catalogue of the Roman pontiffs except for the purpose of fixing the dates. For who could assert that persons lawlessly intruded by such courtesans were legitimate pontiffs? There is no mention anywhere of the clergy electing or subsequently assenting. All the canons were thrust down into silence, the decrees of Popes were strangled, the old traditions were banned, the ancient customs, the sacred rites, and the early usages in the election of the Supreme Pontiff were completely annulled. And what sort of cardinals, deacons, and priests do you suppose were chosen by these monsters?"

by the absence of any schism, when a schism would have had so much to assist it, and by the speedy recovery of the lost position.[1]

But the conclusion a canonist must draw is a very different one; namely, that if any Petrine succession or privilege ever existed in the Roman Church, **it was extinguished** irrecoverably at the close of this period; for **it** extended over sixty years, during which not one lawfully-elected Pope ascended the Papal Chair. None of them **could** canonically appoint to any dignity **or benefice in the** Roman Church; many of them are known to have sold **them.** Consequently, it is certain that, at the close of the sixty years' anarchy, not one single clerical elector in Rome was qualified to vote, for not one **could** show a just title to his position; and the lay vote, even if it was given at all, was invalid by itself. The election of Leo VIII. or of Benedict V. (whichever be accounted the true Pope), in 963, was, therefore, void also; for even if conducted in due form, the clerical voters had no status. And as no act of indemnity was ever passed by any authority whatsoever— **leaving out of account** the very difficult problem of deciding what authority would have been competent for the purpose —the defect has been incurable. It is precisely analogous to a break of two generations of established bastardy in a pedigree by which it is sought to make good a claim to a peerage. Failing the production of some collateral heir (impossible in the case before us), there is no choice but to declare the family honours extinct. The Petrine line, **if** ever a reality, ended in the tenth century. The later Popes may just conceivably have been Bishops of Rome in some canonical sense for a few centuries longer, though **that is** made highly improbable by causes yet to be set **down;** but if so, they had **no** more **connexion** with **the** older **line than** the Napoleonic dynasty **has with** the Carolingian **emperors.**

A second series of intruding Popes, who secured their

---

[1] Baron., *Ann.* 912, ix.

throne by simony, meets us in the eleventh century; Benedict VIII., John XIX., Benedict IX., and Gregory VI. This Gregory was withstood by Benedict and two other anti-Popes, and was deposed for simony in the Council of Sutri in 1046; and thus another canonical vacancy of thirty-four years was caused in the Papacy, enough (even if the former gap of sixty years had not occurred) to throw the gravest doubt on the status of the Roman electorate which elected Clement II. in 1046; for it is not probable that more than a very small minority of the voting clergy could have held their appointments from a date earlier than the simoniacal intrusion of Benedict VIII. in 1012. And the statement of Bonizo, Bishop of Sutri, about thirty years later,[1] is that the Germans charged the local Roman clergy with being, almost to a man, either illiterate, simoniac, or immoral; and the second (for legal purposes the most serious) count of this indictment is amply borne out by the admissions made at the Synod of Rome in 1047, wherein a vain attempt was made to check this crime,[2] and by the indignant language of Pope Victor III. while still Abbot of Monte Cassino.[3]

In 1059 a great innovation on the mode of electing the Popes was introduced by Nicolas II. in a Synod in the Lateran at Rome, which transferred the right of nominating the candidates for the Papacy and voting for them to the College of Cardinals, instead of the clergy and people of Rome; and Alexander III. in 1179 enacted a canon that any election made by two-thirds of the cardinals should be valid. Nevertheless, it was not till the election of Lucius III. in 1181, that the new regulation was carried out so as to exclude the old constituency from voting.[4]

The motives for the change seem to have been all good:

---

[1] Ætelius, *Rer. Boic. Script.* ii. 801.
[2] St. Petri Damiani, *Epist. ad. Henric. Ravenn.*
[3] Desider. Montis Cass. ap. Muratori, *Rer. Ital. Script.* iv. 396.
[4] Muratori, *Ann. d'Italia*, vii. 124.

to avoid the rioting and venality which had too often discredited popular elections in Rome ; to insure certainty as to the actual result of the voting, by a method which made personation and other electioneering artifices impracticable ; and above all (now that the dignity of Cardinal was no longer restricted to the collective presbytery of the city of Rome, but was conferred on representative prelates of all the Latin Churches, and of the titular Oriental ones also) to give a quasi-œcumenical character to the election. In fact, scarcely any proof is stronger to a canonist that no universal jurisdiction was attributed by the ancient Church to the Roman Bishopric than that the election of the Pope should have been for the first thousand years a purely local one. The maxim, "Nemo invitis detur," would have been called into operation had the remaining Patriarchates thought for a moment that the Roman clergy and people could give them a master when they pleased. And though the Imperial licence and consent, which formed an element in all Papal elections for many centuries, may be conceivably taken as standing for the assent of all the laity of the Empire, there was no expression of any kind provided for the yet more important vote of the dispersive clergy.

Unimpeachable as the new electoral scheme appeared, it dangerously narrowed the constituency,[1] and made it actually easier to tamper with, and even to vitiate and disqualify altogether ; while, far from its attaining the anticipated certainty of result and avoidance of double returns, two remarkable cases of disputed elections occurred within a century. The first of these was at the death of Honorius II. in 1130. Sixteen Cardinals, who were in the late Pope's palace, concealing the fact of his death from their colleagues and the Roman clergy and people, clandestinely

---

[1] The cardinals were long before normally even approximating to their present standard number of seventy. There were but twenty-four alive when Pius II. was elected, thirty-one at the election of Innocent VIII., twenty-seven at that of Alexander VI., thirty-three at that of Leo. X.—Ciaconius, *Vitæ Pontificum*.

elected Cardinal Gregory Guidone [1] on the following day by the title **of Innocent II.** Thirty-two Cardinals, with the approval of the whole body of the Roman clergy and of the nobility, except the Corsi and Frangipani, elected Cardinal Peter Leonis, by the title of Anacletus II., and both were consecrated to the Papacy on the same day, Innocent in St. Mary Major, and Anacletus in St. Peter's. It is indisputable, as a legal question, that under either the older or the newer system of electing, Anacletus was the lawful Pope; but Innocent contrived to secure the help of the all-powerful St. Bernard, who induced the Emperor Lothar II. to lead an army to Rome, and put Innocent forcibly into possession; and this imported another defect into his title, as noted above, although he is reckoned as the lawful occupant, and Anacletus as the anti-Pope. The second instance occurred after the death of Hadrian IV. in 1159, **when there** was again a double election; and though Alexander III. had fourteen votes in the conclave of Cardinals as against nine for his competitor, Victor IV., yet the latter had the whole body of the Roman clergy, and the assent of the great majority of the laity, on his **side;** while the only tribunal before which their rival claims **were** tried, that of the Council of Pavia in 1160, gave judgment **in** his favour. It is true that Alexander's refusal, and Victor's consent, to recognise the authority of the Council may have gone far in swaying its decision; but the fact that it did **so decide** must **be held to leave** Alexander's election doubtful at best.[2]

A doubt of yet another kind, not hitherto touched upon, arises in connexion with the seventy years' session of the Popes at Avignon, from 1309 to 1379, often styled the "Babylonian Captivity." It is concerned with the canon-

---

[1] This family was later known as De Paparesca, and still exists as the **Mattei.**

[2] **Labbe,** *Conc.* xiii. 265.

ical duty of residence at their Sees, imposed on all Bishops; and as it is obvious that the Avignonese Popes did not **profess to be** Bishops of that city, nor to have transferred to it any of the privileges of Rome, their episcopate was purely titular, representing no actual fact, and in particular, entirely dissociated from the local Roman clergy and people, whose right to share in Papal elections, however neglected and indeed over-ridden in practice, was yet formally reserved to them by the constitution of Nicolas II. It is more probable than not, that this protracted severance **of** the Bishops of Rome from their See constitutes a fresh breach in the succession, even had the two huge gaps already mentioned been bridged over. For the Roman contention is that St. Peter, by his twenty-five years' residence and death in Rome, and by that alone—as no documentary proof exists—transferred his primacy from Antioch to Rome, his ultimate *residence* being the sole nexus between the Universal Primacy and the local bishopric. They admit that he might have fixed it in any other Church, but that by his final residence in Rome he established it for ever there.

Accordingly, when the Popes went to Avignon, permanently resided there, and died and were buried there, they did in regard to Rome precisely what St. Peter **is** said to have done in regard to Antioch; they broke up the Roman succession, and created a new primacy at Avignon. For *residence* being an essential condition of the episcopate, that condition failed utterly during the Avignon period, and its resumption could not rehabilitate the succession. The Popes living in Avignon could no more be considered Bishops of Rome, than St. Peter living in Rome could be considered as still Bishop of Antioch. And Pope Benedict XIV. says: " **No** one who **is not** Bishop of Rome **can be styled Successor of Peter, and for that** reason the words **of the** Lord ' Feed my sheep ' **can never be** applied to him " (*De Synod. Diœces.* II. i.). Thus the Petrine principle is *Ubi Roma, ibi Papa*, whereas, to make the line of Avignon valid, the converse proposition, *Ubi Papa, ibi Roma*, has to be asserted, as it is in fact by Ferraris and some other Papal canonists.

Furthermore, by the canons of all the Councils, from Nice I. to Trent, and from that to the Bull of Pius IV., *In supremâ militantis Ecclesiæ speculâ*, every Bishop, even of Patriarchal rank, is compelled to a *personal* residence, under pain of deprivation; the Popes, therefore, as Bishops of Rome, and even as Patriarchs, fall under the universal law, and the See of Rome was *ipso facto* void during the Avignon Papacy.[1]

But there is no need to press heavily upon this point, since there is a more serious flaw behind—that due to the Great Schism. From 1379 to 1409, or more strictly till 1417, two and sometimes three rival Popes disputed the Papacy. It is impossible to decide which had the better claim in any case, and the conduct of the Councils of Pisa and Constance, which undertook to settle the matter, does but complicate it further. Thus every Pope within this period is doubtful; and the maxim of Bellarmine, cited above, that "a doubtful Pope is accounted as no-Pope," bars any falling back on the conjecture that one or other must have been the true Pope in any given year of the schism, and compels the rejection of all alike. Such was, in fact, the decision arrived at both at Pisa and Constance; for the former deposed both Gregory XII. and Benedict XIII., electing Alexander V. in their place; and the latter deposed Gregory and Benedict over again, and also John XXIII., representative of the new line set up at Pisa. The Council of Pisa is rejected by Ultramontanes on very strong legal grounds, chiefly that it was not convened by any competent authority, being merely summoned by the Cardinals

---

[1] See this whole question discussed at length by the great canonist Bartholomew Carranza de Miranda, Archbishop of Toledo, in his treatise "De Residentia Episcoporum," read before the Council of Trent, and printed in Le Plat's *Monum. Conc. Trid.*, iii. 521-84.

of the two factions; and that its proceedings were irregular in themselves, and without due process of law. But if Pisa was no true Council, neither was Constance, for it was summoned by John XXIII., whose own title rests on Pisa alone, he being successor to the line of Alexander V.; and the mode of voting at it was entirely novel, being by nations, and others than bishops and cardinals being allowed a vote. The two councils stand or fall together (Bossuet, *Defens. Declar. Cleri Gall.* II. ix. 12). What this means in law is that there had been no true Pope after the death of Gregory XI. in 1378; and therefore that all persons claiming to be cardinals by any subsequent creation were mere pretenders, without any electoral powers. The extreme Italian Papalists went much further, and held that, as all jurisdiction proceeds from the Pope, and invalidly elected Popes could not give what they did not themselves possess, there had been no validly ordained bishops or priests after the death of Gregory XI., and consequently all orders and sacraments ministered by such persons were null and void.

"After the death of Gregory XI., of happy memory, no person belonging to the party of the invalidly elected Pontiff has obtained the priestly dignity, nor can lawful sacraments be had from any such Priests, seeing that the jurisdiction for conferring priestly orders has failed. Consequently, those who are in the obedience of a false Pontiff, though in good faith and a pure conscience, if they fall in with any one ordained by the new bishops, if they adore the Host and chalice, will not adore the Body and Blood of Christ, but the mere substance of bread and of wine mingled with water, as it were an idol."[1]

This theory, and the confirmation it derives in part from the rejection of both lines of Pontiffs, rather than the selection of either, by the two Councils, has a very important bearing on the election of Martin V. at Constance. That

---

[1] Coluccio Salutato, Papal Secretary, writing in 1398 to Jodocus, Margrave of Brandenburg and Moravia, apud Martene (*Thes. Anecd.* ii. 1160).

election was made by the joint action of the twenty-three titular Cardinals present, and thirty electors chosen by the Council itself, six from each of the five nations represented. But there was only one Cardinal then living who had been created before the death of Gregory XI., and he was that very Peter of Luna who claimed to be Benedict XIII., and refused to acknowledge the right of the Council to question his title, inasmuch as the submission of his two competitors, Gregory XII. and John XXIII., left him the only possibly valid Pope.[1] Thus all the votes cast for Otto Colonna (Martin V.) as Pope by nominal Cardinals were void; and it does not appear how the Council (whose own validity is so gravely doubtful) could create for this one turn a wholly new constituency, having no relation to either the ancient one of the Roman clergy and people, or the newer one of the College of Cardinals. If the thirty conciliar electors were only assessors to the Cardinals, they effected nothing, as none of those Cardinals had a right to vote at all, and the election is void on that ground. If, on the other hand, they had a substantive vote, and in fact made the election, then they created a wholly new Papacy, having no legal or historical continuity with the older one, and tracing back not to St. Peter and his alleged Divine privilege, but no further than the Council of Constance itself.[2]

It might be thought that so many breaches in the Pontifical succession would have sufficed, but yet another and crowning one still remains to be recorded. Innocent VIII. was simoniacally elected in 1484,[3] and his next successor,

---

[1] Maimbourg, *Histoire du Grand Schisme d'Occident*, ii. 253.

[2] It is not unworthy of remark that former elections of Popes had been challenged as invalid, on the ground of the elect not being in Holy Orders, and that this throws fresh doubt on Martin V.'s election, for, though a Cardinal, he was not even a Deacon when chosen, but was passed through the three grades of the hierarchy on three successive days, before being consecrated as Pope upon the fourth. Von der Hardt, *Magn. Conc. Constant.* iv. 1486–90. This contravened a decree of Stephen IV. in 769.

[3] Creighton, *History of the Papacy*, iii. 14.

the infamous Cardinal Roderic de Borgia, was elected in the conclave of 1492 by a majority of twenty-two out of the then twenty-seven Cardinals, whose **votes** had **been** purchased by Cardinal Ascanio Sforza, as recorded by Von Eggs, the Roman Catholic historian of the Cardinals, in his *Pontificium Doctum* (p. 251) and *Purpura Docta*, in *Vita Card. Ascan. Sforzæ*, iii. 251. As Pope Alexander VI., Borgia openly sold the cardinalate itself to the highest purchasers,[1] so that both his own popedom and their membership of the Sacred College were all void by reason of simony. But Julius II. was elected in 1503 in a conclave of thirty-seven Cardinals, of whom twenty-six, or rather over the two-thirds necessary for a valid choice, were of Alexander VI.'s invalid creation, while the same Cardinal Sforza is known to have managed that conclave also in the same simoniacal fashion as the previous one.[2] And Leo X. was elected in 1513 in a conclave consisting entirely of Cardinals created by either Alexander VI. or Julius II., and therefore incompetent to elect. And Leo repeated the crime of Alexander VI. in selling the cardinalate; while, finally, Clement VII. was simoniacally elected in 1523.[3]

The electoral body was thus utterly vitiated and disqualified by Canon Law at least so far back as 1513, and no conceivably valid election of a Pope has taken place since that of Sixtus IV., in 1471, even if every defect prior to that date be condoned, and it be conceded that the breaches in the tenth, eleventh, and fifteenth centuries were made good somehow.

There has not been any retrospective action taken in regard to this final vitiation by simony; and to Alexander VI. belongs the responsibility of having made any assertion of unbroken and canonical devolution of a Petrine privilege in the line of Roman Pontiffs impossible for any honest canonist or historian since his time. And consequently, not only have the specific Divine privileges alleged to be

---

[1] Guicciardini, *Istor. d' Italia*, v.
[2] Palatii, *Fasti Cardinalium*.
[3] Guicciardini, *Istor. d' Italia*, xv.

attached to the person and office of the Roman Pontiff all utterly failed, but the whole ecclesiastical jurisdiction appertaining to or derived from the See of Rome has failed throughout the entire Latin obedience. All acts done by the Popes themselves, or requiring Papal sanction for validity, since 1484 (just thirty-three years before the outbreak of the Lutheran revolt), have been inherently null and void, because emanating from usurping and illicit Pontiffs, every one of whom has been uncanonically intruded into the Papal Chair by simoniacal or merely titular electors, having no legal claim to vote at all. Those orders and sacraments in the Latin Church which depend on the valid succession of the dispersive episcopate and priesthood may continue unimpaired, but all that is distinctively Papal died out four centuries ago, and continues now as a mere delusive phantom.

The defence set up on the Ultramontane side against this proof that the Papacy has ceased to exist as a *de jure* institution, is that the mere fact of recognition and acceptance of an invalidly elected Pope by the Roman Church at large suffices to make good all defects and to validate his position. But this is in the teeth of all the legal facts. For (1) there is no such provision to be found in the Canon Law, which could not omit so important a legal principle, did it exist; (2) no opportunity of expressing either assent or dissent is afforded to the dispersive Roman Church, seeing that the election in conclave is not conditional but final,[1] and the result is publicly signified at once in words denoting that the new reign has begun; (3) the absence of any schism, or any public challenge of the title of any one of the thirteen intruded Popes between 903 and 963, is legally equivalent to acceptance of them all by the dispersive Roman Church, but Baronius is most precise in denying their status; and (4) there are Bulls of Julius II. and Paul IV. which categorically contradict this assertion, in that they enact that no recognition, homage,

---

[1] Ferraris, *Prompta Bibliotheca*, s.v. *Papa*, art. i., n. 61.

or obedience shown to an invalidly elected Pope shall avail to legitimate his status, when his disqualification has been either simony or heresy.[1]

The only plea which can be set up in defence of the Ultramontane theory is that of begging the whole question, and saying, "As it is certain that St. Peter did receive the privileges of infallibility and sovereign jurisdiction over the whole Church, and that he conveyed and transmitted them indefeasibly to the Popes of Rome, who are his successors, it is necessary to believe as matter of faith, in despite of any seemingly adverse testimony, that God took care that the gates of hell should never prevail against His Church, and that the succession on which all true jurisdiction depends has been preserved unimpaired amidst all the troubles and dangers which have beset it."

This, of course, does not meet the difficulty at all; and the truer way of regarding the question is to say, "If God have indeed attached such inestimable privileges to the Papal Chair, and if, as all theologians and canonists agree, the occupant of that chair must be validly elected in order to exercise them, then we shall find on inquiry that the line has been regular and undisputed from the first; that no doubt, and, above all, no invalidity, attaches to any one of those reckoned in the succession. And the superabundant proof that such is not the case, that actually no See in the whole world has so many flaws of the gravest kind in its pedigree, none has ever sunk morally so low and so often in the person of its pontiffs, is the final disproof of the Petrine claims, as a mere human legend, destitute of any Scriptural, legal, or historical basis."

The remarkable weakness of the line of Papal succession can be most clearly exhibited in a chronological table of the flaws in legitimate transmission of the Chair, which are precisely analogous to failures of proof of regular descent, or actual proofs of bastardy, in a family pedigree on which titles and estates depend. Their number may be usefully

---

[1] *Cum tam* divino and *Ex Apostolatus officio*.

contrasted with the two intrusions (Stigand and Tillotson), and the one doubtful election (Pole) in five hundred years of the See of Canterbury. It is to be remembered that intrusion and simony are absolute disqualifications, heresy an almost equal one, and that all questions of doubt, either where the result of an election has been reasonably questioned, or invalidity may attach to the election itself, are ruled against the claimant by Bellarmine's maxim, "A doubtful Pope is counted no-Pope." All persons reckoned, whether justly or unjustly, as anti-Popes, are excluded from the following table; and merely legendary stories, such as that of Pope Marcellinus's apostasy, and rigidly technical objections, such as apply, for instance, to the orthodoxy of Nicolas I., and to the election of Gelasius II., are omitted also; so as to state the case for the prosecution as moderately as possible. The names in Roman letters mark the highly doubtful Popes, those in *italics* the certainly invalid and irregular ones.—See Table (p. 343).

The Electoral College of Cardinals was completely vitiated by simony under Alexander VI.; and thus, even if it could be conceded that the Papacy was saved somehow through former irregular transmissions, or was validly reconstituted by the Council of Constance, there has been by Roman Canon Law no *de jure* Pope since 1484 at latest, consequently no *de jure* Cardinal created, and thus no means exist on Ultramontane principles for restoring the Petrine succession; though a General Council of the Latin Church might probably set up a new and canonically valid episcopate in the See of Rome, but with no shadow of claim to any Divine charter of privilege, nor any heirship to St. Peter.

To sum up: The points successively raised, and (it is submitted) proved, in the foregoing inquiry, are as follows:—

I. That the claim to teach and rule the Church Universal, as of privilege, in virtue of a special inheritance from St. Peter, made on behalf of the Popes of Rome, does not satisfy any one of the seven conditions required by Roman Canon Law in all cases of privilege.[1] For,

---

[1] See *ante*, chapter i., p. 6.

(*a*) No document constituting them such heirs, and annexing the privilege to the inheritance, is producible, or so much as thought to have ever existed.

(*b*) The document alleged as conferring this privilege upon St. Peter himself is not certain and manifest in wording for this purpose, but obscure and enigmatic; so as to have **been** diversely interpreted from **the earliest to the** latest time **since** its promulgation.

(*c*) When strictly and literally construed, it contains **no** express gift of either teaching or ruling authority; which accordingly cannot be legally read into it.

(*d*) It is exclusively personal in wording, and is therefore limited to St. Peter singly.

(*e*) It contains **no** clause contemplating or empowering its extension **to** any other person **than** St. Peter.

(*f*) The interpretation actually put upon it by Ultramontanes denies, interferes with, and encroaches upon, **the** rights and privileges of all other Patriarchs, Metropolitans, and Bishops of the Church Universal.[1]

(*g*) It has been habitually **exercised with excess and** abuse, and has **thus been long since forfeited, assuming** that it ever existed.

II. **Holy** Scripture, construed as a legal document tendered in evidence of the Petrine claims, not only fails **to** corroborate, but directly contradicts, them.

III. The Liturgies, as evidence of the mind of whole Churches, and remounting to remote antiquity, recognise no supreme authority as vesting in St. Peter himself, not **to** say any persons claiming to inherit from him.

---

[1] Thus, **not** merely do the Vatican decrees **assert that** the Pope has direct and immediate jurisdiction in every **diocese of the** Church Universal; but in the course of the debates **it was alleged** that bishops are merely the Pope's officials; and one of the cardinals, speaking to **a** French priest about the letter of **censure** addressed by the Pope to the Archbishop of Paris, said:—"Just consider the monstrosity, this Archbishop dares to speak of rights which belong to him. What would you say if one of your lackeys were to talk of his rights when you gave him **your** orders?" — *Letters of Quirinus*, xlvi., **last** sentence.

IV. The great majority of the eminent Fathers of the Church interpret the three great Petrine texts in St. Matthew xvi., St. Luke xxii., and St. John xxi., in a sense contrary to the Ultramontane gloss; and thus make that gloss untenable by Roman Catholics, who are bound to interpret Scripture only "according to the unanimous consent of the Fathers."

V. The Canons and Decrees of the undisputed General Councils of the Church, and those of a large number of provincial and other local Councils, down to the middle of the fifteenth century, are wholly incompatible with any belief in the Petrine Claims having been currently received throughout the Church.[1]

VI. The Acts (as distinguished from the formulated decrees) of the Councils, those of many Popes and of many eminent Fathers, are incapable of being reconciled with the Petrine Claims.

VII. No trustworthy or even probable evidence is adducible for the fact that St. Peter was ever Bishop of Rome.

VIII. Not only is the case for a Petrine Privilege destroyed, but the breaks in the chain of prescription are so numerous and serious as to make it impossible to establish the Petrine Claims on that basis.

IX. Even if there ever had been a Petrine succession, with devolution of the Petrine Privilege, in the See of Rome, it has been entirely annulled and voided by demonstrable and incurable flaws, so that no valid Pope has sat for more than four centuries, or can be secured in the future by any now existing machinery in the Church of Rome.

---

[1] It may be added here that the Papal interpretation of the words "Whatsoever thou shalt bind," &c., was challenged on behalf of the English Church at the Council of Constance, in a petition officially presented by Richard Ullerston. Herein, after disputing the restriction of the power of binding and loosing to St. Peter and his successors, he adds the following interesting sentence: "Quod utinam quidem crebro allegantes, non tamen in toto intelligentes, non allegarent in contumeliam legis Christi."—Von der Hardt, *Magn. Conc. Const.*, I. p. 27, page 114.

CHAP. VIII.] COLLAPSE OF THE PAPAL SUCCESSION. 343

Name of Pope.	Date.	Nature of defect.	Authority for fact.
Victor I. or Zephyrinus	193–202 202–219	Heresy[1]	Tertullian, *Adv. Prax.* i.
Callistus I.	219–224	Heresy	St. Hippolytus, *Ref. Hær.* ix. 6.
Liberius	352–367	Heresy	St. Jerome, *Chron.* ann. 357
Felix II.	367	Heresy and invalid election	St. Athanasius, *Ad Monachos*.
Damasus I.	367–385	Disputed election, and homicidal entrance on see	Marcellin. et Faust. *Libellus*.
Zosimus	417, 418	Heresy	His Letter acquitting Pelagius and Cælestius
Boniface I.	418–423	Disputed election, and forcible entrance on see	Baronius, *Ann.* 419
Hormisda	511–523	Heresy	His Letter to Possessor, Baronius, *Ann.* 520, xvi.–xviii.
Boniface II.	530–532	Disputed election, and probable simony	Cassiodorus, *Var.* ix. 15
John II.	532–535	Probable simony	*Idem*, ibid.
Vigilius	540–555	Intrusion and simony	Liberatus, *Breviar.* xxii.
Pelagius I.	555–559	Intrusion	Anastasius, Bibliothec.
Honorius I.	626–640	Heresy	His Letters, burnt at Sixth General Council
Eugenius I.	655–657	Intrusion[2]	Anastasius, Bibliothec.

[1] The reference is not to the Pope's temporary encouragement of Montanism, as to which Tertullian's wishes may have deceived him, but to complicity with the Sabellian teaching of Praxeas, a wholly distinct charge.

[2] There was no moral guilt in this case, and the intrusion was condoned ; but it is a legal flaw all the same.

Name of Pope.	Date.	Nature of defect.	Authority for fact.
Sergius I.	687–701	Simony[1]	Anastasius, Bibliothec.
Eugenius II.	824–827	Disputed election	Anastasius, Bibliothec.
Formosus	891–896	Doubtful election	Baronius
Boniface VI.	896	Intrusion	Baronius
Stephen VI.	896, 897	Intrusion	Baronius
John IX.	898–900	Disputed election	Flodoard
Christopher	903, 904	Intrusion	Baronius
Sergius III.	904–911	Intrusion	Baronius
Anastatius III.	911–914	Intrusion	Baronius
Lando	914	Intrusion	Baronius
John X.	914–929	Intrusion	Baronius
Leo VI.	929–931	Intrusion	Baronius
Stephen VII.	931	Intrusion	Baronius
John XI.	931–933	Intrusion	Baronius
Leo VII.	936–939	Intrusion[2]	Baronius
Stephen VIII.	939–943	Intrusion	Baronius
Martin III.	943–946	Intrusion	Baronius
Agapetus II.	946–955	Intrusion	Baronius
John XII.	955–963	Intrusion	Baronius
Leo VIII.	963–965	Disputed election	Liutprand
Benedict V.	964, 965	Disputed election	Liutprand
Benedict VIII.	1012–1024	Intrusion and simony	Desider Cassin. Radulphus Glaber.
John XIX.	1033–1046	Intrusion and simony	
Benedict IX.	1033–1046	Intrusion and simony	
Gregory VI.	1044–1046	Simony	Acts of Council of Sutri
Benedict X.	1058–	Simony	Leo Ostiensis, l. iii. c. 8.
Innocent II.	1130–1143	Disputed election	Arnulf. Lexov. *De Schism.*
Alexander III.	1159–1181	Disputed election	Acts of Council of Pavia

[1] This was rather technical than actual simony. The money was not paid to secure election, but was extorted by the Exarch after the election, as the price of the necessary civil sanction.

[2] There was an interregnum of three years between John XI. and Leo VII.

Name of Pope.	Date.	Nature of defect.	Authority for fact.
Hadrian V.	1276	Only a deacon[1]	Raynaldus
Boniface VIII.	1294-1303	Doubtful election[2]	Raynaldus
Clement V.	1305-1314	Simony	Raynaldus
John XXII.	1316-1334	Heresy and Non-residence.	Raynaldus, ann. 1331-34
Benedict XII.	1334-1342	Non-residence	Raynaldus
Clement VI.	1342-1352	Non-residence	Raynaldus
Innocent VI.	1352-1362	Non-residence	Raynaldus
Urban V.	1362-1370	Non-residence	Raynaldus
Gregory XI.	1370-1378	Non-residence	Raynaldus
Urban VI. (Rome)	1378-1389	Doubtful election	
Clement VII. (Avignon)	1378-1394	Doubtful election	
Boniface IX. (Rome)	1389-1404	Doubtful election	
Benedict XIII. (Avignon)	1394-1409	Doubtful election	Maimbourg, *Histoire du Grand Schisme d'Occident*
Innocent VII. (Rome)	1404-1406	Doubtful election	
Gregory XII. (Rome)	1406-1409	Doubtful election	
Alexander V.	1409, 1410	Doubtful election	
John XXIII.	1410-1415	Doubtful election and heresy	
Martin V.	1417-1431	Irregular election	Von der Hardt, *Magn. Conc. Const.*
Innocent VIII.	1484-1492	Simony	Raynaldus, ann. 1484, 28, 31

[1] He was a dying man **when elected, and** did **not live long enough for** consecration. But, **as he** made some important **changes in the** mode of electing the Popes, it is clear that he was **fully Pope without** being successor to any episcopate of St. Peter.

[2] The doubt arises from the questionable validity of the abdication of his predecessor, Celestine V., which created the vacancy; and Boniface's title was challenged in his lifetime **on** that ground, nor has the doubt **ever been** authoritatively **cleared up.**

Name of Pope.	Date.	Nature of defect.	Authority for fact.
Alexander VI.	1492–1503	Simony	Von Eggs, *Purpura Docta*, iii. 251
Julius II.	1503–1513	Simony	Palatii, *Fasti Cardin.*
Leo X.	1513–1521	Invalid election	Palatii, *Fasti Cardin.*
Clement VII.	1523–1534	Simony	Giucciardini, *Istor. d' Italia*, xv.

No valid election has been possible since.

NOTE ON THE FALSE DECRETALS.

(*See p.* 324.)

THERE is one salient difference between the conception of ecclesiastical law as entertained in Oriental and Latin Christendom. In the East, nothing was at any time accepted as law save what had been formally enacted by councils, and those large ones. But in the West it was the aim of the Popes of Rome, from an early time, to attribute equal authority, and to secure the like acceptance, for their own injunctions, whether colourably validated by their local synod, or issued on their single responsibility. Thus there grew up a body of Pontifical law side by side with the Synodical law, and carefully fused therewith, or made to override it. This pontifical law was for the most part embodied in formal epistles, usually addressed as Rescripts in reply to some bishop who had applied for advice on some moot point ; at first, most probably, only to such bishops as belonged to the suburbicarian provinces, but later to prelates in no respect under Papal jurisdiction ; and as these epistles were worded as decrees, and were intended to carry with them the same authority as the canons of Councils, they were styled Decretals. As the papal power increased, it was thought expedient to manufacture a long prescription for these Decretals, and to extend as widely as possible the range of subjects with which they were concerned. And this was fully effected by the forgery of the False Decretals, which issued from the school of Boniface of Mentz, and were first published by one Isidore Mercator, or Peccator (there is some uncertainty as to the agnomen) about the year 850, being at once accepted at Rome, and made a part of the body of pontifical law. It has been argued, now that the spuriousness of these documents is allowed on all hands, that the Pope and the Roman Curia were as much deceived as every one else, and were not to blame in the matter of this reception. But the reply is conclusive : (1) there were ample means at Rome, far more than anywhere else, for detecting the fraud, chiefly in that no documents of the kind were in the Roman archives, precisely where attested copies must have been enrolled, had they been genuine ; (2) the Roman Church had much interest in promoting the fraud ; (3) nothing has been done up to the present moment to withdraw any part of these forgeries from the Canon Law, into which they are now interwoven, far less to abate, not to say renounce, any pretension based on them as its original warrant.

Some account of the subject-matter of these Decretals will usefully illustrate much already put before the reader. The first part consists of about sixty epistles of Popes, beginning with St. Clement (*circ.* A.D. 95), and ending with Melchiades (A.D. 314), and for the most part professedly addressed to all the bishops of the Church Universal. The epistles ascribed to St. Clement are ancient forgeries, but all the remainder are the work of Isidore.

I. The first epistle of Clement to St. James of Jerusalem, with which the series begins, contains the following propositions: (*a*) St. Peter is the foundation of the Church; (*b*) In the presence of the whole Roman Church he ordains Clement its bishop as his own successor, and makes over his chair of preaching and teaching to him; (*c*) and also his special power of binding and loosing, so that whatever Clement decreed on earth should be ratified in heaven; (*d*) Resistance to Clement, clothed with this authority, is rebellion against God; (*e*) in virtue of his new powers, Clement prepares to consecrate and give mission to bishops for Gaul, Spain, Germany, Italy, and other countries of the West, whither St. Peter had not already sent them, and directs James to do the like in the East; (*f*) and also to parcel out the territory under him into patriarchal, primatial, metropolitan, and episcopal jurisdictions, in an ascending scale of rank, "because not even amongst the apostles was there parity, but one was above all the others"; (*g*) appeals were to lie to the metropolitans, and from them to the patriarchs; (*h*) the laity, even those of princely rank and power, are to obey the clergy; (*i*) and the clergy cannot be lawfully tried before lay tribunals; (*j*) nor can any ecclesiastic be called to account, or put on his trial, by his inferiors, unless he err from the Faith.

The First Epistle of Anacletus, after ruling that each province shall have its own judges, and that suits are to be conducted where they arose, and not carried elsewhere, adds: "But if more difficult questions should arise, be they judgments of bishops and magnates, or suits of much importance, if there be an appeal, let them be referred to the Apostolic See. For the Apostles enjoined this, by order of the Saviour, that greater and more difficult questions should always be referred to the Apostolic See, upon which Christ built the Church Universal."

The Third Epistle of Anacletus states that "this sacrosanct and Apostolic Roman Church did not obtain its primacy, or acquire its eminence of power, over all Churches and the whole flock of the Christian people, from the Apostles, but from our Lord and Saviour Himself. . . . If, then, any more difficult cases arise amongst you, refer them to the supreme tribunal (*apicem*) of this Holy See, that they may be terminated by the Apostolic judgment, because such is the Lord's will, and so He has appointed. For this Apostolic See has been made the hinge and head of all Churches by the Lord Himself, and no other; and, as a door is guided by the hinge, so, through the Lord's institution, all Churches are guided by the authority of this Holy See."

The Second Epistle of Sixtus I. declares that whoso disobeys the decrees of the Holy See works his own destruction.

The First Epistle of Hyginus, decreeing that no Metropolitan shall hear causes without the assessorship of comprovincial bishops, makes the exception, " Saving the privilege of the Roman See in all things"; thus asserting the right of the Pope to sit as judge without assessors.

The Epistle of Soter alleges that it is the duty of the Pope, if he learns that anything wrong is done in any of the Churches, to interpose without delay for its correction. This extends the claim to hear appeals into the larger demand of direct and immediate jurisdiction of first instance in all dioceses.

The Epistle of Eleutherius enacts that as it is impracticable to refer all ecclesiastical suits to the Apostolic See, only cases which have been decided by bishops shall be referred thither, to be decided by its authority, in conformity with the rules laid down by the Apostles; and that no promotions or ordinations in any Church may take place prior to a decision on the matter at Rome.

The first Epistle of Victor I. lays down that any bishop accused or condemned by the bishops of his province shall have an appeal to the Pope, who may try the case in person or by his vicars; and, while the cause is pending, no other bishop can be put in his see, because, though it is lawful for the comprovincial bishops to inquire into the presentment against an accused bishop, yet it is not permitted them to decide the case without consultation of the Pope of Rome.

The Epistle of Zephyrinus, repeating this decree, adds, as a further reason for its original enactment by the Apostles, over and above the privilege of Peter, that the Church of Rome is the Mother of all Churches, and it is thus her right to receive appeals and calls for help from all, that they may be nourished from her breasts and defended by her authority, since a mother cannot, and should not, forget her child.

The First Epistle of Fabian alleges that the duty incumbent on the Pope to oversee all Churches, makes it necessary that every Church should know what is the usage of the Holy Roman Church, that they all, as her true children, may follow the example of their Mother.

The Second Epistle of Cornelius forbids any appeal of bishops outside their province, except to the Roman See.

The Epistle of Lucius alleges that the Roman Church, by a peculiar grace, never has erred, and never will err, from the path of Apostolic tradition, and is the Mother of all Churches, so that it is the Pope's special function and duty to teach all Christian people.

The Second Epistle of Marcellinus, addressed (as several other false decretals are) to all the Bishops of the East, alleges that a legation from them had recently come to Rome to receive a Papal edict for their guidance; and the present letter is now sent them as a brief summary of what the Pope had then been pleased to order, lest the members of the legation should have made any mistakes in reporting it upon their return, whether from forgetfulness through the lapse of time in the long journey, or any original misunderstanding on their own part.

The First Epistle of Marcellus, addressed to the Bishops of the province of Antioch, tells them that they are bound to adhere to the teaching of blessed Peter, their first teacher, and not to abandon their father, who is Head of the whole Church. For his See was originally at Antioch, but by the Lord's command was transferred to Rome. Accordingly, they must keep to the path thus marked out for them, and are in all respects to obey that See to which by Divine grace all important cases are to be referred, even as it is there they really began. And if even Antioch, once the first of all Sees, has had to yield to Rome, much more are all others subject to its jurisdiction, and all bishops are entitled to appeal to it as the Head, and to obtain from it protection and deliverance, just as it is thence they derive their instruction and their consecration.

And it was also decreed at the same time by the Apostles through Divine inspiration that no synod should be held without the authority of the Apostolic See, and that no Bishop could be tried for any offence whatsoever except in a legitimate Synod convoked at a fitting time by Apostolic authority; because there is no doubt that all Episcopal judgments and other matters of the first class can be conducted and terminated only by the authority of the Holy See; so that all provincial affairs are to be reviewed by the authority of the Holy Universal See, if it pleases the Pope so to command. Nor may recourse be had by those of one province to the bishops and clergy of another province without the previous sanction of the Apostolic See.

The Epistle of Melchiades alleges that the Lord reserved to Himself the right of judging bishops, whom He willed to be the eyes and pillars of the Church, and that He made over this privilege to the blessed key-bearer Peter exclusively in His stead. And this prerogative of Peter has rightly come by succession to his See, to be inherited and possessed for all time to come; because, there was some distinction of power amongst the blessed Apostles, and though their election was alike, yet it was granted to blessed Peter that he should take precedence of the others, and wisely decide all matters among them which had occasioned disputes, contentions, or questionings. And that this was ordained so by God's ordinance, in order that no one in time to come should claim to manage all matters, but that for all time the more important pleas, such as those of bishops and other weighty subjects of concern, should come together to one place only—the See of blessed Peter, prince of the Apostles—that they might receive the final decision from that place whence they had derived the origin of their appointment, so that they might never be at variance with their head.

Many of these assertions recur over and over again in different decretals, often in the same words, and the text "Thou art Peter," etc., is frequently cited as their justification and proof; but it is unnecessary to give more than specimens.

The second part of the False Decretals consists of Papal decrees of the period between Sylvester (314-336) and Gregory II. (715-731), of which thirty-nine are spurious, and of the acts of several Councils which are quite unauthentic. It opens with the Donation of Constantine, wherein, after declaring that the authority of the Vicar of Christ is superior to the Imperial power and dignity, he decrees that the Popes of Rome for all time are to have precedence and authority over the four other principal Sees, Antioch, Alexandria, Constantinople, and Jerusalem, and over all other Churches throughout the world.

Amongst the spurious synods is one at Rome under Pope Sylvester, coincidently with the Council of Nice, wherein the Pope by his apostolical authority reinstated in their Sees a number of bishops who had been deprived, whether by ecclesiastical or civil action. A spurious correspondence between St. Athanasius and Pope Mark represents the former, in union with all the Egyptian bishops, addressing the Pope as holding the Apostolic and Universal See, and makes St. Athanasius profess entire obedience to him; and the Pope in his reply asserts the inerrancy of the Roman See in matters of faith, as a consequence flowing from the clause of the Petrine charter in St. Luke xxii. 31-32. A letter of Pope Julius I. to the Eastern bishops claims for the Roman See the right of convoking General Councils and of deciding all episcopal causes, in right of a privilege granted in the Gospel, and also by the Apostles and the canons of synods alleges that the Roman Church is higher and greater than all other Churches, and obtained its sovereign rank not merely from the decrees of canons and Fathers, but from the very words of the Lord Himself spoken to St. Peter; so that it is Head of all Churches precisely as Peter was Head of all Apostles, and by the same direct institution of the Lord; consequently nothing, great or small, could be lawfully done anywhere in the Church without the advice and co-operation of the Bishop of the Roman Church. Accordingly, all bishops are to remember that the one way for them to avoid all error of belief or action is to take the rule of their observance from that See of blessed Peter whence their own rank is derived, and which is not only the Mother of their priestly dignity, but also their mistress in all ecclesiastical procedure.

Another rescript of Pope Julius to the Oriental bishops who had taken part in the condemnation of St. Athanasius has appended to it a number of decrees thrown into the form of canons, and inclusive of clauses making the See of Rome the supreme court of appeal, having also direct jurisdiction in all provinces, and the right of rehearing all causes by its vicars, and especially of reviewing the acts of provincial synods, as also of being the only tribunal with a right to condemn and deprive bishops. St. Athanasius is represented as appealing to Pope Liberius for his support against Arianism, on the ground that it is owing to his teaching and that of the Roman See, to which all peoples resort, that the orthodox faith prevails. And Liberius replies to his "son" Athanasius that, since he has himself received such steadfastness of faith from the very beginning, derived from blessed Peter, Prince of the Apostles, as to have authority to defend the true faith on behalf the Church Universal, he will act for and with him as a father for his children.

Another forged letter from St. Athanasius to Pope Felix II. states that a canon was unanimously enacted in the Council of Nice that no council could be held, and no bishop condemned, without the assent of the Pope of Rome; and that another unanimous decree provided that any bishop who had reason to suspect the impartiality of his Metropolitan or the comprovincial bishops assembled to try him, might appeal to the Holy See of Rome, to which the power of binding and loosing is committed above all others by special privilege granted by the Lord. "For thou art Peter, as the Divine Word truthfully attests, and upon thy foundation the pillars of the Church—that is, the bishops, who uphold the Church and are bound to bear it on their shoulders,—are there established, and to these He committed the keys of the kingdom of Heaven, and publicly enacted that thou shouldst bind and loose with power whatsoever is in earth and Heaven." And the reply of Felix entirely corresponds to this declaration of Roman privilege.

So much will suffice to exhibit the general tone and object of the False Decretals, which revolutionised the polity of the Western Church, and which were formally embodied in the Canon Law (of which they had for centuries practically formed a large effective factor) in respect of all their legislative matter by Pope Gregory IX., under the editorship of St. Raymond de Pennaforte, in 1234. They are the sole basis and justification of those claims and exceptional powers asserted by the Roman Chair, which culminated in the Vatican decrees of 1870.

INDEX.

INDEX.

AARON, 21
Abraham, 21
Acacius of CP., 95, 107, 251, 253, 255, 264, 277, 280, 282, 283
Accemetæ, 252, 292
Acquittal, Synod of the Incongruous, 269
Aetius of CP., 241
Aetius the Prefect, 227, 230 n.
Africa, Church of North, 209, **211, 214,** 295, 300, 302
African Canons, 214, 295
Agapetus I., Pope, 289, 294, 298
Agapetus II., Pope, 328, 344
Agatho, Pope, 83, **114, 115, 116,** 118
Agilulf, King, 302 n.
Alberic, son of Marozia, 328
Albertus Magnus, St., 79 **n.**
Alexander III., Pope, 330, 332, 344
Alexander V., Pope, 120, **123,** 335, 345
Alexander VI., Pope, 337, 346
Alexandria, Church of, 65, 93, 102, 103, 235, 237, 258
Alexandria, Council of, 196
Allies, Rev. T. **W., 221 n.**
Allnatt, Mr., 140 n.
Alypius of Tagaste, 97, 103 n.
Amalasuintha, Queen, 288, 295
Ambrose, St., 75, 82, 84, 86, 167
Ambrosian Missal, 67
Anacletus I., Pope, 176, 182, 185, 192, 193, 346
Anacletus II., Anti-Pope, 332

Anastasius the Librarian, **117,** 186, 305
Anastatius, Emperor, 271, 272, 277, 280, 283
Anastatius II., Pope, 263
Anastatius III., Pope, 328, 344
Anatolius of CP., 235, 237, 239, **243, 246**
Andrew, St., 19, 20
Andrew of Thessalonica, 255
Anicetus, Pope, 126
Ante-Nicene evidence **on the** Petrine **texts,** 71-74; on St. Peter's **Roman** episcopate, 175-181
Anthimus, 297, 298
Antioch, Canons of, 159
Antioch, Church of, 66, 69 n., 102, 103 n., 185 n., 213, 235, 237, 258
Antioch, Councils of, 93, 104, 141, 158, 196
Anti-Popes, 307 n.
Antitypes in Gospels, 16
Antonina, 299
Apiarius, 97, 98
Apostles, equality of their commission, 13, 15, 71, 134
Apostolical Canons, 92, **196**
Apostolical Constitutions, 66, 73, 178, 179, 187, 192, 194, 199
Apostolic See, title of, 103 n.
Appeals to Rome, 97, 139, 146, 150, 162-3, 167-8, 208, 212, 217, 218, 224, 249, 291
Appellate Jurisdiction, 93, 252

2 A 2

Aquileia, Patriarchate of, 300, 302
Aquinas, St. Thomas, 83
Aratus of Carthage, 95
Arian Controversy, 148, 159, 296
Arles, Church of, 216
Arles I., Council of, 150, 196
Armorica, 290
Arnobius, 177
Ascholius of Thessalonica, 167
Athalaric, King, 288, 289, 295
Athanasius, St., 155, 158, 159, 161, 167, 168, 351, 352
Augustine of Canterbury, St., 316, 317
Augustine of Hippo, St., 77, 83, 84, 86
Aurelian, Emperor, 141
Aurelius of Carthage, 214
Auxiliarius, 229
Auxilius, 327 n.
Avignon, Papacy at, 332
Avitus of Vienne, 270

BABYLON, 57, 58
Baluze, 140, 183
Baronius, Cardinal, 115, 182, 184, 185 n., 205, 212, 246 n., 265, 274 n., 298, 299, 300, 305 n., 324 n., 328, 339
Basil the Great, St., 74, 82, 84, 107
Basilius the Prefect, 266
Basilian Liturgy, 66
Basilides and Martial, 139
Basle, Council of, 119, 121-124
Bede, Venerable, 78, 85, 161, 200, 316
Belisarius, 296, 298, 301
Bellarmine, Cardinal, 46, 83, 205, 239 n.
Benedict I., Pope, 112, 303
Benedict V., Pope, 329, 344
Benedict VIII., Pope, 330, 344
Benedict IX., Pope, 119, 330, 344
Benedict X., Pope, 309, 344
Benedict XII., Pope, 345

Benedict XIII., Anti-Pope, 334, 336, 345
Benedict XIV., Pope, 333
Bernard, St., 4
Bishop of Bishops, title, 130 n.
Boethius, 287
Boniface I., Pope, 97, 217, 237, 301
Boniface II., Pope, 288, 289
Boniface VI., Pope, 344
Boniface VII., Pope, 326
Boniface VIII., Pope, 1, 2, 305
Boniface IX., Pope, 345
Boniface of Mentz, 312
Bonizo of Sutri, 330
Bossuet, 335
Bower, 213
Breviary, Roman, 117, 162, 194, 195
Bribery in Roman Church, 288-290, 291, 330, 337
Britain separated from Roman Empire, 230
British Church, 316, 317
Bulls, Papal, 2, 146 n.

CÆCILIAN, 156
Cælestius, 209, 210, 214, 215
Callistus I., Pope, 131, 132, 343
Calixtus II., Pope, 140
Cæsarea, 105
Cæsarius of Arles, St., 110
Caius, Pope, 176
Canon Law, 4, 61, 85, 91, 92, 104, 189, 196, 224, 227, 242, 247, 259, 295, 309, 312, 340, 341
Canons of Councils, evidence of, 91-124; how validated, 156, 209
Canterbury, 340
Cardinals, 26, 155, 288, 307, 330, 331 n., 336
Caroline Books, 118, 322
Carranza, 334 n.
Carthage, Councils of, 97, 98, 209, 215, 217, 296
Cathari, 295
Cassiodorus, 222

INDEX.

Catacombs, evidence of, 189
Celestine I., Pope, 98, 106, 217, 218, 241 n.
Celestine V., Pope, 345 n.
Celidonius of Besançon, **106, 224, 244**
Chalcedon, Council of, 95, 99, 159, **165,** 196, **204, 236-243**
Charlemagne, Emperor, **118**
Charter, Petrine, 7, 45
Charters in Scripture, 21, 189
Christopher, Pope, 327, 344
Chromatius of Aquileia, 207
Chronicle of Eusebius, 182, **187,** 193
Chronicle of Nicephorus, 186
Chrysostom, St., **77, 168, 204,** 205, 255
Ciampini, 305
Claudius, Emperor, **181, 182,** 187
Clement of Alexandria, St., 176 n., 177
Clement I., Pope, **178,** 179, 180, 182, 192-194
Clement II., Pope, 330
Clement V., Pope, 345
Clement VI., Pope, 345
Clement VII. (Avignon), Pope, 345
Clement VII. (Rome), Pope, 337, 346
Clement XI., Pope, 221
Clementine Homilies, 71, 90 n., 178, 179, 192
Clementine Recognitions, 186
Coadjutor Bishops, 196
Code of Justinian, 293, 298
Constance, Council of, 119, 120, **335**
Constantine the Great, Emperor, 151, 156
Constantine Pogonatus, Emperor, 320, 342 n.
Constantine VI., Emperor, 323
Constantinople, Church of, 65, 66, 96, 100

Constantinople, General Councils of, 95, 96, 101, 103 n., 111, 115, 157, 163, 238, 244, 319
Constantinople, Lesser Synods of, 117, 246, 280
Constantius III., **Emperor,** 228 n.
Cornelius, Pope, **132-135,** 349
Councils, incompatible with later Papacy, **144-146**; claims of Popes over, **149**
Creed, Nicene, 244
Creed of Pius IV., **3, 70, 80, 91**
Cresconius the Canonist, **221**·
Cresconius of Todi, 264
Cyprian, St., 71, 73, 86, 103, 107, **132-140,** 177
Cyril of Alexandria, St., 78, 84, 219, 239, 251
Cyril the Archimandrite, 252
Cyril of Jerusalem, St., 86
Cyrus of Phasis, 318

DAMASUS I., Pope, 79, 152, 162, 167, 168, **169** n., **187, 196,** 310
Damiani, St. **Peter, 44** n., **184**
Dante, 265
David, House of, **16, 17, 21**
Decentius of **Gubbio, 208**
Decentralisation of Christian worship, **53, 54**
Decretals, False, 83, 208, 324, 347-352
Decretal, **first genuine, 169 n.,** 324
Deposition of bishops, 204
Dinoth, Abbot, 316
Dionysius Exiguus, 96, 221
Dionysius of Corinth, 175, **180**
Dionysius, Pope, **221**
Dioscorus of Alexandria, 238, 241 n., 253
Dioscorus, Anti-Pope, 288
Doctor of the Church, 70
Domnus of Antioch, 141
Donation of Pippin, 144
Donatists, 150, 151, 295

Dorotheus of Thessalonica, 275, 279, 285
Dupin, 224
Durandus, 68

ECTHESIS of Heraclius, 319
Edict of Gratian, 163; of Valentinian III., 227, 230, 248 n., 270
Eggs, Von, 337
Eleutherius, Pope, 349
Elvira, Council of, 296
Emperors, position of, in the Church, 147–149, 301
Ennodius of Pavia, 270, 275, 279
Ephesus, Canons of, 99, 227
Ephesus, Church of, 103, 105
Ephesus, Council of, 98, 218, 239, 241 n.
Ephesus, Robber Synod of, 232
Epiphanius, St., 74, 84, 185, 192, 199
Epiphanius of CP., 289
Episcopate, dual, at Rome, 200
Erwiga, King, 321
Eudoxia, Empress, 206, 233, 235
Eugenius I., Pope, 343
Eugenius II., Pope, 322, 344
Eugenius IV., Pope, 121—124
Eulalius, Anti-Pope, 217, 301
Euphemius of CP., 255, 256, 272, 280, 282, 283
Eusebius of Cæsarea, 126, 129, 142, 150, 154, 181, 193, 194
Eusebius of Rome, 161
Eutychianism, 231, 240, 251, 257, 272, 299
Eutychius of Alexandria, 186
Excommunication of bishops, its meaning, 252

FABIAN, ST., Pope, 143, 349
Fathers of the Church, 4, 62, 69
Faustinus of Potenza, 97, 98, 218
Felix II., Pope, 95, 343, 352
Felix III., Pope, 107, 165, 252, 253, 263
Felix IV., Pope, 110, 287, 288

Felix V., Anti-Pope, 123
Felix and Sabinus, 139
Ferrandus of Carthage, 292
Filioque clause in Nicene Creed, 245 n.
Firmilian, St., 71, 136, 141
Flavian of Antioch, 169, 274
Flavian of CP., 231, 233, 235, 237 n.
Fleury, 142, 246 n., 299
Florence, Council of, 171 n.
Forcible entry on benefice, 310
Forgeries, Roman, in St. Cyprian, 140; in St. Clement of Rome, 208; in Nicene Canons, 242
Formosus, Pope, 326
Formulary of Hormisda, 278–284
Frankfort, Council of, 322
Fravitta of CP., 255, 283
Fulgentius of Ruspe, St., 291

GALLICAN Church, 270, 300, 302, 322
Gallican Missal, 68, 110
Gammarus, Auditor of the Rota, 311
Gaudentius of Brescia, St., 86
Gelasius I., Pope, 107, 166, 254, 256–259, 263
Gelasius of Cyzicus, 153, 219
German Missal, 68
Germanus of Auxerre, St., 106
Gerson, 26 n., 38 n.
Grado, Patriarchate of, 302
Gratian, Decretum of, 309, 312
Gratian, Emperor, 130 n., 162, 163
Gratry, F., 315 n., 320 n.
Gregory of Antioch, 303
Gregory the Great, St., Pope, 78, 91, 106, 112, 113, 166, 241 n., 303, 323
Gregory II., Pope, 117, 320, 323, 351
Gregory VI., Pope, 119, 330, 344
Gregory VII., Pope, 1, 78, 130 n., 270, 305

INDEX.   359

Gregory IX., Pope, 352
Gregory XI., Pope, 335, 336, 345
Gregory XII., Pope, 335, 336, 345
Gregory Nazianzen, St., 75, 83, 164, 167
Gregory Nyssen, **St.,** 79 n.
Gregory Thaumaturgus, St., 141

Hadrian, **Emperor, 37**
Hadrian I., **Pope, 79** n., **119, 149, 323**
Hadrian II., Pope, 118
Hadrian IV., Pope, 79 n., 332
Hadrian V., Pope, 345
Hefele, Bishop, 153, 157, 161, **162,** 233, 254
Henoticon of Zeno, 251, 272
Henry IV., Emperor, 79, 148
Heraclea, 105, 258, 275
Heraclius, Emperor, 318
Heresy, legal effect of, 312-314
Heros and Lazarus, 214
Hesychius, **90 n.**
Hilarus, Pope, 247
Hilary of Arles, St., **106, 224-** 229
Hilary of Poitiers, St., **74, 81, 86,** 160
Himerius of Tarragona, 169 n.
Hippolytus, St., 71, 131, 132, 176
Hippolytus, Pseudo-, 177
Holiness, note of, 315, 316
Honoratus of Marseilles, 229
Honorius, Emperor, 230, 268, 301
Honorius I., Pope, 114-118, **317- 321,** 343
Honorius II., Pope, 331
Hormisda, Pope, 274-287, 290
Hosius of Cordova, 151, 153, **161** n., 219
Hugo, Cardinal, 79 n.
Hugo of Ferrara, 313
Hurter, F., 140 n.
Hyginus, Pope, 349

Ibas of Edessa, 111

Ignatius, St., 73, 175
Illyricum, Eastern, 152, 207, 237, 240, **255, 258,** 278, 289, 294, 300, 302
Image-worship, controversy upon, 118, 322-324
Infallibility, Papal, **5, 115, 16**?, 221, 240, 320, **321**
Innocence, hereditary, **of the** Popes, 270
Innocent I., Pope, **196, 205, 207** -214, 255, 296
Innocent II., Pope, 332
Innocent III., Pope, 1, 247, 305, **312,** 325
Innocent VIII., Pope, 336, 345
Inquisition, 231
Intrusion, legal effect of, 309
Irenæus, St., 104, 126, 128, 176, 191, 192, 194
Irenæus of Barcelona, 249
Irene, Empress, 323
Isidore Mercator, 347
Isidore of Pelusium, St., 77
Isidore of Seville, St., 79 n.

James, St., **the Apostle, 14, 19,** 20, 30, 39
James, St., **the Just, 27,** 37, 43, 90 n., 179
Jansenism, 221
Jerome, St., 37, 76, 83, 159, 161, 173 n., 182, 194, 208, 210 212
Jerusalem, 26, 27, 37, 51-56, 102
Jerusalem, Council of, 23, 26, **27**
Johannes, Andreæ, 313
John, St., the Apostle, 9, 14, **19,** 20, 21, 31, **37, 127,** 128
John I., Pope, **286**
John II., Pope, 290, 296, 343
John III., Pope, 112, 303
John VIII., Pope, 79 n., 326
John IX., Pope, 327, 344
John X., Pope, 328, 344
John XI., Pope, 328, 344
John XII., Pope, 328, 344

John XIX., Pope, 328, 344
John XXII., Pope, 345
John XXIII., Pope, 120, 335, 345
John Damascene, St., 79 n.
John the Faster, of CP., 241 n., 303
John Talaia of Alexandria, 251
John of CP., 283
Julius Africanus, 176 n.
Julius I., Pope, 93, 95, 155, 158, 168, 244, 351
Julius II., Pope, 311, 337, 346
Jurisdiction, St. Peter's, 19, 21, 36, 37
Justin I., Emperor, 130 n., 280, 284-288
Justinian, Emperor, 111, 281, 286, 292-294, 299, 301
Juvenal of Jerusalem, 219

KENRICK, Archbishop, 80 n.

LACTANTIUS, 176, 177, 182
Lando, Pope, 328, 344
Laodicea, Council of, 92
Lateran Synods, 149, 309, 319, 330
Latin language, ambiguity in, 103 n.
Launoi, 149
Laurentius, Anti-Pope, 266, 268
Leander of Seville, 113
Legates, Papal, 122, 151, 153, 154, 155, 219, 220 n., 233, 236, 252, 255, 264, 275, 279, 281, 285, 291
Leo the Great, Pope, 1, 78, 86, 106, 165, 196, 221-247, 280
Leo II., Pope, 113, 116, 117, 157, 320
Leo III., Pope, 245 n.
Leo V., Pope, 327
Leo VI., Pope, 328, 344
Leo VII., Pope, 328, 344
Leo VIII., Pope, 329, 344
Leo X., Pope, 149, 337, 346
Leontius of Arles, 247, 248

Liber Diurnus, 92, 117, 320
Liber Pontificalis, 200, 264, 265, 301, 305
Liberian Catalogue, 193
Liberius, Pope, 159-162, 343
Liberatus of Carthage, 246 n., 298, 300
Linus, St., Pope, 107, 179, 185, 186, 192-195, 200
Liturgies, evidence of the, 64-69
Lothar II., Emperor, 332
Lucius I., Pope, 349
Lucius III., Pope, 330
Ludwig the Pious, Emperor, 322
Lyons, Church of, 108, 110
Lyons, Council II. of, 110

MABILLON, 186
Macedonius of C.P., 272, 274, 280, 282, 283
Mamertus of Vienne, 248
Manichees, 231
Manning, Cardinal, 24, 35, 121, 320
Marcellinus, Pope, 340, 349
Marcellus, Pope, 350
Marcian, Emperor, 235, 236, 246
Marcian of Arles, 133, 138
Marinus, Pope, 326
Mark, St., 11, 102, 235
Mark, Pope, 351
Marozia, 328
Martin I., Pope, 319
Martin III., Pope, 344
Martin V., Pope, 121, 123, 124, 335, 336, 345
Martyrologies, 161, 162
Matrix, 132 n.
Matthias, St., 23, 43
Maxentius, 291
Maximus of Antioch, 240
Maximus the Cynic, 167
Maximus, Emperor, 231
Melchiades, Pope, 150, 295, 348
Meletius of Antioch, 164
Mennas of CP., 298, 318
Michael II., Emperor, 322

INDEX.

Michael III., Emperor, 239 n.
Milan, 105, 108
Milevis, Synod of, 209
Missal, Ambrosian, 67
Missal, Gallican, 68, 110
Missal, German, 68
Missal, Mozarabic, 67
Missal, Roman, 69 n., 80, 81, 195
Monothelism, 318
Montanists, 130
Moses, 16, 17
Muratorian Fragment, 178

Narses, 301, 302
Nectarius of CP., 167
Nero, Emperor, 177, 178, 182, 183, 187
Nestorius, 98, 106, 218, 253
Nice I., Council of, 93, 151, 196, 244, 295
Nice II., Council of, 117, 119, 322
Nicene Creed, 99, 163, 244, 245 n.
Nicolas I., Pope, 239 n., 305, 324, 325
Nicolas II., Pope, 330
Nicolas V., Pope, 302, n.
Novatian, 135
Nullity, various forms of, 307-315

Oak, Synod of the, 205
Oak, Synod of St. Augustine's, 316
Ockham, William of, 313
Odoacer, King, 266, 267
Œcumenical bishop, 241 n., 303
Optatus of Milevis, 185, 194
Orange, Council II. of, 110
Origen, 72, 86, 177
Ordo Romanus, 245 n.
Orleans, Council I. of, 295
Otto I., Emperor, 328

Pagi, 182, 183, 299, 300
Papebroch, 300
Papias, 182
Paris, See of, 106
Paris, Council V. of, 112
Parisian Divines, report of, 323
Paschal I., Pope, 322
Paschal Chronicle, 182
Paschasinus, 236 n., 237 n., 238, 240, 242
Patriarch, 253
Patriarch, Jewish, 244
Patriarchates, 226, 246
Patripassians, 136
Patroclus of Arles, 216
Paul, St., 36-44, 172-182, 208
Paul of Samosata, 141
Paul II., Pope, 130 n.
Paul III., Pope, Bull of, 146 n.
Paul IV., Pope, 69 n., 312, 339
Pauline Scriptures, 33, 34
Paulinus of Antioch, 164
Paulinus of Nola, St., 103 n.
Pavia, Council of, 332
Pelagius, 209
Pelagius I., Pope, 112, 300
Pelagius II., Pope, 83, 112, 149, 166, 301
Peter, St., 5-13, 17-40, 43-47, 62-69, 71-90, 133, 146, 172-201, 333
Peter, Second Epistle of St., 173 n.
Peter of Alexandria, St.. 177
Peter of Altino, 268, 269
Peter the Fuller, 251
Peter Mongus, 251, 256, 257
Peter de Palude, 313
Petrus and Petra, 45-47
Philippopolis, Synod of, 95, 158
Philostorgius, 161
Photinus, 264, 265
Pilgrimage, 305
Pisa, Council of, 119, 120, 335
Pitra, Cardinal, 154
Pius I., Pope, 128
Pius IV., Pope, Creed of, 3, 70
Pius IX., Pope, 1, 13
Placidia, Empress, 226 n., 233
Platina, 265, 327
Polycarp, St., 127, 128, 208
Polycrates of Ephesus, 128

Pontifex Maximus, 130 n.
Possessor, 291
Praxeas, 130
Presbyter, early Popes styled, 128, 129
Prescription, 61, 126
Primates, 92
Prince of the Apostles, 63, 68
Priscillian, 231
Privilege, 4, 6, 61
Proculus of Marseilles, 107, 216
Profession by Pope at coronation, 117
Prosper, St., 83
Protesius, St., 284 n.
Prudentius, 193 n.
Pulcheria, Empress, 165, 235, 243, 246

QUARTODECIMANS, 127, 129
Quirinus, 13 n.

RAVENNA, 251, 269
Reparatus of Carthage, 296
Renouf, Mr., 313 n.
Residence, law of, 333, 334
Rescripts, Papal, 347
Robber Synod of Ephesus, 232
Rock, 44–49
Roman Church, 2, 50, 145, 174, 222, 223
Romans, Epistle to the, 173
Rome in the New Testament, 54, 55
Rome, Synods of, 106, 108, 109, 112, 114, 118, 119, 150, 250, 258, 267, 270, 271, 288, 289, 295, 330, 351
Rosellis, Antonio de, 313
Rufinus, 93, 152, 186, 192, 194, 199
Ryder, F., 313 n.

SABELLIUS, 131
Saints, doctrinal authority of, 69, 70
Salome, 14

Sanhedrin, 144, 145
Sardica, Canons of, 93–96, 227
Sardica, Council of, 93, 95, 155, 158, 196
Scaliger, 181
Schism, the Great, 334
Sergius of CP., 114–117, 318
Sergius III., Pope, 327, 328, 344
Severus of Antioch, 274, 279, 280, 299
Seville, Council II. of, 113
Sforza, Ascanio, 337
Silvanus of Calahorra, 249
Simon Magus, 177, 178, 181
Simony in Roman Church, 288–290, 296, 330; legal effect of, 310
Simplicius, Pope, 250, 252, 266
Sinaitic MS. of New Testament, 57
Siricius, Pope, 47, 107, 169, 244
Sixtus I., Pope, 349
Sixtus IV., Pope, 337
Solomon, 17, 21, 23, 51
Socrates, 95
Sophronius, St., 318
Soter, Pope, 128, 349
Sozomen, 95, 161, 222, 256
Spanish Church, 139, 169, 249
Stephen I., Pope, 132, 135–139
Stephen of Larissa, 112, 289, 295, 296
Stephen IV., Pope, 336 n.
Stephen VI., Pope, 326, 344
Stephen VII., Pope, 328, 344
Stephen VIII., Pope, 328, 344
Stephen X., Pope, 309
Subdivision of dioceses, 37, 114
Suburbicarian sees, 93, 226
Succession in Roman See, 306
Sutri, Council of, 119, 330
Sylverius, Pope, 290, 292
Sylvester I., Pope, 95, 151, 152, 351
Symmachus, Pope, 108, 109, 265, 270–274
Syncellus, George, 183

INDEX. 363

Synodus Palmaris, **108**
Syriac Churches, 32 n.
Syriac Liturgies, 67
Syriac New Testament, 46, **47 n.**

TELESPHORUS, Pope, **128**
Tertullian, **72**, 73, 87, **103 n.**, 129, 130, **176 n.**, 190–**192**, **194**
Theodahat, King, 297, 299
Theodora, Empress, 297, 299
Theodora, Roman courtesan, **328**
Theodore of Mopsuestia, **111**
Theodore of Pharan, 116
Theodore II., Pope, 327
Theodore the Studite, 322
Theodoret, 78, 95, 111, 234
Theodoric the Ostrogoth, **108**, 256, 266, 268, **269**, 275, **285**
Theodosius of Alexandria, **299**
Theodosius I., Emperor, 164, 165, 167
Theodosius II., Emperor, 218, 232, 235, **237**
Theophilus of Alexandria, 205–207, 255
Three Chapters, 111, 300
Tillemont, 225 n., 246 n.
Timothy Ælurus, 284
Timothy of Alexandria, 164
Timothy of C.P., 272, 276
Titles of Apostles, 90 n.
Titles of St. Peter, 63, 88
Toledo, Councils of, 113, 157, 245 **n.**
Turrecremata, Cardinal, 313
Tome of St. Leo, 234, 239, 240, **251**, 276, 299
Trent, Council of, 46, 81, 146 n.
Tours, Council II. of, 69 n.
Turin, Council of, 107, 216
Tutus, Roman legate, 255

ULRIC of Strasburg, 313
Unam Sanctam, Bull, 2, 305
Unigenitus, Bull, 221
Universal bishop, 241 n., 303
Urban III., Pope, 79 n.
Ursicinus, Anti-Pope, 162, **310**

VAISON, Council II., of, 110
Valentinian III., **218**, **233, 235**. See "Edict."
Valerius of Hippo, **201**
Valesius, 152 n., **184**, **194 n.**
Venerius of Milan, 207
Venice, patriarchate of, 302 n.
Vicar of Christ, 16, 17, 204
Vicars, papal, 207
Victor I., Pope, 128-130
Victor III., Pope, 119, 330
Victor **IV.,** Anti-Pope, 332
Victorinus, 193, 224
Vigilius, Pope, 111, 166, 298, 318, 343
Vincenzi, Aloysius, 96
Vincentius and Vitus, **153**, **154**
Vitalian, 274, **278**
Vizirs of right and left hand, 14
Vulgate, **45, 46**

WHITBY, Synod of, **317**
Wilfrid, St., **114, 317**
Witiges, King, **299**

XYSTUS, Pope, 128

ZELLA, Council of, 107
Zeno, Emperor, 251, 252, 284
Zenobia, Queen, 141
Zephyrinus, Pope, 129, 131, 349
Zoega, 154
Zosimus, Pope, 97, 214, 224, 268

✢ PUBLICATIONS ✢

OF THE

Society for Promoting Christian Knowledge.

A Friend's Hand.

	s.	d.
Short Texts and simple Prayers as Consolation for the Sick and Weary, and Comfort for the Dying. With five page Woodcuts. Royal 16mo. .... Cloth boards	1	0

Alone with God; or, Helps to Thought and Prayer.

For the Use of the Sick; based on short passages of Scripture. By the Rev. F. BOURDILLON, M.A., Author of "Lesser Lights." 12mo. .... Cloth boards	1	0

Being of God, Six Addresses on the.

By C. J. ELLICOTT, D.D., Bishop of Gloucester and Bristol. Small post 8vo. .... Cloth boards	1	6

Bible Places; or, The Topography of the Holy Land.

By the Rev. Canon TRISTRAM. With Map and numerous Woodcuts. Crown 8vo. .... Cloth boards	4	0

Bible Thoughts for Daily Life; or, Family Readings from St. Mark's Gospel.

By Mrs. COLIN G. CAMPBELL. Post 8vo. ...... Cloth boards	2	0

Called to be Saints: the Minor Festivals Devotionally Studied.

By CHRISTINA G. ROSSETTI, Author of "Seek and Find." Post 8vo. .... Cloth boards	5	0

Christians under the Crescent in Asia.

By the Rev. E. L. CUTTS, B.A. With numerous Illustrations. Crown 8vo. .... Cloth boards	5	0

Church History, Illustrated Notes on English.

Vol. I.—From the Earliest Times to the Reformation.
Vol. II.—Its Reformation and Modern Work. By the Rev.
C. A. Lane. With numerous illustrations. Crown 8vo.
Cloth boards, each Vol. **1 0**

Church History, Sketches of.

From the First Century to the Reformation. By the late Rev.
Canon Robertson. With Map. 12mo. .... Cloth boards **2 0**

Council of Trent, A Short History of the.

By the Rev. R. F. Littledale. Post 8vo. ...... Cloth boards **1 0**

Daily Readings for a Year.

By Elizabeth Spooner. Crown 8vo. .... Cloth boards **3 6**

Englishman's Brief, The.

On behalf of his National Church. New, revised, and enlarged edition. Small post 8vo. .... Paper boards **0 6**

Faithful Soldiers and Servants.

Twenty Addresses to Young Men. By Mary A. Lewis.
Post 8vo. .... Cloth boards **1 6**

God's Englishmen: Lectures on the Prophets and Kings of England.

Edited by the Rev. C. W. Stubbs, M.A. Post 8vo.
Cloth boards **2 0**

Gospels, The Four.

Arranged in the Form of an English Harmony, from the Text
of the Authorised Version. By the Rev. J. M. Fuller, M.A.
With Analytical Table of Contents and four Maps. Post 8vo.
Cloth boards **1 0**

History of the English Church.
In Short Biographical Sketches. By the Rev. Julius Lloyd, M.A. Post 8vo. ....Cloth boards 1 6

History of the Jewish Nation, A.
From the Earliest Times to the Present Day. By the late E. H. Palmer, M.A. With Map of Palestine and numerous Illustrations. Crown 8vo. ....Cloth boards 4 0

Land of Israel, The.
A Journal of Travel in Palestine, undertaken with special reference to its Physical Character. By the Rev. Canon Tristram. With two Maps and numerous Illustrations. Large post 8vo. ....Cloth boards 10 6

Lectures on the Historical and Dogmatical Position of the Church of England.
By the Rev. W. Baker, D.D. Post 8vo. ......Cloth boards 1 6

Letter and Spirit: Notes on the Commandments.
By Christina G. Rossetti, Author of "Called to be Saints." Post 8vo. ....Cloth boards 2 0

Litany, The.
With an Introduction, Explanation of Words and Phrases, together with Illustrative and Devotional Paraphrase. By the Rev. E. J. Boyce, M.A. Fcap. 8vo. ....Cloth boards 1 0

Narrative of a Modern Pilgrimage through Palestine on Horseback, and with Tents.
By the Rev. A. C. Smith, M.A. Numerous Illustrations, and four Coloured Plates. Crown 8vo. ....Cloth boards 5 0

Paley's Evidences.
A New Edition, with Notes, Appendix, and Preface. By the Rev. E. A. Litton. Post 8vo. ....Cloth boards 4 0

Paley's Horæ Paulinæ.
A New Edition, with Notes, Appendix, and Preface. By the Rev. J. S. Howson, D.D., Dean of Chester. Post 8vo. .... *Cloth boards* 2 0

Parochial Work, A Manual of.
For the Use of the Younger Clergy. By various Authors. Large Post 8vo. .... *Cloth boards* 7 6

Peace with God.
A Manual for the Sick. By the Rev. E. BURBIDGE, M.A. Post 8vo. .... *Cloth boards* 1 6

Plain Reasons against Joining the Church of Rome.
By the Rev. R. F. LITTLEDALE, LL.D., &c. Revised and enlarged edition. Post 8vo. .... *Cloth boards* 1 0

Plain Words for Christ.
Being a Series of Readings for Working Men. By the late Rev. R. G. DUTTON, B.A. Post 8vo. .... *Cloth boards* 1 0

Seek and Find.
A Double Series of Short Studies of the Benedicite. By CHRISTINA G. ROSSETTI. Post 8vo. .... *Cloth boards* 2 6

Servants of Scripture, The.
By the Rev. JOHN W. BURGON, B.D. Post 8vo. .... *Cloth boards* 1 6

Some Chief Truths of Religion.
By the Rev. E. L. CUTTS, B.A., Author of "Pastoral Counsels," "St. Cedd's Cross." Crown 8vo. ...... *Cloth boards* 2 6

Thoughts for Men and Women: The Lord's Prayer.
By EMILY C. ORR. Post 8vo. .... *Limp cloth* 1 0

PUBLICATIONS OF THE S.P.C.K.

Thoughts for Working Days.

Original and Selected. By EMILY C. ORR. Post 8vo.
Limp cloth — **1 0**

True Vine, The.

By the Author of "The Schönberg Cotta Family," &c. Post 8vo. ....*Cloth boards* — **1 6**

Turning-Points of English Church History.

By the Rev. EDWARD L. CUTTS, B.A. Vicar of Holy Trinity, Haverstock Hill. Crown 8vo. ....*Cloth boards* — **3 6**

Turning-Points of General Church History.

By the Rev. E. L. CUTTS, B.A., Author of "Pastoral Counsels," &c. Crown 8vo. ....*Cloth boards* — **5 0**

Under His Banner.

Papers on Missionary Work of Modern Times. By the Rev. W. H. TUCKER. With Map. Crown 8vo. *Cloth boards* — **5 0**

London:

NORTHUMBERLAND AVENUE, CHARING CROSS, W.C.;
43, QUEEN VICTORIA STREET, E.C.
BRIGHTON: 135, NORTH STREET.

www.ingramcontent.com/pod-product-compliance
Lightning Source LLC
Chambersburg PA
CBHW022333230426
43664CB00040B/480